mediation ETHICS

A PRACTITIONER'S GUIDE

OMER SHAPIRA
—EDITOR—

AMERICAN BAR ASSOCIATION
Dispute Resolution Section

Cover design by Kelly Book/ABA Design

Printed in the United States of America.

25 24 23 22 21   5 4 3 2 1

A catalog record for this book is available from the Library of Congress.

Discounts are available for books ordered in bulk. Special consideration is given to state bars, CLE programs, and other bar-related organizations. Inquire at Book Publishing, ABA Publishing, American Bar Association, 321 N. Clark Street, Chicago, Illinois 60654-7598.

www.shopABA.org

Contents

CHAPTER 13
Disciplining Mediators 295
Michael Moffitt

PART V
DEVELOPING ETHICAL SKILLS

CHAPTER 14
Continuing Mediation Ethics Education 321
Gregory Firestone, Ph.D.

Introduction

Ethics is a vital element in the development of professional mediation practices and an important factor in gaining public trust in the emerging profession of mediation. Tens of thousands of mediators conduct mediations in numerous types of disputes and in various settings. Commercial, family, workplace, medical malpractice, and construction mediations are conducted across the United States, Europe, Australia, and East Asia in court-related disputes and in conflicts that have not been filed in court. They are mostly conducted by mediators who come from already established professions and occupations, many of whom are lawyers. These mediators need to develop a new professional identity and follow different rules of conduct than those applying to their other profession or occupation. Lawyer-mediators should be aware of the different values, goals, role definitions, skills, and techniques of legal practice and mediation. They must be flexible enough to move between these sometimes contradictory orientations when they take off the hat of a lawyer and put on the one of the mediator and vice versa.

This book is aimed at lawyer-mediators who care about their clients, professions, and the general public and want to conduct mediations ethically. It takes a practical, concise, and coherent approach to mediation ethics to make lawyer-mediators aware of their ethical obligations while serving as mediators. The book has been written by 15 leading mediation scholars, with special expertise in mediation ethics, each contributing a chapter on a topic within his or her expertise. Each chapter provides a careful examination of a topic related to the practice of mediation and suggests ethical guidelines grounded in ethical theory, codes of conduct for mediators, and mediator ethics advisory committees' (MEAC) opinions. The topics are arranged in four clusters:

Part I offers the readers the "Basics" required for ethical conduct. In Chapter 1, Omer Shapira discusses "What Mediators Need to Know to Mediate Ethically." The chapter describes key concepts in professional ethics, identifies general principles of mediators' ethics that can be applied to mediation practice, suggests specific guidelines to ethical conduct, and acquaints readers with a perspective of mediators' ethics that will assist them in finding their way when ethical problems are encountered.

In Chapter 2, James Alfini contrasts "Lawyer Ethics and Mediator Ethics," analyzes the similarities and differences between the two sets of ethical standards, and demonstrates that although legal ethics and mediator ethics use similar terms for ethics standards (e.g., competence, conflicts of interest, confidentiality), the meaning of these terms is different and might require different conduct in the context of either a mediation or a client representation. In Chapter 3, Susan Nauss Exon gives the reader a better "Understanding of Codes of Conduct for Mediators and MEAC Opinions," provides guidance regarding general themes found in mediation ethical codes of conduct and advisory opinions, and constructs a detailed source of state mediation codes of conduct and mediation ethical advisory opinions in the United States.

Part II takes the reader to the "Outset of Mediation." In Chapter 4, titled "Accepting a Case or Refusing to Mediate: Ethical Considerations," Ellen Waldman and Donna Erez-Navot consider the circumstances in which mediators ought to refuse a case or withdraw at the outset of mediation and the reasons for doing so. The chapter runs through key ethical principles and issues that mediators should be aware of and able to consider, including the mediator's competence, integrity, and conflicts of interest and the ability of parties to exercise self-determination.

Part III takes the reader forward in time to the point of "Conducting Mediation" and looks at "Ethical Aspects in the Use of Mediator Techniques." In Chapter 5, titled "Evaluating Ethically," Kristen M. Blankley considers what it means to evaluate, how it is distinguished from common mediator techniques such as reality testing, and what are the ethical considerations surrounding the use of evaluative techniques. In Chapter 6, titled "Meeting the Parties Separately," Elayne E. Greenberg looks behind the caucus door and highlights the ethical issues that mediators should address when they caucus. In Chapter 7, Sharon Press guides mediators on an ethical practice of "Making Proposals," and in Chapter 8, Bill Eddy explores ethical ways of "Dealing with Difficult Parties," addressing three issues: ethically communicating with difficult clients; reasons to turn down a case or withdraw because of concerns related to one or both parties' behavior or mental capacity; and adaptations to the process when the parties are identified as difficult by a mediator.

Next, in Chapter 9, Jacqueline Nolan-Haley discusses "Lawyer Representation in Mediation." She reviews the ethical duties of lawyers representing parties in mediation, both prior to and during the mediation; explains why lawyer representation in mediation should be deliberative and based on client informed consent; and describes the responsibilities of the lawyer-mediator who believes that a representational lawyer in mediation is engaged in unethical behavior or serious misconduct. In Chapter 10, Nancy A. Welsh describes the practice variations of med-arb, reviews the ethical difficulties associated with these practices, and considers "The Ethical Choices Required to Protect Process Integrity" when mediators change roles after the mediation has begun.

Part IV situates the reader at the "Conclusion of Mediation and Its Aftermath." As most lawyer-mediators try to assist the parties to reach an agreement, in Chapter 11, Fran Tetunic focuses on "The Mediated Agreement." The chapter provides information on the qualities and requirements for mediated agreements; addresses the ethical obligation of the mediator to prevent the formation of illegal, unconscionable, and grossly unfair mediated agreements; and discusses mediators' continuing ethical obligations in the event an agreement is not reached or following the agreement formation process.

In Chapter 12 on "Mediation Confidentiality: Mediators as Witnesses," Ellen E. Deason delves into the ethical expectations of mediators who are subpoenaed to testify about issues that arose in the mediation, applying norms of confidentiality, privilege, and impartiality. The chapter examines disclosures a mediator might make outside a mediation session when serving as a witness in an adjudicatory proceeding and outside legal proceedings, such as to public officials or the mediation program that sponsors her work.

In Chapter 13, titled "Disciplining Mediators," Michael Moffitt reviews several forms of accountability for mediators. He describes the avenues of possible civil action against mediators, assesses the prospects of institutional discipline, and looks at the accountability of mediators who are members of voluntary mediation organizations.

Part V concludes the book with the topic of "Developing Ethical Skills." In Chapter 14, titled "Continuing Mediation Ethics Education," Gregory Firestone addresses the extent to which continuing mediator ethics education is required in some U.S. jurisdictions and why it is necessary, explores how mediators can increase their professional ethics capacities and knowledge, makes recommendations for continuing mediator ethics education, and offers a sample of resources for pursuing it.

This book differs from and may supplement other available full-length books that cover mediation ethics. It focuses on specific ethical issues that arise in the mediation practice of lawyer-mediators. It addresses these issues in a developing order, from the beginning of the mediation to its end, enabling mediators to consult the topic relevant to them at any given point in time. It then provides concise ethical guidance through a diversified yet reasoned ethical approach grounded in ethical theory, codes of conduct for mediators, and ethics advisory opinions.

The book's primary audience is lawyer-mediators and mediators in general. It would also be useful to lawyers representing clients in mediation, administrative staff and mediators in ADR court programs, scholars and students in ADR academic programs, and mediator trainees and trainers.

I would like to thank the contributors for their commitment to produce high-quality works. Reading and commenting on their contributions and the discussions that followed have enriched my knowledge of mediation ethics as I am confident they will enhance our readers'. Special thanks go to Ellen Waldman and Sarah Craig, who were involved in the book project from its very start and offered their continued, kind, and thoughtful support along the way. Finally, I thank my wife Shirly and my children Matan and Daniel for their patience, support, and love.

Omer Shapira

Part I

Basics

Chapter 1

What Do Mediators Need to Know to Mediate Ethically?

*Omer Shapira**

1.1. Introduction

The purpose of this chapter is to give mediators a brief explanation of what it means to mediate ethically. To do that, we have to clarify what it means to engage in mediation and what makes this engagement ethical or unethical. Essentially, mediators' ethics and the ethical practice of mediation are the marriage of two concepts: the concept of role (acting as a mediator) and the concept of ethics (doing the right thing). The law that governs mediators becomes part of mediators' ethics as well through the general ethical obligation to obey the law. This chapter describes key concepts in professional ethics, identifies general principles of mediators' ethics that can be applied to mediation practice, and suggests specific guidelines to ethical conduct that complement existing codes of conduct for mediators, such as the Model Standards of Conduct for Mediators (2005) (hereinafter Model Standards).[1] In addition, it will acquaint readers with a perspective of mediators' ethics that will assist them to mediate

---

*I would like to thank Ellen Waldman, Gregory Firestone, and the reviewers from the ABA Dispute Resolution Section for their valuable comments. The sole responsibility for the content of this chapter lies with me.

1. Model Standards of Conduct for Mediators (2005), https://www.americanbar.org/content/dam/aba/administrative/dispute_resolution/dispute_resolution/model_standards_conduct_april2007.pdf [hereinafter Model Standards].

ethically in the absence of an applicable code, in interpreting codes that apply to them, in filling in gaps in these codes, and in finding their way when ethical problems are encountered.

1.2. Law and Mediators' Ethics

When the term "ethics" is attached to a professional or even occupational activity, it usually means the moral obligations and ideals of those engaging in that activity. This sense of ethics may be termed professional ethics or role-ethics.[2] Applied to mediators, mediators' ethics means the moral obligations and ideals of those who engage in the conduct of mediation. If ethics, therefore, is primarily based on morality, what is the place of law within ethics?

From a professional ethics perspective, the law becomes part of mediators' ethics because of the general moral obligations to follow the law, keep promises, and act with fairness.[3] Therefore, to act ethically you must know and follow the legal rules that apply to mediators in the performance of their role in the jurisdiction in which you operate. These legal rules may consist of (1) legislation (e.g., Alabama Mediator Confidentiality Act for Alabama mediators[4]) and case law,[5] (2) court rules that serve as mandatory mediator standards or codes of conduct for mediators (e.g., Ethical Guidelines for Mediators adopted by the Supreme Court of Texas for court mediators in Texas[6]), (3) mediator ethics opinions (e.g., Florida Mediator Ethics Advisory Committee (MEAC) Opinions[7] for Florida court mediators), and (4) codes of conduct for mediators that mediators choose or are required to submit to by virtue of joining a professional organization (e.g., the Model Standards[8]) (see Figure 1.1). On

2. OMER SHAPIRA, A THEORY OF MEDIATORS' ETHICS: FOUNDATIONS, RATIONALE, AND APPLICATION 3–5 (2016).

3. *Id.* at 27–30, 66–71 (discussing the links between law and professional ethics).

4. *Alabama Act 2008-387*, ALA. CTR. FOR DISPUTE RESOLUTION, https://alabamaadr.org/web/roster-documents/med_Ala_Med_Confidenality_Act.php (last visited Feb. 19, 2021).

5. *E.g.*, Alfieri v. Solomon, 358 Or. 383 (2015) (Oregon Supreme Court construed the statutory meaning of "mediation communications" and held that attorney-client communications before and after the mediation proceedings are not protected).

6. *Ethical Guidelines for Mediators*, SUP. CT. OF TEX. (amended Apr. 11, 2011), http://www.txcourts.gov/media/514701/Eth-Guideline-Amended Order.pdf.

7. *Florida Mediator Ethics Advisory Committee Opinions (MEAC)*, https://www.flcourts.org/Resources-Services/Alternative-Dispute-Resolution/Mediator-Ethics-Advisory-Committee-Opinions-MEAC (last visited Feb. 19, 2021).

8. MODEL STANDARDS, *supra* note 1.

top of these legal sources of mediators' ethics come (5) mediator professional role-ethics obligations independent of law, discussed next.

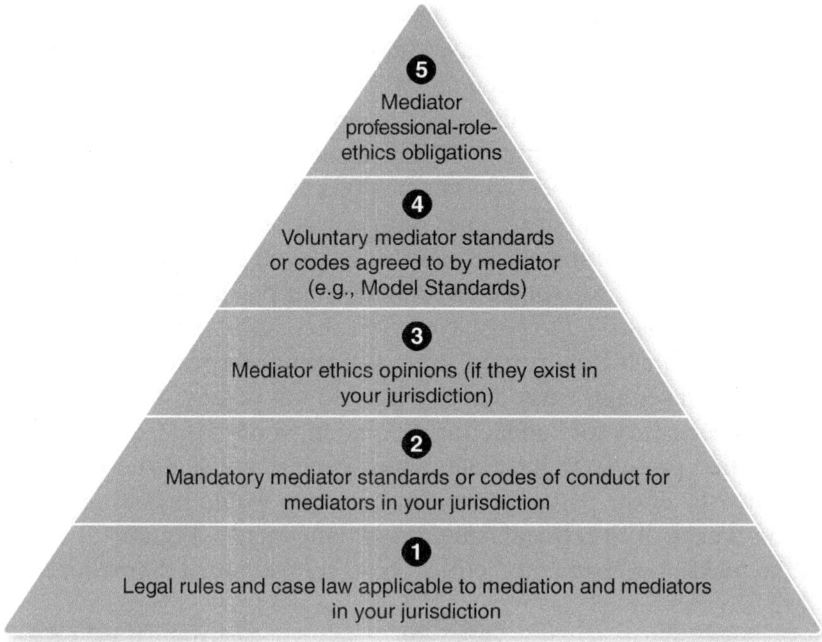

Figure 1.1: Mediators' Ethics and Law

1.3. The Making of Mediators' Ethical Obligations

Satisfying the *legal* threshold of obligations is only the first level of ethical practice. According to professional role-ethics, holding a role comes with responsibilities. Ethical obligations flow from professional roles. By holding the role of a mediator, you are placed in a position of power and influence vis-à-vis your clients and other individuals and groups who develop legitimate expectations of you to conduct yourself in ways that will not harm them. Furthermore, by holding yourself out as a mediator, you are making an implied promise to act "as a mediator."[9] The content of this promise—to act as mediator—has already been determined by other mediators, mediation scholars, legislators, and code drafters who established certain meanings of "mediator" and "mediation" that limit

9. Shapira, *supra* note 2, at 38–40, 106–08 (discussing the normative basis of duties toward clients and the mediator–parties relationship).

your freedom of action. Therefore, to mediate ethically you must also meet a *moral* threshold of obligations that are attached to your role as mediator.

For example, when you offer mediation services, you in effect represent to the parties that you have the knowledge, skills, and expertise required to conduct a mediation and assist disputing parties to negotiate their differences and make decisions regarding the dispute. In addition, the knowledge and expertise you have or have represented to have are sources of power that place you in a position to perform your role, move the parties forward, and overcome communication and negotiation obstacles. In fact, the disputing parties have come to you *because* of these powers. They need your assistance and rely on your presumed ability to help them. They are *entitled* to trust you. And they have a legitimate expectation of you to act in a trustworthy way and refrain from abusing your position of power and trust. Thus, if you do not possess the knowledge and skills necessary for conducting mediation, you would be in breach of your implied promise to have the competence to conduct the mediation *and unworthy* of the parties' trust. In short, you would be acting unethically, in breach of the ethical standard of competence. Figure 1.2 visualizes the making of mediators' ethical obligations toward their clients.

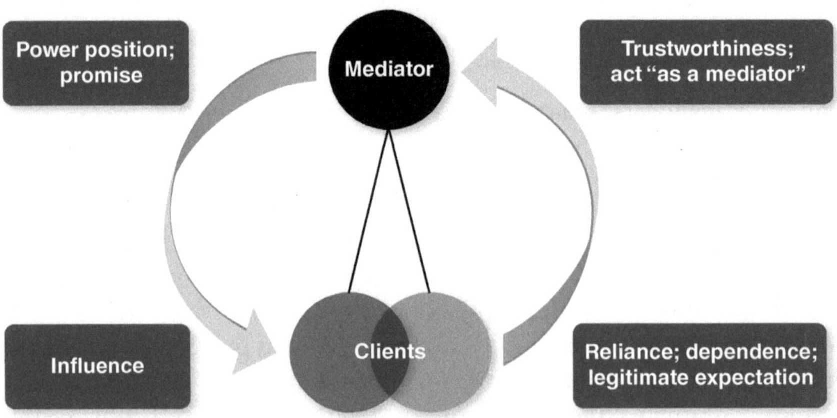

Figure 1.2: The Ethical Relationship between Mediators and Mediation Parties

1.4. Between Ethical and Legal Thresholds of Duties

The ethical threshold of obligations described previously stands regardless of the existence or nonexistence of a parallel legal obligation.

Therefore, you have an ethical duty of competence as a mediator whether competence is required by law or not. This is so because ethical duties have their own standing and force. They are independent of law, though their content is affected by the law when relevant legal rules exist.

For example, if you are a court-connected mediator in Florida, you must, according to Florida Rule 10.630, "acquire and maintain professional competence in mediation."[10] The rule, therefore, sets a legal obligation of competence that defines the minimum level of competence required of a Florida certified or court-appointed mediator. This level of competence will normally satisfy the ethical obligation of competence (which stems from role-morality, that is, from the mediator's position of power and trust and her implied representations to the parties and the public at large), unless the circumstances set the ethical threshold higher than the legal one. For example, if you conduct the mediation through a video-conference platform, there is a legitimate expectation that you will have knowledge of the digital platform you utilize and the skills for operating it. It is part of your ethical obligation of competence, which is not dependent on the foresight of the legislature, which did envision the possibility of remote mediation.

Similarly, if you are a Florida mediator who is not court certified or court appointed, the legal rules for court mediators do not apply to you, but this is not to say you have no ethical obligations. Again, as ethical obligations are attached to role, once you hold yourself out as a mediator and act as a mediator, you are bound by the ethics of mediators. It is true that in the absence of enforcement bodies with legal powers, you might not face legal sanctions for failing to follow your ethical obligations. However, the absence of sanctions does not release you of ethical responsibility. You are still under an ethical obligation to be competent to provide mediation services even though you are a private mediator. The content of this obligation, that is, the minimum qualifications for conducting a mediation, will be determined in accordance with the core definition of mediation and the role of mediators (see later), with reference to the common practices of mediation in the state in which you practice (in our example, Florida), including legal rules applicable to court mediators. As noted previously, the ethical threshold of responsibility need not be the same as the legal one, but both affect one another.

---

10. *Florida Rules for Certified and Court-Appointed Mediators* (Mar. 2018), Rule 10.630, https://www.flcourts.org/content/download/216763/file/rules-certified-court-appointed-mediators.pdf.

1.5. Between Ethical Threshold of Duty and Ethical Bar of Aspiration

An understanding of ethics as a statement of *obligations* that *must* be obeyed is key to ethical practice. An ethical obligation is as mandatory as legal obligation, and following it is not a matter of personal choice or conscience. An ethical obligation should not be mistaken for an ethical *aspiration* or ideal. Ethical ideals signify excellence in ethical conduct that exceeds the demands of duty.[11] Mediators are *encouraged* to reach that ethical bar but cannot be criticized for failing to do so (see Figure 1.3). For example, mediators can be held ethically responsible only for behaviors that may be avoided. A realistic and practical view of impartiality as an ethical concept must be based on a separation between an internal aspect of partiality, which cannot be avoided, and an external aspect, that is, external expressions of bias—in speech or behavior—that can be controlled. An *ideal* mediator may be a "clean slate" in terms of his thoughts while dealing with the parties, but a flesh-and-blood mediator can only be expected to control the external expression of bias. Therefore, a mediator's ethical *duty* of impartiality can only relate to a prohibition on giving external expressions of preference or discrimination.[12]

1.6. The Diversity of Ethical Relationships

Role-ethics draws attention to another important aspect of holding the role of mediator, and that is the formation of *multiple ethical relationships* you have beyond the one with the mediation parties. There are other individuals and groups that might be affected by your conduct and have legitimate expectations that you will conduct yourself in a manner that will not harm them. One such group is made of other mediators and mediation organizations, which together comprise the *profession* of mediation. Belonging to the community of mediators provides you with access to economic and social-status opportunities. The conduct of your fellow mediators has a potential effect on your prospects and vice versa. As a matter of fairness, you are expected to conduct yourself in a manner that preserves and protects the standing of the profession.[13]

---

11. On the distinction between ethical obligations and ethical aspirations or ideals, see Lon L. Fuller, The Morality of Law 5–6 (rev. ed. 1969); Bernard Gert, Common Morality: Deciding What to Do 22–23 (2004); Shapira, *supra* note 2, at 12–19.

12. Omer Shapira, *On the Meaning and Justification of Mediators' Ethical Duty of Impartiality*, 28 Bar-Ilan Law Studies 259, 299 (2012) (Heb.).

13. *See* Shapira, *supra* note 2, at 60–63, 108–10 (discussing the normative basis of duties toward the profession and the mediator–profession relationship).

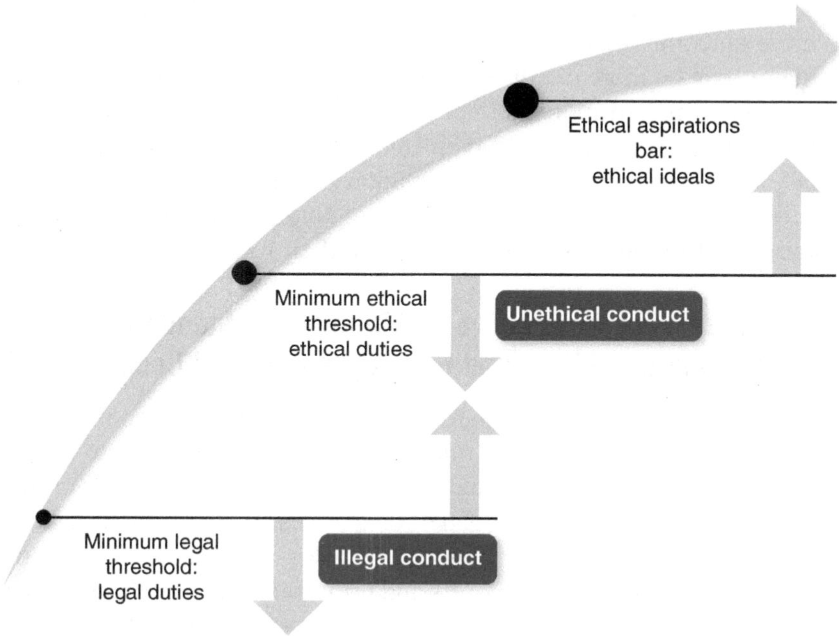

Figure 1.3: Legal and Ethical Thresholds of Obligation and Ethical Bar of Aspiration

Similarly, role-ethics establishes ethical duties of mediators toward the public, employers, and principals. Briefly, the *public* has legitimate expectations of mediators to obey the law, act morally, and refrain from abuse of the mediation process and from harming nonclient members of the public. *Employers* of mediators and bodies that refer cases to them, such as the courts (*principals*), have ethical relationships with mediators as well, creating duties to act in a trustworthy manner.

1.7. The Core Definition of Mediation and the Role of Mediators

Mediation practice is pluralistic. There are various mediation styles of practice and different views of the role of the mediator. Moreover, mediators describe their style with different labels, such as problem-solving, facilitative, evaluative, transformative, and narrative mediation. Still, while these styles may be distinguished by their philosophy, jargon, techniques of intervention, and professional ideals, my research has identified a core, *factual* definition of mediation that is shared by all mediators regardless of their style. According to that factual definition, mediation is *a process conducted by a third party, who assists parties to a dispute to communicate and make decisions regarding the dispute and reach an agreement when they wish to do so.*[14] A facilitative mediator might be more outcome oriented than a transformative mediator; an evaluative mediator may be more directive than a facilitative mediator; and a narrative mediator may be more inclined to use caucuses than a transformative mediator. However, the core of their role is the same: helping parties in a dispute to communicate and make voluntary decisions; and the guidance required to ensure ethical performance of that role is satisfied by one unitary *set* of moral obligations attached to their role.

1.8. Perspectives from Above and Below: The Standards of Mediators' Ethics and My Proposed Model Code

It is useful to think of the standards of mediators' ethics as coming from two sources. The first source is role-ethics. Role-ethics applies to mediators *"from above"* because it is independent of legal rules that may or may not apply to them through state codes, court rules, or professional associations' codes. The ethical obligations of mediators toward their clients, the profession, the public, and employers and principals (when applicable) stem from role-ethics. Thus, all mediators have these ethical obligations by virtue of their role, irrespective of legal regulation of their conduct.

This perspective from above can be developed to establish a list of *minimum ethical standards* that are attached to the core role of mediators. This list includes, alongside competence, which has already been mentioned previously, respect for party self-determination (consisting of party competency, voluntary decision making, and informed consent), impartiality, conflicts of interest, professional integrity (consisting of the exercise of professional discretion, separation of professional roles, dealing with appropriate cases, and prevention of process abuse or substantial defects in the process), diligence, respect and dignity, honesty, maintaining confidentiality, maintaining the standing of the profession, maintaining obligations to employers and principals, and fairness.[15]

Most mediators will be familiar with many of these standards, which are part of numerous national codes of conduct for mediators in the United States, including the Model Standards. These codes provide a second source of mediators' standards of ethics: a view *"from below"* of the obligations of mediators that is widely held by the field of mediation practice. It is the view of mediators' code drafters, legislatures, mediators' professional

14. *Id.* at 94. For a detailed analysis establishing the core descriptive definition of mediation and the role of mediators, see *id.* at 85–95.

15. *Id.* at 105–15 (discussing the perspective from above of professional ethics and its content).

organizations, policy makers, and mediation experts and practitioners (see Figure 1.4). A close examination of this view provides a list of *shared norms of mediators' ethics* according to the field.[16] This list largely replicates and supports the list of the role-ethics obligations "from above." It contains ethical norms that mediators are accustomed to find in codes of conduct for mediators, such as self-determination, impartiality, conflicts of interest, and confidentiality, as well as standards on solicitation, advertising, and fees that do not originate from the "above" role-ethics perspective.[17]

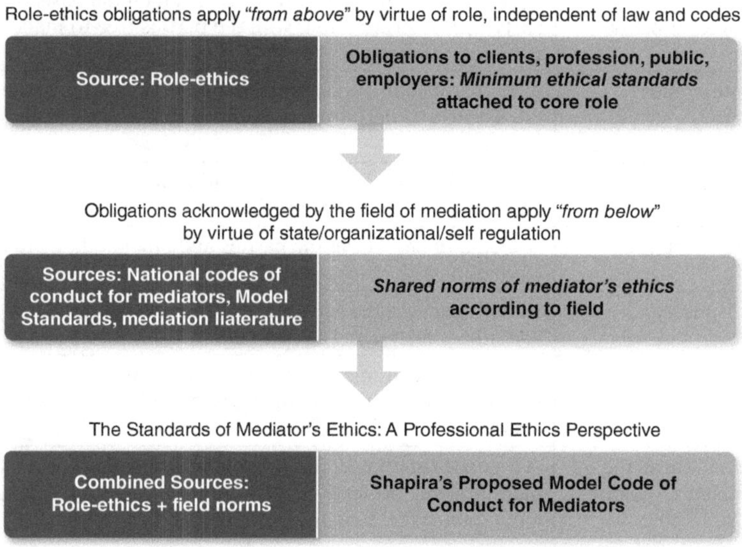

Figure 1.4: Sources of the Standards of Mediators' Ethics

Taken together, the two sources inform a *professional mediator ethics perspective* and provide the Standards of Mediators' Ethics that apply to all mediators, including you. These Standards are attached to your role as mediator and are supported by national codes of conduct for mediators, the Model Standards, and mediation literature. They are described in brief in Figure 1.5, and their full text is contained in my Proposed Model Code of Conduct for Mediators (hereinafter Proposed Model Code).[18]

16. *Id.* at 101–05.

17. *Id.* at 114–15.

18. Proposed Model Code of Conduct for Mediators [hereinafter Shapira's Proposed Model Code], *id.* at 397–411. The Proposed Model Code is also available at https://www.academia.edu/35892350/A_PROPOSED_MODEL_CODE_OF_CONDUCT_FOR_MEDIATORS.

The Standards of Mediators' Ethics in Brief

I. Competence	A mediator shall mediate only when he has the knowledge and skills necessary for carrying out his role.
II. Impartiality	A mediator shall exercise his role without external manifestations of favoritism or bias between parties in word or action.
III. Conflicts of Interest	A mediator shall avoid a conflict of interest or the appearance of a conflict of interest at all stages of mediation or act to neutralize it.
IV. Party Self-Determination	A mediator shall conduct the mediation on the basis of party self-determination, with the parties free to make voluntary, uncoerced, and informed decisions.
V. Professional Integrity	A mediator shall conduct mediation while committed to the nature and definition of both his role as a mediator and mediation.
VI. Diligence	A mediator shall conduct a mediation with the availability and attention necessary for carrying out his role.
VII. Respect and Dignity	A mediator shall treat the parties and others related to the mediation with respect and dignity.
VIII. Honesty	A mediator shall be honest in his contacts with the parties and others related to the mediation.
IX. Confidentiality	A mediator shall maintain the confidentiality of information that came to his knowledge in the exercise of his role.
X. Maintaining the Profession's Standing	A mediator shall exercise his role in a manner that maintains the profession's standing and public trust in the mediation profession and process.
XI. Obligations to Employers and Principals	A mediator shall exercise his role consistent with the rules of his employer or principal, in a manner that will not undermine the employer's or principal's standing and public trust in it.
XII. Advertising and Solicitation	A mediator shall be truthful and refrain from misleading in advertising, solicitation, or provision of information about his qualifications, experience, the type of services offered, and fees.
XIII. Mediator Fees	A mediator shall discuss with the parties, before the mediation begins, the mediation fees and any charges that may be incurred in connection with the mediation.
XIV. Advancement of the Profession	Advancement of the mediation profession is an ideal in the realization of which every mediator should assist.
XV. Fairness	A mediator shall perform his role fairly, following the standards of mediation in accordance with their spirit and purpose.

Figure 1.5: The Standards of Mediators' Ethics from a Professional Ethics Perspective (Source: Proposed Model Code)

The Standards of Mediators' Ethics do not replace the Model Standards or a code of conduct for mediators that you are bound to follow by law—if, for example, you are a court-connected mediator—or by agreement—if, for example, you are a member of a professional organization of mediators. Instead, the Standards help you *understand* more fully your ethical obligations, *supplement* a code that applies to you but has gaps or requires interpretation, and offer you *guidance*, if you are not subject to a code of conduct at all.

1.9. The Content and Meaning of the Standards of Mediators' Ethics

For these goals to be realized, a detailed *meaning* of each of these Standards or ethical obligations must be ascertained. Most mediators will not question that they have an ethical duty of impartiality but might find it hard to define what mediator impartiality means. Similarly, there is a consensus among mediators about the right of mediation parties to self-determination, but they might differ as to the extent of that right and its limitations.[19] Here, again, role-ethics and the perspectives from above and below of mediators' ethics provide a step-by-step process of inquiry that yields the content of these obligations.

Take the Standard of Impartiality as an example. What does mediator impartiality actually mean?[20] Our starting point is the mediator's role. The role of the mediator *shapes the meaning* of impartiality. In mediation, the mediator provides services to several parties in the same matter, while the interests of these parties contradict each other at least in part. In addition, the mediator is in a position of power and influence, and the parties are relying on the mediator to use his powers in a trustworthy way. Therefore, focusing on the relationship created between the mediator and the parties, any party receiving mediation services has a legitimate expectation that the mediator will refrain from giving preferential treatment to the other party in the affairs he is dealing with. This legitimate expectation is translated into an ethical duty toward mediation parties *to avoid favoritism and bias.*

The next step follows from the multiplicity of the mediator's ethical relationships. As discussed previously, alongside the duties toward the

---

19. *See, e.g.*, MEDIATION ETHICS: CASES AND COMMENTARIES (Ellen Waldman ed., 2011) (highlighting how differently well-respected mediators and scholars understand the established norms of mediation).

20. For a full exploration, see SHAPIRA, *supra* note 2, at 207–30.

mediation parties, the mediator has an ethical relationship with her *profession* and fellow mediators. She is under an obligation to maintain the standing of the profession. If the mediator were to favor one party over another or even give an *impression* of partiality, she would jeopardize the reputation of mediation and public confidence in it. Therefore, while the mediator's ethical relationship with the parties establishes a duty to refrain from party favoritism, her relationship with the profession enhances that duty and establishes an ethical duty to avoid an *appearance* of favoritism and bias. This is the basis for holding that in conducting a mediation and exercising her role, "[a] mediator shall avoid partiality in fact, and any conduct that might reasonably appear as an act of partiality."[21] This guidance is reflected in the Model Standards, which provide in Standard II (Impartiality) that "[a] mediator shall conduct a mediation in an impartial manner and avoid conduct that gives the appearance of partiality."[22]

The mediator's duty toward the profession, to maintain the standing of the profession and refrain from actions that undermine it, receives support from the mediator's relationship with *society.* As a matter of fairness and reciprocity, the mediator must exercise his role in a manner that avoids harming important social interests, such as the maintenance of the rule of law and the institution of mediation.[23] Taken together, the duties toward the profession and the public guide the mediator to *decline a case or withdraw* if he cannot conduct the mediation impartially.[24] This rationale is echoed by the Model Standards, which provide that "[a] mediator shall decline a mediation if the mediator cannot conduct it in an impartial manner"[25] and "[i]f at any time a mediator is unable to conduct a mediation in an impartial manner, the mediator shall withdraw."[26]

We can glean additional understandings of the duty to maintain impartiality by focusing on the earlier noted distinction between satisfying minimal ethical duties and following ideal aspirations. The ethical *duty/aspiration* distinction yields ethical guidance to mediators to avoid *explicit* favoritism and bias in word or action as a matter of duty, while realistically treating implicit feelings and thoughts of favoritism, bias, and prejudice as a matter of aspiration, the fight against which is to be encouraged. If you feel that Party A is right and Party B is wrong, or that

21. Shapira's Proposed Model Code, *supra* note 18, Standard II.B.1

22. Model Standards, *supra* note 1, Standard II.B.

23. *See* Shapira, *supra* note 2, at 66–71, 111–13 (discussing the normative basis of duties toward the public and the mediator–public relationship).

24. Shapira's Proposed Model Code, *supra* note 18, Standard II.A.

25. Model Standards, *supra* note 1, Standard II.A.

26. *Id.* Standard II.C.

Party B takes advantage of Party A, you have not breached your obligation of impartiality. Mediators are human beings and, as such, are bound sometimes to experience feelings of sympathy for one party or resentment toward another. What can legitimately be expected of mediators is to refrain from *external* manifestations of favoritism or bias between parties in word or action. If you separate your feelings and views from your conduct, you are within the duty of impartiality. You must, of course, be aware of your feelings and views, keep an open mind, and refrain from any manifestations of favoritism or bias. Moreover, you are encouraged to develop a higher sense of impartiality that involves purity of mind and nonjudgmental feelings. However, you cannot be criticized for failing to reach the ethical bar of ideals. As a realistic normative guide for mediator conduct, the obligatory part of the Standard of Impartiality must be understood as limited to external manifestations of favoritism or bias.

Another analytical tool in the process of establishing the content of mediators' ethical standards is the lack of hierarchy between standards. It is demonstrated on the Standard of Impartiality next.

1.10. No Hierarchy of Standards of Ethics

One of the aspects of the professional ethics perspective of role-ethics, and therefore of mediators' ethics as well, is that there is no hierarchy of standards, no standard is absolute, and no standard has a prima facie priority over another.[27] For example, it cannot be maintained that mediator impartiality is more important than party self-determination or that mediator impartiality is more important than confidentiality. The weight of each norm must be ascertained in context, and no norm always trumps the others.[28]

Therefore, the duty of impartiality should not be considered an absolute obligation (equal treatment at all costs) and should be refined or balanced with other obligations of the mediator, such as the obligation to conduct a mediation based on the parties' right to self-determination and the obligation to conduct a mediation in a manner that preserves the standing of the profession and public trust in it. The result is a concept of impartiality that *justifies different treatment* of mediation parties in

27. *See, e.g.*, Bernard Gert, Morality Its Nature and Justifications 116 (rev. ed. 2005); Tom L. Beauchamp & James F. Childress, Principles of Biomedical Ethics 15 (6th ed. 2009).

28. *See, e.g.*, Mediation Ethics (Waldman ed.), *supra* note 19, at 6–7; Omer Shapira, *A Theory of Sharing Decision-Making in Mediation*, 44 McGeorge L. Rev. 923, 936 (2013); Shapira, *supra* note 2, at 117.

certain circumstances, such as significant imbalance of power and information between the parties that undermines one party's ability to make a voluntary and informed decision.

For example, if you realize that Party A inclines to accept an offer of Party B while unaware of a legal right that has decisive effect on her case, you cannot proceed with the mediation as usual, justifying your action with your obligation of impartiality. You might not want to favor Party A, but "doing nothing" and proceeding with the mediation would in effect favor Party B. A conventional understanding of mediator impartiality as freedom from favoritism is simply inadequate as a guide.

Moreover, if you stay passive and allow uninformed Party A to enter a mediated agreement, you risk violation of some other ethical obligations you owe. First, your duty to respect each party's right to self-determination, which is another expression of your duty to exercise your role as mediator in a manner worthy of the parties' trust. Party A trusts you to conduct the mediation based on the principle of party self-determination. Party A cannot exercise self-determination if she lacks relevant information and is unaware of its existence. Being the one in charge of the mediation, if you become aware of Party A's state of ignorance, you have responsibility to intervene and act, notwithstanding your obligation of impartiality (which therefore should not be interpreted and understood as a formal requirement to equal treatment irrespective of the circumstances). Moreover, there is a second reason supporting your duty to act: your obligation to the *profession*. From a reasonable bystander's point of view, by allowing Party A to enter a mediated agreement, you and the mediation profession have at least some responsibility for the agreement and its implications on Party A. Depending on the degree of harm caused to Party A, your conduct might jeopardize the standing of the profession and public trust in the profession, thereby triggering a duty to take some action.

Your obligation of impartiality must, therefore, allow you some room to treat parties differently, otherwise you will not be able to mediate ethically and keep your other obligations. This is not a license to do whatever you like. You must exercise professional discretion and choose that intervention that would be limited to the *minimum necessary* for Party A to make a self-determined, informed decision whether to accept or decline the offer and that would not result in a loss of public trust in the profession and process of mediation.

For example, giving the missing information to Party A would be a blatant act of favoritism, which is beyond what is necessary to ensure minimum conditions for the exercise of self-determination and which poses a risk to the public perception of mediators as neutrals. Instead, suggesting that the parties consult outside experts before deciding would be a much more minor, and therefore acceptable, intervention. Another possibility could be to hold separate meetings with the parties and ask Party A some questions to stimulate her to expand her sources of information or verify that her choice to make a decision based on the available information is made with awareness that the decision might be ill-informed. If Party A then chooses to accept that risk and its implications and proceed with Party B's offer, this decision would be an exercise in self-determination because it was made with an awareness of the possible implications of making an uninformed decision.[29]

1.11. An Ethical Compass for Mediators: Using the Proposed Model Code of Conduct for Mediators

What we have been doing here is engaging in the ethical analysis of the meaning of *one* mediator ethical standard from a professional ethics perspective: the standard of mediator impartiality. This analytical process has been based on the core, factual meaning of mediation and the role of mediators. It relied on the multiplicity and temporal coexistence of the ethical relationships and obligations of mediators toward the parties, the profession, and the public. It has been grounded in an understanding that ethics is about obligations that go beyond mere good intentions and is binding in ways that ideals or aspirations are not and that obligations must be limited to behavior that mediators can reasonably be expected to exhibit and distinguished from ideals that inspire professionals but do not bind them. And it has been conducted on the basis that there is no set hierarchy of values, no absolute values, and each obligation must be understood and shaped by its interaction with the other obligations of the mediator. In other words, the ethical obligations are interconnected, and their content is the product of mutual influence.

A summary of the analysis of the meaning of mediator impartiality would look something like this:[30]

> A mediator shall exercise his role impartially. Impartiality means freedom from external manifestations of favoritism or bias between parties in word or action.

29. SHAPIRA, *supra* note 2, at 143–44 (discussing the waiver of self-determination).

30. Shapira's Proposed Model Code, *supra* note 18, Standard II. For further explanation of the language of the standard and its full version, see SHAPIRA, *supra* note 2, Chapter 7.

A. Accepting Cases and Withdrawal

A mediator shall not accept a case for mediation or withdraw if:

1. He cannot conduct the mediation impartially; or
2. . . .

B. In Conducting a Mediation and Exercising his Role –

1. A mediator shall avoid partiality in fact, and any conduct that might reasonably appear as an act of partiality . . .
2. A mediator shall treat parties differently where –
   a) Same treatment would favor the interests of one party and disadvantage another; and
   b) The mediator's intervention is (1) required in order to give effect to an ethical right of a party (in particular self-determination), or (2) necessary for the preservation of public trust in the profession and process of mediation.

   Any such intervention shall be limited to one that is –
   a) The minimum necessary for the realization of the party's right; and
   b) Can be reconciled with other mediator obligations; and
   c) Would not be perceived as an act of partiality in the eyes of a reasonable person and thus would not result in a loss of public trust in the profession and process of mediation.

Why should you accept this formulation of mediator impartiality as a guiding principle? The answer is that this formulation is openly and rationally explained, justified, and grounded in both theory and practice. It is attached to the *role* of mediators and based on the legitimate expectations of mediation parties, the profession, and the public that mediators act without favoritism, bias, and prejudice. And it is supported by codes of conduct for mediators and mediation literature in the United States and other Anglo-American countries.

But what if you are already subject to a code of conduct that has a standard of impartiality? And how does this standard relate to the Model Standards? As codes of conduct for mediators are often vague and abstract and have gaps, this formulation and the perspective of professional ethics provide an *additional* source to complement and interpret other codes and for thinking critically about their content and your conduct. For example, reading the Standard of Impartiality of the Model Standards with the professional ethics perspective in mind, together with the previous formulation of impartiality, would help you interpret its provisions and better understand what is expected of you as an impartial mediator.[31]

The analytical process of ascertaining the meaning of the standard of mediator impartiality, utilizing the perspective of professional role-ethics, can be repeated regarding the meaning of the other standards of mediators' ethics: competence, party self-determination, conflicts of interest, professional integrity, diligence, respect and dignity, honesty, confidentiality, standing of the profession, obligations to employers and principals, and fairness. For obvious reasons, we cannot conduct this analytical process here. However, the summary of this process can be found in my Proposed Model Code,[32] and the full analysis is described in detail in *A Theory of Mediators' Ethics*.[33]

1.12. General Guidance to Ethical Decision Making

As a mediator, you make decisions all the time. You decide whether to accept or decline a case, whether you are competent to conduct a mediation, and whether you are in a conflict of interest.[34] You often have to determine the type of information that should be disclosed to parties, the appropriateness of a separate meeting, the conditions for making a mediator proposal, and the right moment to terminate a mediation. Decision making becomes *ethical* when it is based on ethical norms and justified by them. Therefore, you must first be *familiar* with the standards of ethics that apply to you, including legal rules that apply to mediators and mediation in your jurisdiction, otherwise you will not be *aware* that an ethical issue has arisen or that ethics can guide you in making a decision (see Figure 1.1). If you are on a court roster of mediators, you will probably have to consult rules of conduct for mediators adopted by the court. If you mediate for a community or private mediation center, check if it has adopted a code of conduct. In any case, whether a mediator ethics code formally applies to you or not, I suggest that as a minimum you familiarize yourself with the Model Standards[35] and my Proposed Model Code.[36]

---

31. *See* Omer Shapira, *A Critical Assessment of the Model Standards of Conduct for Mediators (2005): Call for Reform*, 100 Marq. L. Rev. 81, 127–30 (2016) (applying the professional ethics perspective to the Model Standards' Impartiality Standard).

32. Shapira's Proposed Model Code, *supra* note 18.

33. Shapira, *supra* note 2.

34. On the constant need to make decisions in the conduct of mediation, see Julie Macfarlane, *Mediating Ethically: The Limits of Codes of Conduct and the Potential of a Reflective Practice Model*, 40 Osgoode Hall L.J. 49 (2002).

35. Model Standards, *supra* note 1.

36. Shapira's Proposed Model Code, *supra* note 18.

Next, establish *the facts* that are relevant for the decision. Different facts yield different results, and therefore you must take care to verify the factual situation that gives rise to the ethical question. For example, if you make a decision regarding your competence to mediate, facts about your knowledge, skills, and experience are relevant, as well as the type of the mediated case and its complexity. A newcomer to the mediation field may be incompetent to mediate a highly complex tax mediation that an experienced mediator with tax expertise is competent to conduct.

Then, identify the *ethical standards* relevant for the decision. For example, a question regarding mediator competence clearly requires you to consult the standard of competence, but familiarity with the map of standards (see Figure 1.5) will make you aware of other potentially relevant standards. For instance, under the standard of party self-determination, the mediation parties have a right to make informed choices as to process and outcome regarding procedural and substantive issues, including mediator selection.[37] Moreover, awareness of your obligations toward the profession and the public, embedded in standards of quality of process[38] and integrity and standing of the profession,[39] alerts you that mediator competence should not be looked at solely through the parties' eyes and preferences, as lack of competence may affect the integrity of the process of mediation.

After clarifying the facts and identifying the relevant ethical standards and relationships, the next stage in ethical decision making is *applying* the ethical standards to the facts and *reaching a conclusion* on the ethicality of the issue at stake (see Figure 1.6).

For example, the standard of party self-determination suggests that the mediation parties have a right to receive information about your competence to make an informed choice as to your suitability to serve as mediator in their case. In addition, your obligations toward the profession and the public, as reflected in the standards of quality of process and integrity and standing of the profession, guide you to take the case only if your competence enables you to conduct the mediation with integrity, in a manner that maintains the profession's standing and is worthy of the public's trust.

37. Model Standards, *supra* note 1, Standard I.A; Shapira's Proposed Model Code, *supra* note 18, Standard IV.A.

38. *See* Model Standards, *supra* note 1, Standard VI.

39. *See* Shapira's Proposed Model Code, *supra* note 18, Standards V, X.

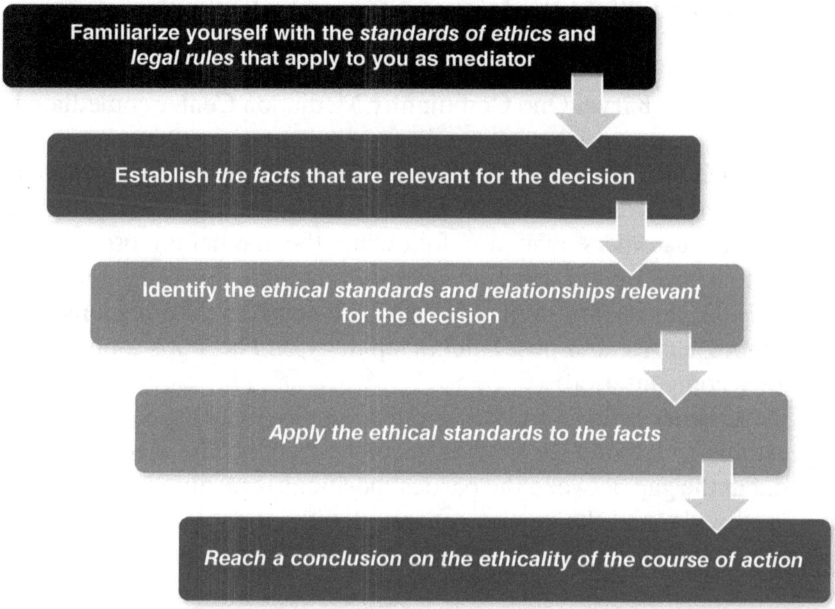

Figure 1.6: A Guide to Ethical Decision Making

This, of course, is a simplified decision-making guide. Ethical questions and dilemmas sometimes require a more nuanced approach, which I discuss elsewhere.[40] Still, to illustrate the ethical analysis and decision-making process I advocate, the next section will take you through a case scenario based on a true mediator query received by a mediator ethics committee I chair.[41]

40. *See* SHAPIRA, *supra* note 2, at 344–62.

41. The Mediator Ethics Forum (Committee) was established in 2012 by the Kiryat-Ono Community and Dialogue Center in cooperation with Ono Academic College as a joint project of Carmela Zilberstein, founder and director at the time of the Kiryat-Ono Community Center, and myself. The forum receives ethical inquiries from practitioners and drafts reasoned ethical opinions that are informed by the professional ethics perspective discussed in this chapter. Since 2012, about 50 ethics opinions have been published in a book—MEDIATION ETHICS: ETHICAL CODES AND COPING WITH DILEMMAS (Omer Shapira & Carmela Zilberstein eds., 2018) (Heb.)—and on the forum's site at https://mediatorethics.com/mediator-ethics-in-israel/.

1.13. Making Ethical Decisions: A Case Illustration

1.13.1. The Facts

Mediators at the Kiryat Ono Community Mediation Center comediated a small-claims court case between a dissatisfied customer ("the customer") and a service provider ("the supplier").[42] During a separate meeting with the customer, the latter stated he is in touch via the Internet with other dissatisfied customers who are following the mediation process. He refused to share this information with the supplier. However, during the joint session, he openly demanded that the supplier take responsibility for the poor service and post a public apology on Facebook along with a monetary compensation.

The supplier refused to issue a public apology but agreed to discuss the customer's demand for monetary compensation. The mediation continued, but the gap between the parties' positions regarding compensation remained wide, and the parties separated without an agreement. Before the parties left the room, the mediators had suggested that the parties reconsider their positions and advised the parties, who did not have legal education and were not legally represented, to consult a lawyer.

Following the timeout and with the assistance of the mediators over the phone, the parties reached an agreement on a monetary sum and the provision of additional services to the customer at a discount rate for an agreed period.

When the agreement was put into writing, the mediators found themselves in a dilemma: the supplier did not make an explicit request that the content of the agreement be kept confidential, presumably because he had no legal background and had not consulted a lawyer. At the same time, the mediators were aware of the customer's intent, expressed during the separate meeting, to bring the content of the mediation to the attention of other dissatisfied clients. The mediators were concerned that in the absence of a confidentiality clause, he would do so.

The mediators debated whether they should raise the issue of keeping the arrangement confidential on their own initiative. They chose to do so to preserve the fairness of the procedure. They contacted the customer and told him that since the supplier had rejected his demand for a public apology on Facebook, the arrangement should include a confidentiality clause that would prohibit the publication of the details of the mediated agreement. The customer took some time to think it over and agreed

42. Ethics Op. 5-2016 (Heb.), https://mediatorethics.com/mediator-ethics-opinion-5-2016/.

to the confidentiality clause. The supplier approved of the agreement as well, and it was signed by both parties. The mediators asked the ethics committee to comment on their conduct.

The ethics committee based its opinion on the Code of Ethics of the Kiryat Ono Community Mediation Center (2014) (KO Code),[43] which adapted my Proposed Model Code to its purposes.[44] Before reading the committee's opinion, let us consider the guidance of the Model Standards on the issues raised.

1.13.2. Discussion under the Guidance of the Model Standards

The Model Standards are made up of nine standards. At least four of them seem relevant for the present case: Standard I, Self-Determination; Standard II, Impartiality; Standard V, Confidentiality; and Standard VI, Quality of the Process.

Standard I, Self-Determination, instructs the mediator to "conduct a mediation based on the principle of party self-determination."[45] Self-determination is defined as an act "in which each party makes . . . informed choices as to process and outcome."[46] If the supplier participated in the mediation and reached an agreement under the wrong assumption that the content and outcome of the mediation would not be disclosed, would he be making an "informed choice as to process and outcome"? And if not—what would be the mediators' ethical responsibility in that case? The Standard of Self-Determination reassures the mediators that "[a] mediator cannot personally ensure that each party has made free and informed choices to reach particular decisions"[47] and further guides the mediators that "where appropriate, a mediator should make the parties aware of the importance of consulting other professionals to help them

43. Code of Ethics of the Kiryat Ono Community Mediation Center (2014) [hereinafter KO Code] *in* Mediation Ethics (Shapira & Zilberstein eds.), *supra* note 41, at 47–62.

44. Shapira's Proposed Model Code, *supra* note 18. In 2018, the KO Code, *id.*, was adopted with few changes by the Israeli Association of Mediation and Dialogue Centers. The revised version of the code has been named the Code of Ethics for Mediators in Community Mediation and Dialogue Centers (2018). *See* https://mediatorethics.com/mediator-ethics-in-israel/ (Heb.). Since then, the 2018 Code has been guiding the mediators of over 40 Community Mediation and Dialogue Centers in Israel, including the Kiryat Ono Mediation Center. For a basically similar version of the code in English addressed to noncommunity mediators, see the Code of Ethics for Mediators (2018) at https://mediatorethics.com/english/code-of-ethics-for-mediators-in-israel/.

45. Model Standards, *supra* note 1, Standard I.A.

46. *Id.*

47. *Id.* Standard I.A.2.

make informed choices."[48] Indeed, the mediators in the discussed case did exactly that, yet the parties chose not to consult a lawyer. Does this mean that the mediators could have moved forward with the agreement as is, without raising the confidentiality issue?

Standard II, Impartiality, directs mediators to "conduct a mediation in an impartial manner and avoid conduct that gives the appearance of partiality"[49] and defines impartiality as "freedom from favoritism, bias or prejudice."[50] The mediators in the discussed case raised the confidentiality issue, an intervention that seems to have favored the *supplier*. Does that mean they have acted with partiality? On the other hand, had they not done so, would not their inaction have favored the *customer*, who indicated his intention to go public with the mediation outcome? Should the mediators have terminated the mediation according to the last subsection of the Impartiality Standard, which provides that "[i]f at any time a mediator is unable to conduct a mediation in an impartial manner, the mediator shall withdraw"?[51]

Next, it is quite clear that the mediators were right not to disclose to the supplier the information shared with them in caucus. The prohibition on such disclosure is found in Standard V, Confidentiality, which states that "[a] mediator who meets with any persons in private session during a mediation shall not convey directly or indirectly to any other person, any information that was obtained during that private session without the consent of the disclosing person."[52] On the other hand, the next subsection of the Standard demands that "[a] mediator shall promote understanding among the parties of the extent to which the parties will maintain confidentiality of information they obtain in a mediation."[53] Could the mediators have done so without displaying favoritism toward the supplier?

Lastly, the Standard of the Quality of the Process provides that "[a] mediator shall conduct a mediation . . . in a manner that promotes . . . procedural fairness."[54] The mediators in our case felt that they had to raise the mediated agreement's confidentiality with the parties because not doing so would have jeopardized the fairness of the mediation. Is that what "procedural fairness," which is not defined by the Standard,

48. *Id.*
49. *Id.* Standard II.B.
50. *Id.* Standard II.A.
51. *Id.* Standard II.C.
52. *Id.* Standard V.B.
53. *Id.* Standard V.C.
54. *Id.* Standard VI.A.

means?[55] Does the mediators' concern provide a good reason to intervene in a manner that appears to have favored the supplier? Alternatively, is this a case that triggers the last subsection of the Quality of the Process Standard, which states that "[i]f a mediator believes that participant conduct, including that of the mediator, jeopardizes conducting a mediation consistent with these Standards, a mediator shall take appropriate steps including, if necessary, postponing, withdrawing from or terminating the mediation"?[56]

1.13.3. Discussion Informed by the KO Code and My Proposed Model Code

Let us now turn to the case analysis according to the professional ethics perspective that has been described in this chapter.[57] This perspective, which is reflected in the Proposed Model Code, informed the opinion of the mediator ethics committee. The committee applied on the facts of the case the standards of the KO Code that is based on the Proposed Model Code.

The committee first noted that the mediators' dilemma stemmed from a tension between conflicting duties: the mediators' duty to prevent an abuse of process by one of the parties in accordance with the Standard of Professional Integrity, their duty to remain impartial in accordance with the Standard of Impartiality, and their duty to conduct a process based on party self-determination consistent with the Standard of Self-Determination.

The committee opened its analysis with the Standard of Professional Integrity that guides mediators on four process integrity issues: Decision-Making and Exercise of Professional Discretion, Separation of Professional Roles, Appropriateness of Case to Process, and Prevention of Process Abuse or Substantial Defects in the Process.[58] The committee identified the fourth issue, which states that "[a] mediator shall prevent an abuse of process (i.e., use of mediation for purposes which it has not been

55. For a critical discussion of the language and clarity of guidance of the Model Standards, see Shapira, *supra* note 31.

56. Model Standards, *supra* note 1, Standard VI.C.

57. For other case illustrations that employ the perspective of mediator ethics and are available in English, see Shapira, *supra* note 2, at 364–96 (discussing five cases); Omer Shapira, *The Challenge of Developing Genuine Pluralism in Mediation Ethics: A Reply to Professor Robert A. Baruch Bush*, 36 Ohio State J. on Disp. Resol. (forthcoming).

58. KO Code, *supra* note 43, Standards 9A–9D; Shapira's Proposed Model Code, *supra* note 18, Standards V.A–V.D.

designed to serve), or a substantial defect in the process,"[59] as particularly relevant to the case in question. The committee noted that

> [a] mediator has a duty *towards the parties to mediation and towards the profession* to carry out, as far as it is under his control, a proper procedure that does not cause harm to the parties. . . . [According to the Standard of Professional Integrity, a mediator shall] "[t]ake appropriate steps, including terminating the mediation, when a participant is abusing the process."[60]

Plainly, the committee appreciated the diversity of mediators' obligations and the idea that the Standards, including the Standard of Professional Integrity, reflect obligations toward the profession as well as toward the parties. Indeed, these obligations are referred to in the Introduction part of both the KO Code and the Proposed Model Code with the effect that the mediator is made aware up front that he "has [both] a duty to exercise his role in a manner worthy of the parties' trust" and "a duty to exercise his role in a manner that maintains the standing of the profession and public trust in the profession and process of mediation."[61] The committee thought that the integrity of the process could have been at stake because

> [t]he mediators felt that the customer might take advantage of the lack of sophistication of the supplier, who despite expressing his opposition to issue a public apology failed to request nondisclosure of the terms of the mediated agreement during the final stage of the agreement's drafting. Unlike the supplier, the mediators were aware of the possibility that the mediation outcome might get publicity on Facebook because this came up in the separate meeting with the customer. However, they were prevented from providing this information to the supplier because of their duty of confidentiality.[62]

The committee cited Standard 5.A.2 (Confidentiality) of the KO Code (the equivalent of the Proposed Model Code Standard IX.A.2),

---

59. KO Code, *supra* note 43, Standard 9D; Shapira's Proposed Model Code, *supra* note 18, Standard V.D.

60. Ethics Op. 5-2016, *supra* note 42 (referring to KO Code, *supra* note 43, Standard 9D.4, which is the same as Shapira's Proposed Model Code, *supra* note 18, Standard V.D.4) (emphasis added).

61. KO Code, *supra* note 43, Introduction; Shapira's Proposed Model Code, *supra* note 18, Introduction.

62. Ethics Op. 5-2016, *supra* note 42.

according to which "[a] mediator shall promote understanding among the parties of the extent to which the parties will maintain confidentiality of information they obtain in a mediation." The committee commented that the mediators would have done better if at the beginning of the mediation they had stressed for the benefit of the parties the distinction between the duty of confidentiality that routinely applies to the *mediators* and the maintenance of confidentiality by the *parties*, which depends on an agreement by the parties.

The committee then moved to consider the Standard of Impartiality and its application to the case. The KO Code slightly rephrased the Proposed Model Code wording to indicate to mediators that under certain circumstances and limitations, preference is a legitimate exception to the principle of impartiality.[63] The committee noted:

> Despite the great importance of the principle of mediator impartiality, which prohibits to favor one party over another, it is not an absolute principle and sometimes there is justification to deviate from it. Standard 2.B.2 (Impartiality) of the [KO Code] states in this context:
>
> "Impartiality is not an absolute principle. Notwithstanding the prohibition on favoritism as aforesaid, a mediator shall treat a party differently in circumstances where same treatment will result in an advantage to a party or in harm to a party and preference is required to ensure the ethical right of a party to self-determination or other right in accordance with the standards. Preference will be justified if the following cumulative conditions are met:
>
> (a) The preference shall be limited to the minimum necessary to ensure the self-determination or other right of a party.
>
> (b) The mediator shall take appropriate measures to prevent, as far as possible, the creation of an appearance of favoritism, for example by separate meeting.
>
> (c) The mediator's conduct shall not violate any other ethical duty.
>
> (d) The preference shall not jeopardize public trust in the process."
>
> Raising the issue of the agreement's confidentiality by the mediators seemingly preferred the interest of the supplier

63. KO Code, *supra* note 43, Standard 2.B.2; Shapira's Proposed Model Code, *supra* note 18, Standard II.B.2.

> over the interest of the customer, but it should be noted that not raising the issue would have created the opposite situation according to which the customer's interest would have prevailed over the interest of the supplier. In the circumstances of the case described, raising the issue by the mediators was justified for two reasons: (a) enabling the supplier to exercise substantive, as opposed to formal, self-determination. The supplier wanted to maintain the confidentiality of the arrangement but did not understand the implications of the agreement and did not realize that to maintain non-disclosure of the mediation information and mediated agreement by the parties required an agreement on that point; and (b) in order to ensure the supplier's right to a proper process in accordance with the Standard of Professional Integrity.[64]

The committee was concerned with the ability of the supplier to exercise self-determination because a self-determined decision is one that is made with knowledge of relevant information. Both the KO Code and the Proposed Model Code include within the Standard of Self-Determination language aimed at sensitizing mediators to the linkage between information and self-determination:

> F. Informed decisions –
>
> A mediator shall conduct the mediation under conditions that enable parties to make informed decisions. An informed decision is a decision that has been made on the basis of the information that is relevant to the decision-making.
>
> 1. A mediator cannot ensure that parties make decisions that are based on complete information. However, the mediator shall take steps, consistent with the Standards, so that party decision-making is based on the information relevant to the decision-making. Relevant information is information the knowledge or ignorance of which could influence the decision or the choice made.[65]

Clashes between conflicting ethical standards are an inevitable phenomenon that practicing mediators should be aware of and trained to face. This concept is reflected in the Introduction to both the KO Code and the Proposed Model Code:

---

64. Ethics Op. 5-2016, *supra* note 42.

65. KO Code, *supra* note 43, Standard 1.F; Shapira's Proposed Model Code, *supra* note 18, Standard IV.F.

> The [Code] should be read, interpreted, and applied in its entirety. The obligations of mediators are relative, not absolute, and no obligation has a prima-facie priority over another. Therefore, when obligations seem to conflict, a mediator shall –
>
> (a) Search for an alternative course of action that is consistent with all of his obligations; and
>
> (b) Terminate or withdraw from the mediation when he cannot prevent the violation, minimizing as far as possible the harm resulting from the violation.

With this approach to the relativity of the standards and the need to understand and interpret them in context, the committee was able to adopt a realistic, practical, and contextual view of impartiality that at the same time is worthy of both parties' trust, respects both parties' right to make informed decisions consistent with the Standard of Self-Determination, and protects the integrity of the process.[66] The mediators' intervention was justified for reasons of self-determination and integrity and could be contained by the concept of mediator impartiality.

The committee, however, finished its opinion with a note of caution on mediators' intervention in parties' agreements:

> The parties' right to self-determination allows them to make decisions regarding the process and its outcome, hence their responsibility for the outcome of the mediation. The mediators recommended that the parties consult a lawyer, and they were given the time required to make a decision regarding the type of arrangement in which they were interested. Apparently, in such situations there is no room for the mediator to intervene in the content of the arrangement.
>
> Indeed, if the circumstances were different, and the mediators had no reason to suspect that one party intended to make public the arrangement the other party indicated he wanted to keep private, there would have been no room for such an initiative on the part of the mediators and the issue should have remained within the parties' responsibility to make their own decisions. However, in the present case there was such a suspicion and it seemed that the supplier had not appreciated that the terms of the agreement could be publicly disclosed.[67]

66. *See* Omer Shapira, *Conceptions and Perceptions of Fairness in Mediation*, 54 S. Tex. L. Rev. 281, 304–10 (2012) (discussing the intersection between substantive impartiality and self-determination).

67. Ethics Op. 5-2016, *supra* note 42.

The committee concluded:

> A decision as to the obligation of the parties to keep the content of mediation and the mediated agreement secret is a matter for the parties to decide in accordance with the Standard of Self-determination. At the beginning of the mediation, the mediator must make it clear to the parties that the mediator is bound by confidentiality regarding information that arises during the mediation and that this obligation does not apply to the parties unless they have chosen to stipulate this in an agreement between them. The mediator is not required to elaborate on this issue unless the parties so request.
>
> However, in circumstances where the mediator has grounds to suspect that one of the parties intends to disclose information from the mediation or about the settlement terms and the other party is unaware of this and is against such disclosure, the mediator should consider raising the issue of confidentiality later in the proceeding subject to the Standard of Impartiality and consider the termination of mediation if appropriate in accordance with the Standard of Professional Integrity.[68]

On further reflection, the mediators might have considered some other options for addressing the issue of confidentiality that could have potentially minimized the intervention in the process even further.[69] For example, they could have asked *both* parties if they wanted to address the confidentiality of the agreement by linking it to the earlier discussion of the public apology, saying something like: "One issue raised during the mediation was a request for a public apology. While you both agreed that an apology need not be included in the agreement, the issue of whether the agreement would or would not be confidential was never discussed. This leaves open to possible misunderstanding the way you like to treat the agreement in terms of confidentiality. What are your views on that?" This intervention could be justified based on the discussion above with the benefit that it might seem more limited and less intrusive compared with the mediators' actual conduct. It also illustrates another characteristic of ethical decision making: ethical questions do not necessarily have one answer. There could be several ethically permissible courses of action that can be justified on a rational and impartial basis.[70] Mediators

---

68. *Id.*
69. I thank Gregory Firestone for suggesting this point.
70. *See* SHAPIRA, *supra* note 2, at 359, 363.

have discretion to choose between them and should strive to mediate in a manner that least compromises party self-determination.

1.14. Conclusion

This chapter offers mediators an impartial and rational approach to the ethics of mediators. It explores key concepts in ethical thinking and decision making and offers practical guidance to ethical conduct. If you follow and apply this approach in the practice of mediation, you will mediate ethically. If mediators in general do so, the profession of mediation will deserve respect and public trust.

Chapter 2

Contrasting Lawyer Ethics and Mediator Ethics: Critical Issues

*James J. Alfini**

2.1. Introduction

Lawyer mediators are subject to at least two ethics standards—rules of professional conduct for lawyers and standards of conduct for mediators. In this chapter, we will focus primarily on the American Bar Association Model Rules of Professional Conduct[1] and the Model Standards of Conduct for Mediators.[2] Both of these sets of model standards have been widely adopted in American jurisdictions. The Model Standards of Conduct for Mediators are often referred to as the Joint Standards because their development was the joint effort of the American Arbitration Association, American Bar Association, and the Association for Conflict Resolution, but we will use the Model Standards shorthand to be consistent with the other chapters in this book. While these sets of standards of ethical conduct bear certain similarities, there are some provisions

*Dean and Professor Emeritus, South Texas College of Law Houston. The author thanks Debra Berman for offering helpful comments on drafts of this chapter.

1. Model Rules of Prof'l Conduct (Am. Bar Ass'n 1983, amended 2001, 2002, 2003, 2012, 2013) [hereinafter ABA Model Rules].

2. Am. Arbitration Ass'n, Am. Bar Ass'n & Ass'n for Conflict Resol., Model Standards of Conduct for Mediators (2005) [hereinafter Model Standards]. The author was an ABA representative on the joint committee that drafted the earlier (1994) Model Standards.

that impose conflicting requirements on the lawyer mediator. Moreover, some ethical issues are not explicitly addressed by either set of standards, leaving the lawyer mediator in an ethics black hole. The purpose of this chapter is to analyze the similarities and differences between the two sets of ethical standards, as well as critical omissions, with particular attention to those standards that present ethical dilemmas for the lawyer mediator. This chapter also demonstrates that although legal ethics and mediator ethics use similar *terms* or labels for ethics standards (e.g., competence, conflicts of interest, confidentiality), the *meaning* of these terms is different and might require different conduct in the context of either a mediation or a client representation. For example, both lawyers and mediators must be "competent," but a competent lawyer is not necessarily a competent mediator: each role requires a different body of knowledge and set of skills.

Therefore, before analyzing specific provisions of the standards of conduct for these two professions, we should consider the core values, roles, and principles underlying these ethics rules. The Preamble to the ABA Model Rules states: "A lawyer, as a member of the legal profession, is a representative of clients, an officer of the legal system and a public citizen having special responsibility for the quality of justice."[3] The lawyer role of client representative does not initially appear to be in line with mediator core values and roles, particularly impartiality and party self-determination. Indeed, because lawyer ethics rules have historically stressed the representational role, there was considerable debate within state and local bar associations during the latter part of the 20th century over whether lawyers could ethically serve as mediators.[4] In particular, if the lawyer mediator was viewed as the representative of the parties to a mediation, the lawyer mediator would be acting unethically by representing clients with conflicting interests, a mainstay of the conflicts rules for lawyers.[5]

Happily, over the past few decades, the ABA Model Rules have been revised to expand the roles that lawyers may perform. In particular, Preamble [3] ("lawyer may serve as a third-party neutral, a nonrepresentational

---

3. ABA Model Rules, *supra* note 1, pmbl.

4. *See, e.g.*, Jay Folberg & Alison Taylor, A Comprehensive Guide to Resolving Conflicts without Litigation 252–56 (1984); Leonard Riskin, *Toward New Standards for the Neutral Lawyer in Mediation*, 26 Arizona L. Rev. 329 (1984).

5. *See* ABA Model Rules, *supra* note 1, R. 1.7 ("A concurrent conflict of interest exists if . . . the representation of one client will be directly adverse to another client.").

role, helping the parties to resolve a dispute or other matter") and ABA Model Rule 2.4 (Lawyer Serving as Third-Party Neutral), adopted in 2002, address a lawyer's responsibilities when serving as a third-party neutral. Even then, however, current ethics standards for the lawyer mediator continue to be criticized for failing to offer adequate guidance to the lawyer mediator and for the general failure to break away from underlying adversarial assumptions in reconfiguring the lawyer's role.[6]

ABA Model Rule 2.4(b) takes pains to separate the lawyer mediator's nonrepresentational role from the lawyer's representational role by warning the lawyer mediator not only to inform unrepresented mediation parties that the lawyer mediator is not representing them but also to "explain the difference between the lawyer's role as a third party neutral and a lawyer's role as one who represents a client."[7] Comment [3] of this rule recognizes that the extent of the disclosure required will depend upon the sophistication of the particular parties and the subject matter involved. However, the comment cautions the lawyer to ensure that the parties clearly understand these important differences in the lawyer's role, particularly the inapplicability of the attorney-client evidentiary privilege to the role of lawyer mediator.

2.2. Competence

Just as it does not necessarily follow that a competent lawyer will make a competent judge, it also does not automatically follow that a competent lawyer is competent to mediate. The mediator's role requires different skills than that of a representational lawyer practicing in an adversarial context. Standard IV(A) of the Model Standards states: "A mediator shall mediate only when the mediator has the necessary competence to satisfy the reasonable expectations of the parties." The standard then goes on to explain: "Training, experience in mediation, skills, cultural understandings and other qualities are often necessary for mediator competence."[8] Standard IV(B) recognizes that a mediator may become concerned, during the course of the mediation, about her ability to conduct the mediation competently and directs the mediator to "discuss that determination with the parties as soon as practicable and take appropriate steps to address

6. *See, e.g.*, Carrie Menkel-Meadow, *The Evolving Complexity of Dispute Resolution Ethics*, 30 Geo. J. Legal Ethics 389 (2017); James J. Alfini, *E2K Leaves Mediation in an Ethics Black Hole*, 7 Disp. Resol. Mag. 3 (2001).

7. ABA Model Rules, *supra* note 1, R. 2.4(b).

8. Model Standards, *supra* note 2, Standard IV.A.1.

the situation, including but not limited to, withdrawing or requesting appropriate assistance."[9]

Professor Omer Shapira criticizes this standard for focusing on parties' expectations[10] rather than criteria that refer to the mediator's role and argues that "basic competence in mediation is *a state of having the knowledge and skills necessary for carrying out the role of the mediator in an effective way*, which will ordinarily require training and experience."[11] While Shapira has stated that mediator competence "generally requires *knowledge and understanding* of conflicts, communication and negotiation theories," he goes on to point out that the "meaning of basic competence varies between the styles of mediation because they offer different accounts of conflicts, communication and negotiation . . . ."[12] Moreover, Shapira explains that mediators are sometimes expected to have "specific competence," such as "subject matter expertise, cultural understanding, and language skills."[13]

Ironically, Professor Shapira's critique and analysis of the Model Standards assist us in understanding why the drafters of the Model Standards chose to use the "reasonable expectations of the parties" language. His analysis implies that it would be difficult to develop a clear consensus over specific indices of mediator competence because of the variety of mediator styles and the fact that an effective mediation may sometimes require "specific competence." If the parties, for example, have informed the mediator that they expect the mediator to employ an evaluative style and the mediator is a committed transformative mediator or a committed facilitative mediator, the mediator arguably would not be competent to mediate because he would be unable to satisfy the reasonable expectations of the parties. Similarly, if the parties to a complex environmental dispute have informed the mediator that they expect the mediator to have knowledge of environmental law and experience in environmental matters and the mediator has neither, the mediator would not be competent to mediate because she would be unable to satisfy the reasonable expectations of the parties. In these contexts, the "reasonable expectations of the parties" criterion would be an important measure of mediator

9. *Id.* Standard IV.B.

10. Omer Shapira, *A Critical Assessment of the Model Standards of Conduct for Mediators (2005): A Call for Reform*, 100 Marq. L. Rev. 81, 133 (2016) ("This seems to be a peculiar and shaky criterion for professional competence.").

11. *Id.*

12. Omer Shapira, A Theory of Mediators' Ethics: Foundations, Rationale, and Application 181 (2016).

13. *Id.*

competence. In any event, the lawyer mediator is well advised not only to keep Professor Shapira's definition of competence in mind but also to assess the reasonable expectations of the parties before accepting a case to ensure that the mediator is competent to mediate the dispute.

2.3. Conflicts of Interest Subsequent to Mediation

Representational lawyers are expected to avoid concurrent conflicts of interest that may exist if "(1) the representation of one client will be directly adverse to another client; or (2) there is a significant risk that the representation of one or more clients will be materially limited by the lawyer's responsibilities to another client, a former client or a third person or by a personal interest of the lawyer."[14] While Rule 2.4 of the ABA Model Rules recognizes that lawyers may serve as third-party neutrals, Comment 3 of Rule 2.4 notes that "lawyers serving in this role may experience unique problems as a result of differences between the role of a third-party neutral and a lawyer's service as a client representative."

Service as a lawyer mediator may raise a number of conflicts-of-interest issues, and the Model Standards present them in straightforward fashion in Standard III. However, the Model Rules only focus on conflicts of interest that the nonrepresentational lawyer mediator could be involved in *subsequent* to the mediation (so-called downstream conflicts). Comment 4 of Rule 2.4 recognizes that the lawyer mediator may subsequently be asked to serve as a lawyer representing a client in the same matter and refers the lawyer mediator to ABA Model Rule 1.12(a), which prohibits a lawyer from subsequently representing "anyone in connection with a matter in which the lawyer participated personally and substantially as a judge or . . . mediator . . . unless all parties to the proceeding give informed consent confirmed in writing."[15] Moreover, Rule 1.12(c) imputes this disqualification to members of the lawyer mediator's firm unless the lawyer mediator is screened and apportioned no part of the fee and written notice is given to the parties to the mediation. Rule 1.12(b) states that the lawyer mediator is also barred from negotiating for employment with a party to a mediation in which the lawyer is serving as a mediator.

By thus referring the lawyer mediator to Rule 1.12 for conflicts purposes, Rule 2.4 is analogizing the lawyer mediator to a former judge and therefore imposing a more permissive ("same matter") test than the "substantially related" test imposed by Rule 1.9. Prior to the adoption of

14. ABA Model Rules, *supra* note 1, R. 1.7(a).
15. ABA Model Rules, *supra* note 1, R. 1.12(a).

Rule 2.4, the preexisting case law had generally analyzed such conflicts under the "substantially related matter" test of Rule 1.9 (former clients).[16] Concerns over grouping the lawyer mediator with other neutrals, particularly those performing adjudicatory roles such as former judges and arbitrators, have been raised in commentary and case law.[17] These concerns generally are raised because mediators are more likely to be privy to sensitive confidential information than other neutrals, and in this way the parties to a mediation are akin to former clients.

The Model Standards also impose conflict-of-interest restrictions on the lawyer mediator but through a different set of lenses and both during and after a mediation. Standard III of the Model Standards calls upon the lawyer mediator to "avoid a conflict of interest or the appearance of a conflict of interest . . . [arising] from any relationship between a mediator and any mediation participant, whether past or present, personal or professional, that reasonably raises a question of a mediator's impartiality."[18] Thus, the animating concerns in the Model Standards are maintaining the impartiality of the mediator and protecting the integrity of the mediation process. Standard III(C) requires the mediator to "disclose, as soon as practicable, all actual and potential conflicts of interest that are reasonably known to the mediator and could reasonably be seen as raising a question about the mediator's impartiality." Standard III(D) imposes this disclosure requirement throughout the mediation, and Standard III(E) calls upon the mediator to withdraw if the conflict "might reasonably be viewed as undermining the integrity of the mediation . . . regardless of the expressed desire or agreement of the parties to the contrary."

The Model Standards carry over this emphasis on maintaining mediator impartiality and protecting the integrity of the mediation to downstream conflicts as well. Standard III(F) prohibits the mediator from establishing a subsequent relationship with any of the mediation participants "that would raise questions about the integrity of the mediation." In an apparent effort to offer guidance to the mediator, Standard III(F) lists the following factors that a mediator should consider to determine

16. *See, e.g.*, Poly Software Int'l, Inc. v. Su, 880 F. Supp. 1487 (D. Utah 1995) ("Where a mediator has received confidential information in the course of a mediation, that mediator should not thereafter represent anyone in the same or a substantially factually related matter unless all parties to the mediation proceeding consent after full disclosure.").

17. *See, e.g.*, Aron H. Schur, *I Never Agreed to This! Reconsidering the Inclusion of Attorney-Mediators under Model Rule 1.12*, 23 GEO. J. LEGAL ETHICS 813 (2010); Moore v. Altra Energy Techs., Inc., 295 S.W.3d 404 (Tex. 2009).

18. MODEL STANDARDS, *supra* note 2, Standard III.A.

whether a subsequent relationship "might create a perceived or actual conflict of interest": "time elapsed following the mediation, the nature of the relationships established, and services offered . . . ." Thus, a lawyer mediator who wishes to enter into a relationship with a mediation party subsequent to the mediation will have to be aware of and comply with both Model Rule 1.12 and Standard III(F) of the Model Standards.[19]

2.4. Misrepresentations, Truthfulness, and Honesty

The ABA Model Rules provide a standard of candor and truthfulness for representational lawyers who engage in negotiations on behalf of their clients and make representations to tribunals.[20] They do not address nonrepresentational lawyers who act as third-party neutrals. Moreover, lawyer mediators should realize they are not considered a tribunal for the purpose of the absolute candor/truthfulness standard in Rule 3.3 that applies to representational lawyers.[21] The practical implication for the lawyer mediator is that she cannot assume that lawyers representing clients in the mediation adhere to the absolute truthfulness standard in ABA Model Rule 3.3 that prohibits lawyers from knowingly making "a false statement of fact or law to a tribunal or fail[ing] to correct a false statement of material fact or law previously made to the tribunal by the lawyer." Instead, the lawyers are bound by the qualified truthfulness standard in ABA Model Rule 4.1 that states that lawyers may not misrepresent a "material fact" when representing a client. This will allow them, according to Comment [2] to Rule 4.1, to engage in "puffery" under generally accepted conventions in negotiation when they participate in mediation. An ABA formal opinion has made it clear that the qualified truthfulness standard of Rule 4.1 applies in a "caucused mediation."[22]

Unlike the ABA Model Rules, the Model Standards explicitly address the standard of candor and truthfulness expected of the lawyer mediator

19. For a helpful discussion of these conflict-of-interest standards, see SHAPIRA, *supra* note 12, at 199–203.

20. See Chapter 9 for a discussion of applicable rules.

21. ABA MODEL RULES, *supra* note 1, Terminology (m) ("'Tribunal' denotes a court, an arbitrator in a binding arbitration proceeding, or a legislative body, administrative agency, or other body acting in an adjudicative capacity."). At least one state (Texas) does include mediation in the definition of tribunal. TEX. DISC. RULES OF PROF'L CONDUCT, Terminology.

22. *See* ABA Formal Op. 06-439, Lawyer's Obligation of Truthfulness When Representing a Client in Negotiation: Application to Caucused Mediation ("[T]he ethical principles governing lawyer truthfulness do not permit a distinction to be drawn between the caucused mediation context and other negotiation settings. . . .").

in the conduct of mediation. The Model Standards mandate a quality process[23] and instruct the mediator to "promote honesty and candor between and among all participants" and mandate that the mediator "shall not knowingly misrepresent any material fact or circumstance in the course of a mediation."[24] The reference to a *material* fact suggests that the drafters may have had Rule 4.1 of the ABA Model Rules in mind when drafting this standard, particularly when coupled with the statement in the Reporter's Notes to this standard that "mediation participants might engage in negotiation tactics such as bluffing or exaggerating that are designed to deceive other parties as to their acceptable positions . . . ."[25] Although there is no other indication that the drafters intended to impose the minimalist standard of Comment [2] to Rule 4.1 on the lawyer mediator, there is some ambiguity here. This ambiguity underscores Professor Omer Shapira's criticism of the Model Standards for failing to elevate honesty to a more prominent place in the Standards.[26] Lawyer representatives and their clients should be able to rely on the lawyer mediator to be truthful and honest, without qualification.

2.5. Conflicts of Interest and Drafting Mediated Agreements

May lawyer mediators assist the parties in a mediation in drafting an agreement or other papers? Unfortunately, neither the ABA Model Rules nor the Model Standards address the circumstances under which a lawyer mediator may participate in the drafting of a mediated settlement agreement or other papers intended to implement the agreement. Because the answer to this question varies widely from jurisdiction to jurisdiction, the lawyer mediator is best advised to look to state bar ethics rules, bar ethics advisory opinions, and court rules in the jurisdiction in which the mediation is to be conducted. After surveying the states, Professor Robert Kirkman Collins reports that the answer to this question, in general

---

23. Model Standards, *supra* note 2, Standard VI.A: "A mediator shall conduct a mediation . . . in a manner that promotes diligence, timeliness, safety, presence of the appropriate participants, party participation, procedural fairness, party competency and mutual respect among the participants."

24. *Id.* Standard VI.A.4.

25. Reporter's Notes to Model Standards of Conduct for Mediators [hereinafter Model Standards Notes], Standard VI.A.4.

26. Shapira, *supra* note 10, at 111 ("the obligation of honesty should not be relegated to a subsection . . . it ought to be upgraded into a separate Standard of Honesty standing in its own right . . .").

terms, is to be found in "an array of rules ranging from 'yes' to 'no' . . . with a bewildering variety of approaches in between."[27]

In his article, Professor Collins views divorce mediation as the principal battleground over the issue of whether the lawyer mediator may draft settlement agreements and related documents. In particular, he views it as part of "the ongoing siege by matrimonial litigators attempting to halt civilian flight away from their traditional gladiatorial matrimonial practice . . . since the inception of divorce mediation . . . ."[28] Histrionics aside, many of the state rules that have emerged in this area do appear to have been influenced by divorce mediation, including unauthorized practice of law (UPL) charges against nonlawyer divorce mediators.[29] Ironically, the Model Standards of Practice for Family and Divorce Mediation, adopted in 2000 by a diverse group of family and dispute resolution organizations, endorses the practice of mediator drafting of settlement agreements.[30] Also, the Committee on Ethical Guidance of the ABA Dispute Resolution Section has issued an opinion titled "Mediator's Duty of Care When Drafting Agreements," which allows a lawyer mediator to act as "scrivener" of points of agreement and draft the settlement agreement if the mediator has the professional experience and competence to do so.[31]

To date, the principal sources of guidance on the issue of lawyer mediators drafting settlement agreements have been state bar and court authorities. Professor Collins identifies 15 states that have "explicitly addressed the issue" and explains that by his count, "approximately twice as many states permit the attorney-mediator to draft than prohibit it."[32] My updated count reveals that none of the states explicitly prohibits the lawyer mediator from participating in the drafting of a settlement docu-

---

27. Robert Kirkman Collins, *The Scrivener's Dilemma in Divorce Mediation: Promulgating Progressive Professional Parameters*, 17 CARDOZO J. CONFLICT RESOL. 691, 695 (2016).

28. *Id.* at 694.

29. *See* David A. Hoffman & Natasha A. Affolder, *Mediation and UPL: Do Mediators Have a Well-Founded Fear of Persecution?*, DISP. RESOL. MAG., Winter 2000, at 20. *See also* Debra Berman & James Alfini, *Lawyer Colonization of Family Mediation: Consequences and Implications*, 95 MARQ. L. REV. 887, 893 (2012) ("the biggest areas of [UPL] risk for a non-lawyer mediator involve . . . drafting documents that can have a legally binding effect").

30. MODEL STANDARDS OF PRACTICE FOR FAMILY AND DIVORCE MEDIATION VI.E (2000) ("the mediator may document the participants' resolution of their dispute").

31. ABA SEC. OF DISP. RESOL. COMM. ON MEDIATOR ETHICAL GUIDANCE SODR-2010-1.

32. Collins, *supra* note 27, at n.4.

ment. Rather, the divide is between states that permit the drafting not only of settlement agreements but also ancillary court documents on the one hand and, on the other hand, those that permit the lawyer mediator to participate only in memorializing or summarizing points of agreement reached in mediation.

To illustrate this difference, let's consider two states that are at the opposite ends of this spectrum: Illinois and Utah. Professor Collins identifies Illinois as a "no" state because an advisory opinion of the Illinois State Bar Association had concluded: "A lawyer who mediated a divorce settlement between unrepresented husband and wife may not prepare a proposed judgment of dissolution of marriage, a marriage separation agreement and joint parenting agreement for husband and wife and allow husband and wife to file said documents as pro se litigants."

The opinion concluded that "such action by the lawyer would constitute representing two parties with adverse interests in violations of IRPC 1.7(a)."[33] In the Illinois advisory opinion, however, the committee said that it "contrasts the facts presented in this inquiry from those of a typical divorce mediation at the conclusion of which the mediator memorializes for the represented parties the agreement reached during the mediation."[34] Thus, Illinois implicitly allows the mediator to memorialize an agreement but not to draft ancillary court documents. In contrast, Utah's Rule 2.4 permits the lawyer mediator not only to memorialize the agreement but also to "prepare formal documents that memorialize and implement the agreement reached in mediation."[35] This would include allowing the lawyer mediator in Utah to "record or file related papers or pleadings with an appropriate tribunal."[36] Comment [5a] to the Utah rule explains: "Because the parties in this situation have fully resolved their issues, they are not considered 'adverse' under Rule 1.7(a)(1)."[37]

The rules and opinions in those states, like Utah, that permit the lawyer mediator to draft and file not only the agreement but also ancillary documents require the mediator to recommend that the parties (if unrepresented) seek independent legal advice before signing and to get

33. Ill. St. Bar Ass'n Prof'l Rules of Conduct, Ethics Op. No. 04-03 (2005, *aff'd* 2010).

34. *Id.*

35. Utah State Bar Rules of Prof'l Conduct R. 2.4(c)(1) (2019).

36. *Id.* cmt. [5a].

37. *Id.*

the informed consent of all parties confirmed in writing.[38] Interestingly, Missouri, New York, and Ohio permit the lawyer mediator to memorialize the agreement in divorce cases and then prepare and file ancillary documents, but only for one of the parties, as long as both parties give informed consent confirmed in writing.[39] The lawyer mediator may not represent *both* parties, because "Rule 1.7(b)(3) forbids a lawyer from representing adverse parties in a proceeding, even with informed consent . . . ."[40]

Texas would not permit the lawyer mediator to subsequently represent either or both parties to a mediation and draws a strict line between mediation and legal representation: "Preparing a draft of a writing to memorialize the parties' oral agreement is part of the normal mediation process and is distinct from drafting court papers or other ancillary legal instruments that may be needed to effectuate the settlement agreement."[41] A number of other states have apparently adopted the Texas approach in distinguishing between drafting or memorializing a mediated settlement agreement and representing one or both parties in effectuating the agreement by drafting court papers or ancillary documents.[42]

Therefore, a clear consensus exists among the minority of states that have addressed the issue that a lawyer mediator may participate in the drafting, or memorializing, of a settlement agreement. However, there is a division of opinion among these states over whether the lawyer mediator may then participate in the drafting of ancillary documents, particularly in divorce cases, or represent one or both of the parties in subsequent proceedings. The lawyer mediator is well advised, therefore, to familiarize herself with the ethics opinions and rules of the jurisdiction as to not only what is *permitted* but also what is *required* of the mediator

---

38. *See, e.g.*, IND. RULES OF CT., *Rules for Alternative Dispute Resolution*, R. 2.7(F) (2015); OR. RULES OF PROF'L CONDUCT R. 2.4(b); Me. Bar Ass'n Ethics Op. 137 (1993); MASS. SUP. JUD. CT. UNIFORM RULES ON DISPUTE RESOL. R. 7(g). *See also* Mass. Bar Ass'n Ethics Op. 85-3 (1985).

39. Mo. Bar Ass'n Informal Advisory Op. 2010-0055; N.Y. St. Bar Ass'n Comm. on Prof'l Ethics Op. 1178 (Dec. 13, 2019); Ohio Sup. Ct. Bd. of Comm'rs on Grievances and Discipline Op. 2009-4 (June 12, 2009).

40. N.Y. St. Bar Ass'n Comm. on Prof'l Ethics Op. 1178 (Dec. 13, 2019).

41. Tex. Ctr. for Legal Ethics Op. 675 (Aug. 2018).

42. *See* Wash. St. Bar Ass'n Advisory Op. 201901 (2019); N.C. St. Bar Ass'n Formal Ethics Op. 2 (Jan. 25, 2013) (mediator may not draft a business contract because joint representation "is a non-consentable conflict of interest"); TENN. RULES OF SUP. CT. 2.4(e); Ky. Bar Ass'n Ethics Op. KBA E-438 (2015).

(e.g., getting informed consent of the parties in writing) before engaging in a particular activity.

2.6. Confidentiality and Reporting Professional Misconduct

A lawyer mediator, like other members of the bar, has a duty to report the misconduct of another lawyer. Rule 8.3(a) of the ABA Model Rules states: "A lawyer who knows that another lawyer has committed a violation of the Rules of Professional Conduct that raises a substantial question as to the lawyer's honesty, trustworthiness, or fitness as a lawyer in other respects, shall inform the appropriate professional authority."[43] Misconduct is defined in Rule 8.4. However, if the lawyer mediator learns of the misconduct through a communication during the mediation, the mediator is presented with a major dilemma. The Model Standards, as well as related state rules and statutes, require the mediator to "maintain the confidentiality of all information obtained by the mediator in mediation, unless otherwise . . . required by applicable law."[44]

The state of Illinois has resolved this dilemma in favor of requiring the lawyer mediator to report the misconduct. An opinion of the Illinois State Bar Association concludes: "A lawyer has an obligation to report violations of Rule 8.4 (c), including when the lawyer is serving as a mediator."[45] The authors of the Illinois opinion pointed out that the Supreme Court of Illinois had emphasized the importance of reporting lawyer misconduct in a leading case.[46] They also pointed out that Illinois had adopted the Uniform Mediation Act (UMA), which provides in Section 6(a)(6) that there is "no privilege under Section 4 for a mediation communication that is . . . sought or offered to prove or disprove a complaint of professional misconduct."[47] They explained that they understood that the mediation privilege established by the UMA would prevent anyone from *forcing* the mediator to testify in a disciplinary proceeding, but "the

43. ABA Model Rules, *supra* note 1, R. 8.3(a).

44. Model Standards, *supra* note 2, Standard V.A.

45. Ill. St. Bar Ass'n Adv. Op. on Prof'l Conduct No. 11-01 (Jan. 2011). For commentary recommending the approach of reporting the misconduct, see Mori Irvine Sub, *Serving Two Masters: The Obligation under the Rules of Professional Conduct to Report Attorney Misconduct in a Confidential Mediation*, 26 Rutgers L.J. 155 (1994).

46. *In re* Himmel, 533 N.E.2d 790 (Ill. 1988).

47. Uniform Mediation Act, 710 Ill. Comp. Stat. 35.

mediator remains capable under this section of disclosing a lawyer's misconduct to disciplinary authorities."[48]

Some states, however, have decided that confidentiality in mediation should trump the duty to report. Accordingly, they have amended their version of Rule 8.3 to include an exception for lawyer mediators. The ABA Model Rules provide only for the following exceptions to Rule 8.3: "(c) This Rule does not require disclosure of information otherwise protected by Rule 1.6 or information gained by a lawyer or judge while participating in an approved lawyers' assistance program." The amended Florida rule reads, in part, "This rule does not require disclosure of information . . . (2) gained by a lawyer while serving as a mediator or mediation participant if the information is privileged or confidential under applicable law."[49] The rules in Oregon[50] and North Carolina[51] have been amended to include similar exceptions. Virginia has also amended its rule to provide for a confidentiality in mediation exception but requires the lawyer mediator to first "attempt to obtain the parties' written agreement to waive confidentiality and permit disclosure of such information to the appropriate professional authority."[52] And Wisconsin's rule limits the exception to "disputes between lawyers arising out of a professional or economic dispute involving law firm dissolutions, termination or departure of one or more lawyers from a law firm where such information is acquired in the course of mediating or arbitrating the dispute between lawyers."[53]

Given this variety of strictures relating to a lawyer mediator's duty to disclose another lawyer's misconduct, the lawyer mediator should become familiar with authoritative statements in his jurisdiction. Even then, however, it is likely that the lawyer mediator will find an absence of official rules or opinions on the subject, leaving the lawyer mediator to find his way out of this ethics black hole by exercising his best professional judgment under the circumstances.

48. Ill. St. Bar Ass'n Adv. Op., *supra* note 45.
49. Fla. Rules of Prof'l Conduct R. 8.3(c)(2) (eff. July 1, 2012).
50. Or. Rules of Prof'l Conduct R. 8.3(d) (eff. Jan. 11, 2018).
51. N.C. Rules of Prof'l Conduct R. 8.3(e) (eff. June 9, 2016).
52. Va. Rules of Prof'l Conduct R. 8.3(c) (eff. Feb. 1, 2016).
53. Wis. Rules of Prof'l Conduct R. 8.3(c)(2) (eff. July 1, 2007).

2.7. Impartiality, Self-Determination, Integrity, and Power Imbalances

One of the most troubling questions faced by a lawyer mediator is what, if anything, she should do to rectify an imbalance of power between the parties to a mediation. The subject of power imbalances in mediation has produced a sizable literature, and it would be folly to attempt a comprehensive discussion of the topic given the space constraints imposed by this book chapter.[54] Therefore, I will attempt to address some of the salient ethics issues related to this topic by posing and discussing a hypothetical that deals with a fairly common scenario, namely, an employment mediation where only one party is represented by counsel.

Power imbalances are often the result of an imbalance of resources between the parties. One of the most significant resources that a mediation party can possess is competent counsel. In our hypothetical, let us assume that the aggrieved party is a woman named Maria who works as an administrative staff member at XYZ Corporation. Maria is claiming workplace discrimination, and she is unrepresented by legal counsel. Her complaint indicates that she had worked at XYZ for ten years in the same position. After her supervisor had denied her request to be promoted with a commensurate raise in salary for the third straight year, Maria had complained to the XYZ Human Resources Office that she was being discriminated against. One month later, she was fired from her job. She filed her complaint, and the dispute was sent to mediation by her local EEOC office. On the opposing side is Maria's supervisor, who is represented by a lawyer from the general counsel's office of the corporation. The corporate lawyer has a long track record of defending workplace discrimination claims against the corporation.

At the outset, there would appear to be a clear imbalance of power between the parties. One might assume that the corporate side possesses information, experience, and advocacy and negotiation skills that are not available to Maria. The lawyer mediator might therefore be inclined to assist Maria to correct this imbalance. However, any intervention by the mediator would bring into question at least two important values reflected in the Model Standards, namely, impartiality and party self-determination. The corporate side might object that the lawyer mediator is favoring Maria and thus violating Standard II(B), which requires the mediator to "conduct a mediation in an impartial manner and avoid

54. For an extensive discussion of ethical considerations in dealing with power imbalances, see Ellen Waldman, Mediation Ethics 87–153 (2011).

conduct that gives the appearance of partiality."[55] However, the mediator also has the duty to conduct a process based on party self-determination. If Maria does not have the knowledge and skills to effectively present her case, her ability to exercise self-determination would be undermined. Thus, mediator intervention would be required to create conditions that would enable Maria to exercise self-determination.

Given these strictures in the Model Standards, the lawyer mediator, when confronting a power imbalance, is presented with a dilemma and faces numerous ethical challenges in seeking to conduct a quality process, particularly to the extent that this anticipates a fair process and outcome. Indeed, the Model Standards have been criticized for lacking a separate Standard of Fairness.[56] Nevertheless, in practice commentaries, mediation educators have attempted to explain how to manage power imbalances while adhering to the dictates of the Model Standards.[57] If the primary objective of the lawyer mediator, in addressing the power imbalance, is to ensure that the parties (particularly Maria) will be able to self-determine by making informed decisions, the mediator may wish to consider using certain techniques aimed at achieving certain goals discussed in the practice commentaries. Two goals discussed in the commentaries that may be applied to our hypothetical are (1) ensuring that Maria has a *voice* during the mediation and (2) making sure Maria has enough information to make informed decisions.

To assist Maria in developing an effective voice during the mediation, the mediator will have to assess both her communication skills and the willingness of the corporate side to allow Maria to find her voice. Maria is likely to feel somewhat intimidated by her boss and her boss's attorney across the table. For that reason, the mediator may wish to arrange separate premediation sessions with each party. During the premediation session with Maria, the mediator will want to have Maria explain the circumstances that led her to bring the complaint and ask her related questions. In this way, Maria will be developing an effective narrative

---

55. Model Standards, *supra* note 2, Standard II.B.

56. *See, e.g.*, Shapira, *supra* note 10, at 119 ("to insist on mediator impartiality (or neutrality) while *ignoring power imbalances* between parties is to award priority to form over substance, that is, to prefer in effect the stronger party over the weaker and sacrifice the 'quality' or substantive fairness of the process").

57. *See, e.g.*, Rick Voyles, *Managing an Imbalance of Power*, Mediate.com (Oct. 2004), https://www.mediate.com/articles/voylesR3.cfm; Max Factor III, *Thirty FAQ's for California Mediators on Ethical Minefields Involving Business, Construction, Employment and Real Estate Mediations*, Mediate.com (Dec. 2003), https://www.mediate.com/articles/factorM2.cfm.

that she can use during the opening joint session. If premediation sessions before the time scheduled for the mediation are not possible, the mediator may wish to confer with the parties as to whether they would prefer an abbreviated opening joint session devoted largely to having the mediator deliver his opening statement and then move to separate sessions that could serve the purpose of premediation sessions. The parties would then move to a joint session where each side would present its opening statements.

A mediator may also use numerous techniques to accomplish the second goal, that of providing Maria with sufficient information to enable her to make informed decisions. In joint session and separate caucus, the mediator might lead the parties in an agenda-setting exercise, listing topics that not only require an open exchange of information but also create focus and structure for communication. In joint session, the mediator may ask the corporate side for clarifying information on particular issues, such as the company's policies or protocols. In separate session with Maria, the mediator might ask whether the company's HR director or personnel manager might be of assistance in filling in information gaps that the boss and his counsel seemed reluctant to mention. Because Maria was terminated, however, contacting the company would be awkward, and the mediator might therefore request the corporate side to fill the information gap by making the calls as needed. In these ways, Maria may become educated and empowered.

Perhaps the most difficult ethical challenge faced by the lawyer mediator in this context is that of offering Maria information or advice when needed. Maria, knowing that the mediator is a lawyer, may press the mediator for legal information and advice. Could the mediator, for example, then explain retaliation in legal terms, apply the law to the facts of Maria's case, and estimate her chances of success on a retaliation claim? Commentators have frequently drawn a line between (permissible) information and (impermissible) advice.[58] In this context, if there is a line to be drawn, it will depend on the lawyer mediator's good judgment in interpreting applicable ethics rules.

---

58. *See, e.g.*, Robert B. Moberly, *Ethical Standards for Court-Appointed Mediators and Florida's Mandatory Mediation Experiment*, 21 FLA. ST. L. REV. 701, 714 (1994) ("distinction the mediator must make here is between giving legal information and giving legal advice"). *But see* James Stark, *The Ethics of Mediation Evaluation: Some Troublesome Questions and Tentative Proposals, from an Evaluative Lawyer Mediator*, 38 S. TEX. L. REV. 769, 784 (1997) ("The (Mostly) False Dichotomy Between 'Information' and 'Advice'").

As discussed earlier, ABA Model Rule 2.4(b) requires the lawyer mediator to inform an unrepresented mediation party that the lawyer mediator is not representing her and to "explain the difference between the lawyer's role as a third party neutral and a lawyer's role as one who *represents* a client."[59] Although Comment [2] to Rule 2.4 states, "Lawyer neutrals may also be subject to various codes of ethics, such as . . . the Model Standards of Conduct for Mediators,"[60] the ABA rules and commentary make no attempt to offer guidance as to how to reconcile provisions of the ABA Model Rules and the Model Standards. In the *Annotated Model Rules of Professional Conduct*,[61] the authors speculate that the "extent to which a lawyer is subject to the lawyer ethics rules when serving in a nonrepresentational role may depend on whether the lawyer/mediator is providing legal advice." They then consider an alternative view that the lawyer mediator is providing "law-related services" as contemplated by ABA Model Rule 5.7, and in that event the lawyer mediator "would have to take reasonable measures to assure that a person obtaining the law-related services knows that the services are not legal services and that the protections of the client-lawyer relationship do not exist."[62] The extent to which the lawyer mediator is *practicing law* under these circumstances has also led to a somewhat confusing array of state bar ethics opinions.[63] Again, the lawyer mediator should therefore become familiar with relevant bar ethics opinions in the mediator's jurisdiction.

In deciding whether or how to offer Maria advice or information, the lawyer mediator will also have to reckon with relevant provisions of the Model Standards and their state counterparts. The most significant standard in this regard is Standard VI(A)(5), which refers to the "provision of information," not advice, and provides in part: "A mediator may provide information that the mediator is qualified by training or experience to provide, only if the mediator can do so consistent with these Standards."[64]

---

59. ABA Model Rules, *supra* note 1, R. 2.4(b).

60. ABA Model Rules, *supra* note 1, R. 2.4, cmt. [2].

61. Am. Bar Ass'n Ctr. for Prof'l Resp., Annotated Model Rules of Prof'l Conduct (9th ed. 2019).

62. ABA Model Rules, *supra* note 1, R. 5.7(a)(2).

63. *See, e.g.*, N.J. Bar Ass'n Ethics Op. 711 (2007) (lawyers handling mediation who advise clients on their legal rights and obligations are practicing limited-representation law under Rule 1.2(c)); N.Y. Bar Ethics Op. 1026 (2014) (lawyer is subject to ethics rules when providing mediation services if those services are provided in a manner not distinct from legal services).

64. Model Standards, *supra* note 2, Standard VI.A.5.

In the Model Standards Notes, the reporter clarifies that the goal of Standard VI(A)(5) is to "distinguish between a mediator's role and such other roles as being a lawyer, mental health counselor, and the like." Yet the standard "recognizes that the insights and training the mediator draws upon to assist parties in mediation" could be beneficial to the parties and therefore "supports the mediator sharing information that he or she is qualified by training or experience to provide," though "only if it is done in a manner consistent with other Standards, most notably promoting party self-determination and sustaining mediator impartiality."[65] To sustain his impartiality, should the mediator offer the information to Maria in joint session or separate caucus? Although some might assume that the information should be imparted in joint session, one might as easily argue that it should be done in caucus given the circumstances of our hypothetical. For example, the mediator may know that the supervisor has already received and discussed information about relevant statutes, regulations, and case law from his lawyer in caucus. The mediator might therefore believe that to be fair, Maria also should be given this information in caucus so that she would have the same opportunity for a private discussion that permits her to consider and discuss the information as it relates to her interests, fears, and goals. By any objective standard, the ethical mandate to be and remain impartial would appear to be satisfied under these circumstances.

As we have seen, a lawyer mediator's attempt to rectify a power imbalance raises many ethics questions. Unfortunately, neither the ABA Model Rules nor the Model Standards offer completely satisfactory answers to these questions. Once again, the lawyer mediator would do well to familiarize herself with ethics opinions and practice commentaries in the mediator's jurisdiction.

2.8. The Judge as Mediator

A sitting judge who decides to mediate a case before the judge's court takes on additional ethical baggage. The judge is subject to not only the two sets of ethical standards confronting the lawyer mediator but also the judicial ethics rules in the judge's jurisdiction. While the role of a judge may bear some similarities to that of a mediator, particularly insofar as *impartiality* is a core value for both, the roles diverge with regard to decision making. Judges are expected to make decisions, while mediators are cautioned to avoid a decision-making role. In this section, I will

65. Model Standards Notes, *supra* note 25.

address the most pressing question raised in this context: "Should a judge be allowed to preside over the trial of a case in which the judge has previously served as a mediator?"

As I have argued elsewhere, we have created a settlement culture in America's courts during the past few decades, but we have not created a judicial ethics infrastructure to support this settlement culture.[66] One of the more troubling aspects of this lack of an infrastructure is that there is little or no guidance for the judge who serves as a mediator in the case assigned to the judge for trial. Commentators have expressed concern that judges exercise a good deal of discretion in deciding how interventionist they will be as far as settlement is concerned and engage in a variety of settlement practices, including mediation, with little in the way of ethical guidance.[67]

The only explicit guidance with regard to settlement activity offered to the judge by the ABA Model Code of Judicial Conduct is an admonition against coercing case dispositions: "A judge may encourage parties to a proceeding and their lawyers to settle matters in dispute but shall not act in a manner that coerces any party into settlement."[68] Comment [2] to Rule 2.6(B) offers the following guidance as to factors a judge should consider when deciding upon appropriate settlement practices: "(1) whether the parties have requested or voluntarily consented to a certain level of participation by the judge in settlement discussions; (2) whether the parties and their counsel are relatively sophisticated in legal matters; (3) whether the case will be tried by the judge or jury; (4) whether the parties participate with their counsel in settlement

66. James J. Alfini, *Risk of Coercion Too Great: Judges Should Not Mediate Cases Assigned to Them for Trial*, 6 Disp. Resol. Mag. 11 (1999). For an opposing view, see Harold J. Baer, Jr., *History, Process, and a Role for Judges in Mediating Their Own Cases*, 58 N.Y.U. Ann. Surv. Am. L. 131 (2001).

67. *See, e.g.*, Peter Robinson, *Opening Pandora's Box: An Empirical Exploration of Judicial Settlement Ethics and Techniques*, 27 Ohio St. J. on Disp. Resol. 53, 107–08 (2012) (the author researched settlement practices of California trial judges and observed: "The data begs many questions for the best practices by individual judges and institutions providing advisory and mandatory guidance for judges."); John C. Cratsley, *Judicial Ethics and Judicial Settlement: Time for Two Strangers to Meet*, 21 Ohio St. J. on Disp. Resol. 569, 570 (2006) ("All of this novel settlement activity engaged in by judges who are assigned to try these matters . . . undermines the traditional judicial role . . . . The time has arrived . . . for the enactment of explicit ethics rules in the Model Code of Judicial Conduct governing judicial settlement activity in civil cases.").

68. Am. Bar Ass'n, Model Code of Jud. Conduct R. 2.6(B) (2007, amended 2011) [hereinafter ABA Model Code].

discussions; (5) whether any parties are unrepresented by counsel; (6) whether the matter is civil or criminal."[69] Factor 3, "whether the case will be tried by the judge or jury," is a significant consideration for a judge who is intending to mediate a case. If the judge will be the ultimate trier of fact, aggressive pretrial settlement negotiation in the context of a mediation may contribute to a perception that the judge has acquired information (and perhaps attitudes) that would not be available to the judge during a trial, making it difficult for the judge to appear impartial at trial.

Both state and federal courts, when faced with disqualification challenges to a judge trying a case after a failed mediation, have generally demonstrated a permissive attitude toward the judge mediator. In *Home Depot v. Saul Subsidiary*,[70] for example, a Kentucky trial judge conducted extensive mediation sessions in an effort to resolve the dispute between the parties. After the mediation failed to resolve the dispute, the judge proceeded to try the case over a party's objection, and the appellate court upheld the judge's actions.

In some federal cases with similar mediation/trial scenarios, reviewing courts have accepted the notion that a judge can "compartmentalize" all the information and attitudes (e.g., confidential facts, inadmissible evidence, attitudes toward parties and attorneys) acquired during mediation that might compromise the judge's impartiality during trial, thus creating a "clean slate" or "open mind" for trial.[71] In one case, however, a federal magistrate judge took issue with this notion of compartmentalization: "No matter how much I am presumed to be able to compartmentalize information I learned while presiding over the settlement discussions . . . I would be obliged to engage in remarkable mental gymnastics."[72]

A number of researchers have addressed the efficacy of a judge's ability to compartmentalize in other contexts. Empirical studies have found that inadmissible information obtained during settlement conferences or preliminary hearings affected judges' views of the matters and parties before them and had an effect on their subsequent decisions.[73]

---

69. *Id.* cmt. [2].

70. Home Depot v. Saul Subsidiary, 159 S.W.3d 339 (Ky. 2004).

71. *See, e.g.*, Bosley v. 21 WFMJ TV, Inc., 245 F. App'x 445 (6th Cir. 2007); Novak v. Farneman, 2011 U.S. Dist. LEXIS 114398 (Sept. 30, 2011).

72. Black v. Kendig, 227 F. Supp. 2d 153 (D.D.C. 2002).

73. *See, e.g.*, Stephan Landsman & Richard F. Rakos, *A Preliminary Inquiry into the Effects of Potentially Biasing Information on Judges and Jurors in Civil Litigation*, 12 Behav. Sci. & L. 113, 122–25 (1994); Andrew J. Wistrich et al., *Can Judges*

I have argued that the ABA Model Code of Judicial Conduct should be amended to offer judges more guidance in this area.[74] Courts might also be well advised to design new procedures that would make a separate judge within the court available to mediate, perhaps upon request of the assigned judge. "Buddy systems" or procedures that separate the settlement function from the trial function have been implemented in some courts. For example, under Maricopa County (Arizona) court rules, a judge pro tem is generally appointed to conduct settlement discussions.[75]

2.9. Conclusion

As a member of two distinct professions, the lawyer mediator must satisfy the ethical imperatives of both the legal profession and the mediation profession. As we have seen, however, the national standards of conduct for these professions are sometimes ambiguous and often silent and may even send conflicting signals. The lawyer mediator should therefore become familiar not only with the national standards but also with the related dictates of state and local bar, court, and legislative authorities.

The lawyer mediator also has the ethical responsibility to "act in a manner that advances the practice of mediation."[76] We have noted significant omissions and ambiguities in national and state ethics standards when searching for answers to critical issues. The lawyer mediator should work through organizations such as the ABA Section of Dispute Resolution and its state and local counterparts to seek the adoption of rules and practice guidelines that offer direction and clarity on these important issues.

Ignore Inadmissible Information: The Difficulty of Deliberately Disregarding, 153 U. Pa. L. Rev. 1251, 1259, 1288–89, 1323–26 (2005).

74. Alfini, *supra* note 66, at 14.

75. *Settlement Conferences*, Jud. Branch of Az., Maricopa Cnty., https://superiorcourt.maricopa.gov/adr/settlement-conferences/ (last updated June 8, 2020).

76. Model Standards, *supra* note 2, Standard IX.A.

Chapter 3

Understanding Codes of Conduct for Mediators and MEAC Opinions

Susan Nauss Exon

3.1. Introduction

Codes of conduct for mediators and mediation ethical advisory opinions offer guidance to ensure a quality mediation process. Codes of conduct, commonly referred to as mediation standards, provide rules to help guide mediator behavior, inform mediating parties, promote public confidence in mediation as a dispute resolution process,[1] and increase access to justice.[2] One jurisdiction aptly states that its ethical standards are "designed to promote honesty, integrity and impartiality" by its neutrals, seeking to promote the highest-quality service.[3]

The standards provide black-letter principles but are often written in imprecise terms to facilitate the flexible nature of mediation. Many standards offer commentary; some add examples or explanations. Nevertheless, mediation ethical advisory opinions are helpful to fill in gaps

1. Model Standards of Conduct for Mediators, Pmbl. (2005), Rules of Conduct for Mediators in Ct.-Connected Mediation Programs for Civil Cases, Cal. Rules of Court 3.850(a) (2009); Standards of Conduct for Mediators in Ct.-Connected Programs, Pmbl. (N.J. Sup. Ct. 2000).

2. Rules of the Cir. Ct. of N.H. – District Div., R. 3.28(A), https://www.courts.state.nh.us/rules/dmcr/dmcr-3_28.htm (last visited April 26, 2021).

3. Unif. Rules on Dispute Resol., Mass. Sup. Jud. Ct. Rule 1:18, R. 9 Ethical Standards (1999).

left open by standards and otherwise assist mediators with their ethical dilemmas, especially when circumstances may create a conflict between two or more values within a single set of standards.[4]

The purpose of this chapter is to provide guidance regarding general themes found in mediation ethical codes of conduct, as supplemented by advisory opinions. Practicing mediators are bound by the codes and opinions aligned with their jurisdiction. Appendix A at the end of this book lists, by state, standards of conduct and ethical advisory opinions available for general civil matters. This chapter does not address codes of conduct for specific subject areas such as family law or probate, nor does it address other types of codes such as qualification or disciplinary standards.

3.2. Mediation Codes of Conduct

The meaning and content of mediation ethics have been discussed in Chapters 1 and 2. This section focuses on mediation codes of conduct, of which there are several main sources. The premier set is the Model Standards of Conduct for Mediators (Model Standards), promulgated by the American Bar Association, the American Arbitration Association, and the Association for Conflict Resolution.[5] Several states, including Colorado, Louisiana, Missouri, Ohio, Pennsylvania, and Rhode Island, have adopted the Model Standards.[6] Many other states, through their court systems or professional mediation associations, have adopted similar standards.

The Uniform Mediation Act (UMA) was promulgated in 2001 and has now been adopted by the District of Columbia and 11 states[7]—Hawaii,[8]

---

4. The mediator ethical standards in Florida and Georgia have extensive commentary and examples. See Appendix A for their respective citations.

5. The Association for Conflict Resolution (ACR) was formed in 2001 as a result of the merger of the Society of Professionals in Dispute Resolution, Inc. (SPIDR); the Academy of Family Mediators (AFM); and the Conflict Resolution Education Network (CREnet), the successor organization to the National Institute for Dispute Resolution (NIDR).

6. See Appendix A at the end of this book for the citation to each respective state's adoption of the Model Standards.

7. Sarah R. Cole et al., Mediation: Law, Policy and Practice § 8:12 (2019); Monica Rausch, *The Uniform Mediation Act*, 18 Ohio St. J. on Disp. Resol. 603, 604 (2003).

8. Haw. Rev. Stat. Ann. §§ 658H-1 to 658H-13 (Westlaw through 2019 Reg. Sess.).

Idaho,[9] Illinois,[10] Iowa,[11] Nebraska,[12] New Jersey,[13] Ohio,[14] South Dakota,[15] Utah,[16] Vermont,[17] and Washington.[18] The UMA deals primarily with mediation confidentiality and privileges; therefore, it is referenced minimally in this chapter regarding discussions of confidentiality.

3.2.1. Legal and Ethical Force of Mediation Codes of Conduct

Each jurisdiction handles the legal and ethical force of its mediation codes of conduct on an individual basis. First, six states have no mediation codes of conduct.[19] Second, some states consider mediation standards of conduct as aspirational in nature, setting goals for mediator behavior in order to promote public confidence; they are not disciplinary in nature.[20] Similarly, voluntary standards are not disciplinary.[21] For example, the Preamble to the Model Standards provides that the Model Standards do not have the force and effect of law unless adopted by a court or other regulatory authority; however, they "might be viewed as establishing a standard of care for mediators."[22]

---

9. Idaho Code Ann. §§ 9-801 to 9-814 (West, Westlaw through Ch. 341 of the 2020 Second Reg. Sess., which convened Jan. 6, 2020, and adjourned Mar. 20, 2020).

10. 710 Smith-Hurd Ill. Comp. Stat. 35/1-35/99 (West, Westlaw through P.A. 101-629).

11. Iowa Code Ann. §§ 679C.101 to 679C.115 (West, Westlaw through legislation effective Mar. 18, 2020, from the 2020 Reg. Sess.).

12. Neb. Rev. Stat. §§ 25-2930 to 25-2942 (West, Westlaw through legislation eff. Mar. 26, 2020, of the 2nd Reg. Sess. of the 106th Legislature (2020)).

13. N.J. Stat. Ann. §§ 2A:23C-1 to 2A:23C-13 (Westlaw, through L. 2020, c. 17).

14. Baldwin's Ohio Rev. Code Ann. §§ 2710.01 to 2710.10 (Westlaw, through File 30 of the 133rd Gen. Assembly (2019–2020)).

15. S.D. Codified Laws §§ 19-13A-1 to 19-13A-15 (Westlaw, through laws of the 2020 Reg. Sess. eff. Mar. 31, 2020).

16. Utah Code Ann. §§ 78B-10-101 to 78B-10-114 (West, Westlaw through May 11, 2020, of the 2020 Gen. Sess.).

17. Vt. Stat. Ann. tit. 12, §§ 5711–5723 (West, Westlaw through acts 1–92 of the Adjourned Sess. of the 2019–2020 Vt. Gen. Assembly (2020)).

18. Rev. Code Wash. Ann. §§ 7.07.010 to 7.07.904 (Westlaw, through Ch. 218 of the 2020 Reg. Sess. of the Wash. Legislature).

19. See notations in Appendix A for the states of Alaska, Arizona, Connecticut, Delaware, South Dakota, and Wyoming.

20. Sup. Ct. of Tex., Approval of Amendments to the Ethical Guidelines for Mediators, Misc. Docket No. 11-9062 (2011); Tex. Ethical Guidelines for Mediators (2011).

21. Colo. Model Standards of Conduct for Mediators (CBA, CJI, DOL, CCMO & Off. of Dispute Resol. of the Colo. Jud. Dep't 2000).

22. Model Standards of Conduct for Mediators, Pmbl. (2005).

Third, some standards of conduct establish a foundation for mediator performance enforced by a court program.[23] These standards distinguish between a violation of law and a breach of one of the standards, which could result in discipline. Many states proclaim that their standards do not create any presumption that a legal duty has been breached, do not give rise to a legal cause of action,[24] and may not be used to challenge a mediated settlement agreement.[25] North Dakota's Code acknowledges that "a violation of a rule *may* be evidence of breach of the applicable standard of conduct" yet does not "give rise to a cause of action nor should it create any presumption that a legal duty has been breached."[26] Although a legal cause of action does not exist in these states, mediator conduct can be enforced through a court's disciplinary procedure.

Fourth, some standards do not focus on legal duties or do not explicitly address their legal or ethical effect. Instead, a mediator may be subject to a spectrum of disciplinary proceedings from a reprimand to disqualification from a mediation panel in response to a violation of a mediation ethical standard.[27] The Florida Rules for Certified & Court-Appointed Mediators consist of three parts: Mediator Qualifications, Standards of Professional Conduct, and Mediation Certification Applications and Discipline.[28] The extensive Mediation Certification Applications and Discipline provide mechanisms to challenge a mediator's good moral character

---

23. Unif. Rules on Dispute Resolution, Mass. Sup. Jud. Ct. Rule 1:18, R. 7 Duties of Approved Programs with Respect to Ct.-Connected Dispute Resol. Servs. & R. 9 Ethical Standards (2005); Standards of Prof'l Conduct for Mediators, N.C. Sup. Ct. Rules, Pmbl. (Dispute Resol. Comm'n 2020), which refers to Rule 7 of the Rules of the Dispute Resolution Commission, https://www.nccourts.gov/assets/inline-files/Rules-of-the-Dispute-Resolution-Commission-Codified-1-March-2020.pdf?n3KxbxjM.r0BoOc.MiXRRD4dGJInhL8P.

24. *See, e.g.*, Ala. Code of Ethics for Mediators, Intro. (Sup. Ct. of Ala., amended 2015); Minn. Gen. R. of Prac. for the Dist. Cts. 114 app., Code of Ethics (amended 2019).

25. Rules of Conduct for Mediators in Ct.-Connected Mediation Programs for Civil Cases, Cal. Rules of Court R. 3.850(b) (2011).

26. Code of Mediation Ethics, N.D. Rules of Court, R. 8.9, app. A, intro. (2007) (emphasis added).

27. Requirements for the Conduct of Mediation & Mediators, Intro. (Ark. Alt. Dispute Resol. Comm'n 2001); Rules for ADR, Ind. Rules of Court, R. 7.1 (amended 2019); Mich. Sup. Ct. Mediator Standards of Conduct, Applicability (Off. of Dispute Resol. 2013); Minn. Gen. R. of Prac. for the Dist. Cts. 114 app., Code of Ethics, intro. (amended 2019); Standards of Conduct for Mediators in Ct.-Connected Programs (N.J. Sup. Ct. 2000).

28. Fla. Rules for Certified & Ct.-Appointed Mediators (Fla. Dispute Resol. Ctr. 2018).

when applying to the court's mediation panel and for investigating claims of ethical violations of the Standards of Professional Conduct.[29]

Finally, some standards recognize that they may conflict with or be affected by applicable law, court rules, regulations, and other applicable professional rules. In such instances, the mediation standards may have to yield to the precedence of the other authorities.[30]

3.2.2. Key Mediation Values

Because the Model Standards are the main ethical standards for mediators, they serve as the focus of this chapter, augmented with a discussion of some state standards. The Model Standards have been discussed extensively elsewhere,[31] so this section will only highlight general themes found in the Model Standards and other mediation ethical codes.

The Model Standards are comprised of nine separate mediation values, although this section details the first six. The last three values are not discussed because they are fairly straightforward. These are Standard VII, Advertising and Solicitation, which includes many of the same requirements as the legal profession; Standard VIII, Fees and Other Charges, which, unlike the legal profession, precludes mediators from charging contingent fees because of the potential to compromise their impartiality; and Standard IX, Advancement of Mediation Practice.

3.2.2.1. Party Self-Determination

Party self-determination is an essential principle of mediation and applies to any stage of the proceeding. Model Standard I designates mediation as a voluntary process in which the parties make "free and informed choices

---

29. *Id.* Part III Mediation Certification Applications & Discipline, R. 10.700 Scope & Purpose.

30. Standards of Practice for Idaho Mediators, Pmbl. (Idaho Mediation Ass'n); Standards of Conduct, Pmbl. (Me. Ass'n of Mediators); Standards of Prof'l Conduct for Mediators N.C. Sup. Ct. Rules, Pmbl. (Dispute Resol. Comm'n 2020); Core Standards of Mediation Practice, Pmbl. (Or. Mediation Ass'n 2005).

31. *See, e.g.*, Laura E. Weidner, *Model Standards of Conduct for Mediators*, 21 Ohio St. J. on Disp. Resol. 547 (2006); Paula M. Young, *Rejoice! Rejoice! Rejoice, Give Thanks, and Sing: ABA, ACR, and AAA Adopt Revised Model Standards of Conduct for Mediators*, 5 Appal. J.L. 195 (2006); Michael L. Moffitt, *The Wrong Model, Again: Why the Devil Is Not in the Details of the New Model Standards of Conduct for Mediators*, 12 Disp. Resol. Mag. 31 (2006); Omer Shapira, *A Critical Assessment of the Model Standards of Conduct for Mediators (2005): Call for Reform*, 100 Marq. L. Rev. 81 (2016).

as to process and outcome."[32] They are not to be coerced into making decisions. A mediator may need to balance party self-determination with the need to conduct a quality process, yet the mediator "cannot personally ensure that each party has made free and informed choices."[33] The mediator may inform parties of their right to consult with other professionals.[34] In short, the mediator controls the process by improving communication, defining issues, exploring alternatives, etc., and parties control other aspects of process including mediator selection, process design, participation in or withdrawal from the process, and outcomes.[35]

As demonstrated in Section 3.3.2, *infra*, notions of party self-determination may collide with other mediation values, especially Quality of the Process. Additionally, some scholars believe that court-mandated mediations essentially erode the autonomous nature of mediation, especially when retired judges and seasoned lawyers become so directive in their style that the mediation begins to assume contours of an adversarial proceeding. Indeed, some mediators and lawyer advocates assume control over mediation communications, shielding clients from speaking and in many instances preventing parties from seeing and interacting with an opposing disputant.[36] Such proceedings restrict party autonomy and appear more like a settlement conference than mediation.

3.2.2.2. Mediator Impartiality

Mediator impartiality is included in every set of standards listed in Appendix A, which is no surprise since impartiality is a guiding benchmark of mediation. Impartiality requirements vary in scope and form depending on the jurisdiction; some are reasonably instructive, while others lack any real benefit.

3.2.2.2.1. Definition of Impartiality

Although some state standards are not very helpful because they simply require a mediator to serve in an impartial manner without describing "impartiality," the Model Standards are fairly instructive, requiring a mediator to be free "from favoritism, bias or prejudice," avoiding even

32. Model Standards of Conduct for Mediators I.A (2005).

33. *Id.* at I.A.2.

34. *Id.*

35. Guidelines for Hawaii Mediators, Pmbl. & Background (Haw. Comm. on Mediation Standards 2002).

36. Nancy A. Welsh, *The Thinning Vision of Self-Determination in Court-Connected Mediation: The Inevitable Price of Institutionalization?*, 6 Harv. Negot. L. Rev. 1, 24–27 (2001).

the appearance of partiality.[37] Additional comments require a mediator to maintain impartiality with respect to the "participant's personal characteristics, background, values and beliefs, or performance at a mediation, or any other reason."[38] Many state standards provide similar guidance. They reiterate some portion of the requirement to be free from favoritism, bias, or prejudice in word, action, and appearance and a commitment to serve all parties rather than any one individual.[39]

Acknowledging impartiality requirements, a mediator may raise questions to enable the parties to consider the "fairness, equity, and feasibility" of proposed settlement options and may withdraw. Some jurisdictions mandate withdrawal from the mediation if the mediator believes he can no longer maintain impartiality.[40]

Some standards commingle impartiality instructions with conflict-of-interest considerations. Thus, a mediator may be required to disclose dealings or relationships that may impact impartiality[41] or may preclude a mediator from participating when she is related to, or employed by, one of the parties.[42]

3.2.2.2.2. Explicit and Implicit Bias

Whether one is consciously aware of his biases (explicit) or not (implicit), it is important to realize that personal biases affect one's ability to maintain impartiality. In fact, some believe that mediators cannot maintain impartiality due to their own biases.[43] The Model Standards refer to bias in the Impartiality Standard,[44] and Maryland specifically cautions that a

37. Model Standards of Conduct for Mediators II.A (2005).

38. *Id.* at II.B.1.

39. *See, e.g.*, Ala. Code of Ethics for Mediators 5(a) (Sup. Ct. of Ala., amended 2015); Requirements for the Conduct of Mediation & Mediators III.5.A (Ark. Alt. Dispute Resol. Comm'n 2001); Fla. Rules for Certified & Ct.-Appointed Mediators R. 10.330(a) (Fla. Dispute Resol. Ctr. 2018); Standards of Prof'l Conduct for Mediators, N.C. Sup. Ct. Rules II.A (Dispute Resol. Comm'n 2020).

40. *See, e.g.*, Guidelines for Hawaii Mediators III.1 (Haw. Comm. on Mediation Standards 2002); Standards of Prof'l Conduct for Rule 31 Neutrals, Tenn. Sup. Ct. R. 31, app. A, § 6(a)(1), (2) (amended 2019).

41. Ethical Guidelines for the Practice of Mediation 4.2 (Wis. Ass'n of Mediators 1997).

42. Rules for ADR, Ind. R. Ct. 7.4(E) (amended 2019).

43. Carol Izumi, *Implicit Bias and the Illusion of Mediator Neutrality*, 34 Wash. U. J.L. & Pol'y 71, 121 (2010).

44. Model Standards of Conduct for Mediators II.A (2005).

mediator should "make an effort to be aware of the mediator's biases and should learn about unconscious and implicit biases."[45]

It is important that mediators acknowledge their own expectations, assumptions, and judgments about people based on cultural, educational, or other diversity-related topics. Mediators should be cognizant of their personal experiences and how those experiences may impact their relationship with mediation participants and the manner in which they approach a problem, all of which may be affected by one's unconscious bias.[46] Finally, mediators should be aware of their personal morals and ethics. Whether based on tradition or education, one's way of life may create biases that impact behavior and communication.

3.2.2.2.3. Overarching Nature of Impartiality Requirements

Impartiality requirements pertain to all forms of communication—both verbal and nonverbal. In order to remain neutral and evenhanded, a mediator should be particularly mindful of how to pose questions and communicate with all participants. A mediator should also remain impartial to the information received from mediation participants. Impartiality considerations apply to other aspects of mediation, such as the use and arrangement of furniture, seating assignments, and methods of greeting mediation participants upon their arrival.[47] Whether by action or word, a mediator should approach all parties with equal respect, transparency, sincerity, and curiosity.

Given the array of understandings illustrated in impartiality standards, rhetoric alone does not provide concrete guidance to mediators. Some MEAC opinions presented in Section 3.3.2, *infra*, address these concerns, especially when impartiality concerns collide with other mediation values.

3.2.2.3. Conflicts of Interest

Conflict-of-interest concerns relate to the subject matter of a dispute and to relationship issues. In either case, the mediator bears the burden of

45. The Md. Standards of Conduct for Ct.-Designated Mediators II.A.3 (Jud. Council ADR Comm. 2020).

46. Izumi, *supra* note 43, at 84–85.

47. Karen A. Zerhusen, *Reflections on the Role of the Neutral Lawyer: The Lawyer as Mediator*, 81 Ky. L.J. 1165, 1169–70 (1993).

disclosure,[48] which continues throughout the mediation process.[49] After the mediator advises of a potential conflict of interest, the parties may agree to allow a mediator to continue to serve,[50] unless the conflict of interest might reasonably be viewed as undermining the integrity of the mediation.[51]

3.2.2.3.1. Subject Matter

A mediator is precluded from having financial or other interests in the outcome of a mediation other than an agreed-upon fee for serving as mediator.[52] Thus, a mediator has a conflict of interest when she owns a condominium in a community in which its HOA Board is a party to a mediation and the mediator would reap a benefit if the HOA prevailed.

3.2.2.3.2. Relationship Issues

Most standards instruct a mediator to avoid a conflict of interest or the appearance of a conflict of interest regarding past or present personal or professional relationships.[53] A mediator must place the interests of parties above those of a court, a referring agency, and himself.[54] It is also important to avoid establishing some type of relationship after the conclusion of a mediation; factors to consider include the time that has elapsed since

---

48. Model Standards of Conduct for Mediators III.C, D (2005); Ala. Code of Ethics for Mediators, Standard 5(b)(6) (Sup. Ct. of Ala., amended 2015); Standards of Prof'l Conduct for Rule 31 Neutrals, Tenn. Sup. Ct. Rule 31, app. A, 6(b) (amended 2019).

49. Requirements for the Conduct of Mediation & Mediators, Standard 5.B.(7) (Ark. Alt. Dispute Resol. Comm'n 2001); Guidelines for Ct.-Connected Mediation Servs., Guideline V.B (N.M. Statewide ADR Comm'n 2016).

50. Model Standards of Conduct for Mediators III.C, D (2005); Fla. Rules for Certified & Ct.-Appointed Mediators, Part II, R. 10.340(b), (c) (Fla. Dispute Resol. Ctr. 2018); Code of Mediation Ethics, N.D. Rules of Court, Rule 8.9, app. A, R. III (2007); Standards of Ethics & Prof'l Responsibility for Certified Mediators G.4 (Judicial Council of Va. 2011).

51. See discussion at Section 3.2.2.3.3, *infra*.

52. Standards of Practice for Idaho Mediators III.4 (Idaho Mediation Ass'n), *available at* https://www.idahomediationassociation.org/Standards-of-Practice (last visited Feb. 24, 2021).

53. Model Standards of Conduct for Mediators III.A (2005); Ethical Standards for Mediators, Ga. Alt. Dispute Resol. Rules, app. C, Ch. 1, III.C (Ga. Comm'n on Dispute Resol., amended 2013); Standards of Conduct, Standard III.A (Me. Ass'n of Mediators), *available at* https://mainemediators.org/Standards-of-Conduct (last visited Feb. 24, 2021); Core Standards of Mediation Practice III (Or. Mediation Ass'n 2005).

54. Standards of Prof'l Conduct for Mediators, N.C. Sup. Ct. Rules VII (Dispute Resol. Comm'n 2020).

the mediation, the nature of the relationship, and services offered.[55] The relationship issue may relate to any mediation participant, whether a disputing party or not.[56] It may be a "direct conflict of interest" involving a relationship between the mediator and one of the participants or an "indirect conflict of interest," which relates to a relationship between the mediator and another person or entity that has a personal, professional, or financial relationship with a mediation participant.[57] Some standards specifically preclude a mediator from accepting or giving a gift, request, favor, loan, or any other item of value to a mediation participant or future participant.[58]

Conflict-of-interest concerns must be consistent with self-determination and impartiality requirements. Thus, a mediator may recommend the services of other professionals as long as she avoids a conflict of interest and may not subsequently represent or provide professional services (including other members of the mediator's firm) to any mediation participant.[59]

Conflicts of interest can exist when a lawyer mediator seeks to mediate with a former client or represented party[60] or subsequently seeks to represent one of the parties. The Mediation Council of Illinois's Standards of Practice preclude a lawyer mediator from "representing either party before, during, or after the mediation process."[61] The Montana Mediation Association's standards preclude a mediator from "subsequently serving as a judge, master, guardian ad litem, attorney ad litem or in any other judicial or quasi-judicial capacity in matters that are the

55. Iowa Sup. Ct. Rules 11.4(6) (2012); Standards of Conduct, Standard III.F (Me. Ass'n of Mediators), *available at* https://mainemediators.org/Standards-of-Conduct (last visited Feb. 24, 2021); Mich. Sup. Ct. Mediator Standards of Conduct, Standard III.A (Off. of Dispute Resol. 2013).

56. Iowa Sup. Ct. Rules 11.4(1) (2012).

57. The Md. Standards of Conduct for Ct.-Designated Mediators, Standard III.A (Jud. Council ADR Comm. 2020).

58. Manual of Standards & Ethics for Ctr. Mediators, Directors & Staff III.B.2 (Neb. Off. of Dispute Resol., amended 2009).

59. Standards of Conduct for Mediators in Ct.-Connected Programs III (N.J. Sup. Ct. 2000).

60. Rules and Procedures for the Dispute Resolution Procedure Act, Okla. Stat. tit. 12, ch. 37, app. A, B.2.b. (Westlaw, current with amendments through Mar. 1, 2020).

61. MCI Prof'l Standards of Practice for Mediators IV.B (Mediation Council of Ill. 2009).

subject of the mediation" absent exceptional circumstances.[62] Moreover, a "mediator shall not use the mediation process to solicit, encourage or otherwise incur future services with either party."[63]

3.2.2.3.3. Severity of Conflict of Interest

Depending on the severity of a conflict of interest, a mediator may be required to withdraw even though parties may consent. According to the Model Standards, when a conflict of interest is viewed as "undermining the integrity of the mediation," the mediator must withdraw; the parties may not consent to the mediator's continued participation.[64] A Massachusetts rule is equally vague; if the "neutral determines that the conflict is so significant as to cast doubt on the integrity of the dispute resolution process," the neutral shall withdraw despite party consent.[65] Similarly, in Florida, a mediator shall withdraw notwithstanding party consent "if a conflict of interest clearly impairs a mediator's impartiality."[66]

3.2.2.4. Competence

Model Standard IV requires a mediator to mediate when possessing the "necessary competence to satisfy the reasonable expectations of the parties."[67] A limited number of state standards mirror this provision, including those of Iowa, Maine, Minnesota, New Jersey, New York, Oregon, and Washington.[68]

As the mediator prepares to mediate, therefore, it is important to inquire as to what the parties are seeking in a mediator. Are they looking

---

62. Code of Ethics & Standards of Practice II.B.4 (Mont. Mediation Ass'n 2014).

63. Manual of Standards & Ethics for Ctr. Mediators, Directors & Staff III.B.4 (Neb. Off. of Dispute Resol., amended 2009).

64. Model Standards of Conduct for Mediators III.E (2005).

65. Unif. Rules on Dispute Resol., Mass. Sup. Jud. Ct. Rule 1:18, R. 9(e) Ethical Standards (1999).

66. Fla. Rules for Certified & Ct.-Appointed Mediators, Part II, R. 10.340(a), (c) (Fla. Dispute Resol. Ctr. 2018).

67. Model Standards of Conduct for Mediators IV.A (2005).

68. Iowa Sup. Ct. Rules 11.5(1) (2012); Standards of Conduct IV.A (Me. Ass'n of Mediators), *available at* https://mainemediators.org/Standards-of-Conduct (last visited Feb. 24, 2021); Minn. Gen. R. of Prac. for the Dist. Cts. 114 app., Code of Ethics III (amended 2019); Standards of Conduct for Mediators in Ct.-Connected Programs IV (N.J. Sup. Ct. 2000); Standards of Conduct for N.Y. St. Cmty. Dispute Resol. Ctr. Mediators IV.A (N.Y. St. Unified Ct. Sys., Div. of Prof'l & Ct. Servs., amended 2009); Core Standards of Mediation Practice V (Or. Mediation Ass'n 2005); Standards of Practice for Mediators IV (Wash. Mediation Ass'n 1997).

for someone to use a directive approach? If so, then the mediator should be well versed in the subject matter and relevant law. Are the parties looking for a mediator who can maneuver sensitive communication issues such as emotional parties or who has the ability to exude empathy, the ability to offer a reality check, or some other specialized communication technique? This type of mediator should possess specialized qualifications in conflict management and communication skills that exceed basic mediation training.

Competence is not solely about satisfying party expectations; it also reflects the interests of the profession, since codes of conduct seek to promote public confidence in the mediation process.[69] A mediator should, therefore, pay special attention to his overall qualifications such as training, mediation experience, cultural understandings, and other qualities of a competent mediator, including communication skills, knowledge of the mediation process and the role of the mediator, theories of conflict, diversity, bias training, and more.[70]

A mediator's special skill set also reflects the needs of a particular type of mediation. For instance, complicated cases such as patent or trust work require specialized legal knowledge. The type of mediator style also requires different mediator skills, such as those essential to problem-solving, transformative, or narrative mediators.[71]

A mediator has a continuing obligation to maintain and enhance her mediation knowledge and skills.[72] This means that a mediator should ensure her competence prior to beginning a mediation practice and continue to enrich her level of competence through continuing education training. Indeed, many state standards require mediation training, including continuing education.[73]

During the course of the mediation, if the mediator determines that he cannot continue in a competent fashion, he should discuss this matter

---

69. Omer Shapira, A Theory of Mediators' Ethics: Foundations, Rationale, and Application 132–34 (2016).

70. Model Standards of Conduct for Mediators IV.A.1 (2005); Shapira, *supra* note 69, at 168, 171–72.

71. Shapira, *supra* note 69, at 169–71.

72. Model Standards of Conduct for Mediators IV.A.2 (2005).

73. *See, e.g.*, Ala. Code of Ethics for Mediators, Standard 9 (Sup. Ct. of Ala., amended 2015); Requirements for the Conduct of Mediation & Mediators, Standard 10 (Ark. Alt. Dispute Resol. Comm'n 2001); Fla. Rules for Certified & Ct.-Appointed Mediators, Part II, R. 10.630 (Fla. Dispute Resol. Ctr. 2018); Md. Standards of Conduct for Ct.-Designated Mediators IV.C (Jud. Council ADR Comm. 2020).

with the parties and take appropriate steps, including withdrawal.[74] For example, if a mediator is asked to mediate in an area in which he has no subject-matter expertise and may not feel competent, he should inform the parties and together they can decide whether the mediator should continue. This author experienced such a situation early in her mediation career. She received a court-connected case involving a personal-injury matter and informed the parties that she had no PI experience despite her mediation process experience. The attorney advocates welcomed the mediator's continuing service; one of the attorneys completed a post-mediation survey indicating it was one of the best mediations he had experienced.

Finally, a mediator should be careful not to let alcohol, drugs, medication, or anything else impair her ability to serve.[75] A mediator should be especially cognizant of medicines such as cold and flu remedies that may cause drowsiness.

3.2.2.5. Confidentiality

Confidentiality applies to everyone who attends mediation and is important to the mediation process. It promotes candor of communication; if parties believe in the process and believe that their statements will remain private, they will be willing to openly communicate with the mediator, increasing the exchange of information.

At the beginning of all mediations, a mediator should explain two levels of confidentiality. The overarching nature of mediation confidentiality means that communications that take place during mediation are cloaked in secrecy. A second level of confidentiality applies to individual caucuses. Mediators should explain that when they meet privately with each party, no information will be conveyed to the opposing party without permission. This second level is particularly important because it is in private meetings that parties are willing to share their secrets with mediators that they trust. Finally, confidentiality may apply beyond the spoken word to actions or behavior conducted during mediation; therefore, a mediator may not discuss how a participant acted with others.[76]

A related issue and part of mediation confidentiality is mediation privilege. When mediation confidentiality serves as a privilege, it allows a person to refuse to disclose and to prevent another from disclosing

---

74. Model Standards of Conduct for Mediators IV.B (2005).
75. *Id.* at IV.C.
76. *Id.* at V.A.2; Iowa Sup. Ct. Rules 11.6(1).b (2012); Core Standards of Mediation Practice IV cmt. 4 (Or. Mediation Ass'n 2005).

particular communications in subsequent legal proceedings, during discovery proceedings, and in administrative proceedings. A privilege is narrower than confidentiality because it does not prevent the disclosure of mediation communications outside of legal proceedings, for example to family members, friends, business associates, and the general public.

Section 4 of the UMA is an example of a mediation privilege. It provides for the inadmissibility of a mediation communication into evidence in a proceeding or otherwise discoverable. The UMA designates parties and mediators as holders of the privilege; only they may waive the privilege. In the case of a privilege of a mediator or nonparty participant, that person must expressly waive the privilege in addition to all parties.[77] Section 8 of the UMA is an example of a rule of confidentiality. It provides that disclosures of mediation communications outside of proceedings are subject to the parties' agreement or to a state's laws or rules.[78]

Notwithstanding the scope of confidentiality or privilege, mediators must carefully discern their jurisdictional requirements, since rules vary significantly among jurisdictions. If a mediator announces that everything said in mediation is confidential when in fact exceptions exist, the mediator could be accused of providing false information. It also might amount to a violation of the confidentiality standard, subjecting the mediator to discipline. Finally, unless the parties have the right to set their own confidentiality provision by mutual agreement, inaccurate recitations in an agreement to mediate could result in mediator liability based on a breach-of-contract theory.

3.2.2.6. Quality of the Process

The individual provisions of Model Standard VI relate to many situations and in some instances overlap with other values. Rather than serve as a potpourri of many ethical values, Professor Omer Shapira opines that this standard could be deconstructed into separate standards of diligence, honesty, respect, professional integrity, and fairness.[79] Some of the provisions of Model Standard VI provide that "[a] mediator shall conduct a mediation . . . in a manner that promotes diligence, timeliness, safety, presence of the appropriate participants, party participation, procedural fairness, party competency and mutual respect among all participants."[80] Standard VI cautions mediators to be clear if they intend to "undertake

77. Unif. Mediation Act §§ 4, 5 (2003).
78. *Id.* § 8.
79. Shapira, *supra* note 31, at 107–18.
80. Model Standards of Conduct for Mediators VI.A (2005).

an additional dispute resolution role," which requires party consent,[81] and to "provide information that the mediator is qualified by training or experience to provide, only if the mediator can do so consistent with these Standards."[82]

Much of the mediator's discretion seems dedicated to ensuring a balanced process because the mediator is to ensure that the parties understand the process, the information received, and settlement options.[83] These concerns relate directly to party self-determination under the rationale that a party cannot exercise autonomy unless he receives appropriate disclosures in order to make fully informed decisions. Many state standards have similar provisions.

Model Standard VI does not refer directly to substantive fairness. Some state standards, however, provide either direct or indirect guidance to ensure a fair result. For example, a mediator may terminate a mediation if a party is unwilling or unable to participate[84] or when a "reasonable agreement is unlikely" due to the inability or unwillingness to participate meaningfully in the mediation process.[85] A mediator may inform parties of difficulties in a proposed agreement, ask parties to consider alternatives, or withdraw when the mediator "knows or has reason to believe" an agreement is contrary to law, grossly inequitable, the result of false information or bad-faith dealing, unenforceable, or not durable.[86] To ensure that parties "reach a fair and fully informed settlement," a mediator may, subject to impartiality requirements, question unrepresented parties whether they have sufficient information.[87] A mediator may indicate nonconcurrence with a decision she finds inherently unfair,[88] should not be a party to an agreement that is illegal or impossible to execute, and should refuse to draft or sign an agreement "which seems fundamentally

81. *Id.* at VI.A.8.

82. *Id.* at VI.A.5.

83. *Id.* at VI.A.10.

84. *See* Standards of Practice for Idaho Mediators IV (Idaho Mediation Ass'n), *available at* https://www.idahomediationassociation.org/Standards-of-Practice (last visited Feb. 24, 2021); Standards of Prof'l Conduct for Rule 31 Neutrals, Tenn. Sup. Ct. Rule 31, app. A, § 4(b) (amended 2019); Ethical Guidelines for Mediators 13 (Tex. Sup. Ct. 2011).

85. Rules for ADR, Ind. Rules of Ct., R. 2.7(D)(1) (2019).

86. Code of Ethics & Standards of Practice IX (Mont. Mediation Ass'n 2014).

87. Unif. Rules on Dispute Resol., Mass. Sup. Jud. Ct. Rule 1:18, R. 9(c)(vii) Ethical Standards (1999).

88. MCI Prof'l Standards of Practice for Mediators IV.A (Mediation Council of Ill. 2009).

unfair to one party"[89] or withdraw if she deems a proposed resolution is unconscionable.[90] California takes a unique approach; "[a] mediator is *not obligated* to ensure the substantive fairness of an agreement . . . ,"[91] which can be interpreted to allow a mediator to address substantive fairness concerns.

The foregoing examples illustrate a conflict between quality of process provisions and party self-determination. One may argue that if parties are to control the final result, the mediator has no duty to question the feasibility of a proposed resolution. If a mediator seeks to ensure justice, how can he comply with impartiality requirements? It is easy to see that a mediator has a very fine line to straddle, and one small slipup can result in a violation of a mediation code of conduct. Model Standard VI provides a safety net: "If a mediator believes that participant conduct, including that of the mediator, jeopardizes conducting a mediation consistent with these Standards, a mediator shall take appropriate steps including, if necessary, postponing, withdrawing from or terminating the mediation."[92]

3.2.3. Tension between Values within a Set of Mediation Standards of Conduct

As shown above, codes of conduct for mediators include a variety of individual values that mediators must follow. The challenge is the ability to comply with all values simultaneously. For example, if one attempts to ensure a quality process by posing questions regarding the feasibility of a final result, might the nature of the mediator's questions threaten party self-determination? Or, if a mediator imposes a directive mediation style, could that style impact her impartiality? And how can a mediator exude her preferred demeanor and style, especially in light of her implicit biases, and simultaneously comply with every value found within a specified code of conduct?

No exact answer exists. This author has previously suggested that ethical values within a single code of conduct could be prioritized by creating an organizational hierarchy of values, acknowledging key mediation values that should be paramount over other values.[93] Additionally,

89. Ethical Standards for Mediators, Ga. Alt. Dispute Resol. Rules, app. C, Ch. 1, IV.A (Ga. Comm'n on Dispute Resol. 2013).

90. Rules for ADR, Ind. Rules of Ct., R. 7.5(B) (2019).

91. Rules of Conduct for Mediators in Ct.-Connected Mediation Programs for Civil Cases, Cal. Rules of Ct. R. 3.857(b) (2011) (emphasis added).

92. Model Standards of Conduct for Mediators VI.C (2005).

93. Susan Nauss Exon, *The Misnomer of a Mediation Value: Why All Mediators Cannot Remain Impartial*, 1 Y.B. Arb. & Med. 164 (2009).

mediators should consult other sources for assistance, such as peers, professional mediation associations, mediation ethics textbooks,[94] and mediator ethical advisory opinions, which offer guidance beyond the black-letter rules of mediation codes of conduct.

3.3. Mediator Ethical Advisory Opinions

When ethical values collide and create tension for mediators, mediator ethical advisory opinions may provide guidance to ameliorate these challenges and shed light on acceptable practice.[95] The American Bar Association's Section of Dispute Resolution has a committee devoted to writing mediation ethical advisory opinions. The Committee on Mediator Ethical Guidance is made up of ADR specialists who have a keen knowledge of mediation ethics and includes a diverse pool of academics and practitioners from across the United States. Their appointment is by invitation only. The committee issues opinions that are well thought out; members analyze a situation, debate the issues, and then write several iterations of an opinion before the opinion becomes final. The opinions can be accessed at the National Clearinghouse for Mediator Ethics Opinions;[96] many state court ADR websites provide links to these opinions.

In addition to the opinions of the ABA Committee on Ethical Guidance, a few states have initiated their own mediator ethical advisory committees (MEACs), and they are designated in Appendix A. If mediators have questions about their conduct, they should contact the appropriate authority in their jurisdiction to request an opinion. If their jurisdiction does not provide MEAC opinions, they should contact the ABA Section of Dispute Resolution's Committee on Ethical Guidance, which is happy to field any questions from across the country.

3.3.1. State Bar Association Opinions Relating to Mediation

Most states do not issue MEAC opinions. State bar associations, however, may issue advisory opinions relating to rules of professional conduct for lawyers, such as a lawyer in a dual role—a lawyer mediator or a lawyer

94. *See, e.g.*, Mediation Ethics: Cases & Commentaries (Ellen Waldman ed. 2011); Susan Nauss Exon, Advanced Guide for Mediators chs. 6–8 (2014); Shapira, *supra* note 69, at 343–63.

95. *See Ethics Information for Registered Neutrals*, Ga. Off. of Dispute Resol., https://godr.org/registered-neutral/ethics-information/ (last visited Feb. 24, 2021).

96. *See* https://www.americanbar.org/groups/dispute_resolution/resources. At the bottom of that page is a link for the National Clearinghouse for Mediator Ethics Opinions.

as a third party neutral—that shed light on acceptable mediator conduct. Such topics address whether a lawyer may serve as a mediator for unrepresented divorcing couples and/or whether the lawyer mediator may draft a settlement agreement agreed to during such divorce mediation.[97] Although most jurisdictions permit this mediator conduct, most have held that it is inappropriate to venture further to draft divorce pleadings for a pro se divorcing couple because such conduct is practicing law and may be violating prohibitions of dual-party representation in a divorce by blending the role of third-party neutral with the traditional role of lawyer.[98] The State Bar of Arizona could not reach consensus on this issue and recommends that lawyer mediators "exercise their own professional judgment . . . ."[99] Additionally, a lawyer mediator may not seek the *consent* of pro se parties to draft ancillary documents at the conclusion of mediation because to do so would inappropriately seek to negate professional responsibility duties owed to clients.[100]

The Mississippi State Bar recognizes that mediation services are not considered the practice of law. When performed by a lawyer, however, they are considered law-related services subject to the Mississippi Rules of Professional Conduct.[101]

3.3.2. State Mediator Ethical Advisory Opinions

The Florida Mediator Ethics Advisory Committee has the most extensive array of MEAC opinions, cataloged by subject and year. They cover the following subjects: advertising/marketing, advice opinions or information, business practices, confidentiality, conflicts of interest, and procedures.[102] They are too numerous to attempt to summarize all of them

---

97. Mass. Bar Ethics Op. No. 85-3 (1985); Comm. of Prof'l Resp. of the Bos. Bar Ass'n, Op. 78-1 (1978); St. Bar of Mich. Ethics Op. RI-351 (2011); Prof'l Ethics Comm. for the St. Bar of Tex., Op. No. 675 (2018).

98. Ky. Bar Ass'n Ethics Op. KBA E-438 (2015); St. Bar of Mich. Ethics Op. RI-351 (2011); Prof'l Ethics Comm. for the St. Bar of Tex., Op. No. 583 (2008); Timothy J. Pierce, *Can a Lawyer-Mediator Draft Documents for a Divorcing Couple after Mediation?*, St. Bar of Wis. (May 14, 2010), https://www.wisbar.org/NewsPublications/Pages/General-Article.aspx?ArticleID=7759; *see* Advisory Op. of the N.C. Dispute Resol. Comm'n, Op. No. 28 (2013).

99. St. Bar of Ariz. Ethics Op. 96-01 (1996).

100. Ky. Bar Ass'n Ethics Op. KBA E-438 (2015) (emphasis added).

101. Miss. Bar Ethics Op. No. 241 (rendered 1997, amended 2013).

102. *See Mediator Ethics Advisory Committee Opinions*, Fla. Cts., https://www.flcourts.org/Resources-Services/Alternative-Dispute-Resolution/Mediator-Ethics-Advisory-Committee-Opinions-MEAC (last visited Feb. 24, 2021) (listing over 100 MEAC opinions dated back to 1994).

in this short chapter. Other states that have established MEACs include Alabama, Georgia, New York, North Carolina, and Tennessee.

This section delineates some examples of the types of questions that have been raised and answered by MEACs. The opinions typically track individual values found in mediator codes of conduct. The opinions are especially helpful to resolve conflicts when several mediation values are involved and seem to collide with one another. Mediators should be aware that the opinions reflect local mediation codes of conduct and legislation and, therefore, vary from one jurisdiction to another.

3.3.2.1. Confidentiality

Many MEAC opinions involve confidentiality issues. The Committee on Ethics of the Georgia Commission on Dispute Resolution has issued two extremely helpful opinions in which it provides a broad overview of confidentiality, including its definition and purpose. In doing so, it held that a mediator may not comment to the media if contacted; any inquiries from the media should be redirected to parties.[103] Additionally, mediators may not report to the court regarding such matters as unresolved issues from mediation, a recommendation to appoint a guardian ad litem in a child custody and/or visitation matter, and information regarding parties' good-faith participation in court-mandated mediations such as verbal and nonverbal behavior.[104] When confidential financial information of parties is stored on a mediator's computer and becomes compromised, the mediator has an implicit duty to notify the parties; this is important to maintain the integrity of mediation.[105]

When a party and attorney in an equitable distribution action admitted to the mediator in caucus that she had withheld information regarding a valuable marital asset, the North Carolina Dispute Resolution Commission instructed the mediator to encourage disclosure and, if that failed, "take appropriate steps including, if necessary, postponing, withdrawing from or terminating the mediation."[106] When withdrawing, the mediator can preserve confidentiality by simply stating, "A dilemma exists that prohibits me from continuing."[107] This generic rationale is a good way for a mediator to announce his intent to withdraw under *any* circumstance.

---

103. Comm. on Ethics, Ga. Comm'n on Dispute Resol., Advisory Op. 8 (2013).
104. Comm. on Ethics, Ga. Comm'n on Dispute Resol., Advisory Op. 6 (2005).
105. Advisory Op. of the N.C. Dispute Resol. Comm'n, Op. No. 9 (2006).
106. Advisory Op. of the N.C. Dispute Resol. Comm'n, Op. No. 16 (2010).
107. *Id.*

A common question exists whether a mediator may testify in court to enforce a mediated settlement agreement. Most jurisdictions cover this issue as part of their codes of conduct or in legislation. Sometimes additional commentary is necessary. For example, under N.C. Gen. Stat. § 7A-38.1(l), a mediator of a court-ordered mediated settlement conference may not be compelled to testify in a proceeding to enforce or rescind an agreement reached in that mediated settlement conference. North Carolina Standards of Professional Conduct for Mediators further provide in Standard 3(a) (Confidentiality) that "[a] mediator shall not disclose to any nonparticipant, directly or indirectly, any information communicated to the mediator by a participant within the mediation process, whether the information is obtained before, during, or after the mediated settlement conference." There, a mediator was subpoenaed to testify to enforce a mediated settlement agreement; no party objected to his testimony. Because the mediator failed to point out to the court his obligation to maintain confidentiality of the mediation proceedings, the North Carolina Dispute Resolution Commission held that his testimony was voluntary. Notwithstanding nonobjection by any party, the Commission held that the mediator's testimony was improper, especially since the confidentiality rule had several exceptions and none allowed parties to expressly waive confidentiality.[108]

This North Carolina advisory opinion offers helpful guidance for all jurisdictions. Since confidentiality and privilege provisions change between jurisdictions, mediators should carefully read the confidentiality provisions in their jurisdiction to ensure the extent of confidentiality that applies to them and ascertain whether any exceptions exist.[109] Aside from specifically stated exceptions, mediators should take all action to ensure mediation confidentiality.

In Alabama, parties can be sanctioned for failing to attend mediation. The Alabama Supreme Court Commission on Dispute Resolution was asked whether a mediator was allowed to report to the court that a party did not attend the mediation. The mediation rules in Alabama refer to confidentiality of communications, not conduct. The Commission stated that "[c]onfidentiality is the backbone of mediation" and held that the remedy of sanctions belonged to the parties, not the mediator. While a party may report the other party's failure to attend mediation, the mediator may not.[110]

---

108. Advisory Op. of the N.C. Dispute Resol. Comm'n, Op. No. 30 (2014).

109. See Section 3.2.2.5, *supra*, for a discussion of different types of confidentiality.

110. Op. of the Ala. Sup. Ct. Comm'n on Dispute Resol., Op. 001-2010 (2010).

3.3.2.2. Ability to Record Mediation Proceedings

The right of a mediation party to record a mediation involves ethical values of party self-determination, confidentiality, and quality of the process. In New York, a mediator was instructed to withdraw rather than allow a party to tape record a mediation to compensate for poor note-taking skills when the party refused to share the recording with the opposing party. The MEAC held that the taping party's refusal to notify the other party of the tape recording would conflict with the mediator's obligation to conduct a quality process; if the taped party was not aware of the recording, he would not be able to participate meaningfully in the mediation process in a manner consistent with the Standards. Additionally, the mediator was encouraged to explore potential accommodations, modifications, or adjustments to help the taping party better understand, participate in the mediation, and exercise self-determination. The fact that the taping party refused to discuss underlying interests for recording the mediation provided additional justification for the mediator to terminate the session. Finally, the MEAC noted that the mediator would compromise his impartiality if he could not report the recording to the taped party. The New York MEAC held, therefore, that the mediator must not allow a mediation party to tape the mediation proceedings without the knowledge and consent of all parties and should terminate the mediation.[111]

On another set of facts, the New York MEAC did not allow parties to video record a mediation for the benefit of one party's attorney who could not attend even though all participants had consented. The Committee reached that conclusion despite the parties' right to self-determination because of the possibility that the video might be viewed by other nonparticipants or find its way to social media or the Internet, thereby compromising the principle of mediation confidentiality and discouraging prospective users from engaging in mediation.[112]

3.3.2.3. Ability to Report Conduct of Mediation Participants

Mediators encounter challenges when they learn of information in a mediation, which is cloaked in confidentiality, yet other laws or rules may require reporting such conduct. For example, while an Illinois lawyer mediator conducted a mediation, he learned that one of the lawyer advocates had committed an act involving dishonesty, fraud, deceit, or misrepresentation, in violation of Illinois Rule of Professional Conduct 8.4(c). The Illinois State Bar Association (ISBA) held that despite the

111. N.Y. Mediator Ethics Advisory Comm. Op. 2010-01 (2010).
112. N.Y. Mediator Ethics Advisory Comm. Op. 2015-01 (2015).

confidentiality provisions of the UMA, the lawyer mediator had to report the other lawyer's conduct because there are no limitations on when the Rules of Professional Conduct apply and the duty to report was absolute. The ISBA also referred to several exceptions found within the UMA and the Not-for-Profit Dispute Resolution Center Act.[113] Similarly, in Tennessee, a mediator may testify regarding alleged unethical conduct of an attorney advocate during mediation. The conduct in question involved an attorney leaving the mediation to eat lunch and take personal telephone calls, which were collateral to the issues in dispute.[114]

Another situation involved a mediator who believed that a party to mediation was engaged in insurance fraud. Noting the importance of confidentiality to encourage candid discussions aimed at resolution, the New York MEAC held that the mediator should refrain from reporting information to authorities unless someone's physical safety is in imminent danger, such as child abuse. Maintaining mediator impartiality was also a concern. The mediator could talk to staff at Community Dispute Resolution Centers for guidance or withdraw.[115]

The same MEAC was confronted with an issue in which, in the course of a mediation between a mother and child, the 12-year-old child told the mediator in caucus that she was sexually active with young men, age 18 and 19. The child stressed that she did not want the mediator to disclose the information to her mother. The New York MEAC held that the mediator must maintain confidentiality pursuant to the Standards of Conduct for New York State Community Dispute Resolution Center Mediators that require confidentiality of information learned in caucus, except for allegations or evidence of child abuse. The mediator was advised to learn more information from the child in caucus to assess whether this was a case of child abuse that involves a duty to report, stop the mediation to consult with Center staff, and determine together whether to report to authorities or resume the mediation. In any event, the MEAC held that the mediator was not allowed to divulge the information he learned about in caucus to the minor's mother without the child's consent.[116]

Physical safety also is important. In Tennessee, a mediator may report to law enforcement if either she or someone else in mediation is assaulted. The rationale is that the information relates to collateral issues

113. ISBA Advisory Op. on Prof'l Conduct, Op. No. 11-01 (2011).

114. Tenn. Alt. Dispute Resol. Comm'n, Ethics Advisory Op. No. 2012-0002 (2012).

115. N.Y. Mediator Ethics Advisory Comm. Op. 2006-03 (2006).

116. N.Y. Mediator Ethics Advisory Comm. Op. 2006-02 (2006).

rather than issues pertaining to the underlying dispute.[117] Georgia also allows a mediator to report to law enforcement regarding an assault in mediation, threats to use a weapon, or situations involving imminent threats. A Georgia mediator may not, however, report the information to the court.[118]

3.3.2.4. Quality-of-the-Process Issues

In New York, a mediator who is also a notary may notarize a document that is required to be signed by one of the mediation parties. A MEAC opinion noted that the quality-of-the-process standard cautions that mixing the role of mediator with another professional role of advising a client is problematic and mediators should strive to distinguish the two roles. A notary, however, performs a ministerial act, and the mediator did not charge for the notary service.[119] In contrast, the Florida MEAC held thrice that a mediator is prohibited from taking on the dual role of mediator and notary.[120] The Committee held that according to the local rules, a mediator is "prohibited from utilizing a mediation to supply any other services which do not directly relate to the conduct of the mediation itself. By way of example, a mediator would therefore be prohibited from providing accounting, psychiatric or legal services, psychological or social counseling, therapy, or business consultations of any sort during the mediation process."[121] The Committee did not consider notarizing ministerial in function because "a notary can and may be asked or required to *attest* to anything related to the mediation in evidence."[122]

The need to distinguish between the role of a mediator and the role of a professional advising a client led the New York MEAC to hold that a mediator had no obligation to advise a party that he may be in violation of an Order of Protection by appearing at the mediation with the other party to the Order; however, the Committee held that the mediator had an obligation to terminate the mediation since the interaction between the two parties appeared to have violated the Order of Protection, thereby

117. Tenn. Alt. Dispute Resol. Comm'n, Ethics Advisory Op. No. 2010-0002 (2010).

118. Comm. on Ethics, Ga. Comm'n on Dispute Resol., Advisory Op. 6 (2005).

119. N.Y. Mediator Ethics Advisory Comm. Op. 2007-01 (2007).

120. Fla. Mediator Ethics Advisory Comm. Op. 2013-009 (2013); Fla. Mediator Ethics Advisory Comm. Op. 2011-004 (2011); Fla. Mediator Ethics Advisory Comm. Op. 2010-004 (2004).

121. Fla. Mediator Ethics Advisory Comm. Op. 2011-004 (2011).

122. Fla. Mediator Ethics Advisory Comm. Op. 2013-009 (2013).

furthering illegal conduct, and may advise the party to seek outside professional advice regarding her obligations pursuant to the Order.[123]

Notwithstanding the requirement to distinguish between roles, a mediator may provide general legal information within his knowledge consistent with his duty of impartiality. The New York MEAC held that if a mediator is aware that a change in custody may trigger a change in child support, he may discuss it with the parties because it is substantial information regarding the dispute and because by doing so the mediator would not provide legal advice specific to the case. The mediator should also raise with the parties the possibility of consulting counsel.[124] Unlike the previous opinions, this MEAC opinion recognizes that it may be ethical for a mediator to provide professional or legal information in some circumstances.

3.3.2.5. Fee Issues

The ISBA was asked whether lawyers who were operating as a mediation firm could share referral fees with a nonlawyer. The ISBA believed the "creation of a 'Mediation Firm' comprised entirely of lawyers, to be a sham designed to circumvent the applicable Rules of Professional Conduct," which prevent lawyers from sharing fees with nonlawyers. It was, therefore, "professionally improper" for the mediation firm to pay a referral fee to a nonlawyer accounting firm.[125] This opinion expands on an earlier opinion in which the ISBA held that because a lawyer did not appear to be using his mediation business as a "'feeder' operation for the divorce practice or any other law practice," he may enter into a business relationship with a nonlawyer in a mediation business or any other business.[126]

North Carolina has addressed attorney's fees. Its Dispute Resolution Commission held that evidence of offers made and rejected in mediation and mediator notes could not be used later in the same action to support a motion for attorney's fees because information about fees as well as mediator notes do not fall within a confidentiality exception and cannot be used to support a claim of fees.[127]

---

123. N.Y. Mediator Ethics Advisory Comm. Op. 2008-01 (2008).
124. N.Y. Mediator Ethics Advisory Comm. Op. 2009-02 (2009).
125. ISBA Advisory Op. on Prof'l Conduct, Op. No. 01-05 (2002).
126. ISBA Advisory Op. on Prof'l Conduct, Op. No. 92-5 (1992).
127. Advisory Op. of the N.C. Dispute Resol. Comm'n, Op. No. 38 (2018).

3.3.2.6. Gifts

Many mediator codes allow a mediator to give or receive a gift of a minimal amount. North Carolina's rule specifically allows a mediator to provide de minimis gifts or favors such as "sodas, cookies, snacks, or lunches" that are intended to further the mediation or show respect for cultural norms to those attending mediation. They may not, however, give away mouse pads that serve as advertising for future business, as this creates an expectation of referral of clients for mediation services and may be perceived by participants or the general public as affecting the mediator's impartiality.[128]

In contrast, Tennessee's ADR Commission specifically precluded a mediator from accepting a Christmas gift from a law firm that frequently employed the mediator.[129] This prohibition seems appropriate since Tennessee forbids a neutral from giving or accepting any type of "gift, request, favor, loan, or any other item of value."

3.4. Conclusion

Mediation codes of conduct and MEAC opinions offer guidance to ensure a quality mediation process, including the promotion of public confidence in mediation as a dispute resolution process. Ethical mediators are instrumental to the credibility and integrity of the mediation field. They should not, therefore, blindly engage in mediation services without first obtaining requisite education and training. They should be intimately aware of the mediation code of conduct in their jurisdiction to help guide them in a successful mediation practice. When ethical dilemmas arise that are not addressed in a code of conduct, a mediator should consult other sources, including MEAC opinions, peers, and professional mediation associations.

128. Advisory Op. of the N.C. Dispute Resol. Comm'n, Op. No. 33 (2016).

129. Tenn. Alt. Dispute Resol. Comm'n, Ethics Advisory Op. No. 2010-0001 (2010).

Part II

At the Outset of Mediation

Chapter 4

Accepting a Case or Refusing to Mediate: Ethical Considerations

Ellen Waldman & Donna Erez-Navot

4.1. Introduction

A mediator's ethical responsibilities attach almost immediately upon being contacted with a request to mediate. Not every dispute should be mediated, and sometimes the "fit" between mediator and case is so awkward that it is best to decline outright. Sometimes, after a brief, tentative entry into the conflict, it becomes clear that the better course of action is to halt the proceedings and graciously withdraw. A mediator who has been tapped to serve should ask the following questions before reflexively moving forward:

1. Am I competent to handle this case?
2. Does this case pose a threat to the integrity of the mediation process?
3. Do I have a conflict of interest, due to either my relationships with one or both of the parties or counsel or my relationship to the subject matter of the dispute? In other words, can I truly mediate impartially?
4. If I mediate this case, can I be certain that I am adequately respecting the parties' rights to self-determination? Does the fundamental principle of party self-determination require I turn this case away?

Each ethical query will be considered in turn.

4.2. Competency—Am I Competent to Handle This Case?

The concept of competence in mediation is generally treated as involving two interrelated capacities—*process* training and experience, and *substantive* education and experience.[1] Court-connected mediation programs seek to assure process expertise by mandating that all providers possess certain qualifications, for example attendance at a 20- or 40-hour training and participation in some minimum number of mediations.[2] But possessing qualifications sufficient to facilitate a simple, straightforward neighborhood dispute does not assure competence in a more complex, legally or psychologically challenging matter.[3] Something more is required.

Competence relates to "[t]he ability to do something successfully or efficiently."[4] At a minimum, in a legal case, this would likely involve some familiarity with court process, the subject matter in dispute, and the vocabulary the parties will be using. It is difficult to add value as a communication enhancer, reality tester, or brainstorming facilitator if one is not fluent in the essential outlines of the conflict, be it construction defect, medical malpractice, securities fraud, or child support.[5]

Most mediation ethics standards declare that mediators should mediate only when competent to do so but do not offer a definition of what competency entails; rather, they enumerate a string of associated attributes or qualities. For example, the ABA's Model Standards of Conduct for Mediators (Model Standards) state that "training, experience in mediation, skills, cultural understandings and other qualities are often necessary for mediator competence."[6] Alabama and Tennessee maintain that competency requires "staying informed of and abiding by all statutes,

---

1. PRINCIPLES FOR ADR PROVIDER ORGANIZATIONS, cmt. 3 to Principle I at 8 (CPR-Georgetown Comm. on Ethics & Standards of Practice in ADR).

2. FLA. RULES FOR CERTIFIED & CT.-APPOINTED MEDIATORS (Fla. Dispute Resol. Ctr. 2018) [hereinafter FLA. RULES], R. 10.100; STANDARDS OF PROF'L CONDUCT FOR RULE 31 NEUTRALS, TENN. SUP. CT., § 14(a)(1)(i) [hereinafter TENN. STANDARDS].

3. *See* W. Lee Dobins, *The Debate over Mediator Qualifications: Can They Satisfy the Growing Need to Measure Competence without Barring Entry into the Market*, 7 U. FLA. J.L. & PUB. POL'Y 95 (1995).

4. Competence, LEXICO, https://www.lexico.com/en/definition/competence (last visited Feb. 24, 2021).

5. *See* FLA. RULES, *supra* note 2, Part I (outlining the criteria for mediator qualifications and certification) & Part II, R. 10.630 (imposing an ethical duty of acquiring and maintaining professional competence).

6. MODEL STANDARDS OF CONDUCT FOR MEDIATORS (Am. Bar Ass'n 2005) [hereinafter MODEL STANDARDS], Standard IV.A.1.

rules, and administrative orders relevant to the practice,"[7] while Virginia cautions its court-certified mediators to ensure they possess the requisite "mediator skill and subject-matter knowledge" to effectively mediate the dispute.[8]

Who should decide whether the mediator is competent? While some codes assert that the mediator must engage in an internal inventory of her skill set and knowledge base,[9] others hold that competence is satisfied so long as the mediator can satisfy the "reasonable expectations of the parties."[10] Ethical mediators should consider the "reasonable expectations" test for mediator competence a necessary, but not sufficient, condition for going forward.[11] In some instances, the parties will have absolutely no expectations regarding what a mediator can and should do. Consider the couple who arrives to family court for the first time and is assigned a mediator. Should a mediator's duty of competence really be pegged to the expectations of parties who enter into the process with an anticipatory blank slate?

It is also true that the mediation field has evolved to serve highly sophisticated parties in specialized fields and these parties often expect and require mediators to have both process expertise and knowledge and experience with the subject matter of the case. Thus, when mediators are considering whether they are competent to handle a case, they should conduct two inquiries, one external, one internal. First, the mediator should ascertain the expectations of the parties. Depending on the setting, the parties' expectations will diverge widely. In a Community Dispute Resolution Center and in some court programs, the parties likely expect the mediator to be a process expert only. In other, more specialized contexts,[12] the parties will expect the mediator to be fluent in the subject matter of the dispute and perhaps even a subject-matter expert.

---

7. ALA. CODE OF ETHICS FOR MEDIATORS [hereinafter ALA. CODE], Standard 1(a)(2); TENN. STANDARDS, *supra* note 2, § 2(a)(2).

8. STANDARDS OF ETHICS & PROF'L RESP. FOR CERTIFIED MEDIATORS, § J (Off. of the Exec. Sec'y of the Sup. Ct. of Va. 2011) [hereinafter VA. STANDARDS].

9. *Id.*

10. MODEL STANDARDS, *supra* note 6, Standard IV.A.

11. *See* OMER SHAPIRA, A THEORY OF MEDIATORS' ETHICS: FOUNDATIONS, RATIONALE, AND APPLICATION 166–67 (2016) (discussing the "reasonable expectation" test).

12. *See* GA. ADR PRAC. & PROC. MANUAL § 11:10 (Ga. Off. of Dispute Resol. 2020) ("If a preferred mediator is not an expert in the disputed subject matter and the subject matter is technically complex, you may want to authorize the mediator to hire a neutral expert. Alternatively, the mediation agreement could provide for the selection of a co-mediator who has expertise.").

When speaking with the parties, mediators must be upfront about their training, experience, and knowledge and experience in the subject matter of the case.

But, even if the mediator can satisfy the parties' expectations, the question of competency is not fully resolved. The mediator should still ask herself: am I sufficiently skilled, knowledgeable, and comfortable with the information and psychological dynamics of the case to do a creditable job? Mediators owe a duty, not simply to the parties, but to the profession itself not to get in "over their heads."[13] Therefore, regardless of the parties' stated presuppositions, the mediator must possess an informed confidence, based on an honest appraisal of her strengths and limitations, that she can meet the *parties'* expectations, the level of competence that is *reasonably* expected of her in the circumstances, and her own standards for what effective service would require. And if she does not possess the necessary competence, she must "decline an appointment, withdraw, or request appropriate assistance."[14]

The mandate of competency interacts with other core values of mediation, such as party self-determination, mediator impartiality, and others. For example, in the Model Standards, Standard VI, Quality of the Process, reminds mediators that the mediation role is distinct from other professional roles, and if a mediator assumes "an additional dispute resolution role," the mediator will be held to have taken on "different duties and responsibilities that may be governed by other standards."[15] Providing legal information is arguably a classic attorney function; however, recognizing that providing information in response to party queries is a recognized feature of proper mediation behavior, and that insight and knowledge gained from a mediator's profession of origin (be it law, psychiatry, engineering, or accounting) may enhance a mediator's ability to assist parties in making informed decisions, the Standards clarify that a mediator "may provide information that the mediator is qualified by training or experience to provide, [but] only if the mediator can do so consistent with these Standards."[16] Thus, attorney mediators who have sufficient subject-matter expertise can provide legal information to

13. *Id. See also* Omer Shapira, *A Critical Assessment of the Model Standards of Conduct for Mediators (2005): Call for Reform*, 100 Marq. L. Rev. 81, 133–34 (2016) (The requirement of competence aims at protecting the institution of mediation and the public, as well as the interests of the parties.).

14. Fla. Rules, *supra* note 2, R. 10.640. *See also* Model Standards, *supra* note 6, Standard IV.B; Ala. Code, *supra* note 7, Standard 1(a)(3).

15. Model Standards, *supra* note 6.

16. *Id.*

parties who request it, so long as they are able to do so congruent with the applicable standards of care governing attorneys in their jurisdiction and can do so sensitively, so as not to compromise the mediator's commitment to other critical mediation values, such as party self-determination or impartiality.[17]

Competence must be not only acquired but also maintained. All mediators "should attend educational programs and related activities to maintain and enhance the mediator's knowledge and skills related to mediation."[18] Continuing education is required and vital for cases where parties have little to no choice of mediator, typically in court-annexed mediation programs. And finally, competence includes being free from drugs and alcohol and having the capacity to mediate effectively: "[I]f a mediator's ability to conduct a mediation is impaired by drugs, alcohol, medication or otherwise, the mediator shall not conduct the mediation."[19]

4.3. Does This Case Pose a Threat to the Integrity of the Mediation Process?

Mediator competence is not the only salient ethical factor to consider when deciding whether to take a case. Mediators also serve as guardians of process integrity.[20] That means, even if the parties are in agreement that they want the mediator's help, sometimes, to preserve the integrity and quality of the process, the mediator must decline. For example, if the parties are planning on using the mediation process to "further criminal conduct," the Model Standards and many state codes dictate that the mediator must take appropriate steps, including ". . . postponing, withdrawing from, or terminating the mediation."[21] Some state codes are stricter. Only termination will do.[22]

Interest in using mediation for questionable purposes arises in the family context when parties seek to minimize the tax consequences of

17. See Chapter 5 (Evaluating Ethically).

18. Model Standards, *supra* note 6, Standard IV.A.2.

19. *Id.* Standard IV.C.

20. Ga. Ethical Standards for Mediators, Standard IV.B; Shapira, *supra* note 13, at 113–18 (discussing the mediator's duty of integrity under the Model Standards); Shapira, *supra* note 11, at 231–33 (discussing the meaning and elements of mediator's duty of integrity in mediation).

21. *See* Model Standards, *supra* note 6, Standard VI.A.9. *See also* Wash. Mediation Ass'n, Standards of Practice for Mediators, Standard VI, cmt.

22. *See* Ala. Code, *supra* note 7, Standard 3(b).

their mergers or dissolutions.[23] Divorce mediators report encountering couples who contemplate tax evasion as part of their postmarital financial strategy, and these mediators typically advise that parties consult with tax experts when considering options that appear to short Uncle Sam. Similarly, where parties to a divorce action fail to properly disclose significant marital assets,[24] mediators who discover the omission are obligated to terminate the mediation, while keeping confidential the reasons for the withdrawal.[25]

In the nonfamily context, Mediator Ethics Advisory Committee (MEAC) opinions suggest that past fraud or criminal activities are not necessarily a reason to decline to accept a mediation case. For example, where a party revealed that he had committed what the mediator determined to be insurance fraud, the New York MEAC counseled the mediator to maintain party confidence, not report the fraud to the police or other authorities, and withdraw if, upon learning of the past fraud, he felt he could no longer remain impartial.[26]

In another opinion, when a New York mediator found himself mediating a case involving two teenagers, one of whom had a valid and ongoing restraining order against the other, the mediator realized that even sitting in the same room violated the terms of the legal order.[27] The MEAC suggested urging the party to get outside professional advice regarding her obligations pursuant to the order and opined that "[o]nce the mediator becomes aware of the Order, the mediator should withdraw from or terminate the mediation process" in order to meet his obligation to ensure a quality process and prevent the mediation being used to further illegal conduct consistent with Standard VI, Quality of the Process, Comment 10.[28]

The decision to accept or decline a case for illegality can be quite complex. Julie Macfarlane has written provocatively about a mediation

23. Brian Shannon, *Confidentiality of Texas Mediations: Ruminations on Some Thorny Problems*, 32 Tex. Tech L. Rev. 77, 96 (2000) (discussing "hypotheticals" based on real cases in which divorce mediation parties engaged in tax fraud).

24. Crupi v. Crupi, 784 So. 2d 611, 614 (Fla. 5th Dist. Ct. App. 2001) (wife seeking disavowal of mediated agreement due to husband's failure to accurately disclose assets).

25. *See* Advisory Op. of the NC Dispute Resol. Comm'n Op. No. 16 (2010), *available at* https://www.nccourts.gov/assets/inline-files/AO-16.2020.pdf?YyaEE97OAwfKGPAhh4fq757mm5aMnyrP.

26. N.Y. MEAC Op. 2006-003 (mediator concerned about possible insurance fraud where party obtained $19,000 in insurance payments for piano purchased for $1,000).

27. N.Y. MEAC Op. 2008-01.

28. *Id.*

she conducted that flowed from a failed drug deal.[29] One party had invested in a shipment of marijuana that was confiscated by the police. The "investor" wanted his money back, and the would-be drug transporter was looking to repay his debt by supplying services, such as painting the "investor's" office. Commentators who were asked to reflect on the case made clear that they would not participate in discussions that contemplated the repaying of funds through *future* drug deals. Indeed, one analyst said that even if no future illegality were contemplated, the mediator should not involve herself in such a distasteful situation: "Faced with . . . unsavory dealings, a mediator should not offer assistance. She should not work with them to tidy up the problem of the unpaid debt or take a gamble that their future interactions will be legally sound. The mediator should not taint the process by using her skills to help parties clean up the messy overflow from a drug deal gone south. Doing so threatens the mediator's integrity and compromises the field in the eyes of the public."[30]

Other ethics experts felt differently. One stated that it is permissible to assist parties with the conflict flowing from *past* commission of a crime, so long as the mediation does not become a vehicle for further wrongdoing.[31] Professor Macfarlane, in discussing her decision to continue mediating even when it became clear that the actions that gave rise to the dispute were illegal, drew a distinction between truly *heinous crimes* that cause physical harm or endanger others and those that do not. The parties, in selling pot, had engaged in illegal behavior but not morally heinous conduct that rendered them and their problems unredeemable. So long as the reparations being contemplated did not involve further illegality, Professor Macfarlane felt comfortable continuing to lend her assistance. While conceding that an argument could be made for withdrawing based on a need to uphold the integrity of the profession, Professor Macfarlane concluded, ". . . my judgment over when, and when not, to offer mediation is responsive first to client needs and only second to the concerns of those who seek to professionalize and promote mediation services."[32] If, early in the case, a mediator senses that the process is being used to heal the rifts stemming from past transgression, it is largely

29. Ellen Waldman, Mediation Ethics Cases and Commentaries 191–96 (2011) [hereinafter Mediation Ethics].

30. John Bickerman, *Mediating on the Wrong Side of the Law*, *in* Mediation Ethics, *supra* note 29, at 183.

31. Jeremy Lack, *Mediating on the Wrong Side of the Law*, *in* Mediation Ethics, *supra* note 29, at 189–90.

32. *Id.* at 193.

up to the individual conscience of the mediator whether to continue or withdraw. But, if the parties are clearly contemplating future illegality, the only course, for the mediator and the profession, is to withdraw.

Quality-of-process standards suggest two other integrity-related considerations for mediators to consider before accepting a case. First, whether the mediator is "prepared to commit the attention essential to an effective mediation"[33] and "can satisfy the reasonable expectation of the parties concerning the timing of a mediation."[34] These provisions reflect a duty of diligence, which includes the intention and ability to both commit the attention necessary for an effective mediation and respond to the parties' needs and expectations regarding timing.[35] If the mediator cannot meet these expectations, he should not accept the case.

Second, the mediator should assess the appropriateness of the case to mediation and decline an inappropriate case. The Florida Rules, for example, provide that "[a] mediator is responsible for confirming that mediation is an appropriate dispute resolution process under the circumstances of each case";[36] the Texas Guidelines note that a mediator should not mediate "if it is apparent to the mediator that the case is inappropriate for mediation";[37] and the Virginia Standards state that "[i]f in the judgment of the mediator the conditions . . . [of appropriateness] are not met, the mediator shall not commence or continue the mediation."[38] The tests for appropriateness are not always clear.[39] In family cases, they may include violence and abuse between parties, child abuse or neglect, drug or alcohol use, and imbalance of power.[40] In nonfamily matters, they could also relate to cases the mediator considers more appropriate to dispute-resolution procedures other than mediation, such as arbitration, neutral evaluation, or counseling.[41]

---

33. MODEL STANDARDS, *supra* note 6, Standard VI.A.1.

34. *Id.* Standard VI.A.2.

35. *See* Shapira, *supra* note 13, at 110. *See also* FLA. RULES, *supra* note 2, R. 10.430; ALA. CODE, *supra* note 7, Standard 3(c) ("A mediator shall refrain from accepting additional appointments when it becomes apparent that completion of mediation assignments already accepted cannot be accomplished in a timely fashion.").

36. FLA. RULES, *supra* note 2, R. 10.400.

37. TEXAS ETHICAL GUIDELINES FOR MEDIATORS (2011), § 13.

38. VA. STANDARDS, *supra* note 8, Standard C.

39. *See* SHAPIRA, *supra* note 11, at 240–43 (discussing the tests of appropriateness).

40. VA. STANDARDS, *supra* note 8, cmt. to Standard C. *See also* MODEL STANDARDS, *supra* note 6, Standard VI.B.

41. *See, e.g.*, MODEL STANDARDS, *supra* note 6, Standard VI.A.7; Shapira, *supra* note 13, at 115–16.

4.4. Do I Have a Conflict of Interest? Can I Mediate Impartially?

A third critical determination that a mediator must make at the outset is whether the mediator can act impartially, that is, with no favoritism or bias in favor of a party or a particular outcome.[42] Mediators must not have, as the old saying goes, a "dog in the race." If a mediator does have a stake in the outcome or a bias in favor of or against a particular party, then the ethical course is clear; she must decline to mediate.

Mediators need to be concerned not simply with what is in their heart, that is, their own assessment of whether they can remain unbiased and impartial. They need to think about whether their impartiality will be obvious to others. Appearances count. Thus, it is important to avoid not simply an *actual* conflict of interest; it is important to avoid even the *appearance* of a conflict of interest.[43]

Conflicts arise from relationships, with either the parties or their counsel—or with the subject matter of the dispute. We will treat each type of relationship separately.

4.4.1. Relationships with Parties

When considering whether to take a case, a mediator must, according to the Model Standards, make a "reasonable inquiry" to determine if facts exist that a reasonable person would consider likely to create a potential or actual conflict of interest.[44] Obviously, what is reasonable is a question of context. If you work for a large law firm, you likely should run the parties' names through the firm's conflict check system. If you are a solo practitioner, your reasonable inquiry will likely be less extensive. But, nonetheless, you should ensure that you have not represented either of the parties (or even any close relatives of either of the parties) and that no relationship exists that could put your impartiality at risk or create the appearance of impropriety.

The fact that the codes only forbid relationships that would lead a "reasonable person" to suspect a conflict is significant. While all types of relationships—personal, professional, financial—should be scrutinized for possible conflicts, transient, superficial, or ephemeral bonds can be disregarded. You needn't worry about mediating a case involving a fellow volunteer at the city orchestra's annual fundraiser or one of the 30 hardy

42. Model Standards, *supra* note 6, Standard II.A.
43. *Id.* Standard III.A.
44. *Id.* Standard III.B.

souls in your four-week cycling class from last summer.[45] More substantial ties should be the focus of your concern. These more substantial ties should be disclosed to the parties, and it will be up to the parties to decide whether they want to continue with you as their mediator. The Model Standards and most state codes suggest that not all conflicts are cured by party consent. If a conflict of interest "might reasonably be viewed as undermining the integrity of the mediation," then the mediator should withdraw, even if the parties wish to proceed.[46]

Ethics opinions from various state commissions as well as case law and the occasional media cause celebre help us better understand which relationships can be ignored, which require disclosure, and which are so detrimental to the appearance of mediator impartiality that the mediator must decline the case, despite party acquiescence.[47]

One incident that attracted significant media attention involves the mediation of wrongful death and personal injury claims stemming from the Las Vegas mass shooting perpetrated by a gunman staying at MGM's Mandalay Bay Hotel on attendees of a music festival in the field below.[48] Nearly 60 died and hundreds were injured. Attorneys for the victims claimed that MGM was negligent in allowing the gunman to stockpile high-powered rifles and thousands of rounds of ammunition in his hotel room. After significant legal skirmishing, counsel for both sides agreed to mediate. They hired two former state court judges to comediate and ultimately reached a settlement in which MGM agreed to pay nearly 4,500 plaintiffs up to $800 million to release their outstanding claims.

Eight months after the settlement was reached, however, a subset of plaintiffs began to express concern that the settlement was not fair. Word had reached them that one of the mediators was the daughter of the vice president of security at MGM, a position he continued to hold until shortly before the mediation took place. Coordinating counsel for the plaintiffs

---

45. *But see* Shapira, *supra* note 11, at 196, 198 (advocating a cautious approach, favoring disclosure in cases of trivial conflicts of interest as well because the line between types of conflicts of interest is often blurred).

46. Model Standards, *supra* note 6, Standard III.E; Rules of Conduct for Mediators in Ct. Connected Mediation Programs for Civil Cases, Cal. Rules of Ct. § 3.855(f) [hereinafter Cal. Rules]; Standards of Conduct for New York St. Cmty. Dispute Resol. Ctr. Mediators (rev. 2009), Standard III.B.

47. *See also* Shapira, *supra* note 11, at 196–200 (suggesting guidelines for disclosure of conflicts of interest and withdrawal).

48. Bill Hutchinson et al., *The Anatomy of the Las Vegas Mass Shooting, the Deadliest in Modern US History*, ABC News (Dec. 23, 2018, 7:49 AM), https://abcnews.go.com/US/anatomy-las-vegas-mass-shooting-deadliest-modern-us/story?id=59797324.

stated that they were aware of and comfortable with the mediator's close familial relationship with MGM security personnel. They averred that they had informed their clients in writing of the family connection and no one had objected. Newspaper inquiries into the case, however, reveal that some of the written disclosures were vague regarding the exact relationship, and even where the written disclosures were clear, individual plaintiffs claim that they did not remember or understand the meaning of the father-daughter tie in the context of the ensuing settlement. As one claimant stated after becoming aware of the father-daughter relationship, "Red flags keep on popping up . . . ."[49]

Ethics experts assert that the MGM mediation provides a classic case of a nonwaivable conflict.[50] Disclosure and consent do not cure a conflict that threatens to undermine "the integrity of the mediation" process.[51] A reasonable person, considering the facts surrounding the MGM mediation, would be led to wonder how the mediator could not help but be concerned with her father's welfare, even as she was trying her utmost to be entirely impartial in her facilitation of the case. How could she not want to push the discussions toward an outcome that was positive, or at least not harmful, to her father's professional status? This type of speculation, this cloud of suspicion, is exactly what the drafters of the Model Standards had in mind when they worried about conflicts that call into question the integrity of the process. It is why, in these instances, disclosure and party consent are almost irrelevant to the mediator's choice of whether to proceed or bow out. Here, the mediator should have bowed out—thereby avoiding the taint, ill will, and concern that ended up contaminating the process.[52]

The Florida MEAC charged with issuing advisory opinions for that state's court-connected mediation program provides additional guidance as to which sorts of relationships create nonwaivable conflicts and which can be managed with disclosure and consent. For example, mediating a case in which your son or daughter is party counsel would create a nonwaivable conflict. On the other hand, if a case came your way from your

---

49. Katie Wilcox & Bianca Buono, *One Mediator in Las Vegas Shooting Settlement Is Daughter to Former MGM Security Vice President*, 12NEWS (updated June 9, 2020, 6:28 PM), https://www.12news.com/article/news/investigations/some-survivors-question-las-vegas-shooting-settlement/75-a30fe101-b4da-4858-8c44-f5b682722821.

50. Art Hinshaw, *An Unquestionable Mediation Conflict of Interest*, 38 ALTS. TO THE HIGH COST OF LITIG. 102 (2020).

51. MODEL STANDARDS, *supra* note 6, Standard III.E.

52. Hinshaw, *supra* note 50.

daughter's law firm and she had no involvement in it at all, that conflict could be waivable after disclosure.[53] In a case where one party's counsel was the brother of the fiancé of the mediator's daughter, the committee took particular notice that "there is no immediate family member involved, but rather a potential extended family relationship [the brother of the mediator's daughter's fiancé]" and "a limited social relationship in which the mediator sees [party counsel] at family gatherings such as dinners . . . two or three times a year . . . ." [54] Upon these facts, the committee stated it did not believe the attenuated personal relationship created a clear (and thus nonwaivable) conflict of interest. However, the relationship could *appear* to compromise the mediator's impartiality, and thus the committee recommended disclosure and procuring the parties' consent.[55]

Personal relationships are not the only types of bonds to watch out for. Professional ties must be scrutinized equally. For example, a mediator who had worked for several decades as in-house counsel for a large insurance company should be wary of mediating a dispute involving his former employer as either a party or a party's insurer.[56] Although this is not the type of conflict that clearly requires the mediator to decline the case, the mediator would need to give close attention to whether there are any personnel that he had worked with in a representative capacity who would be participating in the mediation and whether any knowledge that he gained as counsel would be implicated or relevant in the mediated case. If so, those facts would require withdrawal. If there were no overlapping personnel and if the mediated matter were separate and distinct from the issues the mediator treated in his role as in-house counsel, then disclosure and party consent should be sufficient.

A mediator who is a member of a law firm must consider not only her own work as an attorney, both past and present, but also the work of her law partners. Ethics committees in various states have determined that under no circumstances should a mediator work on a case when one of the mediator's law partners is currently performing transactional work for one party's legal counsel.[57]

53. Fla. Mediator Ethics Advisory Comm., Formal Op. 2004-008 (2005) (citing R. 10.330(a), R. 10.340(a)–(c)).

54. Fla. Mediator Ethics Advisory Comm., Formal Op. 2018-003 (2018).

55. *Id.*

56. Fla. Mediator Ethics Advisory Comm., Formal Op. 2019-007 (2020).

57. Fla. Mediator Ethics Advisory Comm., Formal Op. 2009-009 (2009); Fla. Mediator Ethics Advisory Comm., Formal Op. 2008-007 (2008); Fla. Mediator Ethics Advisory Comm., Formal Op. 2002-005 (2002).

Timing is critical. If facts exist that could create the appearance of a conflict, the mediator should disclose them to the parties as soon as possible. Ideally, the parties would be afforded maximal time to absorb the information about their chosen mediator's relationships and make a considered decision as to whether they remain comfortable going forward.

4.4.2. Relationships with Subject Matter

Mediators should be careful not to take on cases where they are secretly—or not so secretly—hoping for a particular outcome.[58] An attorney who has spent his career advocating for tenants in landlord-tenant disputes should interrogate whether he can really handle a security deposit dispute or threatened eviction in an evenhanded fashion. Can he avoid favoring the tenant given the many years spent as an advocate for renters' interests? Similarly, a parent who has founded and served as president of a nonprofit advocacy group for families with autistic children should think carefully before taking on a special education mediation between a school district and the parents of an autistic student. Certainly, in either circumstance, the mediator should inform the parties of her prior work and volunteer history and give the parties a chance to decide if they would be more comfortable with someone who does not have a history working and advocating in the area. Even if the parties decide they are unfazed by the mediator's prior involvement in the general subject-matter area—be it housing policy or disability rights—the mediator may determine that she is unable to conduct the mediation without bias or partiality and decline the case.

4.4.3. Dual Functions

Mediators who are contemplating taking on a dual role while facilitating party discussion should realize that such multitasking is frowned upon by most ethics codes and opinions. For example, although it would be exceedingly convenient in polyglot court-connected programs for mediators to serve as both conversation facilitators and translators, ethics committees that have considered the question have condemned the practice for impartiality and conflicts-of-interest considerations.[59] Even adding on the primarily ministerial task of notary is prohibited in some

58. Model Standards, *supra* note 6, Standard III.A.

59. Fla. Mediator Ethics Advisory Comm., Formal Op. 2017-021 (2018) (Applying rules 10.330(a) and 10.340(d) as mentioned in MEAC 2017-002, a mediator is prohibited from serving in the dual roles of mediator and an oral interpreter for a deaf pro se defendant who reads lips.).

jurisdictions.[60] In many jurisdictions, mediators are mandatory reporters of child and elder abuse. If a mediator is the first to make a report to authorities regarding suspected abuse of a vulnerable person, then the mediator should inform the parties of her action and thereupon withdraw from the case.[61] In addition, lawyer mediators should not accept a representational role when they serve as mediators.[62]

In sum, upon being asked to serve, a mediator must consider both his relationship with the parties and other mediation participants and his relationship with the topic of the mediation. He must search his conscience to ensure that these relationships do not, in any way, impair his ability to act impartially throughout the process or create any appearance of partiality. Where a nontrivial relationship exists that might lead one or the other party to question the mediator's neutral stance, the mediator should explicitly disclose that relationship and offer the parties the opportunity to choose another neutral. When the relationship threatens to undermine the integrity of the mediation, the mediator must withdraw. Finally, a mediator should avoid taking on professional functions that are properly viewed as outside the traditional mediation role, such as serving simultaneously as a language interpreter, therapist, or legal advisor.

---

60. Fla. Mediator Ethics Advisory Comm., Formal Ops. 2011-004 (2011), 2010-004 (2010); *but see* N.Y. Formal Op. 2007-01 (A mediator-notary is not precluded from acting as a notary under the facts presented. Looking under Standard VI, Quality of the Process, Comment 5, as well as the NYS Notary Public License Law, a notary is not considered a "professional" in the way Standard VI intended. A notary's role is ministerial in nature. Therefore, the mediator may notarize the document in this situation.).

61. Fla. Mediator Ethics Advisory Comm., Formal Op. 2017-0016 (2018) (Interestingly, the ethics committee concluded that "[i]f the mediator is not the initial reporter and the mediator believes they can be neutral and impartial despite making the report, the MEAC believes the appearance of bias or partiality under rule 10.330 may not exist and the mediator may mediate the case with the parties' consent; however, the mediator shall not disclose the identity of a party who has made a prior abuse report.").

62. *See, e.g.*, CAL. RULES, *supra* note 46, R. 3.857(d); GA. ETHICAL STANDARDS FOR MEDIATORS, *supra* note 20, Commentary to § I.E at 26. *See also* Chapter 5.

4.5. If I Mediate This Case, Can I Be Certain That I Am Adequately Respecting the Parties' Rights to Self-Determination? Does the Fundamental Principle of Party Self-Determination Require I Turn This Case Away?

A mediator must be alert to the possibility that parties will not be able to adequately exercise their autonomy throughout the mediation process. Party self-determination—the maximal exercise of party autonomy—is the first and arguably primary ethical imperative of mediation.[63] Defined by the Model Standards as "the act of coming to a voluntary, uncoerced decision in which each party makes free and informed choices as to process and outcome,"[64] self-determination embodies mediation's commitment to vest primary decisional authority with the parties and to nurture party agency to the greatest extent possible.

But sometimes parties are not well situated to exercise their autonomy. Illness, disability, age-related decline, or substance abuse can all impair a disputant's ability to act congruent with deeply felt values and long-term interests. Upon being asked to serve, it is the mediator's immediate task to assess whether parties can negotiate in a self-determining fashion or whether a party's autonomy is so compromised that beginning to mediate is ill advised. This assessment will require the mediator to scrutinize party capacity as well as threats of undue influence and unacceptably large power imbalance.

4.5.1. Party Incapacity

According to the Model Standards, "[i]f a party appears to have difficulty comprehending the process, issues, or settlement options, or difficulty participating in a mediation, the mediator should explore the circumstances and potential accommodations, modifications or adjustments that would make possible the party's capacity to comprehend, participate and exercise self-determination."[65] When the mediator's intervention is not successful, she must postpone the mediation (where the incompetence is temporary) or bring it to an end.[66] The Montana Mediation Association Code of Ethics and Standards of Practice, for example, provides that "[i]f, in the opinion of a mediator, the process is impeded by a party's use of a drug, alcohol or by other physical or mental incapacity, the mediator

63. Model Standards, *supra* note 6, Standard I.A.
64. *Id.*
65. *Id.* Standard VI.A.10.
66. Shapira, *supra* note 11, at 146.

shall postpone a mediation session and/or withdraw from the mediation process and/or refer the parties to appropriate resources."[67]

Capacity is a decision-specific function; that is, a party may lack the capacity to engage in complicated financial transactions but retain sufficient cognitive and emotional function to participate in mediation and bind himself to the resulting agreement.[68] Capacity assessments focus on three areas of function: understanding, appreciation, and communication.[69] First, parties must be able to *understand* the nature and goals of the mediation process, the role of the mediator, the issues to be discussed, and the identity of each participant present.[70] Second, they must be able to *appreciate* the consequences of their decisions, to appraise and consider options,[71] and to realize that signing on the dotted line in mediation will impose duties and obligations, dictating one set of outcomes while foreclosing others. Finally, parties must be able to *communicate* their preferences clearly to both the mediator and the other participants.

If capacity is fragile, the mediator should give thought to whether accommodations can be made to bolster it. Premediation sessions with the vulnerable individual and counsel can explore if and what sorts of modifications to the process would be helpful. Would the inclusion of support people—relatives, friends, medical assistants, or disability advocates—make the process more comprehensible and less intimidating?[72]

For example, mediation of neglect petitions or termination of parental rights petitions sometimes involve parents with mental-health issues, thereby requiring the mediator to engage in capacity assessment. Accommodations frequently involve extensive use of premediation sessions with the inclusion of support people, such as mental health professionals, parent advocates, trusted family members, or clergy.

4.5.2. Extreme Power Imbalance

Self-determination can also be undermined in situations of extreme power imbalance. Parties must be able to reach voluntary, uncoerced decisions as to the mediation process and outcome; if this is not possible, mediators

67. Mont. Mediation Ass'n Code of Ethics & Standards of Practice (2014), § IX.

68. Mediation Ethics, *supra* note 29, at 32–33 (noting that parties' capacity relates to the decision to participate in the mediation and to make an agreement).

69. *Id.* at 30.

70. ADA Mediation Guidelines § D (Kukin Program for Conflict Resol. and the Cardozo J. of Conflict Resol.).

71. *Id.* at 6.

72. Mediation Ethics, *supra* note 29, at 31.

should not proceed with the session.[73] As one of us has observed elsewhere, "[W]hen the power imbalance is too great, most commentators would say that mediation is inappropriate. Mediators confronting such an imbalance should simply refuse to proceed."[74]

Recent case law makes clear that judges trust mediators to level the playing field and keep power imbalances in check. Rebuffing claims from disgruntled mediation participants that the agreements they reached in mediation were the product of duress[75] or "overreaching,"[76] courts in both New York and California pointed to the presence of the mediator as a safeguard against bullying and unconscionable outcomes.[77] In one case, the judge went so far as to say that "the presumption of undue influence cannot properly be applied to marital settlement agreements reached through mediation because family law mediators not only level any imbalance of bargaining strength between the parties, they consider it their duty to attempt to determine whether the parties are 'acting under their own free will' in the mediation."[78]

Since objections to mediation settlement agreements will be seen in this light, it is imperative that mediators correctly assess severe power imbalances from the start and decide at the outset if mediation is appropriate for the dispute in front of them. The question is, when is a power imbalance so great that the mediator should decline to proceed?[79]

Relationships between people are both dynamic and complicated, and rarely do disputants enter mediation with exactly equal amounts of power. Some degree of power asymmetry is to be expected. But, if the imbalance becomes too acute, then the mediation should terminate, for fear that the disempowered party will be railroaded into a resolution that does not represent her autonomous will. The mediator must diagnose the power sources and then decide if the risks of going forward outweigh the

---

73. *Id.* at 89.

74. *Id.* at 87.

75. *In re* Marriage of Kieturakis, 138 Cal. App. 4th 56 (2006).

76. Irizarry v. Hayes, 121 N.Y.S.3d 854 (N.Y. Sup. Ct. 2020).

77. *In re Marriage of Kieturakis*, 138 Cal. App. 4th at 85 (". . . since voluntary participation and self-determination are fundamental principles of mediation, it can be expected that most mediators would work to minimize unfairness in the process . . . ."); *Irizarry*, 121 N.Y.S.3d at 854 ("The mediator is the steward and protector of the process."); *In re* Marriage of Cooke, No. B257791, 2016 WL 6069190, at 6 (Cal. Ct. App. Oct. 17, 2016).

78. *In re Marriage of Kieturakis*, 138 Cal. App. 4th at 85.

79. Mediation Ethics, *supra* note 29, at 88.

benefits, while keeping in mind that litigation can also produce problematic outcomes where power is inequitably distributed.

Power derives from diverse sources, including money or property; knowledge of the subject matter in dispute; merit in the eyes of the law; moral certainty; advantageous personality traits, such as eloquence, analytical prowess, and tenacity; and the power to inflict pain or irritation.[80] In the case of a mediated divorce, a husband's greater knowledge of the couple's finances may be balanced by the wife's greater authority and experience in tending to the needs of the children.[81] But where one party possesses all or even the vast majority of the available sources of power, the mediator should proceed with caution. If it is determined that the possible benefits of allowing the parties to negotiate with each other outweigh the risks, then she should focus on the use of best practices to mitigate the power imbalance to the greatest extent possible, including use of a comediation model; thorough intake; premediation caucuses; a thorough opening statement outlining all aspects of mediation, including the voluntary nature of mediation and the parties' right to terminate; the use of multiple sessions to allow frequent breaks; caucusing often to ensure comfort and informed decision making; and encouraging the assistance of outside counsel for consultation and advice.[82]

The decision whether to decline or proceed in the face of imbalance of power is a complex one, as evidenced by the case of domestic violence or Intimate Partner Violence (IPV). Domestic violence advocates early on believed that mediation should categorically be avoided when couples had a history of violence. More recently, especially with the new understanding of the different types of IPV, the approach of mediation in these cases has become more nuanced.

Once considered monolithic, violence between intimates can actually take a number of forms, including physical, verbal, emotional, economic, and sexual. Additionally, there exist four discrete types of IPV—Coercive Controlling Violence, Violent Resistance, Situational Couple Violence, and Separation-Instigated Violence, each having different markers that make them more or less amenable to mediation.[83] Mediators must be

---

80. *Id.* at 94–95.

81. *Id.* at 96.

82. Comm. on Ethics of the Ga. Comm'n on Dispute Resol., Ethics Op. 1 (1998). For measures to help cope with power imbalance, see MEDIATION ETHICS, *supra* note 29, at 100–01.

83. Michael P. Johnson & Joan B. Kelly, *Differentiation among Types of Intimate Partner Violence: Research Update and Implications for Interventions*, 46 FAM. CT. REV. 476 (2008).

well trained and able to distinguish between these different types of IPV and not conflate all forms of physical violence into one blurred image of abuse within a "battering culture." Mediators should be able to identify the type of IPV implicated in the case in order to fully understand if mediation should be considered. To that end, before meeting with the parties, a mediator must engage in a robust intake process to identify IPV and, if found, utilize specialized screening instruments for reliable differentiation between the types of IPV.[84] The primary question for the mediator is whether the victim of violence has become so accustomed to the disparate power that he or she is unable to advocate for him- or herself in a confidential mediation session.

In cases of Coercive Controlling Violence, which most closely resembles the generalized image of domestic violence, one party feels so systematically and completely disempowered that he or she is unable to speak honestly or assert his or her interests at all. Mediation should be avoided in these cases unless methodical planning and robust supports are in place.[85]

The second type of IPV, Violent Resistance, is violence predominately perpetrated by female partners in response to male-instigated control or violence, so it may often be found within a relationship identified as Coercive Controlling Violence. More research about this type must be conducted to understand whether mediation is ever safe or appropriate.[86]

Situational Couple Violence generally results from situations or arguments between partners that escalate on occasion into physical violence. Situational Couple Violence is not embedded in a relationship-wide pattern of power and control. A majority of couples who have a history of

---

84. Loraine J. Bacchus et al., *"It Doesn't Freak Us Out the Way It Used To": An Evaluation of the Domestic Violence Enhanced Home (DOVE) Intervention to Inform Practice and Policy*, J. INTERPERS. VIOLENCE 3, 32 (2019), https://researchonline.lshtm.ac.uk/id/eprint/4649346/1/It_doesnt_freak_us_out.pdf; V.A. Moyer, *U.S. Preventive Services Task Force Screening for Intimate Partner Violence and Abuse of Elderly and Vulnerable Adults: U.S. Preventive Services Task Force Recommendation Statement*, 158 ANN. INTERN. MED. 478–86 (2013); Frederick D. Edwards et al., *More Than Meets the Eye: The Importance of Screening for Intimate Partner Violence*, 23 J. OF WOMEN'S HEALTH 275 (2014).

85. Johnson & Kelly, *supra* note 83, at 492. Some commentators believe that the traditional adversarial system often fails to protect victims of Coercive Controlling Violence and that, when mediation is provided in safe settings, victims of IPV may have more opportunities to be heard and feel empowered with respect to addressing the needs of their children.

86. Connie Beck et al., *Patterns of Intimate Partner Violence in a Large, Epidemiological Sample of Divorcing Couples*, 27 J. FAM. PSYCHOL. 743, 750 (2013).

Situational Couple Violence are able to mediate and can do so safely and productively with appropriate safeguards. According to researchers, these couples have been found to be quite willing to vigorously express their opinions, differences, and entitlements.[87]

Finally, Separation-Instigated Violence involves unexpected and uncharacteristic acts of violence perpetrated by a partner with a history of civilized and contained behavior. It is unlikely to recur, and protection orders often result in compliance.[88] Couples with Separation-Instigated Violence will benefit from mediation with appropriate safeguards, including referrals to counseling for the violent partner to help restabilize psychological equilibrium.[89]

IPV can show up in guises that take a mediator by surprise. IPV's complexity highlights the importance of premediation discussions, reliance on sophisticated screening instruments that identify different patterns of partner violence, the early and frequent use of caucus, and sensitivity to the fact that IPV does not always follow the stereotyped forms that we expect.

Effectively managing issues of incapacity and extreme power imbalance requires the mediator to become more active than in a typical mediation. To ensure self-determination for both parties, the mediator must utilize best practices to assess at the outset of mediation whether the parties are able to exercise self-determination and to be methodical in arranging the session from the start.

4.6. Conclusion

A mediator's decision to take on a new case should be made thoughtfully and with deliberation. She should engage in an ethical inventory that entails a series of inquiries: Am I competent to handle the procedural and substantive complexities posed by this dispute? Am I free of conflicts of interest such that I can treat each disputant with complete impartiality? Are the parties capable of participating adequately in the process, and, if a power asymmetry exists, can it be managed without threats to the integrity of the process? At this early stage, the mediator has the opportunity to put ethical considerations front and center in her practice, a habit of thought and action that will redound to her individual benefit and the field's at large.

87. Johnson & Kelly, *supra* note 83, at 492.

88. *Id.* at 487.

89. *Id.* at 492.

Part III

Conducting Mediation: Ethical Aspects in the Use of Mediator Techniques

Chapter 5

Evaluating Ethically

Kristen M. Blankley

5.1. Introduction

The self-reflective mediator should understand the underlying philosophies that guide the mediator's decisions as the process progresses. These decisions are not necessarily right or wrong because there is no one best way to mediate. Mediators can choose to mediate in accordance with a wide variety of values, such as settling cases, improving communication, repairing relationships, finding creative outcomes, satisfying interests, and empowering parties, among others.

The evaluative form of mediation, famously contoured by Leonard Riskin, involves a mediator orientation defined by analysis of strengths and weaknesses of legal claims and case values, as well as "strategies and techniques that evaluate issues important to the dispute or transaction."[1] Although early scholarship questioned whether evaluative mediation was ethical at all,[2] the evaluative form of mediation has stood the test of time as a popular choice, particularly in litigated cases in which all parties

---

1. Leonard L. Riskin, *Understanding Mediators' Orientations, Strategies, and Techniques: A Grid for the Perplexed*, 1 Harv. Negot. L. Rev. 7, 9, 23–24 (1996) (citing James Alfini & Gerald S. Clay, *Should Lawyer-Mediators Be Prohibited from Providing Legal Advice or Evaluations?*, Disp. Resol. Mag. Spring 1994, at 8).

2. Alfini & Clay, *supra* note 1; *see also* Kimberlee K. Kovach & Lela P. Love, *"Evaluative" Mediation Is an Oxymoron*, 14 Alts. to High Cost Litig. 31 (1996).

are represented by legal counsel.[3] Today, the better question is whether a mediator acts ethically while in the evaluative role.

This chapter begins by considering what it means to evaluate and how it is distinguished from common mediator techniques, such as reality testing. The remainder of the chapter discusses the ethical considerations surrounding the use of evaluative techniques, drawing from national ethics guidelines, state and local law, and ethics opinions.

5.2. What Does It Mean to Evaluate?

The field of mediation does not have a standard definition of "evaluative mediation," and its boundaries are difficult to define. Evaluative mediators tend to make evaluations, predictions, and estimates of a wide variety of legal issues or settlement values.[4] Mediators use many different techniques to communicate those ideas to the parties so they can make more informed decisions on whether to settle a case. "'Evaluation' is not one behavior, but a continuum of behaviors."[5] Evaluative mediation is not limited to one area of the law. Although evaluative mediation is often practiced in monetary disputes, many family law and other types of cases are resolved with evaluative mediators as well.

Most mediators have a large toolbox of techniques to use during a case, and some of the tools of evaluative mediation are also used in classic, facilitative mediation.[6] This overlap of mediation techniques is one of the reasons that the various mediation orientations are difficult to define with precision. For example, the technique of asking challenging questions of parties and counsel, often called reality testing, is a

---

3. James H. Stark, *The Ethics of Mediation Evaluation: Some Troublesome Questions and Tentative Proposals, from an Evaluative Lawyer Mediator*, 38 S. Tex. L. Rev. 769, 770–71 (1997) (noting in 1997 that evaluative mediation "seems quite likely here to stay"); *see also* Dwight Golann & Marjorie Corman Aaron, *Beyond Abstinence: Safe and Impartial Evaluation Can Be Effective in Mediation*, 25 Disp. Resol. Mag. 22, 22 (2019) (noting in 2019 that they "believe that most mediators evaluate constantly, from the moment of their first contact with a dispute").

4. Riskin, *supra* note 1, at 26 ("A principal strategy of the evaluative-narrow approach is to help the parties understand the strengths and weaknesses of their positions and the likely outcome of litigation or whatever other process they will use if they do not reach a resolution in mediation.").

5. Stark, *supra* note 3, at 774.

6. Leonard L. Riskin, *Decisionmaking in Mediation: The New Old Grid and the New New Grid System*, 79 Notre Dame L. Rev. 1, 14 (2003) ("It is quite clear, however, that many—probably most—mediators engage in behaviors that fit into both categories.").

common technique used by nearly every mediator. Most, but certainly not all, mediators find caucusing to be an acceptable tool used in a wide variety of circumstances. In addition, facilitative mediators may offer a limited amount of legal information to parties to balance power or foster informed decision making. For the purposes of this chapter, evaluative mediation describes mediators who commonly assess legal strengths and weaknesses and provide information regarding case value. However, the discussion is also relevant for facilitative mediators who use evaluative techniques.

Evaluative mediators are best known for providing "information sufficient [for the parties to] make reasonably informed decisions about their rights and responsibilities."[7] Evaluative mediators who are lawyers usually help parties understand strengths and weaknesses of their legal case and settlement options through either evaluative questions or statements.[8] Evaluative mediators from different professions, such as the mental-health or financial fields, may make different types of evaluations consistent with their training. Consider the following illustration of a legal evaluation.

A plaintiff customer sues a retail establishment after a slip-and-fall accident, alleging not only negligence but also gross negligence with a request for punitive damages. Assume that an objective assessment of the situation would uncover a high likelihood of recovery on negligence but only a slight chance of recovery on gross negligence and punitive damages. In a caucus in a facilitative mediation, a mediator might pose the following question to plaintiff's counsel: "How likely do you think it is that you can recover punitive damages in this jurisdiction in this case?" The purpose of the question is to help plaintiff's counsel consider, and admit, the weakness of the claim. A mediator who uses evaluative statements would be more direct: "Counsel, in this jurisdiction, juries rarely award clients punitive damages in slip-and-fall cases." The purpose of this statement remains the same—to encourage counsel and parties to determine an accurate, objective view of the case.

Mediators can evaluate a wide variety of legal issues in a case, including overall case value, strength of a claim or defense, credibility of parties or witnesses in attendance at the mediation, jury tendencies, chance of success on a motion, or even the likelihood of success on appeal. Some evaluative mediators focus almost exclusively on the settlement case or

7. Stark, *supra* note 3, at 772.

8. *Id.* at 774 (describing evaluative techniques) (citing Margaret L. Shaw, *Evaluation Continuum*, prepared for meeting of CPR Ethics Comm'n, May 6–7, 1996).

the question of what a party would likely need to accept a certain offer. In the previous scenario, an evaluative mediator might ask a question such as "Do you think that the defendant corporation would ever agree to a settlement that involves a payment of punitive damages?" or make a statement such as "I think $300,000 would settle this case." While the former statement evaluates objective case worth, the latter question considers settlement options between these parties.

Evaluative mediators tend to work largely, if not exclusively, with the parties in a caucus or shuttle-style mediation. By meeting with the parties separately, the mediator has greater flexibility to ask hard questions and sow doubt, without bolstering the other side's case. The mediator can engage in various levels of arm twisting to exact a new offer during each caucus.

Some evaluative mediators use the technique known as the mediator proposal as an impasse-breaking device at the end of a mediation. If the parties have reached an insurmountable impasse, the mediator may suggest one last offer to both sides to see if they will agree. The mediator determines the offer, based on the negotiations to that point. The mediator provides the offer confidentially to each side separately, and each side indicates to the mediator whether the offer is acceptable. Mediators generally only provide a proposal upon the parties' request or after receiving consent from all parties to try this technique. The proposal is conveyed either in writing, such as a letter or e-mail, or in person. Both parties receive the exact same proposal.

If the offer is acceptable to all parties, the mediation is concluded with an agreement. If any party rejects the proposal, the mediation concludes with no agreement, and the mediator does not disclose the parties' responses to one another. In other words, if a party rejects the proposal, that party will never learn if the other party or parties accepted.

Returning to the slip-and-fall mediation, assume that the parties have mediated for nine hours, and everyone is growing weary. The mediation proceeded slowly but steadily through caucus-style mediation for the first six or seven hours. The last few hours proved more difficult, with smaller concessions and increased frustration. The last demand from the plaintiff was $325,000, and the last offer from the defendant was $280,000. Despite making significant progress throughout the day, neither party is willing to budge at the late hour. At this point, the parties ask the mediator for a proposal, and the mediator agrees. The mediator goes home to consider what happened during the session. The next day, the mediator composes a letter to both parties and puts forth a mediator proposal to see if the case could settle for $302,500 plus a guarantee of confidentiality.

The mediator e-mails the proposal to both parties and their attorneys and requests that the parties reply within 48 hours. Two days later, the mediator will alert the parties either that the case is settled or that the proposal did not result in a mutual agreement.

Evaluative mediation and the use of evaluative techniques provide many benefits for parties. Attorneys and clients have a difficult time making accurate assessments of case values because of common psychological barriers, such as being overconfident in one's own case or only seeking information that bolsters one's side. An evaluative mediator is neutral and should not suffer from those biases and should be in a better position to provide an objective assessment. Evaluative mediation can also help combat reactive devaluation, or the psychological phenomenon that people discount information heard from someone who is not trusted—such as an opposing party in litigation. Parties and their attorneys may be able to listen to the assessment of a mediator and not automatically devalue the message based on the messenger.

An evaluative mediator may also be able to help lawyers manage any of their clients' unreasonable expectations.[9] Lawyers with overly optimistic clients may have a difficult time expressing doubt in their own clients' cases out of fear of appearing disloyal or even being fired. The evaluative mediator has the potential to deliver bad news in a way that lawyers cannot.

Further, evaluation can be used as an impasse-breaking device.[10] Many evaluative mediators save the most evaluative techniques until the end of a mediation, particularly to overcome impasse. Parties who are communicating well and working together in mediation rarely need evaluation—those parties can work cooperatively without additional help.

On the other hand, evaluative mediation is not without its downsides. Most of the concerns about evaluative mediation are rooted in ethics, such as questions about neutrality, party autonomy, and confidentiality, and those concerns are detailed in the next section. Another downside of evaluative mediation is its almost singular focus on monetary settlements in litigated cases. This focus has the potential to neglect the parties' feelings, relationships, and nonmonetary interests, which, in turn, limits the

---

9. Golann & Aaron, *supra* note 3, at 24 ("Lawyers often admit that their efforts to convey a realistic evaluation to a client have fallen on deaf (or at least resistant) ears.").

10. *Id.* at 23 ("Simply put, a mediator's explicit evaluation can help parties overcome impasses caused by divergent views of the likely outcome in adjudication of a single legal issue or the entire case.").

creativity and flexibility of the parties.[11] In addition, parties may not disclose as much information with an evaluative mediator out of the fear that the information may be used to that side's detriment when the mediator makes an evaluation.[12] Further, if the goal of mediation for the parties is to receive a good evaluation, the mediation is positioned to be adversarial—not collaborative.[13] Because evaluative mediation requires subject-matter expertise, the pool of available mediators may be more limited if the parties seek an evaluation.[14]

Evaluative mediation is a popular form of dispute resolution, particularly in litigated cases involving parties represented by counsel who seek a nonbinding assessment of their case.[15] The remainder of this chapter considers the ethical implications of evaluative mediation and the use of evaluative techniques.

5.3. Ethical Rules Implicated

All mediators work under the same ethical standards. Codes of ethics do not distinguish between the different styles but apply to mediation generally. For the most part, mediators are permitted to practice evaluative mediation, although a minority of jurisdictions contemplate a facilitative style within their courts or affiliated programs.[16]

---

11. Omer Shapira, *A Critical Assessment of the Model Standards of Conduct for Mediators (2005): Call for Reform*, 100 MARQ. L. REV. 81, 112–13 (2016) (discussing how evaluation has the potential to limit party choice, rather than expand it); Riskin, *supra* note 1, at 44 (noting that evaluative mediation may restrict a "party's flexibility").

12. Golann & Aaron, *supra* note 3, at 24 (noting the possibility that the parties "may withhold confidential information and mistrust the mediator's actions" when the mediator evaluates the case); *see also* Riskin, *supra* note 1, at 45 ("In addition, if the parties or lawyers know that the mediator will evaluate, they are less likely to be candid either with their counterparts or with the mediator.").

13. Lela P. Love, *The Top Ten Reasons Why Mediators Should Not Evaluate*, 24 FLA. ST. U. L. REV. 937, 940 (1997) (arguing that in evaluative mediation, the parties "are in a competitive mind-set seeking to capture the evaluator's favor and win the case").

14. Riskin, *supra* note 1, at 46 ("The need for subject-matter expertise typically increases in direct proportion to the parties' need for the mediator's evaluations."); Love, *supra* note 13, at 941–42 (arguing that evaluation requires legal expertise, and the profession would lose significant talent and valuable perspective if nonlawyers are reduced to a limited role).

15. *See* Ellen A. Waldman, *The Evaluative-Facilitative Debate in Mediation: Applying the Lens of Therapeutic Jurisprudence*, 82 MARQ. L. REV. 155, 156 (1998) (describing the practice of evaluative mediation as "growing," over two decades ago).

16. *See, e.g.*, Michigan Court Rules, which note that both parties must consent to evaluative mediation in domestic-relations mediation. MICH. CT. R. 3.216(A)(2)

This section primarily relies on national model ethics codes, such as the 2005 Model Standards of Conduct for Mediators, jointly approved by the American Arbitration Association, the American Bar Association, and the Association for Conflict Resolution;[17] and the Model Standards of Practice for Family and Divorce Mediation, approved by the American Bar Association, Family Section, and the Association of Family Courts and Community Professionals, among others.[18] This section also references ethics opinions and state law, as appropriate.

5.3.1. Self-Determination and Informed Consent

Informed consent is a "core value" of mediation,[19] based on "disclosure and consent."[20] Consent can only be "informed" if the parties understand what is happening.[21] Informed consent has a long and important history as a key element of alternative dispute resolution, particularly mediation.[22] Model Standard I provides:

> A mediator shall conduct a mediation based on the principle of party self-determination. Self-determination is the act of coming

(2019) (requiring consent for evaluative mediation); ILL. COOK CNTY. CIR. CT. R. 13.4(e)(v)(g) (2017) (same).

17. MODEL STANDARDS OF CONDUCT FOR MEDIATORS (2005) [hereinafter MODEL STANDARDS].

18. MODEL STANDARDS OF PRACTICE FOR FAMILY & DIVORCE MEDIATION (2001) [hereinafter FAMILY STANDARDS].

19. Jaqueline Nolan-Haley, *Does ADR's "Access to Justice" Come at the Expense of Meaningful Consent*, 33 OHIO ST. J. ON DISP. RESOL. 373, 386 (2018).

20. Jaqueline M. Nolan-Haley, *Informed Consent in Mediation: A Guiding Principle for Truly Educated Decisionmaking*, 74 NOTRE DAME L. REV. 775, 778 (1999) ("At a minimum, the principle of informed consent requires that parties be educated about the mediation process before they consent to participate in it, that their continued participation in mediation be voluntary, and that they understand and consent to the outcomes reached in mediation.").

21. The Model Rules of Professional Conduct for lawyers define "informed consent" as "the agreement by a person to a proposed course of conduct after the lawyer has communicated adequate information and explanation about the material risks of and reasonably available alternatives to the proposed course of conduct." MODEL RULES OF PROF'L CONDUCT R. 1.0 (Am. Bar Ass'n 1980).

22. Carrie Menkel-Meadow, *The Lawyer as Consensus Builder: Ethics for a New Practice*, 70 TENN. L. REV. 63, 88 (2002), Donna Shestowsky, *When Ignorance Is Not Bliss: An Empirical Study of Litigant's Awareness of Court-Sponsored Alternative Dispute Resolution Programs*, 22 HARV. NEGOT. L. REV. 189, 194 (2017) ("The concept of party self-determination plays an important role in the history of ADR."); *see also* Nolan-Haley, *supra* note 19, at 391 ("Informed consent is a foundational principle that promotes human dignity, advances autonomy, and enhances party self-determination.").

> to a voluntary, uncoerced decision in which each party makes free and informed choices *as to process* and outcome. Parties may exercise self-determination at any stage of a mediation, including mediator selection, process design, participation in or withdrawal from the process, and outcomes.[23]

Importantly, informed consent applies to the process as well as the outcome. For this reason, the parties must make a choice after disclosure of the relevant information regarding how the process should proceed, and the parties have the ability to withdraw their consent at any time.

Mediators who evaluate should be open and honest with the parties about what these techniques are and how the parties should use them to help settle their case.[24] Parties should know that the mediator's evaluations are simply that—a mediator's evaluation based on the information provided and not necessarily the view of any judge or jury who would receive different information prior to making a decision.[25] The parties should also know that the evaluations they receive may not be favorable to them[26] and that the parties consent to listening to these aspects of their case that may be difficult to hear.[27]

A best practice is for mediators to discuss their mediation styles with the parties and any attorneys during intake and again during the mediator's opening remarks. Prior to making any evaluations, the mediator may want to preface them with a reminder about the purpose of evaluation and that the mediator will be evaluating all parties. By following

23. Model Standards, *supra* note 17, at I.A; *see also* Family Standards, *supra* note 18, at I ("A professional family mediator shall recognize that mediation is based upon the principle of self-determination by the participants.").

24. Omer Shapira, A Theory of Mediators' Ethics 153 (2016) (stating that "parties should know the style of mediation that the mediator practices, information that is closely connected to the mediator's duty to provide the parties with information about the process of mediation that will take place").

25. Golann & Aaron, *supra* note 3, at 24 ("[T]he mediator's prediction of the likelihood of success at trial may not reflect the way the judge or jury will look at it . . . . No mediator should think his evaluation is the only reasonable one."); *see also* Stark, *supra* note 3, at 797 ("Mediators who evaluate should also be required to tell disputants how their advice may differ from an advocate's advice.").

26. Stark, *supra* note 3, at 798 ("Litigants entering the mediation room ought to be informed that if the mediator evaluates, the information provided might help them or hurt them.")

27. Shapira, *supra* note 24, at 155 ("An informed decision must be based on the hazards of mediation as well if it is to be a true exercise of self-determination.").

these practices, the parties can ultimately make an informed choice about the substance of their dispute.[28]

5.3.2. Self-Determination and the Decision to Settle

Unlike litigation and arbitration, mediation is a consensual process, and the decision-making power belongs in the hands of the parties, not the mediator. Mediation ethics are grounded in party self-determination and party autonomy. These concepts are rooted in the "act of coming to a voluntary, uncoerced decision in which each party makes free and informed choices as to the process and the outcome."[29] Self-determination gives the parties the ability to choose whether they settle their dispute and on what terms.

Evaluative mediators can have a reputation for not only making evaluations but also pushing parties into making concessions.[30] Some mediators engage in various levels of arm twisting to exact new offers or terms from the parties as the mediation progresses. Certainly, nearly all mediators use some level of pressure and persuasion to help their clients move toward resolution. Evaluative techniques, however, if utilized too strongly, may cross the line and become coercive. In addition, a mediation agreement may be subject to rescission if the mediator engages in unethical coercion.[31]

---

28. SUSAN NAUSS EXON, ADVANCED GUIDE FOR MEDIATORS 190 (2014) (considering the divide between legal information and legal advice); Stark, *supra* note 3, at 776 ("Legal evaluation affirmatively facilitates the goal of party self-determination. Indeed, meaningful self-determination is not possible without adequate legal information.").

29. MODEL STANDARDS, *supra* note 17, at I; *see also* FAMILY STANDARDS, *supra* note 18, at I.A ("Self-determination is the fundamental principle of family mediation. The mediation process relies upon the ability of participants to make their own voluntary and informed decisions.").

30. Riskin, *supra* note 1, at 31 (noting that the evaluative mediator may engage in techniques such as urging or pushing parties to arrive at a settlement). In his 2003 *New Grid* article, Professor Riskin admitted that while the behaviors of urging and pushing are evaluative, many of the other techniques defined as "evaluative" were better described as "directive." Riskin, *supra* note 6, at 20.

31. Cases requesting rescission of a mediated agreement due to undue pressure or coercion are rare, and courts are reluctant to grant such relief absent unusual circumstances. *See* Boyd v. Boyd, 67 S.W.3d 398, 403 (Tex. Ct. App. 2002) (noting that a court could not enforce a mediation agreement "procured by fraud, duress, coercion, or other dishonest means"); Vitakis-Valchine v. Valchine, 793 So. 2d 1094, 1099 (Fla. Ct. App. 2001) ("We believe that it would be unconscionable for a court to enforce a settlement agreement reached through coercion or any other improper tactics utilized by a court-appointed mediator.").

Any number of techniques may push the boundaries into unethical practice. As noted by the Florida Rules for Certified and Court-Appointed Mediators: "While mediation techniques and practice styles may vary from mediator to mediator and mediation to mediation, a line is crossed and ethical standards are violated when any conduct of the mediator serves to compromise the parties' basic right to agree or not to agree."[32]

"Line crossing" may take various forms. Mediators may cross the line when they engage in techniques such as using a raised voice; guilt techniques; prohibiting the parties from leaving the room without an agreement; withholding food, drink, or restroom services; convincing participants to stay well into the night; urging participants to continue mediating even after they have asked to leave; and similar techniques.[33] These types of tactics are coercive because they invoke feelings of helplessness, distress, and an inability to choose.[34] Further, mediators bring a certain power into the mediation, and using that power to reduce the parties' choices is not only coercive but also an illegitimate use of mediator power.[35]

Evaluative mediation also has the natural tendency to limit the amount and types of resolutions that are available for the parties. Professor Ellen Waldman expressed a concern that if "a mediator brings legal or social norms into the discussion, it is argued, these norms will assume a predominant role in the discussion. The conversational focus will shift from the parties' own values and definitions of fairness to consideration of the norms" brought into the conversation by the mediator.[36] The parties may have been willing to engage in broader settlement discussions involving items such as apologies and nonmonetary settlements, but an evaluative mediator may be more interested in steering the conversations toward a monetary settlement. An evaluative mediator can certainly mediate any of these types of solutions, and the best practice for a mediator would be to remain open to all possible solutions and to follow the parties' lead regarding settlement options.

The better practice, therefore, is that every mediator, no matter the type of mediation practiced, should ensure that the decisions made by the parties are made voluntarily and uncoerced. Mediation participants

---

32. Fla. Stat. Ann. § 10.310 Comm. Notes (West 2000) [hereinafter Fla. Rules].

33. Exon, *supra* note 28, at 240–46 (discussing pressuring tactics such as withholding comfort items, such as lunch or snacks, from the participants in a mediation).

34. Shapira, *supra* note 24, at 147 (discussing coercion in mediation).

35. Golann & Aaron, *supra* note 3, at 23 (discussing mediator power).

36. Waldman, *supra* note 15, at 164–65.

should be given ample time to process decisions and consult resources, such as attorneys, to help those parties make decisions.[37] Mediators should also ensure that basic comforts, including restroom access and meals, are not neglected. If parties are not willing to come to an agreement, the mediator should respect the autonomy of the parties to choose to reach impasse, rather than unduly pressuring a party to make an offer with which he is not comfortable.

5.3.3. Mediator Competence

Mediator competency is another core ethical consideration.[38] Although all mediators must have the basic competency relating to the process of mediation, evaluative mediators must have additional competencies relating to the subject matter of the dispute.[39] Family law mediators may or may not be competent to provide evaluations in cases involving railroad accidents. Similarly, an intellectual property mediator may not be competent to resolve custody disputes. In some instances, particularly in family mediation, the law of a given jurisdiction may impose additional competencies required for mediators.[40]

Mediators must also be competent in making evaluations, which is an element of competency often overlooked when discussing evaluative mediation. Mediators must understand the risks associated with evaluation as well as learn how to evaluate without losing the perception of impartiality[41] within the "norms of mediation."[42] To date, little training

---

37. The Uniform Mediation Act, for instance, gives all parties the right to have a lawyer or other support person attend the mediation with them. UNIF. MEDIATION ACT § 10 ("An attorney or other individual designated by a party may accompany the party to and participate in a mediation. A waiver of participation given before the mediation may be rescinded."); *see also* FAMILY STANDARDS, *supra* note 18, at I.C ("A family mediator should inform the participants that they may seek information and advice from a variety of sources during the mediation process.").

38. MODEL STANDARDS, *supra* note 17, at IV ("A mediator shall mediate only when the mediator has the necessary competence to satisfy the reasonable expectations of the parties.").

39. SHAPIRA, *supra* note 24, at 169 ("When the mediator engages in evaluation of the parties' cases he or she must have a knowledge of, or expertise in, the subject-matter of the content of the mediation as well."); *see also* Riskin, *supra* note 1, at 46 ("'Subject-matter expertise' means substantial understanding of the legal or administrative procedures, customary practices, or technology associated with the dispute.").

40. *See, e.g.*, NEB. REV. STAT. ANN. § 43-2938 (West 2019) (describing requirements for approved mediators under the Parenting Act).

41. Golann & Aaron, *supra* note 3, at 24.

42. SHAPIRA, *supra* note 24, at 175.

has focused on evaluation, so additional training on evaluation and the ethics of evaluating would be a tremendous addition to the profession.

5.3.4. Impartiality

The Model Standards place a high priority on impartiality. Mediators are expected to act with "freedom from favoritism, bias or prejudice."[43] In addition to actual impartiality, the mediator must also "conduct a mediation in an impartial manner and avoid conduct that gives the *appearance of partiality*."[44] Similarly, the Florida Standards require a "balanced process,"[45] treating the parties in an evenhanded manner.[46] Impartiality helps ensure trust in the process. If the parties trust the mediator, they participate in a meaningful way and disclose information helpful to settling the dispute. The evaluative mediator relies on such full participation to learn the necessary information to make a realistic evaluation of the case.

Mediators who determine that they are actually biased must withdraw. The Model Standards state: "If at any time a mediator is unable to conduct a mediation in an impartial manner, the mediator shall withdraw."[47] Under the Family Standards, impartiality is held in such a high regard that the parties cannot consent to a mediator who cannot act impartially.[48] Mediators who begin to notice a bias as they mediate must examine whether they can set aside the bias and continue their work. Evaluative

43. MODEL STANDARDS, *supra* note 17, at II.A; *see also* FAMILY STANDARDS, *supra* note 18, at IV ("A family mediator shall conduct the mediation process in an impartial manner.").

44. MODEL STANDARDS, *supra* note 17, at II.B (emphasis added); *see also* FAMILY STANDARDS, *supra* note 18, at IV.A ("Impartiality means freedom from favoritism or bias in word, action, or appearance, and includes a commitment to assist all parties as opposed to one individual.").

45. FLA. RULES, *supra* note 32, § 10.410 ("A mediator shall conduct mediation sessions in an even-handed, balanced manner. A mediator shall promote mutual respect among the mediation participants throughout the mediation process and encourage the participants to conduct themselves in a collaborative, non-coercive, and non-adversarial manner.")

46. *Id.*

47. MODEL STANDARDS, *supra* note 17, at II.C; *see also* FAMILY STANDARDS, *supra* note 18, at IV ("If a bias or conflict of interest clearly impairs a mediator's impartiality, the mediator shall withdraw regardless of the express agreement of the participants.").

48. FAMILY STANDARDS, *supra* note 18, at IV. The Model Standards should be understood in the same way. *See* Shapira, *supra* note 11, at 96 ("the *Reporter's Notes* note that the Standard of Impartiality in section II.C will not allow the mediator to conduct a mediation if he is unable to conduct it in an impartial manner, *even if the parties agree that he may proceed*").

mediators must always work to remain impartial, even in cases when the evaluation will likely be lopsided. Although evaluative mediators can certainly provide an ethically unfavorable evaluation to parties, they must not let those evaluations sway their ability to be impartial as they do so.

Additionally, evaluative mediators run the risk of appearing biased when they make their evaluations, in breach of their obligation to "avoid conduct that gives the appearance of partiality."[49] In the slip-and-fall example, the mediator may come to the conclusion that the case is worth roughly $300,000 and that punitive damages are not supported by law. Assume, for the moment, that the mediator was actually impartial when making these determinations. Although the mediator may remain impartial, the plaintiff may not believe that the mediator is impartial when hearing that the punitive damages would be difficult to obtain or that the case is not worth an amount closer to $500,000. The more forceful the mediator is when giving an evaluation or extracting a concession, the greater the danger that a party or attorney may view the mediator as biased.[50]

A best practice for evaluative mediators is to tell the parties at the beginning of the mediation, and throughout the mediation as necessary, that the mediator will be engaging the parties in difficult conversations, will be asking both sides to make difficult concessions, and will be pushing both sides equally to come to settlement. The mediator should also make clear that the ultimate decision belongs to the parties and that the mediator is not committed to and has no stake in any particular outcome.[51]

The parties should intuitively understand that the law impacts each party in an unequal way and that the mediator's assessment of those strengths and weaknesses is not an endorsement of any given party. The mediator should enhance *both* parties' knowledge of the strengths and weaknesses of their claims.[52] In addition, the evaluation should be a

---

49. MODEL STANDARDS, *supra* note 17, at II.B (emphasis added); *see also* FAMILY STANDARDS, *supra* note 18, at IV.A ("Impartiality means freedom from favoritism or bias in word, action, or appearance, and includes a commitment to assist all parties as opposed to one individual.").

50. Golann & Aaron, *supra* note 3, at 24 ("The largest, most obvious risk is that a disputant receiving an unfavorable evaluation will then perceive the mediator as aligned with the other side, no longer neutral, and may withhold confidential information and mistrust the mediator's actions from that point on.").

51. Stark, *supra* note 3, at 776 ("Providing information and advice is not the same thing as being committed to a particular outcome, and a competent evaluator can readily make this distinction clear.").

52. *Id.* at 777 ("In most legal disputes, there will be strengths and weaknesses to each party's position. The evaluative mediator can enhance both parties' knowledge

"prediction about *someone else's* viewpoint" such as a judge or jury rather than about the mediator's personal opinion.[53] Professors Dwight Golann and Marjorie Aaron suggest that "good evaluation does *not* include a mediator voicing his personal opinion about what is 'right' or 'fair,' or a 'just' outcome, in a dispute . . . [because] once a mediator suggests to a disputant that a claim or defense is less than 'just,' the listener may see [her] as biased."[54] In addition, mediators who help their parties evaluate their own cases through questions proceed on safer ethical ground than those who make evaluative statements.[55]

If attorneys are present in the mediation, those attorneys can also help upset parties understand that the mediator is likely acting in a similar manner with all parties. If the mediator is acting impartially and the participants all consider the mediator to be acting equally, the mediator will be practicing within this ethical rule.

5.3.5. Quality of the Process and Integrity of the Role of the Mediator

Ethical codes generally require the mediator to provide a quality process and remain in the role of a mediator. In the Model Standards, the concept of role integrity is found in the standard on "quality of the process." The standard provides:

> The role of a mediator differs substantially from other professional roles. Mixing the role of a mediator and the role of another profession is problematic and thus, a mediator should distinguish between the roles. A mediator may provide information that the mediator is qualified by training or experience to provide, only if the mediator can do so consistent with these Standards.[56]

---

of the strengths and weaknesses of their claims, without necessarily appearing to be a proponent for one side over the other.").

53. Golann & Aaron, *supra* note 3, at 24; *see also* Exon, *supra* note 28, at 164 (noting that using a third-party viewpoint for an evaluation can help with mediator impartiality).

54. Golann & Aaron, *supra* note 3, at 23.

55. *See, e.g.*, Mediator Ethics Advisory Comm., Op. MEAC 2010-006 (Oct. 2010) (interpreting Florida rules on what it means to "direct" a party).

56. Model Standards, *supra* note 17, at VI.A.5; *see also* Cal. St. Civ. Rules R. 3.857(d) [hereinafter Cal. Rules] (stating that a mediator must work in the role of a mediator but that a mediator "may provide information or opinions that he or she is qualified by training or experience to provide"); Standards of Conduct for N.Y. St. Cmty. Disp. Resol. Ctr. Mediators, Standard VI cmt. 5 ("Mixing the role of a mediator and the role of a professional advising a client is problematic, and mediators should strive to distinguish between the roles. A mediator should therefore refrain from providing professional advice.").

In addition, a mediator is not permitted to switch to another type of dispute-resolution role, such as an arbiter, without informed "consent of the parties."[57] The standards also seek to ensure that a mediator does not slip into a different role, such as an attorney, therapist, accountant, clergy, et cetera, thus keeping the process "pure."[58] If a party needs additional services, the mediator should make referrals rather than provide the services directly.[59]

Although mediation is not the practice of law,[60] lawyer mediators must take care to not accidentally slip into the practice of law. An evaluative mediator is more likely than a facilitative mediator to cross the boundary from a neutral to an advocate because of the active role of the neutral and the directive nature of the process. Mediation ethics, however, require the mediator to stay in the role of a neutral and not "give legal or other professional advice during the mediation."[61] Although this section considers the provision of legal advice, similar concerns regarding

57. MODEL STANDARDS, *supra* note 17, at VI.A.8; *see also* CAL. RULES, *supra* note 56, R. 3.857(g) (discouraging a mixing of roles but allowing parties to make informed decisions regarding the process if they would like the mediator to undertake a different role in the process).

58. Love, *supra* note 13, at 940.

59. *See* Deborah Thompson Eisenberg & Noam Ebner, *Disrupting the Eviction Crisis with Conflict Resolution Strategies*, 41 MITCHELL HAMLINE L. J. POL'Y & PRAC. 125, 139 (2020) (describing the phenomenon of mediators switching from mediator to advocate as "role slippage").

60. *Resolution on Mediation and the Unauthorized Practice of Law*, AM BAR ASS'N SECTION OF DISP. RESOL. (Feb. 2, 2002) [hereinafter *ABA Section of DR Resol.*] ("Mediation is not the practice of law. Mediation is a process in which an impartial individual assists the parties in reaching a voluntary settlement. Such assistance does not constitute the practice of law. The parties to the mediation are not represented by the mediator.").

61. STANDARDS OF PROF'L CONDUCT FOR MEDIATORS, Standard 6 (Office of Admin. Counsel, N.C. Sup. Ct. 2020), *available at* https://www.nccourts.gov/assets/inline-files/Standards-of-Professional-Conduct-for-Mediators-Codified-1-March-2020.pdf?MTGctiiCw3Btgkw6qx3EEFnJoUJBWGZQ [hereinafter N.C. STANDARDS]; *see also* NEB. STANDARDS OF PRACTICE & ETHICS FOR FAMILY MEDIATORS, Standard VI.B (2008) ("The mediator shall not provide therapy or give legal advice."), *available at* https://supremecourt.nebraska.gov/sites/default/files/Programs/mediation/Reports/standards_and_ethics_revised_10-31-08.pdf; N.Y. STANDARDS, Standard VI cmt. 5; CODE OF ETHICAL STANDARD FOR MEDIATORS (Multi-Door Disp. Resol. Div. D.C. Super. Ct.) ("A mediator shall limit him/herself solely to the role of mediator, and shall refrain from giving legal, financial, or therapeutic advice and otherwise engaging in counseling or advocacy during mediation.").

the proper role of mediators also apply to mediators of other professional backgrounds.[62]

The boundary between acting as a neutral and creating an attorney-client relationship is a fine one. A mediator is ethically permitted to "discuss legal issues" with participants[63] and even provide legal information.[64] A Florida ethics opinion notes that a "mediator may assist in that endeavor by providing relevant information or helping the parties obtain such information from other sources."[65] On the other hand, the definition of practicing law is broad. The Restatement (Third) of the Law Governing Lawyers notes that an attorney-client relationship exists when a person, i.e., the client, "manifests to the lawyer the person's intent that the lawyer provide legal services for the person" and the lawyer manifests consent *or* "fails to manifest lack of consent to do so, and the lawyer knows or reasonably should know that the person relies on the lawyer to provide the services."[66] Whether an attorney-client relationship exists is determined from the vantage point of the client—not the attorney.[67] Some jurisdictions include the application of law to fact or expressing legal

---

62. *See, e.g.*, MASS. COUNCIL ON FAMILY MEDIATION, STANDARDS OF PRACTICE 6(B)(1)(a) (1997), https://mcfm.org/sites/default/files/sites/default/files/mcfm_standards_of_practice.pdf ("Without exception during the mediation process, no mediator shall represent or provide therapy, financial or other professional services to either or both parties or serve as a Guardian Ad Litem during the mediation process.").

63. *ABA Section of DR Resol.*, *supra* note 60 ("In disputes where the parties' legal rights or obligations are at issue, the mediator's discussions with the parties may involve legal issues. Such discussions do not create an attorney-client relationship, and do not constitute legal advice, whether or not the mediator is an attorney.").

64. *See, e.g.*, FLA. RULES, *supra* note 32, § 10.370(a) ("Consistent with standards of impartiality and preserving party self-determination, a mediator may provide information that the mediator is qualified by training or experience to provide.").

65. Mediator Ethics Advisory Comm., Op. MEAC 2018-002, at 1 (Aug. 2018); *see also* Eisenberg & Ebner, *supra* note 59, at 139 ("It is widely accepted, however, that mediators are not the parties' lawyers, and that they are not to dispense legal advice or confuse the roles of advocate and neutral. Nevertheless, in seeking to address power imbalances, it is easy to envision mediators providing parties . . . information about their rights.").

66. RESTATEMENT (THIRD) OF THE LAW GOVERNING LAWYERS § 14 (2000).

67. *See, e.g.*, Rubin & Norris, LLC v. Panzarella, 51 N.E.3d 879, 891 (Ill. App. Ct. 2016) (stating that the "analysis focuses on the client's viewpoint rather than that of the attorney"); Morris v. Margulis, 718 N.E.2d 709, 718 (Ill. App. Ct. 1999), *rev'd on other grounds*, 754 N.E.2d 314 (Ill. 2001) (noting that the determination of an attorney/client relationship considers the "client's viewpoint rather than that of the attorney").

opinions within the definition of practicing law.[68] In those jurisdictions, a mediator who gives legal advice specifically applicable to the parties at the table may cross the line and unwittingly engage in the practice of law.

Evaluative techniques, such as predicting court outcomes, estimating settlement values, and providing mediator proposals, have the potential to be misinterpreted as legal advice, as opposed to simply legal information. Evaluative mediation is particularly troublesome when the mediator utilizes evaluative techniques with an unrepresented party. Many codes of mediation ethics *and* legal ethics rules require that a lawyer mediator disclose the mediator's educational background with an assurance that the mediator will not engage in the practice of law.[69]

When a client is represented, however, the party can more easily differentiate between the client's lawyer and the mediator. The representative can clarify the roles if the client becomes confused. The lawyer can also explain the role of evaluation in mediation and can advise the client on whether the mediator's evaluations are warranted, accurate, overstated, or even reasonable. The lawyer, who may have more experience in mediation than the client, can also explain the mediator's goals and provide context for the techniques used in a particular mediation.

In 2002, the American Bar Association Section of Dispute Resolution, in its resolution on mediation and the unauthorized practice of law, gave guidance on the issue of evaluative mediation and the creation of attorney-client relationships.[70] The resolution notes that many parties and their counsel hire mediators "precisely to obtain feedback about their case."[71] The Section determined that "this conduct is not the practice of law because the parties have no reasonable basis for believing that the mediator will provide advice solely on behalf of any individual party."[72] The Section likened the evaluative mediator to a judge in a settlement

68. *See, e.g.*, Ariz. S. Ct. R. 31(a)(2) (2003) (including "expressing legal opinions" in the definition of practicing law); Ga. Code Ann. § 15-19-50 (West 1976) (including "the giving of legal advice" within the definition of practicing law); Del. St. Bar Ass'n v. Alexander, 386 A.2d 652, 661 (Del. 1978) (including in the definition of the practice of law furnishing "to another advice or service under circumstances which imply the possession and use of legal knowledge and skill."); *In re* Welch, 185 A.2d 458, 459 (Vt. 1962) (same).

69. Model Rules of Prof'l Conduct R. 2.4(b) (1980); Cal. Rules, *supra* note 56, R. 3.857(d) (requiring disclosure and a statement that the mediator cannot represent either party); Fla. Rules, *supra* note 32, § 10.420(a) (requiring the mediator to describe the process and role); Ind. St. Alt. Disp. Resol. Rules R. 2.7(A)(3) (requiring a disclosure that the mediator is not providing legal advice).

70. *ABA Section of DR Resol.*, *supra* note 60, cmt. 5.

71. *Id.*

72. *Id.*

conference who provides information and insight to all participants while still maintaining neutrality.[73] Although this guidance represents the dominant view that evaluative mediation does not create an attorney-client relationship, the mediator should still be mindful of the potential for confusion on the part of the clients and other participants.

Whether mediators should use evaluative techniques with unrepresented parties is a debated topic. On the one hand, an unrepresented party is more likely to misunderstand the mediator's role, even with disclaimers made by the mediator. On the other hand, unrepresented parties may need legal information to make legally informed choices.[74] Stated another way, this question pits two important ethical considerations against each other—ensuring that parties do not misunderstand the role of the mediator and access to justice.

In addition, the most evaluative techniques should only be used for impasse breaking or otherwise as a last-ditch effort.[75] If providing an evaluation or mediator opinion, the mediator should also clearly state that it is not intended to be legal advice and that clients should refer to their attorneys for such advice.[76] The mediator may also want to be candid that the mediator is using similar techniques with both sides, which may help the clients realize that the mediator is not on either "side" but simply working in an evenhanded way with both parties as a neutral. Further, the evaluative mediator will be on far steadier ground ethically by limiting opinions to a discussion of strengths and weaknesses of legal issues and settlement options, as opposed to making predictions of outcomes.

5.3.6. Confidentiality

Confidentiality is one of the most important benefits of mediation. The guarantee of confidentiality builds trust in the process, and it provides

73. *Id.*

74. *See* Stark, *supra* note 3, at 777–78 (noting concern about unrepresented parties making decisions without legal information).

75. The North Carolina Standards of Professional Conduct for Mediators state that evaluation ordinarily should be a "last resort." Standard 5(c) states: "This subsection does not prohibit a mediator from expressing his or her opinion as a last resort to a party or attorney who requests it, as long as the mediator has already helped that party utilize the party's own resources to evaluate the dispute and options for settlement." N.C. STANDARDS OF PROF'L CONDUCT FOR MEDIATORS R. 5(c) (N.C. Sup. Ct. 2020).

76. *See, e.g.*, FLA. RULES, *supra* note 32, § 10.370(b) ("[W]hen a mediator believes a party does not understand or appreciate how an agreement may adversely affect legal rights or obligations, the mediator shall advise the party of the right to seek independent legal counsel.").

parties the confidence needed to make concessions and move toward settlement. The Model Standards provide: "A mediator shall maintain the confidentiality of all information obtained by the mediator in mediation, unless otherwise agreed to by the parties or required by applicable law."[77] Similar statements can be found in many state mediator standards of ethics.[78] The Uniform Mediation Act additionally provides a privilege for mediation communications and provides mediators with the general ability to refuse to testify in a later proceeding about what was said at a mediation.[79]

In addition to general confidentiality, caucus sessions may be entitled to an additional level of confidentiality—meaning that the contents of one caucus may be confidential even from the other mediation participants. In practice, many mediators have one of two defaults for confidentiality in caucus: (1) everything is confidential *unless* the party gives permission to disclose or (2) nothing is confidential unless the party expressly requests the mediator to refrain from disclosure. The Model Standards prefer the first of these options. The applicable standard states: "A mediator who meets with any persons in private session during a mediation shall not convey directly or indirectly to any other person, any information that was obtained during that private session without the consent of the disclosing person."[80] North Carolina, Florida, and New York rules have a similar presumption of confidentiality within caucuses.[81] However, given

---

77. MODEL STANDARDS, *supra* note 17, at V.A; *see also* FAMILY STANDARDS, *supra* note 18, at VII.

78. *See, e.g.*, FLA. RULES, *supra* note 32, § 10.360(a) ("A mediator shall maintain confidentiality of all information revealed during mediation except where disclosure is required or permitted by law or is agreed to by all parties."); N.C. STANDARDS, *supra* note 61, at 3 ("A mediator shall, subject to the exceptions set forth below, maintain the confidentiality of all information obtained within the mediation process."); CAL. RULES, *supra* note 56, R. 3.857(d) ("A mediator must not use information that is acquired in confidence in the course of a mediation outside the mediation or for personal gain.").

79. UNIF. MEDIATION ACT § 4(b)(2) (providing that a mediator may refuse to testify regarding mediation communications and may also prevent others from testifying as to what a mediator said during a mediation).

80. MODEL STANDARDS, *supra* note 17, at V.B.

81. N.C. STANDARDS, *supra* note 61, at 3(b) ("A mediator shall not disclose to any participant, directly or indirectly, any information communicated to the mediator in confidence by any other participant in the mediation process, . . . unless the other participant gives the mediator permission to do so."); FLA. RULES, *supra* note 32, § 10.360(b) ("Information obtained during caucus may not be revealed by the mediator to any other mediation participant without the consent of the disclosing party."); STANDARDS OF CONDUCT FOR N.Y. ST. CMTY. DISP. RESOL. CTR. MEDIATORS,

the value of party autonomy, the norms of confidentiality can be flexible and allow the parties and the mediator to dictate the confidentiality norms for an individual case.[82]

The ethical guidance varies on the question of *when* a mediator must inform the parties of the level of confidentiality afforded to caucus sessions. The Family Standards note that a mediator who intends to caucus should agree with the participants regarding the confidentiality of those private sessions "prior to the sessions"[83] to avoid any confusion as to the nature of statements made in caucus. The Model Standards, in contrast, do not give guidance on when these determinations need to be made, but certainly a decision must be made to change the default rule of confidentiality within the caucus.[84] California rules note that a mediator must "first discuss with all participants the mediator's practice regarding confidentiality for separate communications with the participants,"[85] but that discussion likely could take place at the beginning of the mediation or before the parties' first caucus.

The best practice for an evaluative mediator is to ensure that the parties understand the ground rules regarding confidentiality and for the mediator to abide by them. The ethical guidelines also prohibit a mediator from disclosing confidential information "indirectly" from party to party,[86] which is significantly more subtle and harder to police. For instance, in the slip-and-fall case, the mediator might caucus with the defendant to discuss the newest offer. The last offer was $250,000, and the defendant was reluctant to make that offer, which it views as significantly more than nuisance value. After the mediator explores the strengths and weaknesses of the case and settlement options, the defendant agrees to offer $270,000 as the next offer. The defendant's attorney also indicated to the mediator that the defendant has room to settle up to

---

Standard V, cmt. 3 (N.Y. Off. of ADR Programs 2009) ("A mediator who meets with a party in private session during a mediation should not convey directly or indirectly to any other party, group or institution any information that was obtained during that private session without the consent of the disclosing party.").

82. Model Standards, *supra* note 17, at V.D ("The parties may make their own rules with respect to confidentiality, or the accepted practice of an individual mediator or institution may dictate a particular set of expectations.").

83. Family Standards, *supra* note 18, at VII.D.

84. Model Standards, *supra* note 17, at V.B ("A mediator who meets with any persons in private session during a mediation shall not convey directly or indirectly to any other person, any information that was obtained during that private session without the consent of the disclosing person.").

85. Cal. Rules, *supra* note 56, R. 3.854(c).

86. Model Standards, *supra* note 17, at V.B.

$300,000, but the defendant does not want the mediator to disclose the $300,000 number to the plaintiff.

When the mediator returns to the plaintiff's room, the mediator begins by disclosing the $270,000 offer. The plaintiff, however, is not happy with the offer because she is interested in a settlement much closer to $350,000. Can the mediator make statements to the plaintiff such as "I think I could get you $300,000 from the defendant" or "After sitting in the room all day with the defendant, I think their max is somewhere right around $300,000"? In one sense, neither of these statements expressly breaches confidentiality. The mediator is simply providing the plaintiff with the mediator's own thoughts and impressions of the defendant's settlement authority. On the other hand, the only way that the mediator could have obtained this impression would be through learning confidential information from the defendant's caucus. This type of disclosure has the effect of indirectly revealing confidential caucus information, which is prohibited under the Model Standards.[87]

The best practice for a mediator is to have a clear—and shared—understanding of the confidentiality afforded to the parties in caucus. The mediator can express those understandings with the parties during the mediator's opening remarks, but the mediator could also include these expectations in an engagement letter or during a premediation phone call with the clients together or separately. In addition, a best practice is to confer with the client at the end of each caucus regarding the information that the mediator may and may not disclose to the other side. Having a shared understanding of what is confidential and what is not will reduce mistakes and ensure trust remains within the session.

5.4. Conclusion

Evaluative mediation and evaluative techniques are neither good nor bad, although they can be performed well or poorly. Provided that mediators have strong ethical grounding and the ability to be self-aware during the process, evaluative mediators can work within the bounds of ethical practice. This chapter seeks to outline the most common ethical pitfalls for mediators using these techniques while also providing practical advice on how to overcome them.

87. *See supra* note 84.

Chapter 6

Meeting the Parties Separately

Elayne E. Greenberg

6.1. Introduction

This chapter looks behind the caucus door and highlights the ethical issues that mediators should address when they caucus. As the chapter unfolds, the reader will learn how the use of caucus is rich with ethical considerations that are also interrelated with *mediation confidentiality,*[1] *party self-determination,*[2] *mediator impartiality,*[3] *and process integrity.*[4]

6.1.1. Defining the Terms

To begin, let's clarify terms. *Caucus*, in its essence, is a private meeting in which the mediator meets with the party and the party's counsel. *Cross caucus* is the term used to describe permeations of this confidential meeting with the mediator. In one type of cross caucus, the mediator

---

1. Standards of Conduct for Mediators, Standard V (Am. Bar Ass'n 2005) [hereinafter Model Standards] (Standard V refers to the mediator's standards of confidentiality).

2. *Id.* Standard I Party Self Determination.

3. *Id.* Standard II Impartiality.

4. *Id.* Standard VI Quality of the Process; Omer Shapira, *A Critical Assessment of the Model Standards of Conduct for Mediators (2005): Call for Reform*, 100 Marq. L. Rev. 81, 113–14 (2016) (discussing the duty to protect process integrity under the Model Standards' Standard VI); Carrie Menkel-Meadow, *Ex Parte Talks with Neutrals: ADR Hazards*, 12 Alts. to Dispute Resol. (CPR Inst. for Dispute Resol. 1994) (raising that caucus, even if used to ferret out a party's interests, may also jeopardize the integrity of the process).

has a private meeting with only the attorneys of each mediation party. In still another variant of cross caucus, the mediator meets privately with only the parties.[5]

6.1.2. Caucus as a Polarizing Discussion

The question of whether or not mediators should caucus has become a polarizing discussion about what constitutes good mediation practice, with dedicated mediators on both sides of this discussion.[6] Those mediators who support a noncaucus model focus on believing that parties themselves, not the mediator, are in the best positions to solve their own conflict.[7] Supporters of the noncaucus model buttress their point of view by referencing the ways caucusing mediators use manipulation and deception when they caucus, at the expense of mediation confidentiality, party self-determination, mediator impartiality, and process integrity.[8] From a different vantage point, those mediators who support a caucus-only or caucus-dominated model justify that caucus cuts through party grandstanding and allows mediators to candidly address with each mediation party the legal and financial issues that will help resolve the case.[9] Still, as with any polarizing discussion, there are those who take a middle-of-the-road stance who, although appreciative of the benefits of caucusing, also warn that caucuses should be used in moderation because of the process dangers they present.[10]

Depending on their mediation philosophy, mediators may opt to use caucus for different reasons. For example, transformative mediators

---

5. *Competition Rules: 13th ICC International Commercial Mediation Competition* at 6, ICC (2018), https://iccwbo.org/content/uploads/sites/3/2017/07/icc-2017-international-commercial-mediation-competition-rules.pdf.pdf.

6. *See, e.g.*, Jay Folberg, *The Shrinking Joint Session: Survey Results*, DISP. RESOL. MAG., Winter 2016 (survey of whether or not JAMS mediators caucused when they mediated); Lynne S. Bassis, *Face-to-Face Sessions Fade Away: Why Is Mediation's Joint Session Disappearing?*, DISP. RESOL. MAG., Fall 2014.

7. *See, e.g.*, GARY FRIEDMAN & JACK HIMMELSTEIN, CHALLENGING CONFLICT: MEDIATION THROUGH UNDERSTANDING (2009).

8. *See, e.g.*, Eric Galton & Tracy Allen, *Don't Torch the Joint Session*, DISP. RESOL. MAG., Fall 2014, at 26.

9. *See, e.g.*, Thomas J. Stipanowich, *Insights on Mediation Practices and Perceptions*, DISP. RESOL. MAG., Winter 2016; Folberg, *supra* note 6, at 16; Bassis, *supra* note 6, at 31.

10. MD. ADMIN. OFF. OF THE CTS., WHAT WORKS IN DISTRICT COURT OF TRIAL MEDIATION: EFFECTIVENESS OF VARIOUS MEDIATION STRATEGIES ON SHORT- AND LONG-TERM OUTCOMES, SJI-12-N-028, at 8 (Jan. 2016).

consider caucus a tool in which the parties get clearer.[11] Many mediators who caucus find it is an essential tool in the mediation process.[12] Caucuses provide mediators an opportunity and a safer space to broach issues that couldn't be discussed in joint sessions and help them develop a deeper understanding of what matters most to the parties, explore viable options for settlement, and overcome impasses.[13] In a rare example of unanimity, all mediators explicitly agree that caucuses should be *confidential unless the caucusing party agrees otherwise*, whatever the mediation theory driving the mediator's caucus and whichever type of caucus the mediator uses.

6.1.3. The ABA Model Standards of Conduct for Mediators Standard V.B, Caucus Confidentiality

Even though the ethical implications of caucusing are far-reaching, the word "caucus" is not explicitly referenced but is implicitly referenced as "private session" in the ABA Model Standards of Conduct for Mediators (Model Standards) under Standard V.B, Confidentiality. Specifically, the standard provides:

> A mediator who meets with any persons in private session during a mediation *shall not convey directly or indirectly* to any other person, any information that was obtained during that private session without the consent of the disclosing person.[14]

This three-sentence ethical guideline, however, is neither simple nor straightforward for mediators to follow. Caucus confidentiality requires a more nuanced understanding of what constitutes direct and indirect communications. Moreover, it compels us to consider how the degree of adherence to protecting confidential caucus communications also implicates a mediator's other ethical obligations. Confidentiality, however, is just one jumping-off point with which to explore the ethical implications of caucusing. This discussion will also alert mediators to consider how the confidentiality obligations regarding mediation's caucus are

11. Dan Simon, *Caucusing in Transformative Media*, Inst. for the Study of Conflict Transformation (Nov. 20, 2019), http://www.transformativemediation.org/caucusing-in-transformative-mediation/.

12. David Hoffman, *Mediation and the Art of Shuttle Diplomacy*, 27 Harv. Negot. J. 263 (2011).

13. Omer Shapira, A Theory of Mediators' Ethics: Foundations, Rationale, and Application 217 (2016).

14. Model Standards, *supra* note 1, Standard V(B) (emphasis added).

interrelated with the mediator's distinct ethical obligations of *party self-determination,*[15] *mediator impartiality,*[16] and *process integrity.*[17]

Unfortunately, there is a paucity of ethical opinions to guide mediators about caucusing. This chapter fills the gap, gently opens the caucus door, glimpses the ethical practice issues, and recommends ethical approaches all mediators should consider in mediation practice when they caucus.

This discussion is framed by first explaining how the separate ethical obligations of party self-determination, mediator impartiality, and process integrity are triggered when a mediator decides to caucus. The second part of this caucusing discussion will continue through the confidentiality prism. It will raise and discuss four ethical questions about caucusing confidentiality that will help heighten a mediator's awareness of the ethical implications of caucusing.

6.2. Part One: Party Self-Determination, Process Integrity, and Mediation Impartiality

6.2.1. Party Self-Determination

The decision about whether or not the parties should caucus is a process design decision. As a threshold issue and throughout the mediation process, a mediator has an ethical obligation to discuss with the mediation participants whether or not they want to caucus. Moreover, when discussing the issue, the mediator has an ethical obligation to ensure that each mediation participant has sufficient information to make an informed decision about whether or not to proceed with a caucus. Specifically, Standard I, Self-Determination, provides:

> A. A mediator shall conduct a mediation based on the principle of party self-determination. Self-determination is the act of coming to a voluntary, uncoerced decision in which each party makes free and informed choices as to process and outcome. Parties may exercise self-determination at any stage of a mediation, including mediator selection, *process design*, participation in or withdrawal from the process, and outcomes.

What is unclear, however, is what happens when a mediation party prefers not to caucus, but the mediator thinks caucusing is a good idea. In

15. *Id.* Standard I.
16. *Id.* Standard II.
17. *See supra* note 4, Standard VI Quality of the Process.

that case, Standard I.A.1 suggests that the mediator's preference for process design, cloaked under the guise of "conducting a quality process," may trump a party's right to self-determination:

> Although party self-determination for process design is a fundamental principle of mediation practice, a mediator may need to balance such party self-determination with a mediator's duty to conduct a quality process in accordance with these Standards.

6.2.2. Quality of the Process

Standard VI, Quality of the Process, states:

> A. A mediator shall conduct a mediation in accordance with these Standards and in a manner that promotes diligence, timeliness, safety, presence of the appropriate participants, party participation, procedural fairness, party competency and mutual respect among all participants.

After reviewing Standard VI, each mediator has to decide for herself whether the decision to caucus rests with the mediation party or the mediator. Furthermore, when a mediator decides to caucus, each mediator should be able to justify how her use of caucus is upholding the quality of the mediation process.

Turning back to party self-determination, the manner in which the mediator engages with mediation participants when they are in caucus will also determine whether or not the mediator honors the participants' self-determination. As will be discussed more fully in section 6.3, a mediator honors participants' self-determination in caucus, for example, when the mediator allows the participants to define the parameters of caucus confidentiality and refrains from coercive actions that compel parties to agree to resolutions that the participants would otherwise reject.

6.2.3. Mediator Impartiality

A mediator's decision to caucus is a value-laden decision that calls into question the mediator's preferences about how mediations should be conducted, how the mediator views his role, and the way the mediator engages with the mediation participants.[18] The Model Standards' Standard II, Impartiality, provides in relevant part:

---

18. *See, e.g.*, Folberg, *supra* note 6, at 15; Stipanowich, *supra* note 9, at 6.

> B. A mediator shall conduct a mediation in an impartial manner and avoid conduct that gives the appearance of partiality.
> 1. A mediator should not act with partiality or prejudice based on any participant's personal characteristics, background, values and beliefs, or performance at a mediation, or any other reason.
> C. If at any time a mediator is unable to conduct a mediation in an impartial manner, the mediator shall withdraw.[19]

As one illustration, a transformative mediator who sees the mediator's role as supporting and empowering the mediation parties in their conflict discourse would use a caucus to help the parties get clearer. A directive mediator, however, who views the mediator's role as using his subject expertise to get a settlement would use the caucus to narrow the legal and financial issues toward a resolution he thinks is just and fair. Consequently, these disparate mediator role definitions will also influence the way the mediator engages with mediation participants in caucus. For example, a mediator's impartiality is also called into question when the mediator conducts overly aggressive evaluations of a party's case[20] or when the mediator intentionally misrepresents a party's stance as he shuttles back and forth between each party's caucus.[21] This will be discussed further in the next section.

6.3. Part Two: Through the Prism of Caucus Confidentiality: Party Self-Determination and Mediation Impartiality

We now look at the ethical implications of caucusing through the confidentiality prism articulated in Standard V.B, Confidentiality. Through this lens, the reader will become more aware of the interrelationship among caucus confidentiality, party self-determination, mediation impartiality, and process integrity. This discussion will be informed by the answers to these four questions: *First, what information should the mediator tell the mediation participants about caucus confidentiality to ensure party self-determination? Second, what types of mediation communications are considered breaches of caucus confidentiality? Third, which types of caucus communications might compel the mediator to consider ending the mediation? Fourth, as more mediators are conducting their mediation online, what additional safeguards must mediators consider to safeguard caucus confidentiality?*

---

19. Model Standards, *supra* note 1, Standard II.
20. Shapira, *supra* note 13, at 213.
21. *Id.* at 268–69.

First, what information should the mediator tell the mediation participants about caucus confidentiality to ensure party self-determination?

Discussion:

The answer to this question implicates both the *confidentiality* of caucusing and each party's ethical right to *self-determination*. As stated in the previous section, the mediation parties, as part of party self-determination, may decide whether or not they want to caucus, and if they do, which caucus communications will remain confidential and which caucus communications may be shared. Therefore, the confidentiality parameters of caucusing, just like the confidentiality parameters of the overall mediation, should be shaped by the mediation participants' preferences, not by the mediator's preference. As stated in the preceding section, however, a mediator may decide not to honor a party's self-determined choice about caucusing if the mediator believes the party's self-determined choices are counter to preserving the integrity of the mediation process. Thus, a mediator's decision on whether or not the parties will caucus and whether or not the caucus information is confidential implicates a party's self-determination and the integrity of the mediation process.

In some states, caucus confidentiality may be subject to legislation or court rules. For example, Florida Rule 10.360(b) of the Florida Rules for Certified and Court-Appointed Mediators provides that "[i]nformation obtained during caucus may not be revealed by the mediator to any other mediation participant without the consent of the disclosing party."[22] An ethics opinion from the Florida Mediator Ethics Advisory Committee (MEAC)[23] highlights the intersection between caucusing confidentiality and party self-determination. The opinion was prompted by a mediator's query asking whether a mediator who has informed the mediation participant, as part of an opening statement or during the mediation, that mediation caucuses are confidential *may still decide to disclose confidential mediation caucuses unless the mediation participant or the participant's attorney explicitly directs the mediator to keep the information confidential* (emphasis added).

The MEAC advised that the mediator is ethically permitted to establish such a ground rule regarding caucus confidentiality with one caveat. The mediation participant must give express verbal or nonverbal consent.

---

22. Fla. Rules for Certified & Ct.-Appointed Mediators, Part II, https://www.flcourts.org/Resources-Services/Alternative-Dispute-Resolution/Rules-Discipline-Sanctions (last visited Feb. 26, 2021).

23. Mediator Ethics Advisory Comm. Advisory Op. MEAC 2003-005.

Lack of objection or silence does not constitute consent. Furthermore, the MEAC guided that a better ethical practice would be for the mediator to secure the express consent for sharing particular caucusing communication as the need arises, rather than as a global ground rule.

The MEAC's recommendation is consistent with the Reporter's Notes to the Model Standards.[24] According to the Reporter's Notes, a mediation participant's informed consent about caucus confidentiality should be "known, meaningful and timely."[25] Mediators should also note that some codes of conduct mandate that the mediator receive the caucusing party's consent before disclosing information obtained in caucus.[26]

Recommendations:

- Prior to caucusing, a mediator should consider what information about caucusing the mediator should provide each mediation participant that would satisfy the informed-consent requirement regarding caucusing.
- Mediators should assume that they are prohibited from disclosing caucus communications unless the caucusing party gives the mediator permission to disclose the information.
- When parties are contracting with the mediator for mediation services, the mediator should ask, as part of the discussion about parties' confidentiality expectations, parties' preferred confidentiality parameters for mediation caucuses. If the mediator and parties do not agree on the confidentiality parameters, the mediator and the parties should try to negotiate a consensus approach.
- These preferences should be memorialized in the written Agreement to Mediate signed by the mediation parties.
- At the beginning and conclusion of each caucus, the mediator should repeat and confirm with the caucusing party the agreed-upon caucus confidentiality parameters.

Second, what types of mediation communications are considered breaches of caucus confidentiality?

Discussion:

Once the mediator familiarizes herself with the law on mediation confidentiality and clarifies with the mediation participants the

---

24. *See* Reporter's Notes to Model Standards of Conduct for Mediators 16, https://www.americanbar.org/content/dam/aba/administrative/dispute_resolution/dispute_resolution/mscm_reporternotes.pdf.

25. *Id.*

26. Shapira, *supra* note 13, at 273.

confidentiality parameters about caucus communications, the mediator is then ethically obligated to adhere to this agreement. The mediator is prohibited from making *explicit and implicit* communications about confidential caucus communications, unless the caucusing party gives the mediator permission to disclose the information. Yet mediators may still inadvertently get around circumscribed confidential caucus communications and communicate these messages to the other party. Such breaches are often caused by a mediator's preexisting biases about her mediator role, the mediation participants themselves, and the appropriate resolution of the case at hand. When these biases are activated, they may cause the mediator to, either unintentionally or intentionally, breach her caucus confidentiality mandate, disregard the mediator's ethical obligation to be impartial, and subordinate a mediation participant's right to party self-determination. In understanding how these biases adversely impact a mediator's role, we note how Standard V, Confidentiality, engages with two other ethical obligations, the Model Standards' Standard I, Self-Determination, and Standard II, Impartiality, cited previously.

First, let's examine how a Partial to My Idea of Settlement Mediator may contravene confidential caucus communications. Some mediators believe that they are effective mediators because they have the substantive expertise to direct mediation parties to the mediator's assessment of the correct settlement, even if the mediation participants hold contrary ideas of what would constitute a reasonable settlement. To direct parties to the predecided settlement that the mediator has deemed is just, the mediator pushes the parties to the mediator's desired goal. Such mediation manipulation, coined "reframe" in mediator parlançe, has become so widespread, dispute resolutions scholars have analogized this tactic to tricksters.[27] This is ethically problematic for three reasons. First, this practice contravenes the ethically required mediator impartiality. Second, the manner in which the mediator reframes may implicitly disclose otherwise confidential caucus communications. Third, if the mediator is using the caucus to achieve the settlement the mediator has assessed is fair, such action may override the causing party's right to self-determination. The following scenario highlights the problem.

> Mighty Mediator is mediating a legal dispute between a customer and the insurance company for a specialty food store.

---

27. *See, e.g.*, James Coben & Lela P. Love, *Trick or Treat: Mediator Manipulation*, DISP. RESOL. MAG., Fall 2010; Robert Benjamin, *The Constructive Use of Deception*, 13 CONFLICT RESOL. MONTHLY, Fall 1995; Robert Benjamin, *Mediator as Trickster*, 13 CONFLICT RESOL. MONTHLY, Winter 1995.

> The customer slipped and fell on the store's newly washed floor, severely herniating the L4 and L5 discs in his back. The customer is seeking $300,000 in compensation to cover unreimbursed medical expenses, physical therapy, and lost wages. The customer brought documentation to the mediation that supports the claim. The insurance company is willing to reimburse the customer $25,000. Take it or leave it.
>
> It turns out that before becoming a mediator, Mighty had a long legal career in insurance defense. Now, Mighty is often chosen as the mediator in negligence cases, because Mighty knows the "true value" of cases.

Mighty's own assessment of the case is somewhat different than that of the injured customer and the insurance company. In Mighty's experience, insurance companies always start with lowball numbers, and injured parties routinely inflate the cost of their losses. In Mighty's judgment, this case should settle at $45,000. In a series of caucuses, Mighty ignores each party's preference and instead coerces the parties in a series of strategic reframes to resolve the matter for $45,000. Mighty also violates the confidentiality of caucus communications and uses the communications to shape his reframes to the other so that the matter is resolved for $45,000. Thus, when the injured victim *confidentially* shared to Mighty in caucus that the party just wanted to resolve the matter quickly, Mighty then caucuses with the insurance company and still discloses the confidential information shared by the injured party: "After my conversation with the injured party, it sounds as if he wants to settle this quickly. What would be the value of ending this quickly so as not to expend company resources defending this in court?"

A different ethical problem than the Partial to My Idea of Settlement Mediator is how a mediator's implicit biases about the mediation participants might cause the mediator to *implicitly* violate caucus communications confidentiality. Mediators, like all human beings, have implicit biases about mediation participants.[28] When mediators caucus, however, these implicit biases may shape which mediation party the mediator believes is credible, what an equitable mediation outcome might be, and which confidential caucus communications warrant protections. The following hypothetical helps bring this ethical conflict to life.

> Marvelous Ms. Mediator is mediating a co-op dispute between the co-op owner, a successful African American entrepreneur,

28. *See, e.g.*, Carol Izumi, *Implicit Bias and the Illusion of Mediator Neutrality*, 34 WASH. U. J.L. & POL'Y 71–156 (2010).

and the co-op board over permissible renovations the entrepreneur may make in her apartment.

Depending on Marvelous Ms. Mediator's own implicit biases, these biases may interfere with her ethical obligation to be impartial and contravene her ethical obligation to honor caucus confidentiality. If Marvelous Ms. Mediator is unconsciously biased against co-op boards, she may inadvertently share in her caucus with the entrepreneur confidential caucus information that the co-op had shared with Marvelous Ms. Mediator. Her reframes of the matter might indirectly convey confidential caucusing information. Alternatively, if Marvelous Ms. Mediator has an implicit bias about moneyed people who waste their time and money fighting over such inconsequential issues as co-op renovations, she may be less interested and less vigilant in preserving caucus confidentiality and more focused on dispensing with the dispute.

Coben and Love prescribe that mediators should self-monitor their interventions for bias by having mediators ask themselves two questions: First, does the mediator's intervention suppress the mediation participants' right to party self-determination? Second, does the mediator's intervention compromise the integrity of the mediation process?[29] A common mediation practice that Coben and Love suggest is of dubious ethics is for the mediator to suggest as his own idea an option that has come from the caucusing party. Although mediators defend this option as a way to minimize the reactive devaluation of the option by the noncaucusing party, Coben and Love suggest such intervention is promoting a deception.[30] Rather, Coben and Love suggest that it might be more ethical if the mediator instead asked the other party to consider if they would regard the option differently if it was suggested by the mediator or the caucusing party.[31]

Recommendations:

The only caucus communications that a mediator might share are those caucus communications that the caucusing party allows the mediator to share. All other communications must remain confidential. In order to minimize the likelihood that a mediator is nonetheless *explicitly or implicitly* sharing confidential caucus information because of the mediator's role bias or implicit bias about the mediation participants, the mediator should do the following:

---

29. Coben & Love, *supra* note 27, at 19.

30. *Id.* at 20. *Compare* Shapira, *supra* note 13, at 268 (distinguishing between a "mild," acceptable misrepresentation as to the *identity* of the proposal's initiator and an unacceptable, dishonest deception as to the *content* of the proposal).

31. Coben & Love, *supra* note 27, at 20.

- Consider how your definition of your mediator role might intentionally or unintentionally affect the way you engage with parties in the mediation caucus.
- Before and during each mediation, develop an awareness of your explicit and implicit biases about people. Try to empathize with each mediation participant to minimize the adverse influence of implicit bias impacting your mediator impartiality.[32]
- Be mindful of the purpose of your reframes to ensure they don't indirectly disclose confidential caucusing information, undermine party self-determination, and threaten process integrity.

Third, which types of caucus communications might compel the mediator to consider ending the mediation?

Discussion:

One peril of caucusing is that during a caucus, a caucusing party may disclose information that compels the mediator to reconsider whether or not the mediator should maintain the confidentiality of the caucus communication and go forward with the mediation. For this problem, the ethical obligation of caucusing confidentiality is in tension with the Model Standards' Standard I, Self-Determination, and Standard VI, Quality of the Process. After all, the mediator might learn as part of a confidential caucus communication some information that, from the mediator's perspective, the mediator believes to be deceptive, unscrupulous, or even criminal. Based on the mediator's professional and personal ethical compasses, the mediator must determine if the mediation could continue without sacrificing the integrity of the mediation. Even though the caucusing party expects that the mediator will keep such caucusing information confidential, the mediator has to weigh, in such a circumstance, whether party self-determination and caucus confidentiality are less important than maintaining the integrity of the process.

The ABA Section of Dispute Resolution Committee on Mediator Ethical Guidance[33] addressed that very issue. The mediator was mediating a dispute about an employee's unauthorized taking of the employer's sensitive electronic data. In a caucus with the mediator, the employer disclosed that they had referred the case to the district attorney. In its decision, the committee analyzed how the prohibition against "directly or indirectly" disclosing confidential caucused communication might be construed

32. *See, e.g.*, Elayne E. Greenberg, *Bridging Our Justice Gaps with Empathic Processes That Change Hearts and Expand Minds about Implicit Discrimination*, 32 Ohio J. of Disp. Resol. (2017).

33. ABA Section of Dispute Resol. Comm. on Mediator Ethical Guidance, SODR-2009-2 (Am. Bar Ass'n 2009).

differently depending on whether a "broad" or "narrow" interpretation of the phrase was used. They reasoned that a broad interpretation of the prohibition against directly or indirectly disclosing such communication would preclude the mediator from asking such reality-testing questions as "Based on your experience, how often might an employer refer a case like this for prosecution?" *unless* such a question was included in the type of questions a mediator would ask in similar employment cases to reality test. However, under a narrow interpretation of the prohibition against direct and indirect caucus communication, such a reality-testing question would be permitted. The committee advised that whichever interpretation the mediator applied, the mediator always retained the option of terminating the mediation.

Sharon Press and Paul Lurie offer a different ethical conundrum that reinforces the mediator's practice challenge. In the middle of a divorce mediation dividing the marital assets, a divorcing partner discloses in caucus the hidden existence of a large bank account that the partner amassed during the marriage. This divorcing partner, however, did not want this fact disclosed and did not include the bank account as part of his or her settlement offer.[34] Should the mediator end the mediation, because failure to disclose such a material fact tainted the integrity of the mediation? Press and Lurie suggest that the mediator should first discuss with the party the impact of withholding such information.[35] If the caucusing party still wants to withhold the information, then the mediator is confronted with deciding whether such withholding is threatening the integrity of the mediation process.[36]

Recommendations:

- A peril of caucusing is that a caucusing party may disclose information that violates your personal values and mediation integrity.
- Be aware that such information may also interfere with your ethical mandate to be impartial.
- When mediators are exercising caution about not disclosing directly or indirectly confidential caucus information to the noncaucusing party, mediators should only use reality-testing questions they would use in similar cases to help a party make an informed decision without being made aware of confidential caucus information. They should not ask reality-testing questions

34. Sharon Press & Paul M. Lurie, *Assessing Risk of Private Caucus*, Disp. Resol. Mag. 38, Fall 2014.

35. *Id.*

36. *Id.*

solely to alert the noncaucusing party to the confidential caucused information.

- When the mediator has serious concerns that keeping the particular caucus disclosure confidential is compromising the integrity of the mediation, the mediator should terminate the mediation.

Fourth, as more mediators are conducting their mediation online, what additional safeguards must they consider to protect caucus confidentiality?

Discussion:

This chapter is being written during the national sheltering in place to contain the spread of COVID-19. During that time, increasing numbers of mediations, along with all the ethical obligations that attach to mediators, have been moved to a remote format. The CIARB Notes on Remote Dispute Resolution Proceeding[37] and the CPR Task Force Guidelines for Video Arbitrations[38] provide welcome guidance about ethical caucusing in a remote format. The central ethical issues that we have been discussing about caucusing—confidentiality, party self-determination, mediator impartiality, and integrity of the process—all continue in a virtual format. However, the preservation of these ethical mandates requires a different application to safeguard these ethical obligations in remote mediation caucuses. A distinguishable concern in a virtual caucus is that the caucusing party may either have unauthorized participants in the virtual caucusing room or be recording the caucus communications.

The CIARB Notes on Remote Dispute Resolution Proceedings are particularly instructive:

> 3.2. A breakout room, or a separate meeting from the virtual hearing room, can be used for caucus proceedings. The other party should not have the ability to hear or view muted caucus proceedings as body language of participants, as well as their reaction might negate the whole idea of confidentiality of caucus meetings. This is particularly important in mediation proceedings.
>
> 6.1. It is imperative to ensure that the technology used allows all participants to feel secure about the confidentiality of the

37. *Guidance Note on Remote Dispute Resolution Proceedings*, CIArb, https://www.ciarb.org/media/8967/remote-hearings-guidance-note.pdf (last visited Mar. 1, 2021).

38. *CPR's Annotated Model Procedural Order for Remote Video Arbitration Proceedings*, CPR, https://www.cpradr.org/resource-center/protocols-guidelines/model-procedure-order-remote-video-arbitration-proceedings (last visited Mar. 1, 2021).

information they disclose in a remote hearing. Access to all virtual hearing rooms and breakout rooms should be strictly limited to their allocated participants.

6.3. Physical rooms occupied by participants in a remote proceeding, either at their homes, offices, or in special hearing venues, should be completely separate from non-participants to the remote proceeding, soundproofed where possible, and have sufficient visibility to eliminate the possibility of the presence of undisclosed non-participating individuals in the room and/or any audio/video recording equipment that has not been agreed to. The use of headsets is recommended to increase both privacy and audibility of participants.

Although the CPR Task Force Guidelines are for virtual arbitrations, there is also relevant information that applies to virtual caucusing. The note explains that if a caucusing party is using a "virtual background," it could jeopardize the confidentiality of the mediation by obscuring the presence of unauthorized others in the room.

Recommendations:

- If mediations are conducted remotely, the mediator and the participants should agree in writing on the confidentiality parameters of caucusing remotely.
- The mediator should provide the parties with a breakout room in which they may have the caucus. This virtual breakout room should allow the mediator and the caucusing participant to communicate privately so that caucusing communication is not heard by the noncaucusing party. The breakout room should also allow the client and attorney to communicate privately.
- Headphones should be encouraged; virtual backgrounds discouraged.

6.4. Conclusion

This chapter focuses the mediator on the ethical obligations that attach when mediators caucus. Yes, caucusing is more than just a private meeting that a mediator has with mediation parties. Rather, *how* mediators use caucus ethically is interrelated with the ethical obligations of party self-determination, caucus confidentiality, mediator impartiality, and the integrity of the mediation process itself. The hope is that readers of this chapter will go forward and caucus in a more ethically centered way, mindful of all the ethical considerations that are implicated when a mediator uses caucus.

Chapter 7

Making Proposals

Sharon Press

7.1. Introduction

This chapter explores the ethical issues surrounding mediator proposals. The ABA Section of Dispute Resolution Task Force on Improving the Quality of Mediation Final Report (2006–2008) reported that 95 percent of mediation users (largely lawyers) surveyed rated making suggestions as an important, very important, or essential characteristic of a mediator, and 70 percent rated giving opinions similarly.[1] Further, 100 percent of those surveyed indicated that a mediator suggesting possible ways to resolve issues would be helpful in half or more of their cases, and 84 percent indicated that recommending a specific settlement would be helpful in half or more of their cases.[2] At the same time, nearly half of those surveyed indicated that it is "sometimes not appropriate to recommend a specific settlement."[3] It is important to note that the opinions of the parties (as opposed to lawyers) were considerably different. 50 percent of the parties thought that mediator comments such as "I think this is the best

1. ABA Section of Disp. Resol. Task Force on Improving the Quality of Mediation Final Report 14 (Apr. 2006–Feb. 2008), https://www.aboutrsi.org/library/aba-section-of-dispute-resolution-task-force-on-improving-the-quality-of-mediation-final-report.

2. *Id.*

3. *Id.*

offer you're going to get" were inappropriate, and 73 percent objected to mediators "telling them what to do."[4]

It is unknown how common mediator proposals are. In 2012, mediator Margaret Shaw reported that in an informal survey of her colleagues, they reported using mediator proposals in between less than 10 percent and 50 percent of their individual cases,[5] while in 2016, mediator Nancy Yeend reported on a sudden popularity and increased use of mediator proposals.[6]

Starting with a definition of what is meant by a mediator proposal, this chapter will include a review of relevant ethical standards for mediators and interpretations of these standards in advisory ethics opinions, case law, and reported mediator grievances. The chapter next will cover the arguments for and against mediator proposals, ending with a series of recommendations for ethical practice if one provides a mediator proposal.

7.2. What Constitutes a Mediator Proposal?

Before one can discuss the ethics of mediator proposals, one needs to define what constitutes a mediator proposal. Mediator Forrest Mosten defines the concept broadly as "a mediator communication that recommends a particular outcome with respect to a disputed issue or a series of issues."[7] Mediator Yeend suggests that

> [m]ediator proposals seem to run the gamut from a specific figure to a range for settlement, presented verbally or in writing, and from a single number to a detailed settlement document. Sometimes the proposal is given in joint session; however, most times it is done in caucus and is presented as a "blind response": where participants only know if it is accepted or rejected.[8]

Mediator Stephen A. Hochman defines a mediator proposal as "a settlement proposal that the mediator makes to all parties, and each party is

4. *Id.* at 15.

5. Margaret Shaw, *Mediator's Proposals: Let Me Count the Ways*, DISP. RESOL. MAG., Winter 2012, at 27.

6. Nancy Yeend, *The Mediator's Proposal*, PLAINTIFF MAG., Aug. 2016, at 1–2, https://www.plaintiffmagazine.com/images/issues/2016/08-august/Reprints/Yeend_The-mediators-proposal_Plaintiff-article.pdf.

7. Forrest Mosten, *Mediator Settlement Proposals*, ACR COM. SECTION NEWSLETTER, Aug. 2015.

8. Yeend, *supra* note 6, at 2. Yeend posits that naming this wide range of practices as mediator proposals has given legitimacy to the practice evaluative mediators have of suggesting terms for settlement.

requested to accept or reject it on the exact terms proposed, in a confidential communication to the mediator."[9] And Yeend correctly observes: "No matter how the technique is defined, the common denominator amongst all of the definitions is that the *mediator* is the one telling the participants what the *mediator* thinks is the case-specific [. . .] solution."[10]

Mediator proposals vary in content with mediators structuring them on multiple bases. A mediator proposal could represent the mediator's view of the likely court outcome, the point where the mediator believes the case *will* settle, the terms the mediator believes to be the "correct/fair" settlement, the point where the mediator believes both parties are "better off than the litigation alternative,"[11] the compromise position (splitting the difference between "final" offers),[12] the settlement that "stretches" both parties beyond where they would otherwise negotiate,[13] and the settlement that the mediator believes the *parties* will accept.[14]

There also is a range of opinions as to what should be contained in a mediator proposal. Mediator proposals tend not to specify all of the terms; rather, they often are broad parameters under which a settlement may be reached and often only include a number,[15] while in some circumstances, depending on the complexity of the dispute, a mediator should consider including all material terms—monetary and nonmonetary—in

9. Stephen A. Hochman, *A Mediator's Proposal—Whether, When and How It Should Be Used*, https://www.mediate.com/pdf/mediatorsproposal.pdf (last visited Mar. 1, 2021). *See also* John DeGroote, *The Mediator's Proposal: A Great Tool for Yesterday's Disputes*, SETTLEMENT PERSP. (Dec. 12, 2008), http://settlementperspectives.com/2008/12/the-mediators-proposal-a-great-tool-for-yesterdays-disputes/; Josh Fruchter, *The Mediator's Proposal: If Both Sides Say Yes, Make Sure It's Binding*, MERGE MEDIATION GRP. (June 14, 2019), https://www.mergemediation.com/the-mediators-proposal-if-both-sides-say-yes-make-sure-its-binding/.

10. Yeend, *supra* note 6, at 1.

11. Hochman, *supra* note 9, at 7.

12. *See* Hochman, *supra* note 9. Thomas I. Elkind points out in *Should a Mediator Ever Make a Settlement Proposal to the Parties?* that the mediator often will propose the midpoint of the difference between the last offers made by the parties to demonstrate neutrality.

13. Rodney A. Max, *Breaking Impasse Part IV: Mediator's Proposal*, UWWM, https://www.uww-adr.com/blog/mediators-proposal (last visited Mar. 1, 2021).

14. *Mediator's Proposals*, JAMS ADR BLOG, https://www.jamsadr.com/blog/tag/mediators-proposals (last visited Mar. 1, 2021).

15. Courts have construed acceptance by both sides of a mediator proposal as full settlement—even if all the details were not clear. *See, e.g.*, Stephenson v. Young, 2011 U.S. Dist. LEXIS 57579, 2011 WL 2112021 (D. Kan. May 26, 2011). See also *In re TFT-LCD (Flat Panel) Antitrust Litig.*, No. 14-15916 (9th Cir. Sept. 1, 2016), which ran into challenges with California's confidentiality statute.

the proposal.[16] Generally, mediator proposals do not include rationales (but they could)[17] and are viewed as "last resort."[18]

7.3. Mediator Proposals: Pros and Cons

There are practical reasons why mediators and advocates support mediator proposals. In this section, I will identify some of them and then follow with the reasons advanced against mediator proposals.

7.3.1. Practical Arguments in Support of Mediator Proposals

Overcoming barriers: Advocates often have a hard time with objective analysis[19] of their case, as do their clients. Receiving a mediator proposal can overcome reactive devaluation. Specifically, the tendency to reject a proposal from an opponent diminishes when a neutral proposes the compromise. A mediator proposal also provides a scapegoat to overcome posturing and "allows the party representative to feel—and to tell their bosses—that they held firm but the mediator 'made them do it.'"[20]

Efficiency: When participants in a mediation get stuck, a way to speed up the process is for the mediator to provide a proposal. This works because a mediator proposal comes with a stamp of objectivity and legitimacy (assuming the parties respect the competence and integrity of the mediator).[21]

Fulfilling expectations: Attorneys have come to expect mediator proposals and negotiate within a mediation "intentionally leaving bargaining room open knowing that the mediator will propose the one final compromise."[22]

---

16. Max, *supra* note 13.

17. *See* Shaw, *supra* note 5, at 28 (quoting a mediator that providing a rationale can be helpful when the "'higher up' individual who did not attend the mediation will be the one making the ultimate decision"; quoting another mediator with a countervailing view that if you provide a rationale, "the parties can always pick apart your reasons, each finding an argument with which it disagrees").

18. *Id.* at 27.

19. *See* Richard Birke & Craig R. Fox, *Psychological Principles in Negotiating Civil Settlements*, 4 HARV. NEGOT. L. REV. 1 (Spring 1999).

20. *Mediator's Proposals*, *supra* note 14.

21. *Id.* at 9.

22. *Mediator's Proposals*, *supra* note 14.

7.3.2. Practical Arguments against Mediator Proposals

Stability of outcome: One of the arguments in favor of mediation is the high compliance rate with mediated settlements, generally believed to be a result of individuals reaching their own agreements. The concern is that participants who "agree" to accept a mediator proposal will be less likely to comply with the settlement and may experience "buyer's remorse." A Maryland Judiciary ADR report found that the more mediators used offering strategies, including offering opinions, advocating for their own solutions, and offering legal analysis, the less participants reported that "the outcome was working, that they were satisfied with the outcome; that they would recommend ADR; and that they changed their approach to conflict."[23]

Legal advice and unauthorized practice of law (UPL) concerns: Some commentators voice concerns that a mediator proposal might be viewed as a form of legal advice, and where the mediator is not an attorney, it could raise a question of unauthorized practice of law.[24] It is worth noting that the American Bar Association Section of Dispute Resolution adopted a resolution that states, "[M]ediation is not the practice of law [and] mediators' discussion of legal issues does not constitute legal advice, whether or not the mediator is an attorney." According to the Association for Conflict Resolution (ACR), "mediators who practice mediation consistent with standards of conduct approved by ACR [the Model Standards] should not be considered to have engaged in the unauthorized practice of law."[25] A cautious approach had been advocated by a report of the Department of Dispute Resolution Services of the Supreme Court of Virginia. The drafters noted: "[M]ediators should note that what constitutes legal advice is highly contextual and may vary according to the nature and type of the statements made by the mediator, the manner in which law-related information is provided to the parties, the purposes for which it is provided, and the expectations of the disputing parties. Furthermore, even when providing permissible legal information, mediators

23. *See What Works in District Court Day of Trial Mediation: Effectiveness of Various Mediation Strategies on Short-Term and Long-Term Outcomes*, Md. Jud. Statewide Eval. of Alt. Disp. Resol., https://www.courts.state.md.us/sites/default/files/import/courtoperations/pdfs/districtcourtstrategiestwopagesummary.pdf (last updated June 2017).

24. Yeend, *supra* note 6, at 3.

25. James Alfini, Sharon Press & Joseph Stulberg, Mediation Theory and Practice 451 (3d ed. 2013).

must be careful to give information only in those areas in which they are knowledgeable because of their training or experience."[26]

Implications for the mediation process: If a mediator gets a reputation for providing a mediator proposal, parties will ask for more caucus time and "spin" the mediator,[27] thus changing the character of the process.

A second impact on the mediation process is that mediator proposals tend to primarily be monetary settlement proposals. This perpetuates the (inaccurate) assumption that "every case is about money."[28] Rather than focusing on the various interests and providing an opportunity for the participants to develop a resolution that accommodates their most important interests, mediator proposals tend to harken back to positional, distributive bargaining where each gain for one side is an equal loss for the other.

Impact on the parties: Some mediation participants may be more resistant than others to mediator proposals. Bill Eddy, a lawyer and licensed social worker who has devoted his professional career to working with high-conflict parties, addressed the impact of a mediator proposal with this population and noted that high-conflict parties tend to get angry when told what to do and are likely to blame the mediator for taking control and resist his suggestion.[29]

7.4. The Ethics of Mediator Proposals

7.4.1. Mediator Proposals and Ethical Standards for Mediators

There is no universally adopted ethical code for mediators; thus, in this section we will explore provisions from a variety of ethical standards that provide guidance on the practice of mediator proposals. In addition to the Model Standards of Conduct for Mediators, which were adopted by the

---

26. Dep't of Disp. Resol. Servs. of the Sup. Ct. of Va., Guidelines on Mediation and the Unauthorized Practice of Law (UPL), ch. 2 § 1,http://www.courts.state.va.us/courtadmin/aoc/djs/programs/drs/mediation/resources/upl_guidelines.pdf (last visited Mar. 2, 2021).

27. Shaw, *supra* note 5, at 28 ("If parties expect that the mediator may make such a proposal at some point, they may intentionally mislead the mediator about their true intentions in an attempt to set the range of the ultimate proposal.").

28. Yeend, *supra* note 6, at 2 ("Accepting that hypothesis as fact narrows the settlement focus, and creative or more encompassing customized solutions are not considered and never see the light of day.").

29. Bill Eddy, *Should Mediators Make Proposals?*, High Conflict Inst. (Jan. 12, 2014), https://www.highconflictinstitute.com/hci-articles/should-mediators-make-proposals (suggesting better ways to help them, such as giving them several alternatives to consider or general approaches to resolve their dispute).

American Arbitration Association, the American Bar Association, and the Association for Conflict Resolution (Model Standards),[30] standards adopted by states and other organizations will be included in this review.

A few codes address mediator proposals directly. The Guidelines for Hawaii Mediators provide that "mediators may make suggestions and may draft proposals for the participants' consideration . . . ."[31] The Minnesota Code of Ethics for neutrals provides, in comments, that "[t]he mediator may . . . draft proposals, and help parties explore options. . . . It is acceptable for the mediator to suggest options in response to parties' request."[32] The North Dakota Code of Mediation Ethics states that "[t]he mediator may . . . draft proposals, and help parties explore options."[33] According to the Kentucky Ethical Guidelines for mediators, "An evaluative mediator might make formal or informal recommendation to the parties as to the outcome of the issues."[34] The New Mexico Ethical Standards for Mediators provide that, "[d]epending on the mediation model utilized, a mediator may make suggestions for the mediation parties' consideration . . . ."[35] The North Carolina Standards provide that "a mediator may suggest options for settlement in addition to those conceived of by the parties."[36] And JAMS Mediators' Ethics Guidelines acknowledge that sometimes a mediator "offers a recommendation with regard to settlement."[37]

---

30. Model Standards of Conduct for Mediators (2005), https://www.americanbar.org/groups/dispute_resolution/policy_standards/ [hereinafter Model Standards].

31. Guidelines for Haw. Mediators (2002), Rule VI Self-Determination 1, https://www.courts.state.hi.us/docs/docs2/guidelines.pdf.

32. App'x to Rule 114, Code of Ethics, cmts. to Self Determination, Minn. Ct. Rules, https://www.revisor.mn.gov/court_rules/rule/gp-114~a0/.

33. N.D. Code of Mediation Ethics, cmts. to Self-Determination (Mar. 1, 2007), https://www.ndcourts.gov/legal-resources/rules/ndrct/appendix-a-to-rule-8-9.

34. Ky. Rules of Admin. Procedure, Part XII Section 3 Ethical Guidelines, § 3(17)(b) https://casetext.com/rule/kentucky-court-rules/kentucky-administrative-procedures-of-the-court-of-justice/part-xii-mediation-guidelines-for-court-of-justice-mediators/section-3-ethical-guidelines [hereinafter Ky. Rules].

35. N.M. Guidelines, Guideline V. Ethical Standards for Mediators, F. Role of Mediator (1), https://adr.nmcourts.gov/wp-content/uploads/sites/31/2020/12/Guidelines_For_Court_Connected_Mediation_Services___September_30_2016_.pdf.

36. N.C. Rev. Standards of Prof'l Conduct for Mediators, Standard 5(b), https://www.nccourts.gov/assets/inline-files/Standards-of-Professional-Conduct-for-Mediators-Codified-1-March-2020.pdf?MTGctiiCw3Btgkw6qx3EEFnJoUJBWGZQ (last visited Mar. 2, 2021) [hereinafter N.C. Standards].

37. JAMS Mediators' Ethics Guidelines, Standard VI, https://www.jamsadr.com/mediators-ethics/ (last visited Mar. 2, 2021).

In contrast, some codes expressly prohibit mediators from making proposals. For example, according to the Montana Standards of Ethics,[38] mediators are prohibited from "mak[ing] a recommendation as to a course of action, or giv[ing] a substantive opinion as to the best course of action for a participant."[39] Furthermore, while a mediator may provide information in a neutral manner, "the information shall not be presented in the form of a recommended course of action."[40] And the Kentucky Ethical Guidelines for mediators state that "[t]he facilitative mediator does not make recommendations to the parties."[41]

7.4.2. Mediator Proposals and the Definition of the Mediator's Role

Most ethical standards for mediators do not address the provision of mediator proposals. One could think, therefore, that understanding the ethical propriety of offering a mediator proposal rests on the role of the mediator in terms of both mediator style and what constitutes ethical "facilitation." Mediator proposals are most often associated with evaluative and directive styles of mediation practice rather than with the facilitative style.[42]

However, while it is commonly recognized that there are different role conceptions[43] and styles of mediation,[44] most ethical standards for mediators do not explicitly acknowledge the different styles of practice and do not suggest that these differences have implications for ethical practice. For example, the Model Standards define mediation without a reference to mediation style as "a process in which an impartial third party facilitates communication and negotiation and promotes voluntary decision making by the parties to the dispute."[45] The mediator's role is commonly described as

38. Mont. Mediation Ass'n, Code of Ethics & Standard of Practice, https://mtmediation.org/wp-content/uploads/2015/04/mtma-code-of-ethics-standards-of-practice-rev-2-13-14-reviewed-by-committee.pdf (last visited Mar. 2, 2021).

39. *Id.* Standard VI Self-Determination, A. Responsibilities of the Participants and the Mediator.

40. *Id.*

41. Ky. Rules, *supra* note 34, § 3(17)(a).

42. *See* Leonard L. Riskin, *Understanding Mediators' Orientation, Strategies, and Techniques: A Grid for the Perplexed*, 1 Harv. Negot. L. Rev. 7 (1996).

43. Robert A. Baruch Bush, *Efficiency and Protection or Empowerment and Recognition?: The Mediator's Role and Ethical Standards in Mediation*, 41 Fla. L. Rev. 253 (1989).

44. Riskin, *supra* note 42; Robert A. Baruch Bush & Joseph P. Folger, The Promise of Mediation (2d ed. 2005).

45. Model Standards, *supra* note 30.

> to facilitate communication and understanding among the parties and to assist the parties in reaching an agreement. The mediator should aid the parties in identifying and discussing issues and in exploring options for settlement. The mediator should not, however, render a decision on the issue in dispute. In mediation, the ultimate decision whether, and on what terms, to resolve the dispute belongs to the parties alone.[46]

A rare exception is the Kentucky Ethical Guidelines for mediators, which contain a provision entitled "Mediation Styles."[47] In this provision, the guidelines provide definitions for facilitative mediation,[48] evaluative mediation,[49] and transformative mediation.[50] However, besides a brief mention of these styles, the definition of mediation[51] and all the obligations of the mediator (e.g., integrity, self-determination, impartiality, conflicts of interest, and confidentiality, with a limited exception of "professional advice"[52]) are the same and equally apply to any mediator regardless of style. The Virginia Standards also acknowledge that there are different mediator styles but do not indicate any ethical implication of mediation styles other than an obligation of the mediator to disclose her style to the parties and record it in the agreement to mediate.[53] The New Mexico Standards acknowledge that differences in mediation styles exist as well, referring to one implication according to which, "[d]epending on the mediation model being utilized, a mediator may make suggestions for the mediation parties' consideration."[54] The New Mexico Standards, however, do not expressly refer to the style of the mediator who may do so.

Because of the limited guidance on mediator proposals that can be drawn from the definitions of mediation and the mediator's role in

---

46. While this language is from North Carolina, N.C. STANDARDS, *supra* note 36, similar language can be found in other ethical standards, including VA. STANDARDS OF ETHICS AND PROF'L RESP. FOR CERTIFIED MEDIATORS (2011), http://courts.state.va.us/courtadmin/aoc/djs/programs/drs/mediation/soe.pdf [hereinafter VA. STANDARDS]; FLA. RULES FOR CERTIFIED & CT.-APPOINTED MEDIATORS (Mar. 2018), https://www.flcourts.org/content/download/216763/1966524/rules-certified-court-appointed-mediators.pdf [hereinafter FLA. RULES].

47. KY. RULES, *supra* note 34, Section 3 Ethical Guidelines (17) Mediation Styles.

48. *Id.* § 3(17)(a).

49. *Id.* § 3(17)(b).

50. *Id.* § 3(17)(c).

51. *Id.* § 3(1).

52. *Id.* § 3(12).

53. VA. STANDARDS, *supra* note 46, D.1.b.

54. N.M. GUIDELINES, *supra* note 35.

ethical standards and from direct reference to mediator proposals, one must undertake a nuanced understanding of those ethical standards that could relate to mediator proposals—specifically, self-determination of the parties, impartiality of the mediator, and the mediator obligations of maintaining the confidentiality, quality, and integrity of the process of mediation. These will be explored next, together with the guidance given by advisory mediator ethics opinions on mediator proposals.

7.4.3. Party Self-Determination

Party self-determination is a fundamental principle of mediation, and mediator standards typically include a provision entitled "Self-Determination."[55] The Model Standards define self-determination as "the act of coming to a voluntary, uncoerced decision in which each party makes free and informed choices as to process and outcome."[56] This suggests at least two elements of an exercise of self-determination: (1) making a *voluntary, uncoerced* decision, which is (2) based on *informed* choices.[57] Mediator proposals raise ethical concerns with regard to both elements: while the mediator's input is stated as a "proposal," many mediation participants view the mediator as an authority figure, and if the participants are not clear on the strength of their position, they might compromise their own self-determination and defer to the mediator;[58] and participants should be able to make an informed choice as to receiving a mediator proposal.[59] Providing a mediator proposal to represented parties who are very familiar with the legal process and capable of making their own assessments about their situation is less

---

55. *See, e.g.*, Omer Shapira, A Theory of Mediators' Ethics: Foundations, Rationale, and Application 127–29 (2016) (illustrating the centrality of party self-determination in codes of conduct for mediators and in the mediation literature).

56. Model Standards, *supra* note 30, Standard I.

57. *See* Omer Shapira, *A Critical Assessment of the Model Standards of Conduct for Mediators (2005): Call for Reform*, 100 Marq. L. Rev. 81, 107–08, 126 (2016) (suggesting a third element of party self-determination—party *competency*, which is the capacity to perceive information, understand it, and participate in the mediation, currently referred to in Standard VI.A (Quality of Process) of the Model Standards).

58. Yeend, *supra* note 6, at 3. On the mediator's position of power and influence see also Omer Shapira, *Exploring the Concept of Power in Mediation: Mediators' Sources of Power and Influence Tactics*, 24 Ohio St. J. on Disp. Resol. 535 (2009).

59. *See, e.g.*, Yeend, *supra* note 6, at 2 (noting that some mediators "provide their opinion, whether asked or not, just as standard practice"). On the importance of informed decision making in mediation, see Jacqueline M. Nolan-Haley, *Informed Consent in Mediation: A Guiding Principle for Truly Educated Decisionmaking*, 74 Notre Dame L. Rev. 775 (1999).

likely to interfere with party self-determination than providing a mediator proposal to an unrepresented party who is unclear about his rights or obligations.[60]

As noted previously, some ethical standards expressly allow mediators to make proposals, a few prohibit them from doing so, and most standards do not refer to mediator proposals at all, seemingly leaving it to the mediator's discretion. A good understanding of the elements of party self-determination can provide mediators who are allowed to make proposals with guidance on the proper way to do so.

Self-determination standards require that "decisions made during a mediation are to be made by the parties"[61] and "a mediator shall not coerce or [unfairly][62] or [improperly][63] influence a party."[64] The Arkansas Requirements limit the prohibition on coercion and unfair influence to "entering into a settlement"[65] but also note that while "[t]he mediator may offer options for the parties to consider as settlement terms[, she] is not to judge or impose settlement terms on the parties."[66] Florida frames the prohibition on coercion or improperly influencing a party broadly as relating to "any decision."[67] Further, in the comments to the Florida Rule on self-determination, the committee noted, "Special care should be taken to preserve the party's right to self-determination if the mediator provides input to the mediation process."[68] The Code of Ethical Standards for Mediators in the Multi-Door Dispute Resolution Division of

60. Paul Lurie & Sharon Press, *On Professional Practice: Protecting Self -Determination in Mediation*, DISP. RESOL. MAG., Spring 2014, *available at* https://www.schiffhardin.com/Templates/media/files/publications/PDF/Lurie_DRM_Spring2014.pdf (immediately offering a suggestion is "ill-advised and not good practice," whereas doing the same with sophisticated parties, represented by counsel, under no time pressure, would not be problematic).

61. FLA. RULES, *supra* note 46, R. 10.310.

62. ARK. ALT. DISPUTE RESOL. COMM'N REQUIREMENTS FOR THE CONDUCT OF MEDIATION AND MEDIATORS, Standard 4 B., https://www.arcourts.gov/sites/default/files/2019-06/CONDUCT%202012.pdf (last visited Mar. 2, 2021) [hereinafter ARK. REQUIREMENTS]; *see also* KY. RULES, *supra* note 34, Section 3 Ethical Guidelines (1) Mediation Defined Comment: "The mediator should not coerce a party in any way."

63. FLA. RULES, *supra* note 46, R. 10.310(b). *See also* KAN. R. 918 (b)(1)(B)(iv), https://www.kscourts.org/KSCourts/media/KsCourts/Rules/Rule-918.pdf?ext=.pdf (last visited Mar. 2, 2021) ("An approved individual must not coerce or improperly influence a party to make a decision.").

64. *See, e.g.*, ARK. REQUIREMENTS, *supra* note 62; FLA. RULES, *supra* note 46.

65. ARK. REQUIREMENTS, *supra* note 62, Standard 4 B.

66. *Id.* Section II.C (Mediator's Role).

67. FLA. RULES, *supra* note 46, R. 10.310(b).

68. *Id.* Committee Notes to R. 10.310.

the Superior Court of the District of Columbia includes a provision in the self-determination standard that a mediator "shall refrain from being directive or judgmental regarding the issues in dispute and options for settlement."[69] And North Carolina Standards add a provision relating to the proper timing and sequence of actions for making a proposal, noting that "[t]his subsection [of the Self-Determination Standard] does not prohibit a mediator from expressing his or her opinion as a *last resort* to a party or attorney who requests it, as long as the mediator has *already helped* that party utilize the party's own resources to evaluate the dispute and the options for settlement."[70] Thus, a mediator respecting the parties' right to self-determination will first encourage parties to participate in the process and develop their own options and proposals.[71] When this phase is exhausted, the mediator may suggest providing the parties with a mediator proposal. It would be the parties' choice whether to accept that suggestion.[72]

Opinions of mediator ethics advisory committees (MEACs) may offer some additional guidance on the meaning of self-determination in the context of mediator proposals. In 2008,[73] a Florida Supreme Court–certified mediator inquired about the ethicality of using an "impasse avoidance technique" of mediator's offer. The mediator described the mediator's offer as a situation in which the mediator picks a number from his own judgment of somewhere between where the parties are, often but not always the midpoint of the parties' last offers, and asks both parties in caucus whether, if the opposing party would be willing to agree to that particular number, they would be willing to accept it. If the answer is yes from both parties, the mediator announces that there is a deal at that number. The mediator stated that the technique would only be used after "substantial (positional) negotiation by the parties." The MEAC opined that

---

69. Code of Ethical Standards for Mediators, Multi-Door Disp. Resol. Div., D.C. Super. Ct., https://www.dccourts.gov/sites/default/files/MultiDoor-PDFs/MD%20Mediators%20Code%20of%20Ethics.pdf (last visited Mar. 2, 2021). *See also* N.C. Standards, *supra* note 36, Standard 5. Self-Determination.

70. N.C. Standards, *supra* note 36, Standard 5(c) (emphasis added).

71. *See, e.g.*, Omer Shapira, *A Theory of Sharing Decision-Making in Mediation*, 44 McGeorge L. Rev. 923, 945–46 (2013) (discussing party self-determination regarding decisions on process).

72. *Id.*

73. Fla. Advisory Op. MEAC 2008-004 (June 30, 2008), https://www.flcourts.org/content/download/216798/1966734/MEACOpinion2008-004.pdf.

> [i]n order to be ethically appropriate, a mediator must employ any impasse avoidance technique consistent with the requirements of impartiality under [the Florida Rules]. Equally important, a mediator must protect the right of willing, fully informed parties to decide all substantive matters before them. Beyond these threshold provisions in the Florida [Rules], the Committee further cautions the inquiring mediator to consider various other limiting provisions in the rules, as well as timing and circumstances specific to any given mediation, prior to employing either technique.[74]

Regarding party self-determination concerns, the MEAC reminded the mediator that "decisions made during a mediation are to be made *by the parties*" with the mediator protecting their right to self-determination and "assisting [them] in reaching *informed and voluntary decisions*."[75] The MEAC considered the timing of the mediator proposal as crucial to effective exercise of party self-determination:

> Timing is critical . . . . Used too soon, the parties will have little opportunity to tell their respective stories and put forward their own proposals. If too late, one or both parties may already have decided to end the mediation, rendering the party/parties unwilling to participate meaningfully in the process. At that point, the mediator must carefully inquire regarding their continued willingness to decide substantive matters necessary to reach a voluntary agreement.

The MEAC was also concerned that the mediator-offer technique ended with the mediator announcing to both parties that there is a deal at the number separately agreed to in caucus and cautioned the mediator that "no case is 'over and settled' . . . because the mediator says so. On the contrary, the mediator must always bring back to both parties the status of the negotiation and advise them the decision to accept, reject, continue, or end the mediation remains theirs and theirs alone."[76]

This is an important point to note. The parties' consent for the provision of a mediator proposal does not turn the mediator into a decision maker. A proposal is not an arbitral award; it is a suggestion, not judgment. The mediator proposal is not binding on the parties, and if they

74. *Id.* (citation omitted).
75. *Id.*
76. *Id.*

want a binding decision, the term "mediator proposal" is not the one to be used.

A second Florida MEAC opinion[77] discussed a mediator's inquiry as to his ability to suggest *with specificity* possible settlement alternatives when the "elements of settlement alternatives were not raised by either party."

The MEAC considered the inquiry in light of the Florida Rules on self-determination; impartiality; and advice, opinions, or information.[78] Specifically addressing the threat to party self-determination, it opined that while a mediator

> may discuss and "explore settlement alternatives," the mediator must assess the interaction of the parties, their demeanor during the mediation and whether making such "suggestions" would be inferred as intimidation or coercion by the parties. The Committee recommends using the tool of "open ended questioning" may be preferable to making specific suggestions.[79]

The committee illustrated its opinion through examples: *asking* a party a question such as "Have you considered the possibility of [specific settlement alternative] as meeting the needs and objectives that you are seeking?" would be appropriate. Making an affirmative *statement* such as "You should consider [specific settlement alternative] as the best alternative presented here today" would be an inappropriate expression of personal or professional opinion, inconsistent with the concepts of impartiality and party self-determination.[80]

The other element of party self-determination relevant to the practice of mediator proposals is *informed* decision making. Decisions that are based on inadequate or erroneous information represent a defective decision-making process involving formal, low-quality exercise of self-determination.[81]

This issue of informed decision making is directly addressed in the Georgia Ethical Standards:

---

77. Fla. Advisory Op. MEAC 2010-006 (Oct. 12, 2010), https://www.flcourts.org/content/download/216796/1966722/MEACOpinion2010-006.pdf.

78. *Id.* R. 10.310 Self-Determination, R. 10.330 Impartiality, R. 10.370 Advice Opinions or Information; FLA. RULES, *supra* note 46.

79. *Id.*

80. *Id.*

81. SHAPIRA, *supra* note 55, at 141; Jacqueline M. Nolan-Haley, *Informed Consent in Mediation: A Guiding Principle for Truly Educated Decisionmaking*, 74 NOTRE DAME L. REV. 775, 776–77 (1999).

> Parties cannot bargain effectively unless they have sufficient information. Informed consent to an agreement implies that parties not only knowingly agree to every term of the agreement but that they have had sufficient information to bargain effectively in reaching that agreement. Self-determination of the parties in a mediation includes not only informed consent to any agreement reached but participation in crafting the agreement as well.[82]

Parties should therefore understand the implications of a mediator proposal and consent to that practice. They should know that it is their choice whether to authorize the mediator to make a mediator proposal; that the proposal comes to break an impasse in the negotiation, not replace the development of options by them; and that the proposal is a suggestion that is not binding, but it could become binding and enforceable if accepted by all parties. It is the obligation of the mediator to provide this information to the parties in order to support the parties' informed decision making regarding the use of the mediator-proposal technique.[83]

Case law on mediator proposals illustrates the deference courts give to mediation settlements, regardless of whether the settlements are the result of mediator proposals. Courts do not seem to provide any greater scrutiny when the mediated settlement involved a mediator proposal both in class-action settlements that were resolved in mediation[84] and in motions to enforce a settlement in individual cases.[85] The courts' approach highlights the importance of mediators providing proposals with close attention to the ability of parties to exercise self-determination regarding both the suggestion of the mediator to provide a settlement proposal and the specific terms of the proposal.

---

82. Ga. Standards I.C, https://godr.org/wp-content/uploads/sites/5/2019/10/Appendix-C-Chapter-1.pdf (last visited Mar. 2, 2021); *see also generally* Jacqueline M. Nolan-Haley, *Court Mediation and the Search for Justice through Law*, 74 Wash. U. L. Q. 47 (1996).

83. *See, e.g.*, Ga. Standards I.A, https://godr.org/wp-content/uploads/sites/5/2019/10/Appendix-C-Chapter-1-1.pdf (last visited Mar. 2, 2021) ("A principal duty of the mediator is to fully explain the mediation process"); Shapira, *supra* note 55, at 155–56 (discussing the duty of mediators to provide parties with information regarding the process).

84. James R. Coben, *Creating a 21st Century Oligarchy: Judicial Abdication to Class Action Mediators*, 5 Y.B. on Arb. & Mediation 162 (2013).

85. *See, e.g.*, Dharia v. Marriott Hotel Servs., No. CV 18-00008 HG-WRP (D. Haw. June 28, 2019); Stephenson v. Young, 2011 U.S. Dist. LEXIS 57579, 2011 WL 2112021 (D. Kan. 2011); *In re* TFT-LCD (Flat Panel) Antitrust Litig., No. C 12-02214 SI, 2013 WL 6326707 (N.D. Cal. Dec. 3, 2013), *rev'd*, 835 F.3d 1155 (9th Cir. 2016); Lee v. Sheldon, 427 P.3d 745 (Alaska 2018).

7.4.4. Impartiality

In addition to concerns around self-determination, mediator proposals also raise issues related to the perceived impartiality of the mediator.

Impartiality is defined in the Model Standards as "freedom from favoritism, bias or prejudice."[86] The Model Standards then provide that "[a] mediator shall conduct a mediation in an impartial manner and avoid conduct that gives the appearance of partiality."[87] Some version of this definition is found in most other ethical standards for mediators.[88] Sometimes it is expanded, as in the Florida Rules, which define impartiality as "freedom from favoritism or bias in word, action, or appearance, and includes a commitment to assist all parties, as opposed to any one individual."[89] The Nebraska Standards of Practice and Ethics for Family Mediators includes the concept of "perceived impartiality,"[90] which is probably similar to an appearance of impartiality.

The connection of impartiality to mediator proposals is whether it is possible for a mediator to propose a resolution while still maintaining freedom from favoritism or bias both actually and in appearance. In other words, does the mere act of a mediator proposing an outcome compromise a mediator's impartiality?

One way to address this real challenge for mediators is to present the proposal in a way that reassures the parties that the mediator does not favor the other side. This requires the mediator to be cognizant not only of the content of the proposal but also of its timing. The Florida MEAC[91] noted that,

> [a]s impasse is frequently preceded by one party's expressed reluctance to continue the mediation absent substantial positional change by the other, the mediator must proceed carefully when using any impasse avoidance technique [such as a mediator proposal] in order to avoid the appearance that the mediator is simply accommodating the party who has threatened to abandon the process.[92]

---

86. Model Standards, *supra* note 30, Standard II.A.

87. *Id.* Standard II.B.

88. *See* Shapira, *supra* note 55, at 201–08.

89. Fla. Rules, *supra* note 46, R. 10.330(a).

90. Neb. Standards of Practice & Ethics for Family Mediators, Standard IV.B (Oct. 26, 2008), https://supremecourt.nebraska.gov/sites/default/files/Programs/mediation/Reports/standards_and_ethics_revised_10-31-08.pdf.

91. Fla. MEAC 2008-004, *supra* note 73.

92. *Id.*

Another way to mitigate the appearance-of-partiality concern is to provide more than one option. Mediator Bill Eddy observed that "[i]f you only provide one option, there is a great risk that one party will like it and the other party will dislike it – and you will appear to have taken sides with the party who likes it."[93]

Another mediator, advocating a one-option proposal, suggested the mediator remind the parties of her impartiality and "agenda [. . .] to help the parties settle on terms that both parties decide is better than their litigation alternative."[94]

7.4.5. Confidentiality, Quality of Process, and Integrity

Mediator proposals are often developed on the basis of information learned by the mediator during caucuses (separate meetings). Moreover, after the proposal is communicated to the parties, the mediator might continue to discuss with them their answers separately. On these occasions, several ethical concerns are raised: confidentiality, quality of process, and integrity.

The confidentiality of caucus information might be compromised if the disclosing party asked that certain information not be shared. The Model Standards provide that "[a] mediator shall maintain the confidentiality of all information obtained by the mediator in mediation, unless otherwise agreed to by the parties or required by applicable law"[95] and that "[a] mediator who meets with any persons in private session during a mediation shall not convey directly or indirectly to any other person, any information that was obtained during that private session without the consent of the disclosing person."[96]

The integrity of the mediation may be undermined if mediators base their proposal on "ex parte" information that only the mediator knows and that the other side may not have been given an opportunity to confront or dispute.[97] Such conduct would jeopardize the quality and procedural fairness of the mediation[98] in breach of the mediator's obligation to

93. Eddy, *supra* note 29.

94. Hochman, *supra* note 9, at 6.

95. Model Standards, *supra* note 30, Standard V.A.

96. *Id.* Standard V.B.

97. Yeend, *supra* note 6, at 3. For similar concerns in the context of "med-arb" where a single neutral serves first as the mediator and then as the arbitrator, see Brian A. Pappas, *Med-Arb and the Legalization of Alternative Dispute Resolution*, 20 Harv. Negot. L. Rev. 157, 169–200 (2015).

98. Model Standards, *supra* note 30, Standard VI.A.

preserve the integrity of mediation.[99] The integrity concern is also related to the protection of the confidentiality of the parties' responses to the mediator proposal. Mediators who use this technique point out that it is critical that a mediator protect the acceptance of the proposal from one side if the other side rejects it "to avoid prejudicing the position of the accepting party in subsequent negotiations."[100]

7.4.6. Mediator Competence

Implicit in considering the ethicality of mediator proposals is that the mediator is competent to make such a proposal. Most jurisdictions that qualify mediators do not require specific legal qualifications;[101] thus a mediator may not be aware of the legal consequences of a particular proposal. In a 2009 New York Advisory Ethics Opinion, the committee noted that

> [a] mediator has no obligation to know that changes in custody may trigger changes in support. However, if the mediator is aware of this information, and deems it essential to the principles of self-determination and a quality process that the parties receive outside legal advice on this issue prior to signing an agreement, then in joint session, as part of reality testing the enforceability of the agreement, the mediator should: (1) give the parties the legal information in his/her possession – namely, that changes in custody may trigger changes in support; and (2) recommend that the parties consult outside counsel for legal advice about their specific case. In addition, the mediator should emphasize that

---

99. *See, e.g.*, GA. STANDARDS, *supra* note 82, Standard IV.B (noting that "[a] mediator is the guardian of the integrity of the mediation process"). *See also* Omer Shapira, *A Critical Assessment of the Model Standards of Conduct for Mediators (2005): Call for Reform*, 100 MARQ. L. REV. 81, 113–14 (2016) (discussing the duty of integrity embedded within the quality-of-process standard).

100. *Mediator's Proposals*, *supra* note 14. *But see* Shaw, *supra* note 5. Shaw describes that an experienced mediator found that it works to disclose the one "yes" (with permission, of course) because the other side knows that the case will be over with a "yes." The mediator made clear that the idea of disclosing the "yes" is not disclosed until the "yes" comes in to avoid "gamesmanship."

101. *See, e.g.*, FLA. STANDARDS, *supra* note 46; MINN. CT. R. 114.02(b), https://www.revisor.mn.gov/court_rules/gp/id/114/ (last visited Mar. 2, 2021); *Become a Mediator*, N.Y. ST. DISP. RESOL. ASS'N, https://www.nysdra.org/page/BecomeA Mediator (last visited Mar. 2, 2021).

(s)he is not acting as any party's attorney and cannot dispense legal advice specific to the case.[102]

This opinion highlights that while a mediator has no obligation to *know* the law, if the mediator does know the law, the mediator should provide the legal information "in his/her possession" and recommend that the parties seek legal *advice* about their specific case from someone other than the mediator.

Ethical standards typically draw a distinction between offering a professional opinion or advice[103] and providing information (even though most do not specifically address mediator proposals), the former (opinion and advice) being more restrictive than the latter (information). Even when providing information, mediators are required to have the necessary knowledge and expertise when providing such information to parties and can only do so if it can be done "consistent with these Standards."[104] This concern has been addressed by the Florida MEAC opinion mentioned previously.[105] The committee noted that, as the mediator stated in his inquiry, if "the mediator picks the number from his/her own judgment," the mediator must make sure that he or she is qualified by training or experience to provide the information and can do so consistent with standards of impartiality and party self-determination, and that in doing so he or she does not offer "a personal or professional opinion intended to coerce the parties, unduly influence the parties, decide the dispute, or direct a resolution of any issue."[106]

While a mediator proposal and mediator providing legal advice or information are not identical, the impact on the parties can be the same, and thus, guidance related to both can be useful by analogy. Further,

---

102. N.Y. Advisory Ethics Op. 2009-20 (Oct. 14, 2009), http://ww2.nycourts.gov/sites/default/files/document/files/2018-07/FormalPublishedOpinion2009-02.pdf.

103. *See, e.g.*, NEB. STANDARDS, *supra* note 90, Standard E.1; GUIDELINES FOR HAW. MEDIATORS, *supra* note 31, Rule VII.1; STANDARDS FOR CONDUCT FOR N.Y. ST. CMTY. DISP. RESOL. CTR. MEDIATORS, Standard IV, cmt. 5; SHAPIRA, *supra* note 55, at 238–39 (reviewing ethical standards prohibiting mediator opinion and advice).

104. *See, e.g.*, MODEL STANDARDS, *supra* note 30, Standard VI.A.5; *see also* ABA TASK FORCE REPORT, *supra* note 1, at 14–15 (factors to consider that include the "extent of mediator's knowledge and expertise").

105. Fla. Advisory Op. MEAC 2008-004, *supra* note 73.

106. *Id.*

parties might interpret a mediator proposal as an impermissible legal opinion or advice.[107]

7.5. Guidelines for Ethically Providing Mediator Proposals

Based on the discussion above, in this last section, I offer some guidelines for ethically providing mediator proposals, if a mediator chooses to do so.

7.5.1. Only upon Request of "Sophisticated" Parties

While some mediators believe that they may suggest or offer a mediator proposal on their own initiative, the safest practice from an ethical standpoint is to only consider a mediator proposal if asked by the *parties*. The use of "parties" here is intentional and meant to signal that it is not sufficient to be asked by the attorneys representing parties because it is the actual parties, and not their attorneys, who have the right to self-determination. Given the perceived position of power mediators occupy, they should only provide proposals to parties who are represented and familiar with the court system to ensure that the mediator proposal does not undermine the parties' self-determination.

7.5.2. Knowledge and Expertise—Mediator

Before offering a proposal, a mediator should be sure that she possesses the knowledge and expertise to provide an appropriate proposal[108] and that doing so is not considered to be the provision of legal advice in violation of UPL provisions.[109]

7.5.3. Timing

Despite the lack of consensus of how to define a mediator proposal, there is general consensus that mediators should only entertain mediator proposals late in the process or as an end game. This guideline is supported

107. *See* Fla. Mediator Qualification Board Consensual Agreements 2010-012 ("The GCC found cause to believe the mediator violated the Florida Rules for Certified and Court Appointed Mediators by . . . indicating his opinion as to how the court would rule . . . ."); 2011-013 (the GCC found the mediator "offered legal advice" in violation of rule 10.370(c)); 2013-014 (the GCC found probable cause that the mediator advised the party that if she went to court, she would get a 50/50 parenting plan).

108. *See also* ABA Task Force Report, *supra* note 1, at 17 (raising concerns that the quality of "analytical techniques var[ies] widely").

109. *See* Section 7.3.2, *supra*.

by a meaningful principle of party self-determination.[110] Specifically, mediators should provide opportunities for parties to be heard and the time and space to make their own decisions.[111] In addition, mediators should encourage parties to discuss and resolve (for themselves) all of the nonmonetary issues before offering a mediator proposal on the monetary issues. Doing so creates buy-in by the parties and leaves less up to further negotiation if other terms and conditions are necessary.

Mediators also need to be careful about providing the option of a mediator proposal after mediation fatigue has set in. Namely, when a mediation goes on so long that participants will do anything to get out of the mediation, a mediator should acknowledge the risk to party self-determination and be wary of recommending a resolution, even when asked to do so.[112]

The final aspect of timing that mediators should consider is the timing and process for decision making once a mediator proposal has been tendered. It has been suggested that depending on the circumstances "parties should be given a reasonable period of time for determining its acceptability and delivering their confidential response to the mediator."[113]

7.5.4. Process

Once a mediator is clear that a mediator proposal is acceptable to all and a mediator feels comfortable that a proposal can be provided in an ethical manner, the mediator should emphasize his impartiality and clarify the process that will be followed.

The final phase of ethically providing a mediator proposal is to be clear with the parties as to the procedure for accepting or rejecting a proposal and protecting the confidentiality of the responses. As a practical matter, this means checking with parties before setting the deadline for responses so that both can come in at the same time.[114] To avoid subsequent legal issues, mediators should ensure there is clarity as to the binding and enforceable nature of the acceptance of the mediator proposal.

110. *See* Section 7.4.3, *supra*.

111. Eddy, *supra* note 29 ("It's important for a mediator to help the parties *exhaust* their own efforts at making proposals – especially in high conflict case. If they are going to make an agreement work and last, they have to have a sense of ownership in it.").

112. Lurie & Press, *supra* note 60.

113. Max, *supra* note 13.

114. Hochman, *supra* note 9, at 10.

Mediators are advised to include language to this effect and avoid including language that the acceptance is "subject to [fill in the blank]."[115]

7.6. Conclusion

Providing a mediator proposal is not inherently unethical; however, mediators should be cautious in employing this tactic to ensure that they do so consistent with the ethical standards for mediators. Special attention should be given to having the competence (knowledge, skills, and subject expertise) for providing a proposal; honoring party self-determination; maintaining confidence of caucus information; and ensuring mediator impartiality, quality of process, and integrity.

115. *See, e.g.*, *Facebook, Inc. v. ConnectU, Inc.*, No. C 07-01389 JW, 2008 WL 8820476, at *1 (N.D. Cal. June 25, 2008), *aff'd*, 640 F.3d 1034 (9th Cir. 2011). The mediated agreement provided that "the parties agree that they may execute more formal documents but these terms are binding and this document may be submitted into evidence to enforce this agreement." The parties failed to agree on the final deal documents. The district court determined that the settlement was enforceable and the Ninth Circuit affirmed, *Facebook, Inc. v. Pac. Nw. Software, Inc.*, 640 F.3d 1034 (9th Cir. 2011), but a great deal of time and expense ensued.

Chapter 8

Dealing with Difficult Parties

Bill Eddy

8.1. Introduction

Dealing with difficult parties in mediation is one of the most worrisome everyday topics for mediators, as well as a potential source for ethical complaints. Yet defining and assessing difficult parties are not easy. Unfortunately for most mediators, they may not see that they are dealing with a difficult party until they are fully engaged in the case. Then they realize it when difficult behavior occurs, often to their surprise, and they must decide how to proceed.

This chapter will address three questions:

1. How to ethically communicate? Whether or not the mediator takes the case, how one communicates with difficult clients from the first contact can be very important.
2. Whether to take the case or not, or whether to withdraw during the case? Based on mediator ethics, there are several reasons it may be necessary to turn down a case or withdraw because of concerns related to one or both parties' behavior or mental capacity.
3. What adaptations should be made to the process? If or when the parties are identified as difficult by a mediator, can adaptations be made so that it is a productive and ethical mediation?

8.2. Definition of Difficult Parties

While difficult clients are frequently discussed by mediators, lawyers, and even judges, there is little in the way of definitions based on statutes or case law. This term is raised primarily in the context of attorney discipline, in which the claim of having difficult clients is generally not a successful argument for a lawyer's inappropriate actions. As the North Dakota Supreme Court stated in *Disciplinary Board v. Kellington* (*In re Kellington*), when a lawyer's license was suspended for 30 days because of charging unreasonable fees: "[D]ifficult clients do not equate with difficult legal issues."[1] Likewise, in suspending a lawyer's license to practice for six months, the Colorado Supreme Court stated:

> Here, there is no question that Respondent's clients presented difficult practical and legal issues for him. His clients may very well have expected too much of him and were "difficult clients" as he testified. However, Respondent did not have to take their cases or continue to represent them if they failed to abide by the terms of his fee agreement by failing to pay him or failing to cooperate with him. Having failed to timely withdraw, Respondent had a duty to act professionally on behalf of these clients.[2]

Without defining difficult clients, other cases refer to them as a "fearful thing" (*Farnham v. State Bar*[3]), having "adamant directives" (*Schofield v. West Virginia Department of Corrections*[4]), often having "mental health issues and substance abuse issues" (*In re Wiederholt*[5]), and "suffer[ing] from a personality disorder that caused him to be rigid, hostile, lacking in trust, and making it difficult for him to compromise" (*In re Wiederholt*[6] in describing a "difficult" disbarred attorney).

Often, especially in family law, such parties are referred to as "high-conflict" parties or clients. "[H]igh conflict cases are those in which 'the parties simply can't resist the temptation to do anything and everything to subvert, attack, demean and literally try to destroy the child's relationship with the other parent'" (*Rosecky v. Schissel*[7]).

A more specific definition of high-conflict parties is the following:

1. Disciplinary Bd. v. Kellington (*In re* Kellington), 852 N.W.2d 395, 400 (2014).
2. People v. Walker, 135 P.3d 71, 81 (2005).
3. Farnham v. State Bar, 47 Cal. 3d 429, 444 (1988).
4. Schofield v. W. Va. Dep't of Corr., 185 W. Va. 199, 206 (1991).
5. *In re* Wiederholt, 182 P.3d 1047, 1058 (2008).
6. *Id.* at 1061.
7. Rosecky v. Schissel, 833 N.W.2d 634, 642 (Wis. 2013).

> High-conflict personalities stand out. Their emotions are often exaggerated. Their behavior is repeatedly inappropriate. Minor problems become major disputes. They persist long after others let go. There is an urgency and drama to their daily lives. And they always have someone to blame. . . . This preoccupation [with blame] drives them constantly into one dispute after another—and enables them to avoid ever looking at themselves or changing their own behavior.[8]

Taking all of these references to the characteristics of a difficult party and applying them to mediation, the following definition will be used in this chapter:

> A difficult party is someone who demonstrates some or all of the following in the mediation process: exaggerated emotions, adamant directives, attacking and demeaning behavior, difficulty compromising, a preoccupation with blaming others, repeated interruptions, bad-faith participation, mental-health issues, substance-abuse issues, and/or a personality disorder.

Yet this definition and those previous emphasize aggressive behaviors, which appear most often in the literature and tend to cause the most fear in mediators. There are also parties who are difficult because they have incapacities related to mental-health issues, such as dementia, depression, and other such passive disorders. Therefore, this chapter will address both aggressive and passive patterns of behavior.

Difficult parties raise a whole range of ethical considerations, from how mediators interact with these parties to whether they should use mediation with the parties and, if they do, how they should adapt their process. Mediators do not need to be mental-health professionals to recognize difficult clients and apply the concepts described in this chapter.

We start with a key tool for interacting with the parties respectfully throughout the process, including when mediators need to stop the mediation or not even take the mediation in the first place.

8.3. How to Ethically Communicate?

One of the most important issues from the start of communicating with potential clients in mediation is calming their emotions. From the first contact, be it by phone, by e-mail, or otherwise, all potential clients should be treated with empathy, positive attention, and respect.

8. Bill Eddy, High Conflict People in Legal Disputes 16 (2016).

When a party has mental-health problems, substance-abuse problems, or a personality disorder, upset emotions are a common problem. Yet, in and of themselves, upset emotions should not be a basis to reject a case or to become disrespectful toward a party. Their upset emotions are often associated with the fight-or-flight response to a feeling of threat, which may or may not be exaggerated. Brain scientists generally associate this fight-or-flight behavior with three key areas of the brain:

Amygdala: This part of the brain is in the limbic system in the middle of the brain below the cortex. As Robert Sapolsky, a stress research biologist, states: "It is central to mediating aggression . . . ."[9] It can quickly send chemical messages to the rest of the body to prepare for fight or flight. It plays a central role in feeling afraid and anxious, which can lead to aggression.[10] Thus, if you can reduce the feelings of fear and anxiety, you should be able to reduce the expression of aggression.

Vagus nerve and polyvagal theory: This cranial nerve is in the brainstem and is connected to the throat, neck, chest, and abdomen. It plays a role with the central nervous system, causing one to stop in one's tracks and shut down, or to flee or to fight. The polyvagal theory emphasizes the importance of the environment in creating a sense of safety for these defensive responses to relax and positive social engagement to occur.[11]

Mirror neurons: Discovered in the late 1990s by Italian brain researchers, mirror neurons are connected to our motor neurons and tend to make us mirror the specific behavior that we see others doing—good or bad. Of course, we do not do everything we see others doing, but we tend to add their behavior to our own repertoire of future behavioral choices.[12] Thus, we may be tempted as mediators to mirror our clients' behavior, when we should communicate in ways that we want them to mirror.

Using this understanding of the brain, the author's High Conflict Institute has developed a technique to use with difficult parties in mediation, or any upset party, as follows.

EAR statements: EAR statements involve giving one or both clients comments showing empathy, attention, and respect (EAR). They

9. Robert Sapolsky, Behave: The Biology of Humans at Our Best and Worst 31 (2017).

10. *Id.* at 34.

11. Steven Porges, The Pocket Guide to the Polyvagal Theory: The Transformative Power of Feeling Safe 30–31 (2017).

12. Marco Iacoboni, Mirroring People: The New Science of How We Connect with Others (2008).

are especially recommended when a party is emotionally upset and cannot seem to manage her own emotions, either because of the content of the dispute or because of her own emotional personality traits. This is a frequent issue with high-conflict people (HCPs), as this author described in 2008:

> With HCPs, you need to really *connect*. You need to make efforts to say or show your E.A.R.: "I *care* that you're upset about such-and-such, and I want to help you. I *respect* the efforts you've made to solve this problem." It's a *giving* process from you to the other person, to help create a connection. It's not just a neutral reflection back to the person, because that's not usually enough to help HCPs feel connected.[13]

Such a statement may be the opposite of what the mediator feels at the moment, because such clients are often blaming the mediator, attacking each other, and taking rigid, unproductive positions. Yet, because of the brain science described previously, such statements have had a calming effect on clients in many cultures according to many years of anecdotal feedback from mediators.

In terms of the brain, it appears that this type of statement may calm the fears of the amygdala, create a sense of safety for the vagus nerve, and have a calming influence when the client mirrors the mediator's sense of confidence and calm. Of course, this takes practice, but such EAR statements can be useful throughout the mediation process to help avoid the emotional escalation that occurs when a mediator criticizes a client or perhaps even just frowns at the statements a difficult client may make.

An ethical concern mediators might have in these instances is a fear of losing their impartiality or appearance of impartiality while connecting with the difficult party and showing him EAR. For example, the American Bar Association's Model Standards of Conduct for Mediators (2005) (Model Standards) state under Standard II, Impartiality, that

A. A mediator shall decline a mediation if the mediator cannot conduct it in an impartial manner. Impartiality means freedom from favoritism, bias or prejudice.
B. A mediator shall conduct a mediation in an impartial manner and avoid conduct that gives the appearance of partiality.

13. Bill Eddy, It's All Your Fault! 12 Tips for Managing People Who Blame Others for Everything 227 (2008).

However, any realistic approach to the mediator's role must recognize that mediation parties cannot always be treated the same. For example, the Model Standards state in Standard VI, Quality of the Process, that "[i]f a party appears to have difficulty comprehending the process, issues, or settlement options, **or difficulty participating in a mediation**, the mediator should explore the circumstances and potential accommodations, modifications or adjustments that would make possible the party's capacity to comprehend, participate and exercise self-determination."[14]

The mediator would therefore be justified in practicing EAR if treating the difficult party differently is required to enable him to participate meaningfully in the mediation. Of course, the mediator must stay mindful of his appearance of impartiality, and this would probably require him to consider showing EAR during separate rather than joint meetings or showing both parties some EAR, even if not the same amount.[15]

Another ethical aspect of EAR statements is an emphasis on respect, which is an expectation of all professionals in their interactions with clients. This is particularly important for mediators, who are providing a guided interpersonal process, not just a legal procedure.

For example, in the Model Standards, Standard VI, Quality of the Process, states:

> A. A mediator shall conduct a mediation in accordance with these Standards and in a manner that promotes diligence, timeliness, **safety**, presence of the appropriate participants, **party participation**, procedural fairness, party competency and **mutual respect** among all participants.[16]

To see a more detailed emphasis on the mediator respectfully interacting with the parties, *A Proposed Model Code of Conduct for Mediators*, proposed by Omer Shapira in his book *A Theory of Mediator's Ethics*, Section VII (pp. 397–411), is titled "Respect and Dignity" and includes the following as the first two terms:

---

14. Am. Bar Ass'n, Model Standards of Conduct for Mediators (2005) [hereinafter Model Standards], Standard VI.A.10 (emphasis added).

15. *See* Omer Shapira, *A Critical Assessment of the Model Standards of Conduct for Mediators (2005): Call for Reform*, 100 Marq. L. Rev. 81, 129–30 (2016) (discussing different treatment of parties under the Model Standards); Omer Shapira, A Theory of Mediators' Ethics: Foundations, Rationale, and Application 213–24 (2016) (discussing the ethics of different treatment in mediation).

16. Model Standards, *supra* note 14, Standard VI (emphasis added).

A. A mediator shall treat the parties, their representatives, co-mediators, and other participants with dignity and respect, and shall endeavor to conduct the mediation with patience and courtesy.
B. A mediator shall refrain in the exercise of his role from the use of abusive, discriminatory, humiliating, and profane language.[17]

Thus, EAR statements give the mediator a simple, but powerful, technique to implement the standards described previously. Mediators trained to use such an approach can often calm the parties by using EAR statements with each of them, so that they feel respected and able to remain in mediation even when hearing difficult comments or proposals from the other party. Without such strong efforts to calm the parties' upset emotions, mediations with difficult parties regularly fail, and they proceed to litigation, where their ability to have self-determination and other values of mediation is significantly curtailed.

The degree to which a mediator can handle her own emotions and her clients' upset emotions should play a major role in deciding whether or not to personally take a case. However, the parties should not be dissuaded from participating in mediation, even if they are difficult. If a mediator does not feel that she can handle a difficult case, a referral to another mediator with skills in working with such clients would be appropriate, if available.

8.4. Whether to Take the Case or Not, or Withdraw during the Case?

Mediation is a structured negotiation process, in which the parties participate in understanding the nature of their interests, negotiate around those interests, and evaluate the pros and cons of various solutions. This raises several ethical concerns, each of which could be the basis for not taking a case with difficult parties.

Where does one draw the line between a party who is merely obnoxious, aggressive, and narrow-minded and a party who lacks the ability to restrain himself, to respect the other party's concerns, and to understand the potential impact of various solutions discussed for his case? Different difficulties present different issues. The following are the most common issues potentially impacting **competence, self-determination, voluntariness, and undue influence.**

---

17. *See* Proposed Model Code of Conduct for Mediators in SHAPIRA, MEDIATORS' ETHICS, *supra* note 15, at 407 [hereinafter Proposed Model Code].

Personality disorders: A mediator does not need a mental-health background to decide whether or not to take or withdraw from a particular case. There is a range of difficulty involved. Generally, the disruptive, high-conflict parties tend to have personality disorders or lesser traits of such disorders. The current diagnostic manual for mental-health professionals (DSM-5) indicates that personality disorders are characterized by an "enduring pattern of inner experience and behavior" that causes internal distress and/or social impairment.[18] Personality disorders affect approximately 15 percent of the adult population in the United States according to the DSM-5.[19] The ten personality disorders are grouped by three clusters. The four personalities included in Cluster B are antisocial, narcissistic, borderline, and histrionic. This cluster is generally considered "dramatic, emotional, or erratic,"[20] in other words interpersonally difficult or high conflict.

Yet the difficulties of clients with such disorders are not due to a lack of intelligence (they have the full range of the general population), an inability to know right from wrong, or occupational incapacity. They can be successful surgeons, politicians, actors, lawyers, and any other occupation. Their problems arise from interpersonal "cognitive errors," which primarily include feeling victimized by others and not seeing the connection of their own behavior to their own life circumstances or how others treat them.[21] This helps explain their blaming behavior and resistance to change, because they appear to truly believe their problems are other people's fault.

In other words, they are not lacking in competence, but rather misunderstanding their own responsibility in conflicts and, at least those high-conflict ones in Cluster B, having a preoccupation with aggressively blaming others. Thus, they are considered by many experienced legal professionals to have a significant presence in all legal disputes, especially prolonged cases that end up in trials rather than settling.[22]

Those with these Cluster B personality disorders tend to see the world through an adversarial lens and are often driven to have power and control over others, to distort ordinary information, to act in bad faith, to

18. Am. Psychiatric Ass'n, Diagnostic & Stat. Manual of Mental Disorders 646 (5th ed. 2013) [hereinafter DSM-5].

19. *Id.*

20. *Id.*

21. Aaron T. Beck et al., Cognitive Therapy of Personality Disorders 4 (2nd ed. 2004).

22. Eddy, *supra* note 8, at 12.

manipulate others, and to lie frequently.[23] Perhaps the most difficult in terms of truthfulness and cooperation are those with antisocial personality disorder, because it is specifically identified by its characteristics of violating the law and social norms, deceit (lying, conning), aggressiveness, recklessness, and lack of remorse.[24]

With this in mind, it may appear that they would not be good candidates for mediation, but they can be even more inappropriate for litigation, as they tend to drive up costs, manipulate procedures, avoid their responsibilities, submit false information, and often not follow court orders. It appears that it would be good to find a way to work with such difficult parties in mediation so that they can stay out of prolonged litigation, for their own emotional benefit as well as to reduce the cost of litigation for society. These cases should be seriously considered for mediation, but possibly with adaptations to the process, such as described in Section 8.6.

However, people with the other six personality disorders in Clusters A and C may be difficult as well, not because they are highly aggressive or dramatic, but because they may be more passive in their sense of being other people's victims, as the following case suggests, raising questions of competency, self-determination, and undue influence. In this case, a former wife, Anna Kieturakis, unsuccessfully sought to overturn a marital settlement agreement (MSA) negotiated in divorce mediation:

> Psychiatrist James Missett testified for Anna that she had a psychological profile consistent with her claims in the case. She suffered from a long-standing depression and had a "**dependent personality disorder** of the passive type." She had **low self-esteem**, exhibited symptoms of **psychological abuse**, and would have been unable to negotiate with Maciej. Missett acknowledged that Anna was **intelligent**, and that people with her psychological profile could **function well** in society. He admitted that Anna was capable of doing things that upset Maciej while the MSA was being negotiated, and that she might have known what she was doing during the mediation.[25]

This case demonstrates the difficulty of determining whether a mediation party is impaired and unable to negotiate or competent and knows what she was doing. This is a common dilemma with personality

23. Charles V. Ford, Lies! Lies! Lies! The Psychology of Deceit (1996).

24. DSM-5, *supra* note 18, at 659.

25. *In re* Marriage of Kieturakis, 138 Cal. App. 4th 56, 73 (2006) (emphasis added).

disorders. The court found that she had competently negotiated a valid agreement and was not under undue influence.

However, the ethical practitioner cannot always wait for a court's decision. She must respond to the situation here and now. Moreover, the ethical practitioner realizes that ethical concepts of party incompetency, coercion, and voluntariness are not equivalent to the legal definitions of these terms.[26] Ethical concepts consider legal determinations as setting minimum thresholds and then go on to consider context and apply a realistic, substantive approach that is more flexible than the legalistic, more technical, and formal approach of the law.[27] For example, an ethical approach to incompetency and coercion does not regard these states as clear-cut. It recognizes that incapacity and voluntariness fluctuate on a continuum ranging from low to high and change in accordance with a variety of factors including the type of information processed or decision made, use of alcohol or drugs, mental illness, age, and pressures that undermine choice.[28]

Therefore, a mediator who feels that a party has difficulty in perceiving information, processing it, and understanding the information and its implications must take steps to assist that party to exercise self-determination, whether that party is legally incompetent or not. Similarly, a mediator who suspects that a party—like Anna—is about to make a decision out of feelings of helplessness and lack of choice as a result of pressures of mediation participants or nonparticipants should discuss it with that party.[29] To support party self-determination, mediators must repeatedly emphasize to the parties—especially those with possible personality disorders—that their agreements are voluntary at every step of the process. "It's up to you" is a good refrain to counter the frequent tendency of those with personality disorders to try to shift blame for their own decisions and behavior to the other party or the mediator. The mediator should also consider postponing the mediation or involving a representative of the party in the process to support the party's exercise of self-determination.[30]

---

26. *See* Nancy A. Welsh, *The Thinning Vision of Self-Determination in Court-Connected Mediation: The Inevitable Price of Institutionalization?*, 6 Harv. Negot. L. Rev. 1, 59–74 (2001) (discussing the legal concept of coercion in the courts and the ethical concept of self-determination in mediation).

27. *See* Shapira, Mediators' Ethics, *supra* note 15, at 27–31.

28. *Id.* at 138–42.

29. Proposed Model Code, *supra* note 17, Standard IV.E (Voluntariness).

30. *Id.* Standard IV.D (Party Competency).

Dementia: Dementia is listed under neurocognitive disorders (NCDs) in the DSM-5. These include Alzheimer's disease, Parkinson's disease, traumatic brain injury, substance-induced neurocognitive problems, and others. However, the term "dementia" can still be used for this category. There is a range of severity of these disorders, from mild to major symptoms, which may include difficulty maintaining attention, planning and making decisions, comprehending concepts, sticking to tasks, coping with multiple stimuli, remembering recent events, doing previously familiar tasks, and abiding by social standards.[31]

Given the importance in mediation of staying focused on discussions and tasks, accurately remembering past events, planning for the future, and following agreements and social standards, people with neurocognitive disorders do not make good candidates for mediation on their own. However, if the symptoms are mild, if they have the assistance of counsel, and if the mediator can structure the mediation to accommodate their needs, some of these cases may be able to be mediated.

> *In a divorce mediation, the retired husband had been a competent and successful bank vice president. While he smiled and nodded during the first mediation session, the mediator did wonder if he was sufficiently understanding and decided to raise this issue at the second session, so as not to put a damper on their initial discussions, which appeared realistic, fair, and fruitful. The husband participated but appeared to be processing slowly. Both he and his wife were eager to proceed and scheduled a second session. At the second session, the husband appeared with an attorney by his side. His wife agreed that this was a good idea. However, the attorney was sharply critical of the mediator for not immediately recognizing the need for the husband to have a lawyer present and requiring this for the second session. During this session, the lawyer remained critical of the mediator and persuaded the husband to cease mediation and have the lawyer negotiate with the wife and/or the wife's lawyer directly.*

This case raises several ethical questions: Should the mediator have raised this issue earlier and required that a lawyer appear with the husband at the second session? Should the mediator have required an assessment for competency before proceeding? Was the husband better off with the lawyer or the mediator? Should the mediator have given the husband a list of mediation-friendly lawyers to consult with, who would have

31. DSM-5, *supra* note 18, at 591–95.

supported continuing in mediation? Is the vulnerable party sufficiently protected if the mediator requires the parties to have attorneys review the final agreement at the end of the process before it is signed?

The ethical standards of mediation enable us to come up with some answers. No, the mediator did not have an ethical obligation to require that a lawyer appear with the husband at the second session or that the husband take an assessment for competency before proceeding. Clearly, the mediator had some concerns about the capacity of the husband to make decisions, and he correctly decided to explore this issue in accordance with his duty to conduct the mediation on the basis of party self-determination. However, as states of incapacity are varying in degree, the previous scenario did not create a clear impression of inability to process information and make decisions that would have required the mediator to insist on legal representation or competency assessment. Moreover, making such a suggestion at that point in time might have alienated the husband and undermined his confidence in the mediator's impartiality. If the husband had come to the second session unaccompanied, the mediator would have had another opportunity to listen to the husband and get a better sense of his level of understanding and his needs for support. In addition, during that session the mediator would have been able to steer the conversation to enable the husband and wife to consider for themselves whether they would feel more comfortable if they were supported throughout the process by friends or professionals, and it is quite possible that the option of legal representation or other supporting professionals or individuals would have been raised. As practice tells us, some lawyers have a positive view of mediation, while others are more cautious. Accordingly, lawyers may be very helpful in moving the mediation forward and supportive of their clients in the mediation, while others may play a disruptive role. The scenario does not tell us much about the lawyer's previous experience with mediation, and notwithstanding his decision to discontinue the mediation, the mediator's conduct was ethically sound. Of course, should the mediator realize in the second meeting that the husband had in fact difficulties in comprehending and participating in the process, he should have postponed the mediation or involved a representative of the husband in the process. The mediator could have provided the husband with a list of mediation-friendly lawyers to consult with but must have given the list to the wife as well in order to comply with the standard of impartiality and avoid favoritism and an appearance of partiality. If the husband and wife were to decide not to involve lawyers in the process, and the mediator was convinced that the decision had been an informed one, he could have proceeded without the presence of lawyers and be satisfied with the parties having attorneys review the final agreement at the end of the process.

Other mental-health issues: Depression, anxiety, bipolar disorder, schizophrenia, and other mental disorders could all cause a mediation party to be difficult and/or lacking in competence to proceed in mediation. However, the presence of a mental disorder does not create a bright-line demarcation between difficult or not and between competent or not. People with mental disorders show impairments that range from very mild (such as temporary depression or anxiety) to very severe (the person cannot even hold a job).

Even bipolar disorder and schizophrenia—considered more biologically based disorders—do not automatically prevent people from working, having meaningful relationships, and negotiating fair agreements, especially if they take appropriate medications. Yet some people with these disorders are barely able to function in society, including people who end up homeless because of their disordered thinking and behavior.

Substance abuse: The DSM-5 lists many substance-use disorders, including those involving alcohol, prescription medications, and illegal drugs. However, this is another gray area with "a broad range of severity."[32] The following example demonstrates how one case was handled:

> *The parties were business partners who owned two taverns and were dissolving their partnership. They appeared appropriate and businesslike for their first mediation session. When they arrived at their second mediation session in the afternoon, one party had obviously been drinking a lot based on the strong smell of alcohol on his breath. He stated that he would prefer to lie down on the floor during the mediation but that he could hear and make rational decisions. The mediator suggested to the parties that this would be a very unusual arrangement and that they would be better off to reschedule the mediation. (They would sacrifice the cost of the first hour, as the mediator's well-known policy for last-minute cancellations, but not any additional time.) The second party stated that she wanted to proceed as well and that this was typical for the first party and might be the same situation next time. With this input from the second party, the mediator decided to proceed, with a watchful eye for any unusual or heavily unbalanced terms of agreement. The parties reached a full and fairly normal business termination agreement,*

32. *Id.* at 484.

which the mediator agreed to write up for signing after they had a reasonable time to look it over and opportunity for attorney review. Several days later, they both signed (in the morning), and both expressed appreciation for the mediator's work with them.

This case raises several ethical issues. Was the first party competent? Both parties thought so, but the mediator told them, as always, that no agreement would be signed and finalized that same day. This would allow them both time to soberly consider their terms of agreement. The mediator was also watchful for unusual or heavily imbalanced terms, in which case she would not have agreed to write it up and would have withdrawn from the mediation.

Was this an appropriate decision for the mediator to make? Would it have been better for the mediator to have refused to proceed while the first party was lying on the floor smelling of alcohol? Yet would that have denied them self-determination, since they both wanted to proceed? Does it matter that the mediator had already met with them once before in a normal and productive session, which may have influenced her decision to proceed? The mediator certainly stretched the boundaries of her professional discretion in deciding to proceed with the mediation in those circumstances. The right of parties to exercise self-determination may legitimately be balanced and sometimes must be restricted, where the quality of the process and the integrity of mediation are at stake.[33] The mediator was obviously impressed by the ability of the intoxicated party to effectively participate and make rational choices during the meeting. Moreover, she took great care to ensure that both parties had an opportunity to review the terms of the nonbinding draft agreement they had negotiated and amend them before committing to the final agreement. Taken together, these precautions met the demands of the ethical values of party self-determination, quality process, and integrity.

Violence and abuse: One of the most troubling questions in regard to difficult parties is whether someone who previously engaged in violent or otherwise abusive behavior should be allowed to use the mediation process. Mediators are divided on this issue, and much has been written about it in the literature over the past several decades, especially in regard to domestic violence between intimate partners.

33. Model Standards, *supra* note 14, Standard I.A.1; Standards of Conduct for N.Y. St. Cmty. Disp. Resol. Ctr. Mediators, Standard I cmts. 1, 2 (rev. 2009), http://ww2.nycourts.gov/sites/default/files/document/files/2018-07/Standards_of_Conduct.pdf; Shapira, Mediators' Ethics, *supra* note 15, at 135–37.

While mediations involving business partners, employees, customers, managers, and others occasionally make mention of a violent incident, most appellate cases address the issue of violence in domestic relations mediation. Furthermore, most states have developed required procedures that mediators must follow in screening cases for domestic violence before and during the mediation, if they go forward with it.

For example, the state of Michigan has the following Court Rule 3.216 (H)(2) for Domestic Relations Mediation:

> The mediator must make reasonable inquiry as to whether either party has a history of a coercive or violent relationship with the other party. Throughout the mediation process, the mediator must make reasonable efforts to screen for the presence of coercion or violence that would make mediation physically or emotionally unsafe for any participant or that would impede achieving a voluntary and safe resolution of issues. A reasonable inquiry includes the use of the domestic violence screening protocol for mediators provided by the state court administrative office as directed by the supreme court.[34]

A Michigan court of appeals analyzed the application of this rule to a claim by a party that she was under duress during her property mediation, so that it should be set aside. Jody Pohlman stated that she suffered from a "mental vulnerability and affliction" and that the mediator did not conduct a premediation screening process, which she believed was required by the previous court rule. However, the court looked at the fact that the mediation was done using "shuttle diplomacy" with the parties in separate rooms and that she was represented by counsel. The court stated:

> The Supreme Court Administrative Office (SCAO)'s Standards of Conduct for Mediators do not specify any particular manner for handling mediation when domestic violence or control exists. However, the SCAO's Model Screening Protocol for domestic-relations mediation when domestic violence or control exists contains a number of suggestions for keeping parties safe, accommodated, and capable of negotiating and making decisions free from fear or coercion. It appears that the mediator took proper care to ensure that the mediation was free from coercion.
>
> Plaintiff's allegations that she was not allowed to leave,

34. Mich. Ct. Rule 3.216 (H)(2) for Domestic Relations Mediation.

> and was pressured to sign the settlement terms agreement by her attorney and the mediator, do not demonstrate the coercion necessary to set aside an agreement based upon duress.[35]

However, a dissenting justice saw it differently and emphasized that the mediator must make a reasonable inquiry "at the beginning, middle and end of the process," rather than simply providing a good process free from coercion during the mediation. History matters according to this justice.

> In a marriage plagued by domestic violence, the victim may be unable to assert her or his needs, or may be particularly susceptible to controlling or coercive tactics. The mediator must be sensitive to that dynamic, because mediation tainted with the emotional residue of domestic violence is inherently imbalanced.[36]

If appellate court justices cannot even agree on how a mediator should assess voluntariness and duress, it makes clear how difficult it is for a mediator to determine whether to proceed and which parties will be difficult or even dangerous. Still, the restrictive legal test for voluntariness and duress for the purpose of determining the legal validity of a mediated agreement should not be taken as a sole guide for the ethical mediator. A mediator is expected to hold a quality process based on party self-determination, which requires more than merely satisfying the law on the annulment of contracts.[37]

This case raises several ethical questions: Should the mediator have taken the case at all? Once the parties are physically living apart, are all future negotiations still inherently imbalanced? Did the plaintiff's lawyer and the mediator truly pressure her to sign, or was that a misperception on her part? Who decides whose perception is accurate and whose is not? What happens if an intimidated party denies that there is a history of abuse, out of fear? How is the mediator to know?

It is helpful to know that there are model protocols that family mediators can use to help in answering these questions. Training and experience are particularly important in this difficult area, now that court systems are encouraging mediation in most family law cases.

It is hard to ethically evaluate the conduct of the mediator in the Pohlman case because ethical evaluations must be based on a clear set

35. Pohlman v. Pohlman, 2020 Mich. App. LEXIS 798, 2020 WL 504775, at 11–12.

36. *Id.*

37. *See supra* notes 27–29 and accompanying text.

of facts, yet we do not know what in fact happened at the mediation between the mediator, the plaintiff's lawyer, and the plaintiff. Obviously, a mere perception, however genuine, of mediator pressure by mediation parties cannot constitute an ethical wrong on the part of mediators. A party might be oversensitive or simply wrong in his perception of the mediator's conduct. However, this case does tell us how important it is that mediators reflect on their conduct in real time and remain attentive to the impacts of their interventions on the parties' ability to exercise choice. Furthermore, it cannot be ruled out that the mediator did pressure the plaintiff to settle, as mediators sometimes do,[38] but the degree of pressure did not meet the legal definition of coercion applied by the courts.[39] If that is the case, the mediator might have very well violated his ethical duty to respect Jody's self-determination and to avoid pressuring her to settle. The North Carolina Standards, for example, provide that "[a] mediator shall not exert undue pressure on a participant . . . to accept a settlement."[40] The Florida Rules provide that "[a] mediator shall not coerce or improperly influence any party to make a decision";[41] and the Proposed Model Code provides that "[a] mediator shall not exert pressure designed to reduce party choice in decision-making."[42] Therefore, the ethical mediator should refrain from exerting pressure on parties to settle even where the pressure does not amount to legal coercion.

In short, a mediator should seriously consider whether she has the knowledge, experience, and skill to take a case with the warning signs of a difficult party, based on a mental disorder, high-conflict personality, substance abuse, or violence. However, all mediators should recognize that there may be no warning signs in advance that a party will turn out to be difficult. Thus, they should be prepared to stop, transfer the case to another qualified mediator, or adapt the mediation process at any time throughout the case.

---

38. *See* Omer Shapira, *Joining Forces in Search for Answers: The Use of Therapeutic Jurisprudence in the Realm of Mediation Ethics*, 8 Pepp. Disp. Resol. L.J. 243, 260–61 (2008).

39. *See supra* note 26.

40. N.C. Rev. Standards of Prof'l Conduct for Mediators, Standard 4(b) (2020),https://www.nccourts.gov/courts/supreme-court/court-rules/standards-of-professional-conduct-for-mediators.

41. Fla. Rules for Certified & Ct.-Appointed Mediators, R. 10.310(b) (Mar. 2018), https://www.flcourts.org/content/download/216759/file/rules-certified-court-appointed-mediators.pdf.

42. Proposed Model Code, *supra* note 17, Standard IV.E.1.

8.5. What Adaptations Should Be Made to the Process?

As mentioned throughout this chapter, there are many ways that a mediation can be conducted that may provide a safer, more patient, and more balanced process when difficult parties may be involved. These can help the mediator manage aggressive behavior by difficult parties, as well as facilitate a voluntary process for passive parties and ones with questionable competence. The following is based on the experience of the author and colleagues with the High Conflict Institute with divorcing families, business disputes, workplace conflicts, and personal injury disputes.

Requiring the presence of lawyers: Many mediations today are conducted with self-representing parties. Some parties have lawyers with whom they merely consult, and others have lawyers who represent them but do not attend the mediation sessions to save money for the client and time for the attorney. If a mediator believes that the parties could benefit from mediation but have competence or safety issues, he should require that lawyers be physically present. The plaintiff had a lawyer in the Pohlman mediation in Michigan discussed previously, which was a key factor in the court's decision to uphold the signed settlement agreement.

Shuttle diplomacy: A substantial number of civil disputes are mediated with the parties in separate rooms and the mediator going back and forth. This helps the mediator manage difficult parties because she can deal with the parties one at a time and does not need to manage their face-to-face interactions. This was another reason that the family mediation in the Pohlman case was considered by the court to be safe and free from fear and coercion—during the mediation. Of course, this does not guarantee safety afterward, which is why a mediator might decide not to take a case at all or withdraw later on.

Premediation screening: Some mediators prefer to meet with each party before meeting with them together. This allows an opportunity to assess whether the mediator should take the case. This also may assist the mediator in designing the process to meet the needs of both parties if there are questions of competence and inappropriately aggressive behavior. This also offers an opportunity to form a stronger relationship with each party individually, to build trust and understanding that will help throughout the mediation process.

Parties arrive separately: In cases of parties representing themselves, some safety concerns and emotion management concerns can be addressed by having the parties arrive 15 to 30 minutes apart. This way, they avoid opportunities to bully each other during the stressful times they are going through. If one has been found to be too aggressive (such as in cases where there is a protective order that allows mediation), that person can be required to arrive first and leave last, so that the protected person is not vulnerable to being alone with the aggressive person.

Allow a support person: In some mediations, a party with a mental-health issue, such as bipolar disorder, can be asked if he wishes to bring a support person who could assist the party in making thoughtful decisions. This has been helpful in several mediation cases but requires the consent of the other party to be successful.

Assess for extreme language: Mediators and lawyers should pay attention to the written and spoken language that the parties use prior to a mediation.

> *Prior to a business mediation between a subcontractor and the CEO of a business he had done work for, the subcontractor swore at and wrote threatening letters to the lawyer for the CEO. He said he would go after him "with every fiber in my being" because he believed he was part of a conspiracy to defraud him. The mediation was held at a mediator's office. At the end of the mediation, which did not reach an agreement, the subcontractor pulled out a gun and shot the CEO and the lawyer for the CEO. They both died. The mediator was unharmed. A day later, the subcontractor shot and killed himself.*[43]

One way to assess for the extreme language that is often displayed by those with high-conflict personalities is the *WEB Method*®: Pay attention to their Words, your Emotions, and their Behavior. If a mediator reads or hears extreme "all-or-nothing" words, feels extreme emotions, or is aware of a client's extreme negative behavior that 90 percent of people would never do, then the mediator and/or the other client(s) are likely to be dealing with a high-conflict person and the possible risks of being blamed and attacked, verbally and/or physically.[44]

In the above case, there were indications of all of these extremes. The lawyer knew there was a pattern of extreme behavior but apparently did not realize the level of danger. The only way that it would have been safe to proceed with this mediation would have been to hold it at a courthouse or law office with a metal detector. When someone repeats threatening

---

43. Bill Eddy, 5 Types of People Who Can Ruin Your Life 16–17 (2018) (citing facts provided by Michael Muskal, *Phoenix Lawyer Shot after Mediation Session Dies*, L.A. Times, Feb. 1, 2013).

44. *Id.* at 21–23.

language, it should always be taken seriously and the mediation process adapted or not held at all.

Focus on proposals: People with personality disorders tend to be preoccupied with defending their past actions and criticizing the past actions of others. One way to avoid the escalation of this type of behavior is to keep the mediation focused on the future and what to do now, rather than who-did-what-when-and-why, which rarely succeeds with high-conflict people. This doesn't totally exclude discussion of the past, which may be necessary, but it puts the emphasis on the future. This tends to minimize defensiveness and maximize investment in problem solving and following through on agreements. Most, if not all, people with mental-health problems tend to be relieved by this reduction of stress and vulnerability.

Structuring the mediation process around proposals also helps the mediator to be less stressed and more effective at managing high-conflict or otherwise emotional parties. Simple, but structured, appears to be the most successful approach, whatever style of mediation the mediator may prefer to use.

8.6. Conclusion

Difficult clients raise challenging issues regarding client competence, self-determination, voluntariness, mediator impartiality, quality process, and integrity, all of which are essential to the mediation process.[45]

Difficult clients are not a clear-cut category when it comes to mediation. Mediators must consider how they communicate with potential difficult clients, in order to calm them in a respectful, ethical fashion. It is easy to be critical of them, but that does not help them, the mediator, or the public's respect for the mediation process. Statements that provide empathy, attention, and respect tend to calm the upset brains of potentially difficult parties or anyone in an ethical way, even when a party is told that she is not a good fit for a particular mediator or possibly the mediation process with any mediator.

The decision of whether to take a case with one or more difficult clients is necessarily a difficult one. While mediation grows in use as a realistic alternative to litigation, it is not for everyone. Potentially difficult clients include those with personality disorders, depression, anxiety, dementia, bipolar disorder, schizophrenia, substance abuse, and domestic violence or abuse. Many of these are commonly known as high-conflict

45. Model Standards, *supra* note 14; Shapira, Mediators' Ethics, *supra* note 15, at 114–15; Proposed Model Code, *supra* note 17.

clients, because they tend to be preoccupied with blaming others. Yet none of these conditions is a clear-cut basis for denying a party the services of a mediator. The severity of the person's problems needs to be assessed, as well as the training, experience, and skill of the particular mediator who is considering taking the case. It is important to remember that a mediator should not determine that a client is not appropriate for mediation, but rather for that particular mediator. A referral to a qualified mediator with skills in working with a particular type of difficult party would be preferred, although that is not always an option.

Lastly, adaptations may enable a mediator to provide a safe, voluntary, and balanced mediation process despite one or more clients having indications of difficulty. These adaptations can assist in managing the behavior of difficult parties who are aggressive as well as those who are passive or may have questionable competence. As more mediators receive training and experience and gain skill in ethically handling difficult clients, almost all people and society will benefit.

Chapter 9

Lawyer Representation in Mediation

Jacqueline Nolan-Haley

9.1. Introduction

There is little doubt that the alternative dispute resolution (ADR) movement, and mediation in particular, is gradually transforming the practice of law. However, insufficient attention has been paid to the normative questions of how that transformation should take place. The role of the lawyer who represents a client in mediation is understudied compared to the role of the lawyer acting as a mediator,[1] and while volumes of articles and books are devoted to exploring the lawyer mediator's role as a third-party neutral in mediation, less attention has been paid to the role of the representational lawyer.[2] This chapter seeks to fill that void and provide the representational lawyer with ethical guidelines for mediation practice

1. It should be noted that apart from direct representation in mediation, lawyers may be involved in more limited functions such as reviewing mediated agreements, sideline coaching, or preparing final settlement documents. The client's written consent is necessary in these arrangements, and states vary in the formalities that are required. Analysis of limited-scope representation in mediation is beyond the scope of this chapter. *See* SARA COLE ET AL., MEDIATION: LAW, POLICY & PRACTICE 757–58 (2018–2019 ed.).

2. Some notable recent exceptions include John A. Sherrill, *Ethics for Lawyers Representing Clients in Mediation*, 6 AM. J. MEDIATION (2012); HAROLD I. ABRAMSON, MEDIATION REPRESENTATION: ADVOCATING AS A PROBLEM-SOLVER 2 (3d ed. 2013). Older publications include JOHN W. COOLEY, MEDIATION ADVOCACY (2d ed. 2002); ERIC GALTON & KIMBERLEE K. KOVACH, REPRESENTING CLIENTS IN MEDIATION (Diane Burch Beckham ed., 1994).

that are grounded in rules, standards, case law, statutes, and mediation ethics advisory opinions. How should lawyers behave? What rules should govern their behavior? Much needs to be done if representational mediation practice is to be distinguished from adversarial-style lawyering so that it may truly respond to clients' goals and underlying interests, and that is what really matters in mediation.

The standard conception of the lawyer's traditional role has been characterized by scholars as one that honors partisanship and nonaccountability. Translated into practice, this has meant zealous advocacy with little moral responsibility for helping clients achieve their goals. Existing models for lawyers who represent clients in mediation are based largely on the dominant ethic of the zealous advocate, and this raises a question of fit. What does zealous advocacy require in mediation? Is the traditional zealous advocate, sometimes "hired gun," model[3] of the adversarial system consistent with the primary participatory and dignitary values of mediation? The short answer is no. Representational lawyering in mediation is different from adversarial-style lawyering, and it should be grounded in a deliberative and problem-solving process. As noted wisely by Professor Harold Abramson, the zealous advocate should be replaced by the zealous problem solver.[4]

The transition to zealous problem solving has not been a smooth one for the legal profession. In many cases, lawyer-controlled mediation still has the appearance of a muscle settlement conference, and negotiation in mediation resembles aggressive trial advocacy. Meanwhile, many clients are kept in the dark. The problem is largely a conceptual one. Many lawyers lack an authentic understanding of the mediation process, the premises and values that drive it, and the creative outcomes that are possible. As a result, when engaging with clients in representational mediation practice, too many lawyers are pouring new wine into old wineskins. This explains why human dignity, mutuality of respect, and responsible client decision making, values that have been absent from much of traditional adversarial practice, are frequently missing in representational mediation practice.

Mediation is a client's process, and a conceptual understanding of the mediation process as a client's process based on informed consent is essential in developing and sustaining an ethical theory of representational mediation practice.

---

3. *See* Joseph Allegretti, *Have Briefcase Will Travel: An Essay on the Lawyer as Hired Gun*, 24 Creighton L. Rev. 747 (1991).

4. *See* Abramson, *supra* note 2.

The first part of the chapter (Section 9.2) argues that lawyer representation in mediation should be deliberative and based on client informed consent. The second part (Section 9.3) reviews the ethical duties of lawyers representing parties in mediation, both prior to and during the mediation. The last part (Section 9.4) focuses on the responsibilities of the lawyer mediator who believes that a representational lawyer in mediation is engaged in unethical behavior or serious misconduct.

9.2. Client Counseling and Representation in Mediation: A Deliberative Model Based on the Principle of Informed Consent

Client counseling is a critical component of representational mediation practice. Too often, lawyers' involvement in mediation is not preceded by any meaningful deliberation with clients. Some lawyers do not listen to their clients but presume to know their goals and then dictate what should occur in mediation. Unfortunately, this behavior has the potential to sabotage the mediation process. Instead, the ethical responsibilities of attorneys who represent parties in mediation should be grounded in what I have described as a "deliberative model" of client counseling based on informed consent.[5]

Informed consent is an ethical, moral, and legal concept that is deeply ingrained in American culture. Where informed consent is required, the legal doctrine requires that individuals who give consent be competent, be informed about the particular intervention, and consent voluntarily.

The principle of informed consent in the lawyer-client relationship is formally rooted in the professional responsibility rules of the legal profession and is explicitly defined in Model Rule 1.0(e). Model Rule 1.4(b) requires that lawyers "explain a matter to the extent reasonably necessary to permit the client to make informed decisions regarding the representation." Model Rule 1.4(a)(2) requires that a lawyer "reasonably consult with the client about the means by which the client's objectives are to be accomplished." And Model Rule 1.2(a) provides that a lawyer must abide by a client's decision about whether or not to settle. In general, the principle of informed consent in the lawyer-client relationship requires that clients be educated about their choices and that they participate in decision making. Deliberation is a necessary precondition to client decision

5. For a description of this model, see Jacqueline Nolan-Haley, *Lawyers, Clients and Mediation*, 73 Notre Dame L. Rev. 1369, 1383–88 (1998). The sections on client counseling in this chapter are largely drawn from this article.

making, both in the mediation counseling relationship and during the mediation process.[6]

9.2.1. Deliberation

Deliberation is a process of careful calculation and reasoned dialogue. It is a method of discourse in which individuals debate the merits of particular activities. Deliberation is a reflective activity, requiring active participant engagement. Deliberation in mediation client counseling and representation does not just happen; there are a series of first information events that precede it. These include lawyers' understanding of their clients' perspective and goals and clients' understanding of what will occur in counseling as well as a general understanding of relevant law.

9.2.2. Preconditions for Deliberation

The first precondition for deliberation is that lawyers understand their clients' perspective—the facts as well as the clients' emotional state. This ability has been recognized in the litigation context as possibly "an ethically required practice skill."[7] As a general matter, the content of attorney-client deliberation takes into account the totality of the clients' circumstances and may include the cultural, economic, social, psychological, moral, political, and religious consequences of actions.

Second, lawyers must attempt to understand and not presume to know their clients' initial goals. Even though clients' goals may change during deliberation, lawyers must be respectful of client preferences from the beginning of the counseling relationship.

Third, lawyers should ensure that clients have a general understanding of what will occur in the counseling interaction. Clients should be informed that the counseling will be based on informed decision making, both in the attorney-client relationship and in the mediation process. They should be advised of the roles that both attorney and client will have in this relationship. Clients must also be educated about the mediation process and understand its essential differences from litigation.

Finally, clients should have a general knowledge about the relevant law governing their case, so that during deliberation they may meaningfully evaluate alternative courses of action and give informed consent, not only to their participation in mediation, but also to any agreement that is reached in mediation.

6. *Id.* at 1381–82.

7. *Id.* at 1383 (quoting Joan L. O'Sullivan et al., *Ethical Decisionmaking and Ethics Instruction in Clinical Law Practice*, 3 Clinical L. Rev. 109, 133 (1996)).

9.2.3. Foundation of Trust

Deliberation brings lawyers and clients together, fostering mutual respect and trust. Clients must be able to trust lawyers to guide them through decision making; clients qua disputants must be able to trust the mediator to guide them in decision making. Trust is an understudied element in mediation.

9.2.4. Informed Consent in the Context of Mediation

Lawyers must appreciate the special role that the principle of informed consent plays in mediation practice, where it functions as a means of exercising self-determination and achieving the fundamental goal of fairness. Fairness requires at least three levels of knowledge. Parties should know what they are doing when they participate in mediation. They should understand all aspects of the decision-making process, including their right to withdraw consent and discontinue negotiations. Finally, they should understand the outcome reached in mediation. Toward this end, the principle of informed consent in mediation protects the psychological and legal interests associated with the values of autonomy, human dignity, and efficiency.[8]

9.3. Legal and Ethical Duties of Representational Lawyers in Mediation

Lawyers' professional conduct is governed by the Model Rules of Professional Conduct of the jurisdiction in which they are licensed. The rules in all U.S. states are based on the ABA Model Rules of Professional Conduct, which do not specifically address the role of the representational lawyer in mediation. Nevertheless, representational lawyering in mediation encompasses the functions that lawyers perform generally for clients: counseling, negotiation, evaluation, and advocacy. As a general matter, therefore, the rules governing lawyer representation of parties in negotiation also apply in mediation.

These rules include the duties to provide competent representation, to avoid conflicts of interest in representing parties, to inform clients of ADR options, to keep clients informed about their case, to exercise candor toward the mediator and refrain from engaging in any material misrepresentation, to participate in good faith, to protect confidentiality, and to avoid the unauthorized practice of law. These responsibilities can be

8. *Id.* at 788.

divided into those that arise prior to the mediation and those duties that arise during and after the mediation.

9.3.1. Lawyers' Ethical Duties Prior to Mediation

9.3.1.1. Competence: Duty to Provide Competent Representation

According to Model Rule 1.1, lawyers have a duty to "provide competent representation to a client. Competent representation requires the legal knowledge, skill, thoroughness and preparation reasonably necessary for the representation." Competent representation in mediation requires specific knowledge and skill with which the lawyer might be unfamiliar. To provide adequate representation at the premediation stage, the lawyer has to consider the agreement to mediate, prepare the client for mediation, select the appropriate mediator, prepare premediation submissions, and decide upon a course of bargaining behavior. In the case of online mediation, lawyers must also be prepared to engage with new technologies and to navigate the ethical issues that arise.

9.3.1.1.1. Agreements to Mediate

Agreements to mediate, while not required in most states, are a common feature of mediation practice, and drafting the agreement requires thoughtful planning. Typical issues to include in the agreement are the following provisions:

(a) identity of the parties
(b) the scope of the mediation
(c) identity of specific issues to be mediated
(d) selection of the mediator or the institution that will govern the selection process
(e) whether the mediator has an option to offer an evaluation
(f) timing
(g) fees
(h) the scope of discovery
(i) rules governing confidentiality
(j) how a party can terminate participation
(k) whether the mediator will bc liablc for ncgligent acts

There are additional considerations involved when mediation will be conducted online. In such cases, the agreement to mediate should also identify what technology or platform will be used and any special rules related to the use of that technology. Consideration should also be given to whether supplemental confidentiality provisions will be included. Examples here would be a rule against recording of the session or a prohibition against the presence of third parties unless all parties give informed consent.

9.3.1.1.2. Preparing the Client for Mediation[9]

Effective client preparation is achieved through a deliberative process of client counseling described previously. Clients need to understand the mediation process, be clear on their goals, understand their options and BATNA, and be clear on the extent of their settlement authority.[10] There are a number of practical and strategic decisions to be considered, including

(a) the timing of mediation
(b) choosing the right mediator
(c) deciding who should attend the mediation
(d) deciding what documentary evidence and witnesses should be produced
(e) determining the client's role in the mediation—would an active role be helpful for this client, or would she benefit more by assistance from an attorney?[11]

9.3.1.1.3. Selecting the Right Mediator

Choosing the appropriate mediator can make all the difference in the outcome of the dispute. Lawyers need to understand the actual and potential barriers to settlement and be familiar with the various models of mediation practice, for example, facilitative, evaluative, transformative, narrative, understanding-based.[12] Then, with their clients, they are prepared to choose the model that best fits the clients' needs. As a practical matter, there is no pure model, and mediators often combine a variety of approaches. In addition to the model of mediation practiced, some clients may also be interested in other mediator-selection factors such as diversity, gender, age, and substantive expertise. While there is no consensus on what qualifications mediators should possess, studies show that

9. COLE ET AL., *supra* note 1, at 736–40.

10. CARRIE MENKEL MEADOW, LELA PORTER LOVE & ANDREA KUPFER SCHNEIDER, MEDIATION: PRACTICE, POLICY, AND ETHICS 147–50 (3d ed. 2020).

11. *See* Jean R. Sternlight, *Lawyers' Representation of Clients in Mediation: Using Economics and Psychology to Structure Advocacy in a Nonadversarial Setting*, 14 OHIO ST. J. ON DISP. RESOL. 269 (1999).

12. For a description of these models, see JACQUELINE NOLAN-HALEY, ADR IN A NUTSHELL 96–97 (4th ed. 2013).

mediators with some experience are more successful in resolving cases.[13] Finally, it may well be that personal trust-building skills make the critical difference in success as a mediator. A study based on interviews with lawyers who represented parties in commercial mediation showed that a "core element" of predicting mediator success was the mediators' skills in creating a relationship of trust and confidence with the parties.[14]

9.3.1.1.4. Premediation Submissions

Premediation submissions offer the opportunity to inform the mediator about the case. Some mediators may request that parties submit statements summarizing the issues and state of the case. Such submissions may also be required in some court-connected mediation programs.[15]

9.3.1.1.5. Mediation Bargaining Behaviors

In accordance with Model Rule 1.4(a)(2), a lawyer shall "reasonably consult with the client about the means by which the client's objectives are to be accomplished." Thus, prior to the beginning of the mediation, lawyers should consult with their clients about what strategic approach they will take. Will they engage in distributive, competitive tactics characteristic of traditional lawyering behavior? Integrative, problem-solving behavior seeking to focus on underlying interests rather than positions? Or will they choose a tit-for-tat strategy that sends the message that their behavior is dependent upon the opponent's behavior? Ultimately, the choice of strategy will depend upon the client's goals. However, there is no free license to engage in hostile or negative behavior. In *Brooks v. The Lincoln National Life Insurance Co.*,[16] sanctions were imposed upon an attorney who engaged in highly aggressive behavior and left the mediation. Sanctions included an order to apologize to all the participants, to take a course on mediation representation within six months and file a certificate of completion, and to inform his client of these sanctions.

---

13. Bobbi McAdoo et al., *Institutionalization: What Do Empirical Studies Tell Us about Court Mediation?*, 9 Disp. Resol. Mag. 8, 9 (2003).

14. Stephen B. Goldberg & Margaret L. Shaw, *Further Investigation into the Secrets of Successful and Unsuccessful Mediators*, 23 Negotiation J. 393–418 (Oct. 2007).

15. Cole et al., *supra* note 1, at 751.

16. Brooks v. The Lincoln Nat'l Life Ins. Co., 2006 WL 2487937 (D. Neb. 2006).

9.3.1.1.6. Additional Considerations in Preparing for Online Mediation[17]

In the rapidly expanding world of online or virtual mediation, representational lawyers will be required to adapt to new technologies. Despite what platform the parties or the court chooses in the case of court-connected mediation, whether it be Zoom, WebEx, Skype, or any other number of newly developing platforms, it is critical to test the platform in advance of the mediation. Other preparations include

(a) having backup technology available (e.g., phone conference call number)
(b) understanding the new ground rules
(c) explaining the virtual mediation experience to your client—the possibility of being sent to breakout rooms—how you will communicate with the client during the mediation session
(d) preparing in a practical way for the new environment—make sure you have a way to execute documents[18]

9.3.1.2. Avoid Conflicts of Interest

Lawyers must not represent a client if the representation involves a conflict of interest.[19] Lawyers who act both as third-party neutrals (mediators) and as advocates should be mindful of Model Rule 1.12(a) and "not represent anyone in connection with a matter in which the lawyer participated personally and substantially as a judge or other adjudicative officer . . . arbitrator, mediator or other third party neutral, unless all parties to the proceeding give informed consent, confirmed in writing." Courts have also held that absent consent, lawyers must refrain from taking on representation of a client if the representation would be adverse to the interests of a former client.[20] Attorneys have been disqualified for conflict-of-interest violations. For example, in *McKenzie Construction v. St. Croix Storage Corp.*,[21] an attorney and her law firm were disqualified from representing a party where the attorney had previously acted as a

---

17. Deborah Masucci, Co-Chair Int'l Mediation Inst., Preparing for Mediation (Apr. 2020), PowerPoint presentation at Fordham Law School (on file with author).

18. Several practice guides are available to assist the representational lawyer. *See, e.g.*, *Mediator Guide to Online Mediation*, CEDR Ctr. for Effective Disp. Resol., https://www.cedr.com/wp-content/uploads/2020/03/Mediator-Guide-to-Online-Mediation-1.pdf (last visited Mar. 4, 2021).

19. Model Rules of Prof'l Conduct R. 1.7.

20. *See, e.g.*, Reading Int'l, Inc. v. Maluani Grp., Ltd., 814 F.3d 1046 (9th Cir. 2016); Cole et al., *supra* note 1, at 721 n.5.

21. McKenzie Constr. v. St. Croix Storage Corp., 961 F. Supp. 857 (D.V.I. 1997).

mediator in a substantially related matter. Likewise, in *Poly Software International, Inc. v. Su*,[22] the court disqualified a mediator-turned-attorney and his law firm from participating in litigation. The court held that without the consent of the original parties, an attorney who serves as a mediator cannot subsequently represent anyone in a substantially related matter.

9.3.1.3. Duty to Inform Clients of ADR Options

In the United States, there is no national rule that requires lawyers to inform clients of ADR options for resolving their disputes. Individual states have addressed this issue with a wide variety of approaches ranging from an explicit duty to inform clients of ADR options, for example, Virginia[23] and New Jersey,[24] to a more limited, contextual approach. For example, Massachusetts Rules of Professional Conduct provide that "when a matter is likely to involve litigation, it may be necessary under Rule 1.4 to inform the client of forms of dispute resolution that might constitute reasonable alternatives to litigation."[25] Some federal court rules go further than imposing a duty to inform and require documentation. For example, a rule in the Northern District of California requires parties and their lawyers to sign an ADR certification document in which they each confirm that they have read the court's handbook describing its ADR procedures and discussed with their clients the procedures offered by the court.[26] The rule even provides for sanctions to be imposed upon attorneys who fail to advise clients of the availability of mediation.[27]

In considering whether to discuss ADR options with a client, it is important to determine whether mediation is appropriate for your client's case. This involves a consideration of many questions. What are the costs and benefits of engaging in mediation? What other options are available? What are the BATNAs and WATNAs? The answer to these questions depends upon your client's ultimate goals and her needs and interests. As discussed earlier, this is information that can be gained through the give and take of deliberative client counseling. As a general matter, in most cases, clients will benefit from a problem-solving approach to dispute resolution. Thus, after lawyers have an understanding of their clients' needs, interests, and goals, they should make them aware of ADR options. As

22. Poly Software Int'l, Inc. v. Su, 880 F. Supp. 1487 (D. Utah 1995).
23. Va. Prof'l Guidelines, R. 1.2 cmt. 1 (2004).
24. N.J. Rules Governing Prof'l Conduct, R. 1:40-1 (1992).
25. Mass. Sup. Jud. Ct. Rules of Prof'l Conduct, R. 2.1 cmt. 5 (2015).
26. N.D. Cal. ADR Local Rules, R. 3.5(b).
27. *Id.*

noted by former law school dean John Feerick over 20 years ago, "[I]n the world of disputes, people seek less trauma, less expense, less delay, greater simplicity, fewer public embarrassments, and more options for reaching agreement. ADR offers a just response to these needs."[28]

9.3.1.4. Beyond the Duty to Inform: Duty to Explain about Mediation

As a practical matter, clients will find themselves in mediation either voluntarily through a predispute or postdispute agreement or involuntarily in the case of a court referral program. With the growth of court-connected mediation programs, some of which are compulsory, and the presence of predispute mediation clauses in parties' contracts, the lawyer's duty shifts from informing clients of ADR options to helping them more fully understand the nature of the mediation and how it fits in their particular case.

9.3.1.5. Duty to Expedite Litigation

Model Rule 3.2 requires that lawyers "make reasonable efforts to expedite litigation consistent with the interests of the client." Some of the traditional selling points for mediation are efficiency, speed, and party satisfaction. Acting in accordance with his client's interests, a lawyer might consider mediation as a process that could help to achieve the goals of Model Rule 3.2. If so, then a discussion of mediation should be included as part of the deliberations in client counseling.

9.3.2. Lawyers' Ethical Duties during Mediation

9.3.2.1. Competent Representation during Mediation

In addition to client counseling, which is ongoing throughout the mediation process, consistent with Model Rule 1.1, the competent lawyer who represents a party in mediation should be prepared to give sound legal advice. Lawyers have been found liable for providing erroneous legal advice during mediation.[29] Lawyers should also be prepared for involvement in at least three other activities: the opening statement, enlisting the help of the mediator, and drafting the mediated settlement agreement.

9.3.2.1.1. Opening Statement

The opening statement is a preview of what the lawyer plans to present at the mediation. It is a unique opportunity to create a favorable climate for the client to achieve her goals both by creating an ally in the mediator and

28. John D. Feerick, *ADR: Worthy of the Appellation "Justice,"* 19 ALTS. TO HIGH COST LITIG. 9, 11 (2001).

29. COLE ET AL., *supra* note 1, at 716–17.

by influencing the opposing party. Whether it is delivered by the lawyer or in some cases the client, the opening statement is an early opportunity to persuade.

It has become common for some lawyers to suggest abandoning the opening statement in the interests of efficiency. The arguments are varied. Why add to the time and cost of the mediation when each side already knows the other's arguments? Or, with emotionally driven clients, why agitate them from the very beginning of the process and invite early impasse? Despite the initial appeal of these arguments, abandoning the opportunity to give an opening statement deprives the lawyer and client of the opportunity to speak directly to the principal on the opposing side and to craft a narrative that could lead to settlement.[30] In fact, this may be the only opportunity to have direct communication with the principal on the other side. However, in the event that a decision is made to omit the opening statement, lawyers should be prepared to get right into the process and begin without it.[31]

9.3.2.1.2. Enlisting the Mediator's Assistance

The mediator can be a valuable asset to the attorney in furthering his client's goals. Therefore, lawyers should take advantage of the mediator's presence and insights. Consistent with the duty under Model Rule 1.6 to keep clients' information confidential, lawyers should carefully plan what information they will share with the mediator and be clear on the extent to which the mediator should keep information confidential.

Other suggestions for taking full advantage of the mediator's expertise include the following:

(a) Consider how you might enlist the mediator in signaling your willingness to compromise to the other side.
(b) Think about how the mediator can help overcome barriers to settlement.
(c) Take advantage of the caucus and request assistance from the mediator in how to make an acceptable proposal or whether a particular proposal is likely to be acceptable or will result in alienating the parties.

---

30. DWIGHT GOLANN & JAY FOLBERG, MEDIATION: THE ROLES OF ADVOCATE AND NEUTRAL 265 (2d ed. 2011).

31. *Id.* at 377.

(d) Take advantage of the time that may exist between caucuses when you have informal opportunities to speak with the mediator as the process unfolds.

9.3.2.1.3. Drafting the Mediated Settlement Agreement

Drafting the mediated settlement agreement involves several considerations. Professor Harold Abramson offers the following guidelines:[32]

(a) Make sure that the agreement reflects your clients' interests and the settlement terms.
(b) Pay attention to implementation details.
(c) Consider including the following provisions:
- a dispute resolution clause in case something goes wrong during implementation
- standard clauses such as releases, indemnification if required, confidentiality protections
- a provision to dismiss pending litigation with prejudice

When reviewing mediated settlement agreements, it is important to keep in mind that in general, these agreements are treated as contracts. Thus, their enforceability is governed by contract law, including the traditional contract defenses of fraud, duress, undue influence, and mistake. However, lawyers should not give too much weight to these defenses. Studies conducted by Professor James Coben and Peter Thompson show that it is very rare that parties are successful in defending enforcement claims based on these defenses.[33]

9.3.2.2. Dealings with Other Parties

Two Model Rules are relevant in considering the representational lawyers' dealings with other parties in connection with mediation. Model Rule 4.2(a) states that a lawyer may not contact the opposing party directly if that party is represented by a lawyer unless the lawyer has the consent of the other lawyer or is authorized to do so by law or court order. Additionally, pursuant to Model Rule 3.4(f), a lawyer cannot request that persons other than her client refrain from giving relevant information to another party.

32. For a complete list of guidelines, see ABRAMSON, *supra* note 2, at 350–52.

33. James R. Coben & Peter N. Thompson, *Mediation Litigation Trends: 1999–2007*, 1 WORLD ARB. & MED. REV. 395, 395–407.

9.3.2.3. Continuing Duty to Keep Clients Informed

Model Rule 1.4 requires that lawyers keep clients reasonably informed about the status of their cases.[34] The ethical duty to keep clients informed extends well beyond the initial client counseling, premediation phase. Lawyers have a continuing duty to inform clients of developments in mediation, including the date and time of upcoming mediations,[35] and the existence of any settlement offers. Lawyers have been subject to disciplinary actions for their failure to convey settlement offers in mediation.[36]

9.3.2.4. Candor toward the Mediator

A lawyer is required to be a zealous advocate for his client in mediation. What does this mean when it comes to truthfulness? How honest should a lawyer be when communicating with a mediator? These questions have generated much discussion and debate by those who believe that mediation is based on good faith, which requires a higher duty of candor than that used in traditional negotiations, and those who argued for the status quo, claiming that deception is inherent in the negotiation process. The American Bar Association issued an ethics opinion in 2006 that directly addressed the issue by considering the following question—what is the extent of a lawyer's obligation to be truthful when making statements on behalf of a client in a caucused mediation?[37] The opinion makes it clear that the truthfulness requirement of Model Rule 4.1, which applies in negotiation, also applies in a caucused mediation. Thus, a lawyer representing a client in a caucused mediation may not make a false statement of material fact to a third person. However, statements regarding a client's negotiating goals or willingness to compromise or statements considered to be "puffing" are not considered false statements of material fact within the meaning of the Model Rules and thus are permitted in mediation.

There are some situations, however, when a higher degree of candor may be required in order to satisfy clients' interests and achieve their goals. The final footnote to Opinion 06-439 provides guidance in this regard:

---

34. Model Rules of Prof'l Conduct R. 1.4(a)(3).

35. *See, e.g.*, Doorstep Beverages of Longwood Inc. v. Collier, 928 So. 2d 482 (Fla. Dist. Ct. App. 2006) (attorney who failed to advise his client that personal attendance was required at mediation was subject to sanctions).

36. *See, e.g.*, *In re* Disciplinary Action against Peterson, 771 N.W.2d 575 (N.D. 2009).

37. ABA Formal Op. 06-439 (Apr. 12, 2006).

> [C]omplete candor may be necessary to gain the mediator's trust or to provide the mediator with critical information regarding the client's goals or intentions so that the mediator can effectively assist the parties in forging an agreement . . . . Thus, in extreme cases, a failure to be forthcoming, even though not in contravention of Rule 4.1(a) could constitute a violation of the lawyer's duty to provide competent representation under Model Rule 1.1.[38]

9.3.2.5. Good-Faith Participation

Good-faith participation by parties and their lawyers contributes to the dignity of the mediation process, and it is unfortunate when lawyers abuse mediation by engaging in aggressive, hostile, or otherwise negative behaviors. In her study of Ontario litigators, Professor Julie Macfarlane offers a vivid account of lawyers who engaged in a variety of bad-faith tactics. In the words of one litigator in her study:

> If . . . I act for the Big Bad Wolf against Little Red Riding Hood and I don't want this dispute resolved, I want to tie it up as long as I possibly can, and mandatory mediation is custom made. I can waste more time, I can string it along, I can make sure this thing never gets resolved because . . . I know the language . . . .[39]

As a corrective to these and other negative behaviors, many states have enacted good-faith participation statutes. Professor John Lande's seminal study of good-faith requirements shows that at least 22 states and the territory of Guam have such statutory requirements.[40] In addition to statutes, good-faith requirements in mediation have been established by court rules, mediation referral orders, and the common law. However, the lack of clarity on the meaning of good faith presents challenges. With few exceptions, what constitutes good-faith participation is never defined in the statutes, leaving courts to wrestle with the problem of explaining its meaning. According to Professor Lande's study, courts have generally interpreted good-faith requirements in a narrow fashion "to require compliance with orders to attend mediation, provide pre-mediation

---

38. *Id.*

39. Julie Macfarlane, *Culture Change? Commercial Litigators and the Ontario Mandatory Mediation Program*, 2002 J. Disp. Resol. 241, 267 (2002).

40. John Lande, *Using Dispute System Design Methods to Promote Good-Faith Participation in Court-Connected Mediation Programs*, 50 UCLA L. Rev. 69, 78 (2002).

memoranda, and, in some cases, produce organizational representatives with sufficient settlement authority."[41]

Some courts have met the good-faith definitional challenge by describing what constitutes bad faith.[42] Similarly, in its *Resolution on Good Faith Requirements* (2004), the American Bar Association Section of Dispute Resolution offered examples of what constitutes bad faith. These include "failure of a[n] . . . attorney . . . to attend a court-mandated mediation for a limited and specified period or to provide written memoranda prior to the mediations."[43] Most courts do not require parties to make an offer at mediation to demonstrate good faith.[44] However, it is good practice for a party with a no-offer position to inform the mediator and opposing party of this prior to the mediation.[45]

9.3.2.6. Confidentiality

Lawyers should be familiar with two aspects of confidentiality protection in mediation. The first relates to the attorney-client relationship, and the second deals with the relationship between the attorney and the mediation process generally.

9.3.2.6.1. Confidentiality in the Lawyer-Client Relationship

As a general matter, Model Rule 1.6 prevents a lawyer from revealing information relating to the representation of a client unless the client gives informed consent. The confidentiality of information acquired in the lawyer-client relationship can be threatened in a number of ways in mediation. Lawyers might be inclined to reveal their clients' interests and information to opposing counsel or to the mediator in the hope of moving closer to a settlement. Or lawyers may be required to safeguard client information from judges who participate in pretrial settlement conferences. It may be that a judge participating in a pretrial settlement discussion inquires about the lawyer's settlement authority or related information. Before disclosing any such information, a lawyer must

---

41. *Id.* at 85.

42. COLE ET AL., *supra* note 1, at 540, 541.

43. *Resolution on Good Faith Requirements for Mediators and Mediation Advocates in Court-Mandated Mediation Programs*, ABA SECTION OF DISP. RESOL. (Aug. 7, 2004), *available at* https://www.pamediation.org/archives/ABA_Resolution.pdf.

44. *See* Avril v. Civilmar, 605 So. 2d 988 (Fla. 4th Dist. Ct. App. 1992); *In re* A.T. Reynolds & Sons, Inc., 452 B.R. 374 (S.D.N.Y. 2011).

45. *See, e.g.*, Apelian v. Allstate Ins. Co., No. LACV164977GHKPLAX, 2016 WL 7388276 (C.D. Cal. Dec. 20, 2016), *aff'd in part, rev'd in part*, 737 F. App'x 327 (9th Cir. 2018). *See also* cases cited in COLE ET AL., *supra* note 1, at 547.

obtain the informed consent of her client. ABA Ethics Opinion 93-370 (1993) makes it clear that absent informed consent, a lawyer should not reveal to a judge the limits of the lawyer's settlement authority or the lawyer's advice to the client regarding settlement. Lawyers should also abide by this rule with respect to mediators and refrain from revealing such confidential information to mediators without the client's consent.

9.3.2.6.2. Confidentiality in the Mediation Process

Confidentiality is considered a standard and attractive feature of mediation. The underlying rationale for confidentiality protections in mediation has been expressed well by Judge Denny Chin in *Bernard v. Galen Group*:[46]

> [I]f participants cannot rely on the confidential treatment of everything that transpires during [mediations,] then counsel of necessity will feel constrained to conduct themselves in a cautious, tight-lipped, non-committal manner more suitable to poker players in a high-stakes game than to adversaries attempting to arrive at a just resolution of a civil dispute.[47]

In counseling clients about safeguarding confidentiality in mediation, lawyers must become familiar with and take note of the various means of confidentiality protection: evidentiary exclusionary rules, privilege, contract, court rules, and private provider organization rules. The Uniform Mediation Act takes a privilege approach. In addition, lawyers must become familiar with any related statutory regulations concerning confidentiality. For example, California law now requires lawyers to obtain written informed consent from their clients indicating that they understand the breadth of confidentiality protection in mediation.[48]

In short, there is no uniform approach to protecting confidentiality in mediation. While every state has enacted confidentiality protections of some type, existing statutes vary by state and even within a given state. Statutes may also differ by type of programs and subject matter of the dispute. Court decisions are inconsistent, and it is difficult to predict

---

46. Bernard v. Galen Grp., 901 F. Supp. 778 (S.D.N.Y. 1995).

47. Cole et al., *supra* note 1, at 784. In this case, an attorney for one of the parties wrote a letter to the judge disclosing the terms of certain settlement offers, including specific dollar amounts. The attorney was fined $2,500 for breaching the confidentiality provisions governing the court's mediation program, and the court ordered that the fine be paid by the law firm and not the client. *See also* Lawson v. Brown's Day Care Ctr., 177 Vt. 528 (2004).

48. Cal. Evid. Code § 1129 (2020).

with certainty how much protection will be afforded to communications made in mediation as well as conduct that may violate confidentiality regulations.[49] It is important, therefore, for the representational lawyer in mediation to become familiar with the specific confidentiality requirements of the jurisdiction in which mediation occurs. Lawyers have been held liable for disclosing privileged mediation communications.[50]

9.3.2.7. Unauthorized Practice of Law

The unauthorized-practice-of-law doctrine restricts the practice of law to licensed attorneys who have satisfied specific educational requirements and have demonstrated good moral character. Model Rule 5.5(a) provides: "A lawyer shall not practice law in a jurisdiction in violation of the regulation of the legal profession in that jurisdiction, or assist another in doing so."

With the expansion and institutionalization of ADR, lawyers frequently represent clients in out-of-state mediations. Several states lack procedures for allowing out-of-state lawyers to enjoy pro hac vice status so that they may represent clients. Thus, the attorney who represents his client in mediation in a jurisdiction where he is not admitted to practice faces exposure to sanctions under unauthorized-practice-of-law statutes. For example, in *In re Non-Member of State Bar of Arizona*,[51] a lawyer who was licensed to practice in Virginia and Florida was found to have engaged in the unauthorized practice of law by representing parties in a mediation in Arizona. As a result, she was sanctioned with an "informal reprimand."[52]

In response to the growing number of out-of-state attorneys representing parties in ADR processes, the ABA adopted Model Rule 5.5(c) to offer some means of protection to attorneys who are in good standing in their home jurisdictions and who represent parties on a limited and temporary basis in ADR processes such as mediation. Several states have adopted some version of this rule.

---

49. For example, in *Toon v. Wackenhut Corrections Corp.*, 250 F.3d 950 (5th Cir. 2001), the plaintiff's attorney was found to have violated confidentiality provisions by not filing its motion to enforce under seal.

50. Cole et al., *supra* note 1, at 1185.

51. *In re* Non-Member of St. Bar of Ariz., 152 P.3d 1183 (2007).

52. *Id.* at 1185.

9.4. Legal and Ethical Obligations of the Lawyer Mediator Triggered by the Lawyer's Conduct

Section 9.3 of this chapter addressed the legal and ethical responsibilities of lawyers acting as representatives of parties in mediation. This section focuses on the lawyer who serves as a mediator, and it addresses different concerns. Specifically, (1) what happens when the mediator believes the lawyer is uninformed or incompetent? (2) What happens when the mediator suspects the lawyer engages in professional misconduct and acts dishonestly or has a conflict of interest? Should the mediator report the representational lawyer's misconduct to the appropriate authority or not? (3) What should the mediator do when he finds the lawyer to be disruptive of the process? These situations raise further questions as to the mediator's responsibilities to represented parties and to the mediation process. The discussion will consider these questions based on mediator ethics sources, including codes of conduct and MEAC opinions.

9.4.1. The Mediator Believes the Lawyer Is Uninformed or Incompetent

It is well settled that mediators are under a duty to conduct the mediation based on the principle of party self-determination (e.g., Model Standards, Standard I). This duty is owed to the parties, and the mediator must take positive steps to assist them in making free and informed choices in a quality process.[53] This means that the mediator has a duty to take measures to generate the conditions for making informed decisions. In some cases, these measures might include preventing a party from making a decision. For example, the Committee to the Florida [Ethics] Rules states that "[a] mediator must not . . . knowingly allow a participant to make a decision based on misrepresented facts or circumstances."[54] Omer Shapira has argued that while mediators cannot ensure that parties will make informed decisions, they should take all available means for helping the parties to do so, including providing information directly, making information accessible through indirect means, and, as a last resort to prevent uninformed decision making, discontinuing the process.[55]

53. Model Standards of Conduct for Mediators, Standard VI (Quality of the Process), VI.A, VI.A.10.

54. Fla. Rules for Certified & Ct.-Appointed Mediators, Comm. Notes to R. 10.310.

55. Omer Shapira, A Theory of Mediators' Ethics: Foundations, Rationale, and Application 152 (2016).

The mediator represents the integrity of the mediation process and owes an obligation to both parties to maintain the integrity of that process.[56] The mediator's duty of integrity, found in several ethics standards,[57] is not extinguished by the presence of the lawyer and the lawyer-client relationship. The lawyer and her mediation client are not the same entity. Ethics opinions have made it clear that the mediator's ethical responsibilities to the parties and the process remain despite party representation. For example, a North Carolina ethics opinion held that in the absence of a party, the mediator had a duty to verify with the party's lawyer that the latter had been authorized by his client, the mediation party, to settle the case.[58] A Florida ethics opinion held that where a party's physical presence in mediation is required, his lawyer's presence will not suffice.[59]

Omer Shapira has suggested that the mediator's duty of integrity holds strong despite representation by counsel—"even where both parties are represented the mediator has a responsibility to ensure that the mediation is not abused by one of the representatives."[60] Of course, in situations where parties are represented by counsel in mediation, the mediator's responsibilities are lessened, presumably because the lawyer will provide relevant information and protect the client's interests.[61] However, if a mediation party is uninformed and cannot engage in effective self-determination based on informed decision making, and her lawyer appears uninformed as well, the mediator should take appropriate steps that would make it possible for the party to exercise self-determination. For example, the mediator could ask questions and engage in a soft reality testing.

Finally, the mediator should be willing to withdraw or terminate the mediation if he realizes that the party and the lawyers are unaware of their ignorance and this jeopardizes the integrity of mediation. Model Standard VI.C is relevant in this context: "If a mediator believes that participant conduct, including that of the mediator, jeopardizes conducting a mediation consistent with these Standards, a mediator shall take appropriate steps including, if necessary, postponing, withdrawing from or terminating the mediation."

56. Jacqueline Nolan-Haley, *Informed Consent in Mediation: A Guiding Principle for Truly Educated Decisionmaking*, 74 NOTRE DAME L. REV. 775, 826 (1999).

57. *E.g.*, GA. STANDARDS IV.B. (mediator must protect the integrity of the process). *See also* SHAPIRA, *supra* note 55, at 231, 232.

58. N.C. Op. MEAC 35-2018.

59. Fla. Advisory Op. MEAC 2002-1.

60. SHAPIRA, *supra* note 55, at 236.

61. *Id.* at 156.

9.4.2. The Mediator Suspects the Lawyer Acts Unethically

9.4.2.1. Conflicting Obligations of Confidentiality and Disclosure of Misconduct

Historically, American attorneys have been reluctant to report their fellow attorneys to disciplinary authorities.[62] Supporting a decision to report misconduct is the language of Model Rule 8.3, which states that "[a] lawyer who knows that another lawyer has committed a violation of the Rules of Professional Conduct that raises a substantial question as to that lawyer's honesty . . . shall inform the appropriate professional authority . . . ."[63] On the other hand, the Model Standards of Conduct for Mediators require that confidentiality be honored. Standard V provides that "a mediator shall maintain the confidentiality of all information obtained by the mediator unless otherwise agreed to by the parties or required by applicable law. A mediator should not communicate to any non-participant information about how the parties acted in the mediation . . . ."[64]

In addition to the Model Standards, state statutes and court rules and regulations all call for confidentiality in mediation. To further muddy the waters, the Preamble to the Model Standards contemplates that other rules and regulations "may create conflicts with and take precedence over these Standards."[65]

Thus, the question is: Should the lawyer mediator act in accordance with the principle of mediation confidentiality or follow the professional responsibility rules of the legal profession that require disclosure of the offensive conduct? The response to this question may well depend upon whether Model Rule 8.3 extends to the mediation process. While there have been efforts by some states to amend Model Rule 8.3 by exempting lawyer mediators from the duty of reporting professional misconduct, the rule remains in effect.[66] Thus, tension continues to exist between rules of professional responsibility and mediation privilege rules governing confidentiality.

---

62. Pamela Kentra, *Hear No Evil, See No Evil, Speak No Evil: The Intolerable Conflict for Attorney-Mediators between the Duty to Maintain Mediation Confidentiality and the Duty to Report Fellow Attorney Misconduct*, 1997 B.Y.U. L. Rev. 715, 744 (1997) (citing study by the ABA Committee on Evaluation of Disciplinary Enforcement).

63. Nonlawyer mediators are not bound by Model Rule 8.3.

64. Model Standards of Conduct for Mediators, Standard V.2.

65. *Id.* pmbl.

66. For example, the North Carolina State Bar proposed such an amendment. *See Proposal: No Reporting for Mediators in N.C.*, N.C. Law. Weekly, 2009 WLNR31182806 (Nov. 2, 2009).

There are exceptions to mediation privilege rules in the case of professional misconduct. The Uniform Mediation Act (UMA) specifically exempts from the privilege communications "sought or offered to prove or disprove a claim or complaint of professional misconduct against a mediation party, a nonparty participant, or a party's representative for misconduct during a mediation."[67] Thus, states adopting the UMA permit reporting of lawyer misconduct that takes place during the mediation process.[68] There are other non-UMA states that also have specific exemptions for misconduct,[69] and a proposal for one has been submitted by the California Law Revision Committee.[70] However, in states where such an exception is not available, lawyer mediators confronted with a representational lawyer's misconduct will be required to manage the tension between two competing policies—the mediation privilege designed to provide for honest exchanges in mediation and the ethical obligation of a lawyer to behave in a professional manner.[71]

9.4.2.2. Response of Courts and State Ethics Committees

Courts and state ethics committees have taken different approaches in resolving conflicts at the intersection of confidentiality statutes and allegations of attorney misconduct. The case of *In re Waller*[72] is instructive. In *Waller*, an attorney mediator was confronted with the conflict between a mediator's confidentiality obligations and the mediator's duty to report unethical conduct of fellow attorneys. In this case, a lawyer mediator reported the possible conflict of interest of another attorney, which he learned about during the course of a court-annexed mediation. The D.C. Board of Professional Responsibility supported the mediator's decision to report misconduct, ruling that the mediation confidentiality requirement was not intended to prevent disclosure of attorney misconduct.

Ethics opinions have taken a variety of approaches to this question. A 2006 Florida ethics opinion held that confidentiality in mediation

---

67. Uniform Mediation Act 6(a)(6).

68. COLE ET AL., *supra* note 1, at 722.

69. *See, e.g.*, FLA. STAT. 44.405(a)(6). There is no confidentiality or privilege for any mediation communication offered to prove professional misconduct.

70. The committee issued a report recommending the creation of a new exception to California's mediation law designed to hold attorneys accountable for misconduct during the mediation process. *Relationship between Mediation Confidentiality and Attorney Malpractice and Other Misconduct*, 45 CAL. L. REVISION COMM'N REP. 19 (Dec. 2017), http://www.clrc.ca.gov/pub/Printed-Reports/Pub240-K402.pdf.

71. COLE ET AL., *supra* note 1, at 722, 723.

72. *In re* Waller, 573 A.2d 780 (D.C. App. 1990).

trumped disclosure of attorney misconduct in a case where an attorney told the mediator that he had misspent funds held in escrow. Noting that the escrow violation did not occur during mediation, the committee concluded that the professional misconduct exception to mediation confidentiality did not apply. Thus, the committee held that mediation rules control over conflicting ethical standards, and the attorney mediator was prohibited from reporting this conduct to the bar.[73]

A few years later, the committee was presented with the question of whether it was possible for a lawyer mediator to report an attorney's misconduct without violating other ethical duties. In that case, counsel for a party acted in an outrageous and excessively rude and aggressive manner with respect to opposing counsel, the opposing party, and the mediator and inflicted emotional distress on one of the opposing parties. The Florida Ethics Committee opined that a certified mediator may report an attorney's misconduct, solely for the internal use of the body conducting the investigation of the conduct, without violating ethical duties. The committee stressed that "[t]he confidentiality of mediation is not intended to cloak or provide protection for the professional misconduct of any party or participant during the mediation process."[74]

Similarly, an ethics opinion from the Illinois State Bar Association held that "[a] lawyer should not be able to subvert the mediation process by engaging in misconduct and then avoid discipline for such misconduct because of . . . confidentiality provisions . . . ."[75]

Further support for a lawyer mediator's duty to report misconduct is found in an opinion of the ABA Section of Dispute Resolution Mediator Ethical Guidance Committee, *The Unprepared Attorney: What Is a Mediator to Do?*[76] The factual scenario in that report described a mediator in the middle of an employment discrimination case with both sides represented by counsel. In the mediator's view, the attorney for the complainant was ill prepared, had grossly undervalued the client's case, and agreed, with minimal negotiation, to a mediated settlement that was significantly below the value of the case. The ABA Ethics Committee Co-Chair, Roger Wolf, opined that "[a]n attorney who is a mediator may have

---

73. Fla. Advisory Op. MEAC 2006-005.

74. Fla. Advisory Op. MEAC 2011-003.

75. Ill. St. Bar Ass'n Advisory Op. on Prof'l Conduct, 11-01.

76. *The Unprepared Attorney: What Is a Mediator to Do?*, ABA Section of Disp. Resol. Mediator Ethical Guidance Comm., *available at* https://www.americanbar.org/content/dam/aba/administrative/dispute_resolution/the_unprepared_lawyer.pdf (last visited Mar. 4, 2021).

an ethical responsibility to report an attorney engaged in malpractice, although it is rarely done."

In addition to the limited case law and ethics opinions, scholars generally support reporting of professional misconduct by lawyer mediators.[77]

9.4.2.3. Withdrawal as Alternative to Reporting Misconduct

In some cases, as an alternative to reporting the misconduct of the representational lawyer, the mediator may be advised to withdraw from the mediation process. An example of this approach is found in a 2010 ethics opinion from North Carolina that described the following scenario. During the course of a mediation session regarding equitable distribution, a mediator learned that the wife and her attorney had intentionally failed to disclose to her husband the existence of a valuable marital asset. The committee held that the proper course of action was for the mediator to engage the parties in a private conversation about the consequences of such actions and, if they persist in nondisclosure, then terminate the mediation session. If the parties' decision still remains the same, the mediator should withdraw from the mediation. However, the mediator should not violate confidentiality in the withdrawal process. In the words of the committee: "A simple statement such as, 'A dilemma exists that prohibits me from continuing' with no further explanation or elaboration would suffice to end the mediator's participation."[78]

9.4.3. What Should the Mediator Do When She Finds the Lawyer to Be Disruptive of the Process?

The mediator has a duty to conduct a quality process and maintain the integrity of mediation.[79] This means that the mediator has responsibility for maintaining the quality and integrity of the process and preventing an abuse of process. This duty is expressed in several ethics codes and guidelines. The Florida Rules provide a clear-cut example—"[a] mediator

---

77. *See, e.g.*, Arthur F. Greenbaum, *The Attorney's Duty to Report Professional Misconduct: A Roadmap for Reform*, 16 GEO. J. LEGAL ETHICS 259, 318 (2003) (in proceedings where the lawyer serves as counsel to a party, there should be reporting of misconduct); Kentra, *supra* note 62; Mori Irvine, *Serving Two Masters: The Obligation under the Rules of Professional Conduct to Report Attorney Misconduct in a Confidential Mediation*, 26 RUTGERS L.J. 155 (1994).

78. Advisory Op. of the N.C. Disp. Resol. Comm'n, Op. No. 16 (2010).

79. MODEL STANDARDS OF CONDUCT FOR MEDIATORS, Standard VI.

is responsible for safeguarding the mediation process."[80] Omer Shapira reminds us that not only do parties expect the mediator to intervene in cases of abuse of process, but the profession and the public also expect a mediator to take action.[81]

Disruption of the process could be the result of the lawyer's unfamiliarity with mediation or inexperience rather than a deliberate attempt at sabotaging the mediation. Thus, the mediator should provide the disruptive lawyer with information about mediation, emphasizing that it is a nonadversarial process and describing expectations for the lawyer's behavior. If disruption persists, with the client's consent, the mediator might caucus with the lawyers without their clients. The mediator could also meet with clients without the lawyers (with the lawyers' and clients' consent). As a last resort, the mediator could withdraw from the process.

9.5. Conclusion

This chapter has provided practical and ethical guidance to the representational lawyer in mediation and addressed some obligations of the lawyer mediator triggered by the representational lawyer's conduct in the mediation.

Working from a deliberative model of client counseling based on the principle of informed consent, the representational lawyer begins first to develop a trust relationship with the client. This relationship will help to guide all aspects of the premediation and mediation phases from the initial client interaction in explaining the mediation process until the end of the mediation process and the drafting of the mediated agreement. The legal and ethical framework within which the representational lawyer works is governed by case law, ethical standards, and statute. There is not one uniform approach, as regulatory statutes vary from jurisdiction to jurisdiction. In general, however, ethical duties require that the representational lawyer provide competent representation *prior* to the mediation (including drafting the agreement to mediate, preparing the client for mediation, selecting the right mediator, preparing premediation submissions, and deciding among strategic behavioral choices) and *during* the mediation process (including being prepared to deliver an opening statement, taking advantage of the mediator's expertise, and drafting the mediated

80. Fla. Rules for Certified & Ct.-Appointed Mediators R. 10.400. *See also* Standards of Conduct for N.Y. St. Cmty. Disp. Resol. Ctr. Mediators, Standard VI.B; Shapira, *supra* note 55, at 244–45.

81. Shapira, *supra* note 55, at 245.

settlement agreement). Other duties require the representational lawyer to avoid conflicts of interest, inform clients of ADR options, keep clients informed about their case, expedite litigation, exercise candor toward the mediator, refrain from engaging in any material misrepresentation, act in good faith, honor confidentiality, and avoid the unauthorized practice of law. To the extent that these duties are honored, representational mediation practice will flourish, and clients' interests will be well served.

Regarding the obligations of the lawyer mediator triggered by the representational lawyer's conduct in the mediation, mediators should realize that representation does not relieve them of their responsibilities to the mediation parties and process to conduct a quality process with integrity. Furthermore, there is no uniform approach to dealing with the question of whether the lawyer mediator may report the misconduct of representational lawyers in mediation without violating confidentiality obligations. However, there is significant support from ethics opinions, some case law, and scholarly commentary that would uphold the lawyer mediator's duty to report professional misconduct that occurs during mediation.

Chapter 10

Switching Hats in Med-Arb: The Ethical Choices Required to Protect Process Integrity

Nancy A. Welsh

10.1. Introduction

Many have written about mediation and arbitration, but there is another alternative that combines these two processes. It goes by the rather inelegant name of "med-arb." As the name implies, this process generally begins as mediation. If the parties resolve their dispute in this phase, there will be a mediated settlement agreement and no need for arbitration.[1] If the mediation phase does not produce a settlement, however, the

---

The author thanks Lexie Ford and Jonah Fritz for their excellent research assistance with this chapter.

1. In some instances, the neutral in a med-arb may adopt the parties' mediated settlement terms as his arbitral award. The resulting "consent decree" or "consent award" may then be entitled to expedited recognition and enforcement just like an arbitral award that resulted from a hearing. *See* Robert J. Rabin, *The Role of Unions in the Rights-Based Workplace*, 25 U.S.F.L. Rev. 169 (1991) (citing *Arbitration and Med-Arb*, 23 PERB News 4, 7, col. 2 (Apr. 1990)) (describing a med-arb program that produced, inter alia, consent awards). The use of arbitration to render a mediated agreement into an arbitral award has been controversial. *See* Ellen E. Deason, *Combinations of Mediation and Arbitration with the Same Neutral: A Framework for Judicial Review*, 5 Y.B. on Arb. & Mediation 219 (2013); Edna Sussman, *The New York Convention through a Mediation Prism*, 15 Disp. Resol. Mag. 10 (2009);

process transforms into an arbitration. In the most common variation—"classic same-neutral med-arb"—the same individual serves as both mediator and arbitrator and, in the mediation phase, uses both facilitative and evaluative interventions and meets with all of the parties in joint (or plenary) sessions as well as one-on-one private meetings (or caucuses). The arbitration phase—if it occurs—will be conducted as a hearing, with the parties presenting evidence to the arbitrator entirely in joint session. The neutral will issue an arbitral award that can be recognized and enforced by a court.[2]

It is worth noting here that classic same-neutral med-arb resembles the situation in which a presiding judge in a lawsuit—who will hear the case and adjudicate its outcome—also facilitates the parties' pretrial settlement negotiations. If the parties settle with the pretrial assistance of the judge, there will be no need for trial. If the parties do not settle, the case will proceed to trial with the same judge presiding. In the United States, many state court judges "switch hats" in this way, which has the potential to assist the parties in achieving a more expeditious resolution guided by the judge's perception of the strengths and weaknesses of their cases.[3] However, judges, lawyers, and academics have also raised serious concerns regarding this practice[4] due to its potentially negative effects in

---

Minkowitz v. Israeli, 77 A.3d 1189 (N.J. Super. Ct. 2013) (arbitration awards based on agreements reached during mediation were deemed in excess of the mediator-arbitrator's power as arbitrator and therefore vacated). Now, under the Singapore Convention on Cross-Border Mediated Settlements, there is no need for the conversion of mediated agreements into arbitral awards in international commercial disputes. *See* Hal Abramson, *New Singapore Convention on Cross-Border Mediated Settlements: Key Choices*, *in* MEDIATION IN INTERNATIONAL COMMERCIAL AND INVESTMENT DISPUTES (Catharine Titi & Katia Fach Gomez eds., 2019).

2. This chapter does not include consideration of a process called "binding mediation," which involves a single neutral who serves only as mediator (using both plenary sessions and caucuses) and never holds an arbitration hearing but nonetheless has the authority to issue a "binding mediation award" if the parties fail to reach their own agreement. *See* Congsi Wu, *Binding Mediation: Not an Oxymoron Anymore?*, 30 ALTS. TO HIGH COST LITIG. 165 (2012).

3. *See* Peter Robinson, *An Empirical Study of Settlement Conference Nuts and Bolts: Settlement Judges Facilitating Communication, Compromise and Fear*, 17 HARV. NEGOT. L. REV. 97 (2012); Peter Robinson, *Settlement Conference Judge—Legal Lion or Problem Solving Lamb: An Empirical Documentation of Judicial Settlement Practices and Techniques*, 33 AM. J. TRIAL ADVOC. 113 (2009); Edward Brunet, *Judicial Mediation and Signaling*, 3 NEV. L.J. 232, 252–54 (2003).

4. *See* Nancy A. Welsh, *Magistrate Judges, Settlement, and Procedural Justice*, 16 NEV. L.J. 983 (2016) (citing John C. Cratsley, *Judicial Ethics and Judicial Settlement Practices: Time for Two Strangers to Meet*, 21 OHIO ST. J. ON DISP. RESOL. 569

terms of the parties' perceptions of procedural fairness,[5] violations of due process,[6] coercion of settlement,[7] conflicts of interest, and lack of impartiality. These same concerns exist when a neutral switches hats in classic same-neutral med-arb.

Besides classic same-neutral med-arb, there are many other practice variations. Parties may choose to modify the number of neutrals, the sequencing of the mediation and arbitration phases, the use of caucusing during the mediation phase, the timing of the parties' election to proceed from mediation to arbitration, and the neutral's use and disclosure of confidential information. Med-arb variations include the following:

- *Sequential med-arb*[8]—involving two neutrals rather than one, with one neutral serving as mediator and, if the parties do not reach a mediated settlement, the other neutral stepping in to serve as arbitrator.
- *Overlapping med-arb*[9]—again involving two neutrals, with one neutral serving as mediator and the other, who will serve as arbitrator, attending and observing the joint sessions of the mediation phase.
- *Standby mediator*[10]—involving two neutrals, but beginning with arbitration rather than mediation, and with the mediator reading the arbitration briefs, observing the arbitration hearing, and available to serve as mediator at any time.
- *Braided arbitration*[11]—involving a single neutral, beginning as arbitrator but pausing at various points to serve as mediator.

(2006); Roselle L. Wissler, *Court-Connected Settlement Procedures: Mediation and Judicial Settlement Conferences*, 26 Ohio St. J. on Disp. Resol. 271 (2011)).

5. *See id.*

6. *Id.*; Ellen E. Deason, *Beyond "Managerial Judges": Appropriate Roles in Settlement*, 78 Ohio St. L.J. 73 (2017).

7. *See* Nancy A. Welsh, *The Thinning Vision of Self-Determination in Court-Connected Mediation: The Inevitable Price of Institutionalization?*, 6 Harv. Negot. L. Rev. 1 (2001).

8. *See* David J. McLean & Sean-Patrick Wilson, *Compelling Mediation in the Context of Med-Arb Agreements*, 63 Disp. Resol. J. 28, 30 (2008) (describing one variation of med-arb as involving "separate sequential processes"); Joshua M. Javits, *Better Process, Better Results: Integrating Mediation and Arbitration to Resolve Collective Bargaining Disputes*, 32 ABA J. Lab. & Emp. L. 167 (Winter 2017).

9. *See* Richard Fullerton, *Med-Arb and Its Variants: Ethical Issues for Parties and Neutrals*, 65 Disp. Resol. J. 52, 57 (2010).

10. *See* Deason, *supra* note 1.

11. *See* Fullerton, *supra* note 9, at 53, 58.

- *Plenary med-arb*[12]—involving a single neutral, but in the mediation phase, using only joint sessions to ensure that all parties are aware of everything that the arbitrator has heard.
- *Opt-in med-arb*[13]—involving a single neutral, but with the parties deciding whether to opt in to arbitration only after completion of the mediation phase.
- *Opt-out med-arb*[14]—involving a single neutral, but with the parties deciding whether to opt out of arbitration after they have completed the mediation phase.
- *Med-arb not incorporating confidential information learned during caucuses*[15]—involving a single neutral using both joint sessions and caucuses during the mediation phase and then, if serving as arbitrator, not disclosing confidential mediation communications and avoiding consideration of confidential information in determining the arbitral award.
- *Med-arb incorporating confidential information learned during caucuses*[16]—involving a single neutral using both joint sessions and caucuses during the mediation phase and then, if serving as arbitrator, not disclosing confidential mediation communications but considering such confidential information in determining the arbitral award.

---

12. *See id.* at 58; Deason, *supra* note 1, at 246 (noting that this approach has been recommended by the CEDR Commission on Settlement in International Arbitration); *Med-Arbitration Rules of Procedure*, Colo. Mediators & Arb. (Nov. 1, 2013), https://coma.com/rules/med-arbitration (Rule MA-9, which provides: "The initial step in Med-Arbitration is a mediation session in which all parties and the med-arbitrator are present together. No ex-parte (private) sessions with the med-arbitrator shall be held.").

13. See the process at issue described in the text accompanying *Spruce Environmental Technologies, Inc. v. Festa Radon Technologies Co.*, 370 F. Supp. 3d 275 (D. Mass. 2019), *infra* page 219.

14. *See* Fullerton, *supra* note 9, at 58. Australia, for example, has a Commercial Arbitration Act that permits med-arb with an opt-out provision. *See Commercial Arbitration Act 2010 No 61 (NSW)*, s. 27D(3), N.S.W. Gov't, https://www.legislation.nsw.gov.au/view/html/inforce/current/act-2010-061#sec.27D (last visited Mar. 15, 2021); *Commercial Arbitration Act 2017*, Austl. Cap. Terr. (effective July 2, 2019), https://www.legislation.act.gov.au/View/a/2017-7/current/PDF/2017-7.PDF.

15. *See* Brian A. Pappas, *Med-Arb and the Legalization of Alternative Dispute Resolution*, 20 Harv. Negot. L. Rev. 157, 177 (2015); Javits, *supra* note 8, at 173.

16. *See* Javits, *supra* note 8, at 173 (citing John Kagel, *Med-Arb after 40: More Viable Than Ever*, *in* Nat'l Acad. of Arb., A Tale of Two Countries, Proceedings of the Sixty-Sixth Ann. Meeting 241, 244 (Matthew M. Franckiewicz et al. eds., 2013)).

- *Med-last offer arbitration (MEDLOA)*[17]—involving a single neutral, using both joint sessions and caucuses during the mediation phase and issuing an arbitral award based on what was learned during both the mediation and arbitration phases, but limited to choosing between the parties' last best offers.
- *Med-arb not promising confidentiality*[18]—involving a single neutral using both joint sessions and caucuses during the mediation phase and then, if serving as arbitrator, disclosing confidences shared by the parties while in caucus if such information may inform the neutral's arbitral award.

Obviously, there are many variations of med-arb, and this list is not exhaustive. Some variations are more problematic ethically than others.

10.2. Contexts in Which Med-Arb Is Used and Legal Questions That Can Arise

It has been reported that in the United States, Sam Kagel first combined mediation and arbitration into one process in the labor-management context in the 1970s when he settled a controversial nurses' strike in a San Francisco hospital.[19] The nurses apparently waived their right to strike, and both parties committed to accept the final settlement.[20] Commentators indicate that med-arb continues to be used to resolve labor-management disputes, but it is also used now in corporate disputes (including disputes between shareholders) and in international commercial arbitration.[21] Use of med-arb—or at least interest in its use—is also growing in

17. *See* Joseph B. Stulberg, *Keeping Commercial Arbitration True to Its Core Values*, 20 Disp. Resol. Mag. 18 (2014) (book review).

18. *See* Deason, *supra* note 1, at 247 (describing the Hong Kong Arbitration Ordinance, which provides that if a neutral learns confidential information during the mediation phase and the case does not settle, "before resuming arbitration he must disclose to all the parties 'as much of that information as the arbitrator considers is material to the arbitral proceedings'").

19. *See* Fullerton, *supra* note 9, at 53–54; *see also* Dafna Lavi, *Divorce Involving Domestic Violence: Is Med-Arb Likely to Be the Solution?*, 14 Pepp. Disp. Resol. L.J. 91, 130–33 (2014) (reporting that med-arb was first used by John and Sam Kagel).

20. *See* Lavi, *supra* note 19, at 131.

21. *See id.* (also reporting that China, Germany, and Switzerland use various forms of med-arb in international disputes).

the context of family[22] and estate disputes[23] as well as online business-to-consumer (B2C) disputes.[24] In the United States, some state statutes and court rules authorize the use of med-arb in, for example, the labor-management[25] and court-connected[26] contexts. In general, however, the process is used in the United States only on an ad hoc basis or due to its incorporation into dispute resolution clauses in contracts. In other parts of the world, in contrast, there is substantially more cultural acceptance of[27] and interest in med-arb, as evidenced by legislation authorizing its use, sometimes accompanied by safeguards.[28]

Unfortunately, there is no definitive information available regarding how frequently med-arb is used in any of the contexts just identified. Focusing particularly on the incidence of med-arb in the corporate

22. *See id.*; Kristen M. Blankley, *Keeping a Secret from Yourself? Confidentiality When the Same Neutral Serves Both as Mediator and as Arbitrator in the Same Case*, 63 BAYLOR L. REV. 317, 320 (2011) (drawing a parallel between neutrals providing med-arb and parent coordinators); Linda D. Elrod, *The Need for Confidentiality in Evaluative Processes: Arbitration and Med/Arb in Family Law Cases*, 58 FAM. CT. REV. 26, 34 (2020).

23. *See* Yolanda Vorys, *The Best of Both Worlds: The Use of Med-Arb for Resolving Will Disputes*, 22 OHIO ST. J. ON DISP. RESOL. 871 (2007).

24. *See* Dafna Lavi, *Three Is Not a Crowd: Online Mediation-Arbitration in Business to Consumer Internet Disputes*, 37 U. PA. J. INT'L L. 871, 930–32 (2016).

25. *See* Karen L. Henry, *Med-Arb: An Alternative to Interest Arbitration in the Resolution of Contract Negotiation Disputes*, 3 OHIO ST. J. ON DISP. RESOL. 385, 395 (1988); *but see* Gerawan Farming, Inc. v. Agric. Labor Relations Bd., 234 Cal. Rptr. 3d 88 (5th Dist. 2015) (holding that a labor med-arb process mandated by California statute in agricultural workers' collective bargaining was unconstitutional).

26. *See e.g.*, 3A MINN. PRACTICE SERIES, GEN. RULES OF PRACTICE ANNOTATED R. 114.02(9) (2020 ed.) (defining med-arb and categorizing it as a hybrid ADR process); N.D. ALA. LOCAL R. 16.1(c) (providing that parties using the med-arb track to settle disputes will switch from mediation to arbitration upon the neutral's determination that "further efforts [in mediation] would not be useful"); N.D. ALA. ALT. DISP. RESOL. PLAN § IV.C.9.e (2006).

27. *See, e.g.*, Carlos de Vera, *Arbitrating Harmony: "Med-Arb" and the Confluence of Culture and Rule of Law in the Resolution of International Commercial Disputes in China*, 18 COLUM. J. ASIAN L. 149 (2004); Gu Weixia, *The Delicate Art of Med-Arb and Its Future Institutionalisation in China*, 31 UCLA PAC. BASIN L.J. 97 (2014); Shahla F. Ali, *The Legal Framework for Med-Arb Developments in China: Recent Cases, Institutional Rules and Opportunities*, 10 DISP. RESOL. INT'L 119 (2016).

28. *See, e.g.*, *Commercial Arbitration Act 2010* (NSW), *supra* note 14, at s 27D (Power of arbitrator to act as mediator); Hong Kong Arbitration Ordinance (2011) Cap. 609 § 33 (both permitting med-arb with certain safeguards). *See also* Lavi, *supra* note 19, at 131 (reporting that Brazil and China have arbitration legislation that includes med-arb provisions).

arena, Tom Stipanowich and J. Ryan Lamare conducted a survey of Fortune 1000 corporations in 2011 regarding their use of various dispute-resolution processes—including "mediation-arbitration." A hefty percentage of respondents—51 percent—indicated that they had experience with the process within the previous three years. Professors Stipanowich and Lamare warn, however, that this percentage likely overstates the use of classic same-neutral med-arb and that it is more likely that these corporations are using med-arb variations that involve two neutrals, such as sequential med-arb or standby mediation.[29]

The use of med-arb—as well as the legal and ethical challenges it presents—is evidenced by court cases challenging the enforcement of arbitral awards. In *Lindsay v. Lewandowski*,[30] a California Court of Appeal refused to enter judgment on a stipulated settlement agreement, finding that there had not been a meeting of the minds between the parties regarding the consequences of a med-arb process (described by the parties as "binding mediation"). In *Bowden v. Weickert*,[31] the Ohio Court of Appeals vacated an arbitral award after similarly finding insufficient evidence that the parties had agreed to classic same-neutral med-arb and, further, that the neutral had exceeded his powers by using a failed settlement proposal made during the mediation as the basis for his arbitral award. Several cases have dealt with both the sufficiency of parties' consent to classic same-neutral med-arb and the sufficiency of their waiver of the mediation privilege when the neutrals considered mediation communications in determining their arbitral awards.[32] Quite recently, for example, a corporate party unhappy with an arbitral award objected to med-arb in *Spruce Environmental Technologies, Inc. v. Festa Radon Technologies Co.*,[33] arguing that med-arb violated public policy, specifically the protection of confidential mediation communications as provided by Massachusetts's mediation privilege, because the neutral used what she had learned in mediation to inform her arbitral award. Citing the "exceedingly deferential" standard of review provided by the Federal Arbitration Act, the federal district court concluded that the parties

29. Thomas J. Stipanowich & J. Ryan Lamare, *Living with ADR: Evolving Perceptions and Use of Mediation, Arbitration, and Conflict Management in Fortune 1000 Corporations*, 19 Harv. Negot. L. Rev. 1, 42 (2014).

30. Lindsay v. Lewandowski, 43 Cal. Rptr. 3d 846, 850 (App. Ct. 2006).

31. Bowden v. Weickert, 2003-Ohio-3223, 2003 WL 21419175 (App. Ct. June 20, 2003).

32. *See* Blankley, *supra* note 22, at 345–60.

33. Spruce Envt'l Techs., Inc. v. Festa Radon Techs. Co., 370 F. Supp. 3d 275 (D. Mass. 2019).

had knowingly waived the mediation privilege and the neutral did not exceed her authority. Therefore, the court confirmed the arbitral award and denied the vacatur motion. Similarly, in *U.S. Steel Mining Company v. Wilson Downhole Services*,[34] the court refused to vacate an arbitral award arising out of a med-arb after finding that the parties had expressly authorized the neutral to rely on confidential information he learned in the mediation phase and had anticipated that ex parte communications would occur.[35] Particularly for same-neutral variations of med-arb, these cases highlight the challenges that can arise when a case proceeds to arbitration after a mediation phase that included parties' disclosure of confidential information while in caucus. These cases also counsel the importance of ensuring parties' informed consent regarding the mechanics and consequences of agreeing to med-arb.

Cases from other parts of the world also attest to the use of med-arb and the legal challenges it can pose. For example, in the 2011 Hong Kong case of *Gao Haiyan v. Keeneye Holdings Ltd.*,[36] one member of a Chinese arbitral panel and the general secretary of the arbitration commission conducted an informal and unsuccessful mediation during the pendency of the arbitration proceeding. After the arbitration resumed, the panel issued an award that was much lower than the settlement amount that had been proposed during the mediation. The challenge to Hong Kong's enforcement of the arbitral award alleged that the arbitrators had acted with bias and had penalized the party who refused to cooperate with the earlier settlement efforts. On appeal, the Hong Kong Court of Appeal found that apparent bias had not been sufficiently established and also took into consideration the cultural norms of Chinese arbitration in determining to allow enforcement of the arbitral award.[37]

10.3. Organizational Rules and Cautions

Major dispute-resolution service providers offer med-arb.[38] JAMS, for example, has neutrals who list examples of providing med-arb services

34. U.S. Steel Mining Co. v. Wilson Downhole Servs., 2006 WL 2869535 (W.D. Pa. Oct. 5, 2006).

35. *See* Edna Sussman, *Developing an Effective Med-Arb/Arb-Med Process*, 2 N.Y. Disp. Resol. Law. 71, 72 (2009).

36. Haiyan v. Keeneye Holdings, Ltd., [2011] 1 HKLRD 627 (C.A.).

37. *See* Edna Sussman, *International Mediation*, 47 Int'l Law. 179 (2013).

38. The American Arbitration Association offers AAA Med-Arb. *See AAA Statement of Ethical Principles*, Am. Arb. Ass'n, https://adr.org/StatementofEthicalPrinciples (last visited Mar. 15, 2021). JAMS offers Med-Arb as one of its binding adjudicative processes. *See JAMS Case Submission Form*, Jud. Arb. & Mediation, Inc., https://www.jamsadr.com/about/submitacase (last visited Mar. 5, 2021).

in disputes over health care-related contracts, national security, environmental/construction issues, antitrust claims, insurance disputes, and landlord-tenant matters,[39] and the American Arbitration Association (AAA) includes "AAA Med-Arb" among the services it offers. However, the AAA acknowledges the controversies that the process can cause.[40] Its Commercial Arbitration Rules provide that "[u]nless agreed to by all parties and the mediator, the mediator shall not be appointed as an arbitrator to the case"[41] and "[a]bsent agreement of the parties, the arbitrator(s) shall not have served as the mediator in the mediation phase of the instant proceeding."[42] Even more pointed is the cautionary advice that the AAA provides in its *Drafting Dispute Resolution Clauses: A Practical Guide*:

> Except in unusual circumstances, a procedure whereby the same individual who has been serving as a mediator becomes an arbitrator when the mediation fails is not recommended, because it could inhibit the candor which should characterize the mediation process and/or it could convey evidence, legal points or settlement positions *ex parte*, improperly influencing the arbitrator.[43]

10.4. Overview of Ethical Difficulties Associated with Med-Arb

As suggested by the med-arb procedures that have been challenged in court, as well as the cautionary words of a leading dispute-resolution provider, there are several ethical difficulties associated with the practice of med-arb. They are listed here and will be referenced in the discussion of relevant ethics provisions:

- Whether the neutral is competent to conduct both mediation and arbitration.
- Whether the parties have made a self-determined, informed decision regarding their participation in a med-arb process.

---

39. *See Search*, Jud. Arb. & Mediation, Inc., https://www.jamsadr.com/search?q=med-arb (last visited Mar. 5, 2021).

40. Organizations' candor in this area would appear consistent with the Principles for ADR Provider Organizations developed by the CPR-Georgetown Commission on Ethics and Standards of Practice in ADR. *See* CPR-Georgetown Comm'n on Ethics & Standards of Prac. in ADR, Principles for ADR Provider Orgs (May 1, 2002).

41. Com. Arb. Rules & Mediation Procedures R-9 (Am. Arb. Ass'n amended 2013).

42. *Id.* at L-2(c).

43. Am. Arb. Ass'n, Drafting Dispute Resolution Clauses: A Practical Guide 33 (amended 2013).

- Whether the transition of the neutral's role is consistent with the parties' exercise of self-determination in making voluntary and uncoerced substantive decisions in mediation.
- Whether the transition of the neutral's role is consistent with maintaining the quality and integrity of both mediation and arbitration.
- Whether the transition of the neutral's role is consistent with the neutral's maintenance of impartiality and integrity in conducting both processes.
- Whether the transition of the neutral's role is consistent with mediation confidentiality obligations.
- Whether the transition of the neutral's role, particularly when the neutral has caucused privately with the parties during the mediation phase, is consistent with the neutral's provision of a fair arbitration hearing.
- Whether the neutral has sufficiently disclosed potential conflicts of interest associated with the transition of roles.

10.5. Relevant Ethics Provisions

There are no rules of ethics that apply specifically to neutrals providing med-arb services. Because the process combines mediation and arbitration, however, the ethics provisions that apply to each of those two processes are relevant here. This chapter will begin with generally applicable and context-specific mediation ethics provisions and then move on to generally applicable and context-specific arbitration ethics provisions.

10.5.1. Relevant Mediation Ethics Provisions

10.5.1.1. Model Standards of Conduct for Mediators

The Model Standards of Conduct for Mediators (Model Standards),[44] which were developed and approved in 2005 by the American Arbitration Association, American Bar Association, and Association for Conflict Resolution, have been used as the basis for mediator ethics codes in a variety of contexts. The Model Standards' provisions regarding self-determination, quality of process, confidentiality, impartiality, and conflicts of interest are applicable to med-arb.

---

44. Model Standards of Conduct for Mediators (Am. Arb. Ass'n, Am. Bar Ass'n & Ass'n for Conflict Resol. 2005).

Self-determination and quality of process. Standard I of the Model Standards—Self-Determination—establishes the central ethical importance of protecting parties' self-determination in mediation. It provides that "[a] mediator shall conduct a mediation based on the principle of party self-determination" and defines self-determination as "the act of coming to a voluntary, uncoerced decision in which each party makes free and informed choices as to process and outcome." In classic same-neutral med-arb, neutrals use both facilitative and evaluative interventions during the mediation phase. Evaluative interventions can include the neutrals' assessments of the strengths and weaknesses of the parties' cases and even settlement recommendations. It is quite likely that a party's decision whether to accept the mediator's assessment or recommendation will be influenced by the knowledge that if the case does not settle, the mediator will transform into an arbitrator. Thus, while the party's choice in deciding whether to settle certainly is "informed" by the neutral's advice, this choice is unlikely to be entirely "free," "voluntary," or "uncoerced."[45]

Importantly, however, Standard I also recognizes party self-determination in making "free and informed choices as to process." The standard notes that "[p]arties may exercise self-determination at any stage of a mediation, including . . . process design . . . ." This language suggests that it can be ethical for a mediator to accept the additional role of arbitrator as long as the parties have exercised self-determination in choosing or designing their med-arb process. However, the standard also limits the effect of parties' self-determination:

> Although party self-determination for process design is a fundamental principle of mediation practice, a mediator may need to balance such party self-determination with a mediator's duty to conduct a quality process in accordance with these Standards.

This of course begs the question: What is a quality process according to these Standards? Would med-arb be considered a quality process?

Standard VI—Quality of Process—is meant to answer this question and includes the language that most obviously applies to a mediator who assumes the role of arbitrator: "A mediator shall not undertake an

45. *See* Welsh, *supra* note 7 (extensive discussion of evaluative interventions' effect on parties' exercise of self-determination); *see also* Omer Shapira, A Theory of Mediators' Ethics: Foundations, Rationale, and Application 140–42, 146–48 (2016) (discussing the meaning of voluntariness and the duties of the mediator regarding self-determination).

additional dispute resolution role in the same matter without the consent of the parties." This is again consistent with self-determination. But there is more: "Before providing such service, a mediator shall inform the parties of the implications of the change in process and obtain their consent to the change. A mediator who undertakes such role assumes different duties and responsibilities that may be governed by other standards." Standard VI thus indicates that a mediator may ethically take on the role of arbitrator, but *only if the mediator ensures the parties' informed consent and recognizes the other duties—and ethics—that may apply to the neutral's second role.*

In two advisory ethics opinions dealing with med-arb, the Florida Supreme Court's Mediator Ethics Advisory Committee (MEAC) acknowledged that parties may exercise self-determination in choosing to have a mediator assume the changed role of arbitrator. However, the MEAC made it clear that a mediator may not ethically change roles unless he is responding to an explicit request from the parties and ensures that (1) the parties' agreement to such changed role is voluntary; (2) the parties "understand[] their alternatives and the legal implications of their decisions";[46] and (3) the parties consent to the resulting changes in the neutral's role and the dispute-resolution process.[47] Later, this chapter will examine the particular disclosures that a mediator should make to ensure the parties' informed consent.

Even for the mediator who takes all of the precautions just described, the MEAC had these cautionary words: "In summary, while it is not expressly prohibited for a mediator to serve as an arbitrator . . . the MEAC believes that doing so is inherently laden with hazards and suggests great caution for any mediator that accepts this change in roles."[48]

Confidentiality. Standard V—Confidentiality—also has the potential to be relevant to med-arb, particularly because a neutral may intentionally or unintentionally disclose some of what she learned in mediation. This may occur as the neutral interacts with the parties or asks questions during the arbitration hearing or discloses the reasoning underlying her

46. Fla. Sup. Ct. MEAC Op. No. 2009-002 (Oct. 23, 2009).

47. Fla. Sup. Ct. MEAC Op. No. 2015-003 (Feb. 4, 2016); *see also* Fla. Rules for Certified & Ct.-Appointed Mediators R. 10.310 Committee Note ("Before providing decision-making services, therefore, the mediator shall ensure that all parties understand and consent to those changes.").

48. Op. No. 2015-003, *supra* note 47.

arbitral award.[49] Standard V provides that "[a] mediator shall maintain the confidentiality of all information obtained by the mediator in mediation, unless otherwise agreed to by the parties or required by applicable law." Specifically regarding the confidentiality of what the mediator learned in caucus, the standard provides: "A mediator who meets with any persons in private session during a mediation shall not convey directly or indirectly to any other person, any information that was obtained during that private session without the consent of the disclosing person." Thus, as with assuming an additional dispute-resolution role, the parties' consent will determine the ethicality of violating this otherwise-applicable ethics rule. Indeed, as Standard V later provides: "The parties may make their own rules with respect to confidentiality . . . ."

Impartiality and conflicts of interest/integrity. Two more ethical obligations borne by mediators under the Model Standards that are relevant to med-arb are the mediator's obligations to maintain impartiality (Standard II—Impartiality) and avoid a conflict of interest that "might reasonably be viewed as undermining the integrity of the mediation" (Standard III—Conflicts of Interest). Standard II provides that "[i]mpartiality means freedom from favoritism, bias or prejudice." A mediator is required to "conduct a mediation in an impartial manner and avoid conduct that gives the appearance of partiality" and "should not act with partiality or prejudice based on any participant's personal characteristics, background, values and beliefs, or performance at a mediation, or any other reason." Meanwhile, according to Standard III, "[a] mediator shall avoid a conflict of interest or the appearance of a conflict of interest during and after a mediation."

As referenced briefly in the discussion of self-determination, the mediator—or a party—could reasonably worry that playing the role of arbitrator will cause at least the appearance of partiality and conflict of interest. The mediator might prefer his recommended solution over the solution that seems to be favored by one of the parties. Thus, the mediator's anticipated power as arbitrator may tempt him to push the resisting party toward the solution that the mediator prefers rather than the one the party favors. Is this mediator truly impartial? The mediator also might benefit financially from serving as arbitrator—that is, holding a series of evidentiary hearings that may take days or even weeks, reviewing the

49. This neutral also may use some of what she learned during the mediation phase as she determines her arbitral award. Such use may violate a mediation privilege, but it would not, in and of itself, violate an *ethical* standard for mediation.

parties' briefs, and drafting his award and opinion, rather than helping the parties reach settlement in a half-day mediation. Could this represent a conflict of interest?

If a mediator has these or other concerns arising out of her dual role, Standard III provides that she "shall disclose, as soon as practicable, all actual and potential conflicts of interest that are reasonably known to the mediator and could reasonably be seen as raising a question about the mediator's impartiality." According to Standard III: "After disclosure [of the actual or potential conflict of interest], if all parties agree, the mediator may proceed with the mediation." This sounds very much like Standards V's and VI's handling of concerns regarding confidentiality and quality of process—relying upon disclosure and the consent of the parties. However, in this instance, even the parties' informed consent will not always be sufficient: "If a mediator's conflict of interest might reasonably be viewed as undermining the integrity of the mediation, a mediator shall withdraw from or decline to proceed with the mediation regardless of the expressed desire or agreement of the parties to the contrary." A mediator's obligation to avoid undermining the integrity of the mediation supersedes the parties' informed consent to the potential perils of med-arb.

Ethics advisory opinions issued in Florida and North Carolina underscore this point. Regardless of the parties' consent, a mediator may not serve as an arbitrator if it would "compromise the mediator's integrity or impartiality."[50] In one advisory opinion, the North Carolina Dispute Resolution Commission focused on impartiality and helpfully recommended that a mediator should

> engage in appropriate self-reflection before agreeing to serve. S/He may have spent several hours with the parties during mediation. In that time, did s/he develop any strong positive or negative feelings toward any of the individuals involved that might cloud his judgment or compromise her/his neutrality? Did s/he learn any confidential information during a caucus session that s/he may not be able to exclude from his[/her] thought process and that may inappropriately affect his/her decision? If the mediator has any concerns about his[/her] ability to be fully neutral, s/he should not serve.[51]

---

50. Op. No. 2009-002, *supra* note 46 (citing Fla. Rules for Certified & Ct.-Appointed Mediators R. 10.620).

51. N.C. Disp. Resol. Comm'n Op. No. 17 (Sept. 28, 2010).

In another advisory opinion, the North Carolina Dispute Resolution Commission actually concluded that a mediator's acceptance of the decision-making role of parenting coordinator in a family matter would represent a conflict of interest and thus would be unethical.[52] The Commission noted that the confidential information that the neutral learned while serving as mediator could influence his decision making as parenting coordinator and thus affect his ability to remain neutral. Two aspects of this case, though, distinguish the situation from med-arb. First, the Commission cited to a bright-line rule in the Association of Family and Conciliation Courts' *Guidelines for Parenting Coordination* (2019) barring a parenting coordinator from providing services if he has already served the parties as a confidential mediator. Second, the Commission perceived the financial conflict of interest to be much more significant for a parenting coordinator, who might have an extended role with the parties, than for an arbitrator whose service would be short-term and "supportive of the resolution of the dispute being mediated . . . ."[53]

The Model Standards and these advisory ethics opinions help us understand how and when med-arb could threaten a neutral's impartiality or create at least the appearance of a conflict of interest. Unfortunately, however, neither the Model Standards nor any of the advisory ethical opinions specify what could threaten the *integrity* of mediation—that is, what is so core, so essential to mediation that its absence or violation would eviscerate the process. Professor Omer Shapira has been the first to observe that the Model Standards lack an independent standard that clearly expresses mediators' duty to "conduct mediation with professional integrity," which he defines as "in a state of true commitment to the role of a mediator and to the wholeness of the mediation process."[54] Professor Shapira helpfully asserts that mediators' ethical duties should be understood to extend beyond the parties, to the mediation profession and the public, and to include a responsibility "to preserve the institution of mediation and public trust in it."[55] Thus, and regardless of the parties' consent, will the public's confidence in mediators and the mediation process be jeopardized by a neutral's use of confidential information, never disclosed and learned only while in caucus, as the basis for her arbitral award? Similarly, and again regardless of the parties' consent, will the

52. N.C. Disp. Resol. Comm'n Op. No. 40 (Mar. 24, 2020).

53. *Id.*

54. Shapira, *supra* note 45, at 233.

55. Omer Shapira, *A Critical Assessment of the Model Standards of Conduct for Mediators (2005): Call for Reform*, 100 Marq. L. Rev. 81, 113 (2016).

public's confidence in the voluntariness of mediated settlement agreements be threatened by the knowledge that a mediator in a same-neutral med-arb process will have the authority to impose the settlement that he is now merely suggesting?

As Professor Shapira urges, the obligations under Standard III to avoid conflicts of interest and subsequent relationships that "might reasonably be viewed as undermining the integrity of mediation" should compel a mediator to make the ethical choice to "decline to serve the parties in another professional capacity where accepting a different role after the mediation would reasonably raise a question about the propriety of the mediator's actions at the time of the mediation, to the effect that a reasonable concern might arise that the process had been faulty and that public trust in the process and profession of mediation could be undermined."[56] This may mean that a neutral should decline to serve in a same-neutral med-arb process or withdraw from such a process.

10.5.1.2. Context-Specific Mediator Ethics Codes

In addition to the generally applicable Model Standards, there are various context-specific mediator ethics codes. Mediators in the U.S. Federal Mediation and Conciliation Service and other public and private labor mediators, for example, practice subject to the Code of Professional Conduct for Labor Mediators,[57] adopted in 1966. The International Mediation Institute Code of Professional Conduct,[58] which was adopted much more recently, applies to those serving as international mediators (largely but not exclusively in commercial matters). The Model Standards of Practice for Family and Divorce Mediation[59] were adopted by the Association of Family and Conciliation Courts, Association for Conflict Resolution, and Mediate.com and generally apply to the mediation of family and divorce disputes.

---

56. Shapira, *supra* note 45, at 240 (including consideration of Standard III.F.—"Subsequent to a mediation, a mediator shall not establish another relationship with any of the participants in any matter that would raise questions about the integrity of the mediation.").

57. 29 C.F.R. § 14000.735-20 (2011).

58. Code of Prof'l Conduct, Int'l Mediation Inst., https://imimediation.org/practitioners/code-professional-conduct/#:~:text=The%20IMI%20Code%20of%20Professional,IMI%20Professional%20Conduct%20Assessment%20Process (last visited Mar. 5, 2021).

59. Model Standards of Practice for Family & Divorce Mediation (Ass'n of Family and Conciliation Cts., Ass'n for Conflict Resol. & Mediate.com 2001).

Overwhelmingly, these context-specific mediator ethics codes are consistent with the Model Standards. There are, however, a few notable omissions. None of the context-specific codes identifies the potential for parties to exercise self-determination in making process decisions, such as the decision to hire a single neutral to serve as both mediator and arbitrator. None addresses directly the potential that a mediator may change roles and become an arbitrator in a med-arb. Finally, none suggests a mediator's ethical obligation to protect the integrity of mediation.[60]

10.5.2. Relevant Arbitration Ethics Provisions

10.5.2.1. Code of Ethics for Arbitrators in Commercial Disputes

The Code of Ethics for Arbitrators in Commercial Disputes (Commercial Arbitrators Code)[61] was approved and recommended by the American Arbitration Association and the American Bar Association in 2004. Although it provides ethical guidance for arbitration in many contexts, it explicitly does not apply to labor arbitration.

Integrity, fairness, and impartiality. The Commercial Arbitrators Code gives priority to the neutral's obligations of integrity, process fairness, and impartiality. Unlike the Model Standards, the Commercial Arbitrators Code explicitly recognizes duties owed to the public. Canon I provides that "[a]n arbitrator should uphold the integrity and fairness of the arbitration process." More specifically:

> An arbitrator has a responsibility not only to the parties but also to the process of arbitration itself, and must observe high standards of conduct so that the integrity and fairness of the process will be preserved. Accordingly, an arbitrator should recognize a responsibility to the public, to the parties whose rights will be decided, and to all other participants in the proceeding.

Further, "[o]ne should accept appointment as an arbitrator only if fully satisfied: (1) that he or she can serve impartially. . . ." There is no provision for parties' consent to overcome the arbitrator's obligation to serve impartially and uphold the integrity and fairness of the arbitration process.

---

60. *But see* Shapira, *supra* note 55, at 113 (observing that two states' mediator ethics codes—the Georgia Ethical Standards for Mediators and the California Dispute Resolution Council Standards of Practice for California Mediators—explicitly reference a duty of integrity).

61. CODE OF ETHICS FOR ARB. IN COM. DISPUTES (Am. Arb. Ass'n & Am. Bar. Ass'n 2004).

Fairness and diligence. Perhaps the most basic ethical obligation of the arbitrator is contained in Canon IV of the Commercial Arbitrators Code: "An arbitrator should conduct the proceedings fairly and diligently." As in the Model Standards, Canon IV explicitly recognizes that neutrals may be asked to play dual roles—that is, that an arbitrator may be asked to play the role of mediator:

> Although it is not improper for an arbitrator to suggest to the parties that they discuss the possibility of settlement or the use of mediation, or other dispute resolution processes, an arbitrator should not exert pressure on any party to settle or to utilize other dispute resolution processes. An arbitrator should not be present or otherwise participate in settlement discussions or act as a mediator unless requested to do so by all parties.

Thus, the ethics of serving as both a mediator and arbitrator depends upon the will of the parties. There is no requirement that the arbitrator ensure the parties' informed consent.

However, one of the comments to Canon IV speaks to the potentially negative consequences of an arbitrator's engagement in mediation, particularly if it includes caucusing. Specifically, this comment provides that "[t]he arbitrator should afford to all parties the right to be heard and . . . should allow each party a fair opportunity to present its evidence and arguments." Assume that the neutral in a med-arb learned something during a mediation caucus and knows she has been influenced by what she learned but cannot disclose what she learned to the other party. The other party then *cannot* present evidence and arguments—or even ask questions—to address this point. That party is not being given a fair opportunity to present his evidence and arguments. Thus, the neutral is not providing and cannot provide a procedurally fair process and is not protecting and cannot protect either the integrity or fairness of arbitration. Under these circumstances, the arbitrator must be aware that she cannot uphold her obligations to the parties, the process, or the public as required by Canon I.[62] A very substantial body of research, primarily involving judges, also indicates that the neutral who has learned particularly vivid information while in a mediation caucus—even information that is not legally relevant—will not be able to ignore what he learned,

62. Interestingly, Canon V.D. also acknowledges that arbitral awards sometimes represent consent decrees but makes the arbitrator responsible for assessing the propriety of the settlement terms reached by the parties.

even if he thinks he can.[63] Regardless of whether this information is particularly negative or particularly positive, it will keep the neutral from being able to provide a procedurally fair arbitration and preserve the integrity of the process.

Confidentiality and ex parte communication. The Commercial Arbitrators Code requires a neutral in med-arb to consider further ethical issues, especially if the mediation phase included caucusing and the neutral learned information that she is obligated to keep confidential from the other party. Canon III provides that "an arbitrator should avoid impropriety or the appearance of impropriety in communicating with parties" and more specifically provides that "an arbitrator or prospective arbitrator should not discuss a proceeding with any party in the absence of any other party, except" for a list of specified circumstances. A caucus necessarily involves discussing a proceeding with one party in the absence of the other party. Service as the neutral in a med-arb is not on the list of exceptions to the bar on such ex parte communications. It is possible that disclosure and the parties' consent may overcome this ethical issue,[64] but that is not explicitly provided in Canon III, and as noted previously, neither Canon I nor Canon IV provides for parties' consent or waiver.

Conflicts of interest. Canon II provides that "[a]n arbitrator should disclose any interest or relationship likely to affect impartiality or which might create an appearance of partiality." Among these, an arbitrator should disclose any known professional relationship "which might reasonably affect impartiality or lack of independence in the eyes of any of the parties" as well as "[t]he nature and extent of any prior knowledge they may have of the dispute." If an arbitrator has previously served as mediator, he certainly will have "past knowledge of the dispute"—and if he has had ex parte meetings with the parties, he will have knowledge about both parties that *neither may have regarding the other.* He also may have developed a particular bias for or against a party.

Canon II by itself suggests that disclosure and the parties' consent provide the cure: "When parties, with knowledge of a person's interests and relationships, nevertheless desire that person to serve as an arbitrator, that person may properly serve." According to Canon I, however, the arbitrator retains the independent obligation to determine whether she

63. *See* Welsh, *supra* note 4, at 1029–30; Chris Guthrie et al., *Blinking on the Bench: How Judges Decide Cases*, 93 CORNELL L. REV. 1, 28 (2007); Deason, *supra* note 6, at 121–27.

64. *See* Metro. Prop. & Cas. Ins. Co. v. J.C. Penney Cas. Ins. Co., 780 F. Supp. 885 (D. Conn. 1991) (failure to disclose ex parte activities by a party-appointed arbitrator violated his ethical disclosure obligations).

can serve impartially and uphold the integrity and fairness of the arbitration process. Further, in making this determination, she must take into account her responsibility to the public, not only the parties. If she cannot meet all of her obligations to all of these stakeholders, she should decline the appointment or recuse herself.

10.5.2.2. Context-Specific Arbitrator Ethics Codes

Beginning with the labor-management context, the Code of Professional Responsibility for Arbitrators of Labor-Management Disputes (Labor Arbitration Code)[65] was adopted by the American Arbitration Association, Federal Mediation and Conciliation Service, and National Academy of Arbitrators in 1974, with occasional amendments over the years. In the international arbitration arena, there are no ethics provisions that are binding on all arbitrators. However, in the late 1980s, the International Bar Association promulgated Rules of Ethics for International Arbitrators (IBA Rules)[66] to reflect "internationally accepted guidelines developed by practicing lawyers from all continents."[67] There are no rules of ethics for family and divorce arbitrators.

The Labor Arbitration Code and the IBA Rules mirror the Commercial Arbitrators Code in their ethics provisions requiring arbitrators to conduct fair hearings, maintain impartiality, and disclose conflicts of interest. However, these context-specific ethics codes vary from the Commercial Arbitrators Code in their treatment of neutrals' dual role in med-arb. The Labor Arbitration Code is strikingly matter-of-fact in discussing the potential for a neutral to engage in med-arb. Standard 2 provides that if the parties request med-arb before the arbitrator's appointment and the arbitrator then accepts the appointment, "the arbitrator must perform a mediation role consistent with the circumstances of the case." On the other hand, if a party requests mediation after the arbitration appointment has been made, the arbitrator may only accept the appointment if all the parties agree; otherwise, the arbitration must be continued to decision. Standard 2 also anticipates that the arbitrator may suggest mediation to the parties. This is "not precluded." However:

> To avoid the possibility of improper pressure, the arbitrator should not so suggest unless it can be discerned that both parties

65. Code of Prof'l Responsibility for Arb. of Lab.-Mgmt. Disputes (Nat'l Acad. of Arb., Am. Arb. Ass'n & Fed. Mediation & Conciliation Serv. 1974, amended Sept. 2007).

66. Rules of Ethics for Int'l Arb. (Int'l Bar Ass'n 1987).

67. *Id.* intro.

are likely to be receptive. In any event, the arbitrator's suggestion should not be pursued unless both parties readily agree.

Clearly, in the labor-management context, med-arb is not outside the norm.

The IBA Rules take a quite different approach, specifically addressing in Rule 8 the ethics and consequences of an arbitrator's provision of settlement assistance in meetings that fail to include all of the parties:

> Although any procedure is possible with the agreement of the parties, the arbitral tribunal should point out to the parties that it is undesirable that any arbitrator should discuss settlement terms with a party in the absence of the other parties since *this will normally have the result that any arbitrator involved in such discussions will become disqualified from any future participation in the arbitration.*[68]

This sentence is particularly noteworthy. If the mediation phase in a med-arb involves caucuses and the discussion of settlement terms—a pairing that is almost inevitable—there "normally" cannot be a med-arb. Proceeding to arbitration will be barred. Of course, we must also note the introductory language that "any procedure is possible with the agreement of the parties."

10.6. Managing the Ethics Issues Raised by Med-Arb

As should be apparent, some med-arb variations are more likely than others to avoid or substantially mitigate the ethics problems identified thus far. Ensuring the parties' informed consent also will be key to neutrals' ability to meet their ethical obligations.

10.6.1. Med-Arb Variations That Are More Likely to Avoid or Mitigate Ethics Issues

Sequential med-arb and standby mediator. These two processes are most effective in avoiding the ethics problems identified thus far. This is because they involve two neutrals—one to serve as the mediator, the other to serve as the arbitrator—and thus avoid all of the ethics issues that could be problematic. The parties' self-determination will not be threatened by the neutral's potential adverse arbitral award. The confidentiality of the parties' mediation communications, both in plenary sessions and caucuses, can be fully protected. The mediator does not have to deal with

68. *Id.* R. 8 (emphasis added).

any threats to her impartiality. If the case proceeds to an arbitral award, such award will be based entirely on the evidence presented at the hearing. The integrity of mediation and arbitration are thus fully protected. Of course, because these processes involve two neutrals, they are likely to be more expensive and may require more time than a process involving just one neutral. In addition, during the mediation, the parties will not get the benefit of the neutral's "signaling" regarding his likely decision, nor will they feel any pressure to settle—except to avoid the additional time and cost involved in arbitration. But these last issues are practical and do not raise ethical concerns.

Overlapping med-arb and plenary med-arb. While overlapping med-arb involves two neutrals and plenary med-arb involves just one neutral, these two med-arb variations share the primary ethical benefit of ensuring that the parties will know exactly what the neutral serving as arbitrator heard during the mediation. In overlapping med-arb, caucuses may occur and secrets thus may be disclosed—but only to the neutral who will serve solely as mediator. The arbitral award will be based on the information presented in everyone's presence, during the joint mediation sessions and the arbitration hearing, thus ensuring a fair arbitration process. As with sequential med-arb and standby mediator, the primary disadvantage of this process is practical—the additional cost involved in using a second neutral.

In plenary med-arb, there will be no caucuses and thus no confidential information disclosed to the single neutral serving as mediator and arbitrator. The prohibition on caucusing is likely to be viewed as a significant practical disadvantage because many parties value the opportunity to speak privately with a mediator. In addition, this variation has the ethical disadvantages that if the single neutral shares her assessments or recommendations during the mediation phase, she may experience more difficulty in maintaining her impartiality, and her power as potential arbitrator may interfere with the parties' self-determination in choosing whether to settle.

Med-arb not promising confidentiality. This med-arb variation uses a single neutral and requires the parties' waiver of mediation confidentiality before they enter into the process. Then, if the neutral learns confidential information during the mediation phase and the case does not settle, the neutral is required—before the arbitration begins—to disclose to all the parties "as much of that information as the arbitrator considers material to the arbitral proceedings."[69] The intent of this provi-

69. Permitted by the Hong Kong Arbitration Ordinance, *supra* note 28.

sion is to ensure that all of the parties are aware of the information that could serve as the basis for an award. This gives them the opportunity to present responsive evidence or ask questions at the arbitration hearing. Obviously, this variation allows for an arbitration that is fairer than one that produces an award based in whole or in part on information communicated ex parte and never disclosed to the parties. In other words, it mitigates the potentially negative effects of a med-arb that includes caucusing during the mediation phase. However, this variation fails to acknowledge that an arbitrator may not recognize or be willing to admit (even to himself) that his judgment or impartiality has been or will be influenced by what he learned during a caucus. In a sense, it fails to acknowledge that arbitrators are human too. It also fails to address the ethical challenge to parties' self-determination during the mediation phase when they may feel subject to undue pressure or coercion to accept the neutral's assessment or settlement recommendation.

Opt-in med-arb, opt-out med-arb, MEDLOA. These three options involve a single neutral serving as mediator and then arbitrator, but each introduces an opportunity for the parties to exercise self-determination regarding the process—for example, deciding, at the conclusion of the mediation phase, whether to opt in or opt out of the arbitration phase or, in MEDLOA, placing limits on the arbitrator's discretion in issuing her award. These represent important safeguards of the parties' self-determination in mediation because the parties need not be concerned (or, in the case of MEDLOA, need not be *as* concerned) about the potential for an adverse arbitral award. Despite this benefit, none of these processes explicitly deals with another ethical issue—the potential for the neutral to learn confidential information during caucuses, with such potential then affecting the neutral's impartiality and her ability to provide a fair arbitration hearing for all parties. This remains a significant ethical problem because, ultimately, the parties may not possess the authority to waive the neutral's ethical obligations.

10.7. The Most Problematic Med-Arb Variations and Practices

Four med-arb variations are extraordinarily likely to yield ethical problems, including violation of the obligations of ensuring impartiality, avoiding conflicts of interest and protecting the integrity of both mediation and arbitration, and ensuring self-determination in mediation and fairness in arbitration. These problematic variations are classic same-neutral med-arb, braided arbitration, med-arb not incorporating confidential information learned during caucuses, and med-arb incorporating confidential information learned during caucuses.

In all four of these variations of med-arb, a single neutral conducts the med-arb and may learn something during the mediation phase, especially in caucus, that will then bias him toward or against one of the parties to such a degree that he will not be able to meet his ethical obligations to remain impartial, protect the integrity of either the mediation or arbitration phase, and provide a fair hearing during the arbitration phase. Also, in all of these variations, particularly if the neutral uses caucuses, he is more likely to engage in behavior—or be perceived as engaging in behavior—during the mediation phase that is coercive, simply because he and the parties are aware that he will transform into an arbitrator and thus have the power to impose a decision upon the parties. Finally, none of these variations incorporates any mitigating safeguards such as opt-in, opt-out, or limitations on the neutral's obligation of confidentiality or discretion in fashioning an arbitral award.

A few examples illustrate this point. Regarding threats to the integrity of the arbitration process, the neutral in one of these same-neutral variations may learn something in caucus that she is quite aware will influence her arbitration award but that she is not permitted to disclose to the other party. To nonetheless proceed to arbitration will violate the fairness and integrity of the arbitration process. One of the parties will not know that he should introduce or contest evidence on this particular issue. The neutral may try to persuade the disclosing party to permit her to share the confidential information with the other party. If she is not successful in these efforts, however, the neutral's only ethical course of action must be to withdraw. In another example, the neutral may learn something in caucus that is extremely provocative or coincides with a stereotype that is likely to bias him or influence his arbitration award. Here, the neutral may be unaware or unwilling to admit that he will be biased or influenced and is therefore unlikely to seek the parties' consent for any mitigating disclosures or avoid considering the information as he determines his award. In many ways, this presents an even worse ethical dilemma.

Turning to examples that threaten the integrity of the mediation process, the single neutral involved in classic same-neutral med-arb, braided arbitration, or med-arb incorporating (or not incorporating) confidential information may realize that as a result of his power to serve as arbitrator, he has used behaviors or threatened consequences that have had the effect of coercing one of the parties to enter into a mediated settlement agreement. In this case, the neutral may use a caucus at the end of the mediation phase to remind the party that she is not required to reach agreement and that she may instead proceed to arbitration. But the intimidated party is likely to continue to fear the consequences that she will suffer if she goes to arbitration. Her mediated settlement agreement is unlikely to represent an act of self-determination. Even worse is the example of the less self-reflective neutral who uses behaviors or threatens consequences that have the effect of coercing a party to enter into a mediated settlement agreement but is unaware or unwilling to admit that he has behaved in this way and with these coercive effects. This neutral will have violated both the party's self-determination and the integrity of the mediation process—but will do nothing about it.

All of these problematic examples involve med-arb variations characterized by the presence of a single neutral, the use of caucuses during mediation, the potential influence of confidential information upon the neutral and her arbitral award, and the neutral's inability or unwillingness to breach confidentiality. These med-arb variations are thus particularly susceptible to ethical problems. Although this chapter will soon turn to what should be disclosed to gain parties' informed consent to med-arb, such consent cannot be sufficient to overcome every ethical issue. Rather, under both the Model Standards and the Commercial Arbitrators Code, neutrals remain responsible for making independent judgments regarding whether they can fulfill their ethical obligations—to be impartial, avoid conflicts of interest, protect the integrity of both the mediation and arbitration phases, and conduct a fair arbitration hearing. In making such judgments, it is up to neutrals—not the parties—to protect public trust in the mediation and arbitration professions and processes.

10.8. Ensuring the Parties' Informed Consent to Med-Arb

As discussed throughout this chapter, many—but not all—ethics obligations can be waived or met through parties' informed consent. Indeed, most of the commentary regarding med-arb involves this topic—that is, what a neutral must disclose in order to ensure the parties' informed consent to the mechanics and consequences of the process. Thus, ensuring the parties' informed consent to med-arb is essential. But as this chapter has revealed, such consent will not be sufficient to overcome certain violations of neutrals' ethical obligations to protect the integrity of the mediation and arbitration processes. Gaining the parties' informed consent to dual service is a precondition, but it is not sufficient in and of itself.

With that warning as preface, to be effective, neutrals' disclosures to ensure the parties' informed consent to med-arb should include all of the following:

(1) An initial agreement of the parties to use med-arb and the services of the neutral (or neutrals) chosen to serve as mediator and then arbitrator.
(2) Confirmation of the impartiality of the neutral(s), absence of conflicts of interest, independence of all the parties, and obligation to act in good faith.
(3) Explanation of the processes and roles of the neutral(s) in each phase of the process, with special emphasis on the neutral's role in the mediation phase to assist the parties to reach their own resolution and not to impose an outcome, as contrasted with the neutral's role during the arbitration phase, when he will adjudicate and impose an outcome that will be binding upon the parties.
(4) Explanation of the specifics of the med-arb variation being used. For example, in opt-out mediation, that at the conclusion of the mediation phase, if a mediated settlement agreement has not been reached, parties are entitled to opt out and not proceed to the arbitration phase, etc.
(5) Confirmation of the parties' understanding of the risks involved in the use of med-arb. For example, in the med-arb variations involving a single neutral and the use of caucuses, these will include the risks that
    (a) the neutral and his arbitral award may be influenced (consciously or subconsciously) by confidential information learned during the mediation phase;
    (b) information learned by the neutral during ex parte meetings (caucuses) in the mediation phase may influence him and his award and will not be disclosed to the other side;
    (c) the process will likely cause the neutral to receive information that might not otherwise have been received as evidence in arbitration;
    (d) the parties might not know of the information the mediator learned in caucus and thus will not know to contest it at the arbitration hearing; and
    (e) the neutral may share his assessments or settlement recommendations during the mediation phase, and parties may feel pressured to accept such assessments or recommendations due to the neutral's dual role and his authority as arbitrator to impose an outcome.[70]

---

70. *See* Lavi, *supra* note 19, at 140–42 (advising additional disclosures to avoid legal, rather than ethical, issues); Lavi, *supra* note 24, at 931–32; Deason, *supra* note

10.9. Conclusion

Increasingly, there is interest in the use of mixed-mode dispute resolution, including med-arb. Med-arb provides the opportunity for parties to reach their own agreements, while also guaranteeing a binding decision. As this chapter has revealed, however, med-arb presents a variety of ethical challenges. Some of these challenges can be met through the use of two neutrals rather than one, providing for the parties' opt-out or opt-in before the commencement of the arbitration phase, the avoidance of caucuses during mediation, and establishing exceptions to the confidentiality of mediation communications. Also essential is careful and thorough assurance of parties' informed consent. But some med-arb variations, including the one that is discussed most often—classic same-neutral med-arb—do not incorporate any meaningful mitigating procedural elements and present ethical dangers that cannot be guaranteed to be overcome by neutrals' self-awareness or the parties' informed consent. This chapter urges the avoidance of these med-arb variations—thus prioritizing the protection of parties' self-determination, neutrals' impartiality, and the fairness and integrity of both mediation and arbitration.

1, at 247–49; Gerald Phillips, *Same-Neutral Med-Arb: What Does the Future Hold?*, 60 Disp. Resol. J. 24, 30 (2005).

Part IV

The Conclusion of Mediation and Its Aftermath

Chapter 11

The Mediated Agreement

Fran L. Tetunic

11.1. Introduction

The familiar expression "The devil's in the details" aptly fits mediated agreements. Reaching agreement, the culmination of the mediation process, is symbolic and ceremonial. Whether celebratory, nerve-wracking, or numbing, it documents closure of the parties' dispute by delineating their future rights and obligations.

Working through the process of mediation for the parties to reach agreement requires the mediator's adherence to ethical standards, from first contemplating acceptance of the case through and following the signing of the agreement. Numerous ethical challenges may bedevil the mediator throughout and beyond the mediated agreement process.

Despite inconsistency in the definition of mediation and the enunciated role of the mediator, the parties' role as decision maker is consistent and unique to the mediation process. Statutory law and applicable rules provide that the parties have self-determination to decide if they will reach agreement, as well as the consensual terms of their agreement. Self-determination stands as the cornerstone of mediation, which arises from the parties' voluntary and informed decision making.[1] The media-

1. Scott H. Hughes, *The Uniform Mediation Act: To the Spoiled Go the Privileges*, 85 Marq. L. Rev. 9, 72 (2001).

tor stands as guardian of the process, protecting the integrity of mediation[2] and meeting ethical obligations to the parties, process, profession, courts, and referring entities.[3] This chapter will address the importance of memorializing mediated agreements, along with the mediator's critical responsibility to honor party self-determination throughout and following the mediation process. It will reflect the significant variation in the law on mediated agreements, as well as the mediator's multiple, and possibly conflicting, ethical obligations regarding mediated agreement formation. Section 11.4 will provide information on the qualities and requirements for mediated agreements, along with the mediator's obligation to follow applicable ethical codes when working with parties to memorialize their agreements. Section 11.5 will address the ethical obligation of the mediator to prevent the formation of illegal, unconscionable, and grossly unfair mediated agreements. Lastly, Section 11.6 will discuss mediators' continuing ethical obligations in the event an agreement is not reached or following the agreement formation process.

11.2. Background: Mediators' Ethical Guidelines—Differing, Yet with a Common Core

Mediation to resolve (or avoid) disputes is widespread, including court cases as well as matters that do not anticipate litigation. Based on the jurisdiction and type of case being mediated, the definition of mediation may vary, along with the mediator's role and ethical obligations.[4] Mediation may be defined simply as "a process in which a mediator facilitates communication and negotiation between parties to assist them in reaching a voluntary agreement regarding their dispute."[5] It may be more specifically defined as "a process whereby a neutral third party called a mediator acts to encourage and facilitate the resolution of a dispute between two or more parties. It is an informal and non-adversarial process with

2. Ga. Ethical Standards for Mediators, Standard IV.B. (Ga. Comm'n on Dispute Resolution 2013).

3. Omer Shapira, *A Critical Assessment of the Model Standards of Conduct for Mediation: Call for Reform*, 100 Marq. L. Rev. 81, 113 (2016) (discussing mediators' obligation to the profession and the public in addition to the parties, with their responsibility to preserve the institution of mediation); Fla. Rules for Certified & Ct.-Appointed Mediators (delineating mediators' responsibility to the parties, Rules 10.300–10.380; to the process, Rules 10.400–10.430; to the courts, Rules 10.500–10.530; and to the profession, Rules 10.600–10.690).

4. Shapira, *supra* note 3.

5. Unif. Mediation Act § 2(1) (Unif. Law Comm'n 2005).

the objective of helping disputing parties reach a mutually acceptable and voluntary agreement. In mediation, decision making authority rests with the parties. The role of the mediator includes, but is not limited to, assisting the parties in identifying issues, fostering joint problem solving, and exploring settlement alternatives."[6]

If the process fits the applicable definition of mediation, the mediator has inherently assumed the ethical obligation of preserving the integrity of the process.[7] Regardless of the style of mediation or type of case, mediators have a shared set of mediation norms based on their codes of conduct and the mediation literature.[8] The shared norms transcend differences in codes of conduct for mediators. Notably, the mediator does not serve as decision maker.[9] Rather, the mediator honors the parties' self-determination as to whether they reach an agreement and the terms of any agreement they may reach,[10] absent a controlling obligation to do otherwise.[11] Mediators are also obligated to know and comply with the law and rules applicable to the cases they are mediating.[12]

Mediators determine many matters consequential to the mediated agreement before and during the mediation.[13] Even if the ethical standards to which a mediator is bound do not specifically address mediated agreements,[14] mediators are guided by principles of party

---

6. FLA. STAT. § 44.1011.

7. *See, e.g.*, GA. ETHICAL STANDARDS, *supra* note 2 (establishing the mediator as the guardian of the integrity of the mediation process); FLA. RULES FOR CERTIFIED & CT.-APPOINTED MEDIATORS R. 10.200 (providing whether parties decide to settle is secondary in importance to whether the mediator conducts the mediation according to the ethical rules).

8. OMER SHAPIRA, A THEORY OF MEDIATORS' ETHICS: FOUNDATIONS, RATIONALE AND APPLICATION 85 (2016).

9. *See, e.g.*, FLA. STAT. § 44.1011(2) (noting that decision-making authority rests with the parties).

10. *See, e.g.*, MODEL STANDARDS OF CONDUCT FOR MEDIATORS, Standard I.A. (Am. Arb. Ass'n, Am. Bar Ass'n, Ass'n for Conflict Resol. 2005).

11. *See infra* Section 11.5.

12. *See, e.g.*, FLA. RULES FOR CERTIFIED & CT.-APPOINTED MEDIATORS R. 10.520 (requiring mediators to "comply with all statutes, court rules, local court rules, and administrative orders relevant to the practice of mediation").

13. Sharon Press & Paul M. Lurie, *A Mediator's Obligation to Memorialize the Agreement*, 22 DISP. RESOL. MAG. no. 1, Fall 2015, at 39.

14. *See, e.g.*, MODEL STANDARDS, *supra* note 10.

self-determination,[15] conflict of interest,[16] competence,[17] impartiality,[18] confidentiality,[19] and quality of the process.[20] They necessarily make important process decisions, including the appropriateness of the case for mediation,[21] whether the parties are able to meaningfully participate,[22] and whether the process is being misused.[23] While some mediators are subject to advisory codes of conduct, others have ethical rules, the breach of which may lead to decertification or delisting. Notably, all mediators have core principles to guide them. While not all mediators are required to follow specific codes of conduct, all individuals conducting a process they call mediation are duty bound to honor the parties' self-determination. Mediators respect the proposition that party self-determination is a critical foundational principle of mediation and the parties' control over their resolution fuels the power of the mediation process.[24]

11.3. The Importance of Memorializing Mediated Agreements

Mediation is not a mere settlement process, and mediated agreements are not merely settlement agreements.[25] Rather, mediation provides the opportunity for the parties to collaboratively structure an agreement uniquely suited to their needs and interests. As mediated agreements may be subject to varying requirements governing their memorialization,[26] mediators will need to know if specific requirements apply to the cases they are mediating. In some jurisdictions, oral agreements will not be recognized or enforced. Further, even if oral agreements are recognized, confidentiality and privilege provisions may prevent parties from introducing evidence needed to prove the existence or terms of the agreement. The question of whether parties reached agreement at mediation is the

15. *Id.* Standard I.
16. *Id.* Standard II.
17. *Id.* Standard IV.
18. *Id.* Standard II.
19. *Id.* Standard V.
20. *Id.* Standard VI.
21. *Id.* Standard VI.A.6, 7.
22. *Id.* Standard VI.A.10.
23. *Id.* Standard VI.A.6, 9.
24. Ga. Ethical Standards for Mediators, *supra* note 2, Commentary; Ga. Rules Uniform ADR app. C, ch. 1.
25. Peter N. Thompson, *Enforcing Rights Generated in Court-Connected Mediation—Tension between the Aspirations of a Private Facilitative Process and the Reality of Public Adversarial Justice*, 19 Ohio St. J. on Disp. Resol. 509, 539 (2004).
26. *See infra.* Section 11.4.2.

most common issue regarding the enforcement of mediated agreements.[27] Courts have difficulty finding a mediated agreement when the parties do not have an executed writing to show the court.[28]

Written documents provide formal recognition of the parties' agreement and provide a comprehensive settlement to avoid misunderstanding and ambiguity.[29] A written mediated agreement brings a sense of closure and certainty to the parties,[30] with legal as well as emotional benefits.[31] With a memorialized agreement, they leave the mediation knowing the specific terms and conditions on which they have agreed.[32] Without a memorialized agreement, the parties may later find themselves turning to the court for relief should the agreement have come undone. Ironically, having sought to problem-solve themselves and avoid court determination, they then find themselves seeking court intervention to decide their mediated-agreement dispute.[33] Further, they may run afoul of confidentiality or privilege provisions that prevent admission of evidence to establish the very existence, let alone terms, of the agreement.[34] Hence, mediators will well serve the parties by discussing with them the appropriate memorialization of their agreement.[35]

11.4. The Mediated Agreement

11.4.1. Basic Qualities

Mediated agreements, as settlement agreements, follow the accepted formality of parties reducing to writing and signing their agreed-upon terms and conditions.[36] However, variations in the law regarding mediated

27. Thompson, *supra* note 25, at 523.

28. *Id.* at 524.

29. Ellen E. Deason, *Enforcing Mediated Settlement Agreements: Contract Law Collides with Confidentiality*, 35 U.C. DAVIS L. REV. 33, 73–85 (2001).

30. Press & Lurie, *supra* note 13, at 39.

31. *Id.*

32. *Id.*

33. The most frequently litigated mediation issue involves parties attempting to enforce mediated agreements. *See* James R. Coben & Peter N. Thompson, *Disputing Irony: A Systemic Look at Litigation about Mediation,* 11 HARV. NEGOT. L. REV. 43, 66–75 (2006).

34. *See, e.g.*, CAL. EVID. CODE § 1119(b).

35. *See, e.g.*, FLA. RULES FOR CERTIFIED & CT.-APPOINTED MEDIATORS ("The mediator shall cause the terms of any agreement reached to be memorialized appropriately and discuss with the parties and counsel the process for formalization and implementation of the agreement.").

36. R. Wayne Thorpe & Jennifer Boyens, *Mediated Settlement Agreements: Legal, Ethical, and Practical Issues*, 16 ALTS. TO HIGH COST LITIG. 93 (1998).

agreements may also result in enforcement, under certain circumstances, of oral agreements[37] or technologically inscribed records of agreement.[38] In addition to satisfying form requirements, mediated agreements must meet certain substantive requirements.[39] As with other settlement agreements, the necessary parties must agree to the terms,[40] and the parties must have the requisite settlement authority.[41] Mediation parties cannot bind parties who were not participating in the mediation.[42]

However memorialized, the mediated agreement should specify whether it is a partial or full resolution of the parties' dispute and whether it represents the complete agreement. Parties often sign a document that contemplates a more formal agreement that would be binding only when agreed upon and executed by the parties.[43] This must be duly noted in their agreement to prevent a party from attempting to enforce a document not intended to be final or binding. Similarly, if the parties merely have "an agreement to agree," that must clearly be stated to prevent future confusion and misinterpretation.[44]

Memoranda of Understanding will suffice to establish the parties' mediated agreement when the terms resolve the crucial issues and are definite enough to be enforced.[45] Language that clearly states that the settlement was intended to be an enforceable agreement will discourage litigation inconsistent with the parties' intent at the time of signing their agreement.[46]

The opportune time for the mediator to assist parties in capturing the terms and conditions of their agreement is during the mediation.[47]

---

37. *See infra* Section 11.4.2.1.

38. Unif. Mediation Act § 6(a)(1); *see infra* Section 11.4.2.1.

39. *See infra* Section 11.4.2.2.

40. Court rules or orders often specify the parties who are required to attend the mediation.

41. *See, e.g.*, Fla. R. Civ. P. 1.720(b)(1) (requiring parties attending mediation to have full settlement authority).

42. Sunshine Props. v. State Dep't of Transp., 900 So. 2d 714 (Fla. Dist. Ct. App. 2005) (deciding the mediated agreement between the department and a lessor did not constitute a settlement of lessee's damages when lessee was not a party to the mediated agreement, even though the settlement was subject to apportionment).

43. Thompson, *supra* note 25, at 524.

44. *Id.*

45. Deason, *supra* note 29, at 21.

46. *Id.*

47. Thorpe & Boyens, *supra* note 36; Comm. on Ethics of the Ga. Comm'n on Disp. Resol., Ethics Op. 1 (1998).

Matters such as waivers[48] and confidentiality provisions are best clarified to avoid future problems.[49] If complete drafting of the final agreement is not possible during the mediation session, the parties should agree on a memorialization plan that identifies who has the obligation to do what, when, and how to avoid confusion and prevent the later casting of blame should the memorialization go awry.[50]

As with other settlement agreements, mediated agreements will, at times, require court approval. Certain types of cases, such as bankruptcy and class actions, may require the court to determine if the mediated agreement is fair.[51] In divorce cases, matters regarding child custody and support are generally subject to court approval with determination of the best interests of the children.[52] Additionally, the parties may, at times, present their mediated agreement as a stipulation for court approval.[53] When mediated agreements are incorporated in a court order or the court retains jurisdiction over the matter, the court may use its contempt powers for enforcing its orders.[54]

11.4.2. Requirements Specific to Mediated Agreements

11.4.2.1. Mediated Agreement Form

Mediated agreements are contracts subject to contract law[55] and will generally be enforceable to the same extent as settlement agreements.[56]

48. *See, e.g.*, Chappell v. Roth, 353 N.C. 690 (2001) (finding mediated agreement was not enforceable because agreement provided for release "mutually agreeable to both parties" and parties did not agree on the release).

49. *See, e.g.*, Gulliver Schools, Inc. v. Snay, 137 So. 3d 1045 (Fla. Dist. Ct. App. 2014) (finding Snay was not entitled to enforcement of the settlement agreement because he had breached the confidentiality provision by telling his daughter that the case was settled to their satisfaction). *See infra* Section 11.4.3.

50. *See, e.g.*, FLA. RULES FOR CERTIFIED & CT.-APPOINTED MEDIATORS ("The mediator shall cause the terms of any agreement reached to be memorialized appropriately and discuss with the parties and counsel the process for formalization and implementation of the agreement.").

51. SARAH R. COLE ET AL., MEDIATION: LAW, POLICY AND PRACTICE § 7:17 (2018).

52. *Id.* § 15:2.

53. *See, e.g.*, COLO. REV. STAT. § 13-22-308 (providing the mediated agreement may be presented as a stipulation and, if approved by the court, will be enforceable as an order of the court).

54. COLE ET AL., *supra* note 51, § 7:19.

55. Mediated agreements are subject to contract law according to state rules. RESTATEMENT (SECOND) OF CONTRACTS § 188 (1981).

56. MINN. STAT. § 572.35 subdiv. 1.

Whether settlement agreements constitute valid enforceable contracts is a matter of state law.[57] The formality required for a court to enforce mediated agreements will differ based on jurisdiction and case type and may exceed the requirements for settlement agreements. Florida, for example, definitively requires that mediated agreements be in writing.[58] The Florida courts will not recognize oral agreements or admit evidence regarding their existence.[59] Similarly, mediation parties in the 12 states that have presently adopted the Uniform Mediation Act (UMA) will require a signed record of mediated agreements.[60] While the UMA provides for privileged mediation communication, it specifically excepts a record of an agreement signed by all of the parties to the agreement.[61] Consequently, if the parties want their agreement to be admissible in subsequent court proceedings, they must have a written agreement signed by the parties or a record "inscribed on a tangible medium" or "stored in an electronic or other medium, and retrievable in perceivable form."[62]

Although oral mediated agreements are commonly not honored or enforced by the courts, some states will recognize them. California does recognize an oral mediated agreement if the agreement is recorded; the terms are recited on the record in the presence of the parties and the mediator; and either the parties state that the agreement is enforceable or binding, or the recording is reduced to writing and signed by the parties within 72 hours after it was recorded.[63]

Written mediated agreements will only be recognized when they have the requisite signatures. The Minnesota statutory definition of mediated settlement agreement is "a written agreement setting out the terms of a partial or complete settlement of a controversy identified in an agreement

---

57. Restatement (Second) of Contracts § 188 (1981).

58. *See* Fla. R. Civ. P. 1.730(b), Fla. R. Juv. P. 8.290(o), Fla. R. Fam. Law 12.740(f) (requiring that mediated agreements be reduced to writing).

59. *See, e.g.*, Hudson v. Hudson, 600 So. 2d 7, 9 (Fla. Dist. Ct. App. 1992) (holding courts will not recognize oral mediated agreements or hear testimony alleging their existence); Cohen v. Cohen, 609 So. 2d 785 (Fla. Dist. Ct. App. 1992) (holding an oral settlement agreement reached during mediation is inadmissible as privileged unless it has been reduced to writing).

60. Nebraska, Illinois, Iowa, New Jersey, Washington, Ohio, Utah, Vermont, the District of Columbia, South Dakota, Idaho, and Hawaii have enacted the UMA. *See* Unif. Law Comm'n, uniformlaws.org/home (last visited Mar. 8, 2021). The states of Massachusetts (HB60) and Georgia (SB7464) have introduced bills in 2020. *Id.*

61. Unif. Mediation Act § 6(a)(1).

62. *Id.* cmt. § 2(8).

63. Cal. Evid. Code ch. 2, § 1118.

to mediate, signed by the parties, and dated."[64] Consistent with Minnesota's definition, Florida[65] and Indiana[66] will recognize mediated agreements only when they are signed by the parties and their counsel, if any.

Significant variation in law and rules exists both among and within states. Court rules may differ within a state depending on the court in which the case is pending. Florida, like Indiana, requires that mediated agreements for circuit civil cases must be in writing and signed by the parties and their attorneys, if any. However, for small-claims cases in Florida, either a party's attorney or nonlawyer representative may appear and enter into the mediated agreement if she has full settlement authority without further consultation.[67] Florida rules require a mediator to "comply with all statutes, court rules, local court rules, and administrative orders relevant to the practice of mediation,"[68] making it essential for mediators to stay abreast of the applicable law and rules.

11.4.2.2. Mediated Agreement Substance

State statutory law may require that mediated agreements include specific clauses to be enforceable.[69] California has conditions for the recognition of written as well as oral mediation agreements, requiring that they be signed by the parties and one of the following applies: the agreement provides that (1) it is subject to disclosure or admissible, (2) it is enforceable or binding, (3) all parties expressly agree to its disclosure in writing or orally, or (4) the agreement is used to show fraud, duress, or illegality related to the dispute.[70]

Similarly, Minnesota law provides that for a mediated agreement to be binding, it must include a provision stating it is binding, and the parties must be advised that (1) the mediator does not have a duty to "protect their interests or provide them with information about their legal rights," (2) "signing a mediated settlement agreement may adversely affect their legal rights," and (3) "they should consult an attorney before signing a mediated settlement agreement if they are uncertain of their rights."[71] This

64. MINN. STAT. § 572.33 subdiv. 4.

65. FLA. R. CIV. P. 1.730(b).

66. IND. ALT. DISP. RESOL. R. 2.7 (E)(2).

67. FLA. R. CIV. P. 1.750(e). The nonlawyer representative would require signed written authority from the party. *Id.*

68. FLA. RULES FOR CERTIFIED & CT.-APPOINTED MEDIATORS R. 10.520.

69. Thompson, *supra* note 25, at 540.

70. CAL. EVID. CODE § 1123. The waiver would need to meet the requirements of CAL. EVID. CODE ch. 2, § 1118.

71. MINN. STAT. § 572.35 subdiv. 1.

provision can lead to a result inconsistent with party intent. For example, a mediated agreement that stated it was a "Full and Final Mutual Release of All Claims" and signed by the parties on each page was determined to be unenforceable by the Minnesota Supreme Court because it did not contain the required provision "stating that it is binding."[72]

As mediated agreements are subject to additional requirements, they may also face additional challenges because the parties resolved their dispute through the mediation process. In addition to the traditional contract-law defenses,[73] mediated agreements may be challenged based on mediator misconduct.[74]

11.4.3. Confidentiality Considerations

Confidentiality issues remain high in importance for party determination when drafting their mediated agreement. Parties often include confidentiality provisions in their mediated agreements to limit future communication about the settlement and provide for consequences in the event of disclosure. For example, a mediated employment discrimination case in which the confidentiality provision was breached underscores the importance of careful drafting and the parties' clear understanding of the provision.[75] The mediated agreement settling the case had a confidentiality provision that read, "[T]he plaintiff shall not either directly or indirectly, disclose, discuss or communicate to any entity or person, except his attorneys or other professional advisors or spouse any information whatsoever regarding *the existence* or terms of this Agreement . . . . A breach . . . will result in disgorgement of the Plaintiff's portion of the settlement Payments."[76] When the plaintiff advised his daughter that the suit had been settled, she posted on Facebook: "[M]ama and papa Snay won their case against Gulliver. Gulliver is now officially paying for my vacation to

---

72. Haghighi v. Russian-Am. Broad. Co., 173 F.3d 1086, 1088 (8th Cir. 1999).

73. *See, e.g.*, Fran L. Tetunic & Gregory Firestone, *Confidentiality and Privilege for Family and Child Protection Mediation: A Roadmap for Navigating the Innovation, Inconsistency and Confusion*, 58 FAM. CT. REV. 46, pt. IV.E., F. (2020) (identifying common challenges to mediated agreements).

74. Vitakis-Valchine v. Valchine, 793 So. 2d 1094 (Fla. Dist. Ct. App. 2011). *See also* Fran L. Tetunic, *The Irony of Mediator as Problem Maker: Mediator Misconduct Setting Aside Mediated Agreements*, 23 HARV. NEGOT. L. REV. 177 (2017).

75. Gulliver Schools, Inc. v. Snay, 137 So. 3d 1045 (Fla. Dist. Ct. App. 2014).

76. *Id.* at 1046.

Europe. SUCK IT."[77] Plaintiff's breach of the confidentiality provision in the mediated agreement led to disgorgement of his settlement payment.[78]

The mediated agreement itself presents a confidentiality decision for the parties. State law is not consistent on the confidentiality of mediated agreements, and parties may want to include an agreement provision regarding the confidentiality of their agreement. For example, in Virginia[79] and Florida,[80] written mediated agreements signed by the parties are not confidential, so parties would need to agree to have their agreement be confidential.[81] In contrast, California considers mediated agreements to be confidential.[82] The parties would have to agree in writing to waive confidentiality.[83]

As mediated agreements may be confidential, mediation communications may also remain confidential. Mediation confidentiality and privilege may preclude parties from introducing evidence they would need to set aside their mediated agreement or to prove wrongdoing occurring during mediation. In some states, parties who sued their attorneys, alleging malpractice during mediation, were unable to admit evidence they needed to prove their case.[84] The courts decided that the attorney-client communication during mediation was confidential and therefore inadmissible in evidence. Had the individuals settled without mediation, the communications would not have been confidential.[85] California has addressed this issue by requiring attorneys to provide notice to their clients in writing in advance of mediation that all of the communications between the client and attorney in preparation for and during mediation will be confidential (except in rare circumstances) even if the client decides to sue the attorney for malpractice based on the mediation.[86] Mediators in the state have no comparable directive.

---

77. *Id.* at 1047.

78. *Id.* at 1046–47 (Mr. Snay did not lose the agreed-upon $10,000 for back pay, and the disgorgement did not affect the agreed-upon $60,000 for attorneys' fees. He lost the $80,000 settlement figure.).

79. VA. CODE §§ 8.01–581.22.

80. FLA. STAT. § 44.405(4)(a).

81. Virginia requires that the parties' agreement regarding confidentiality be in writing. VA. CODE §§ 8.01–581.22.

82. CAL. EVID. CODE § 1119(b).

83. *Id.* § 1123.

84. *See* Alfieri v. Solomon, 365 P.3d 99 (Or. 2015); Grubaugh v. Blomo, 359 P.3d 1008 (Ariz. Ct. App. 2015); Amis v. Greenberg Traurig, 185 Cal. Rptr. 3d 322 (2015).

85. *Id.*

86. CAL. EVID. CODE § 1129.

Mediation parties require the necessary information about confidentiality to decide whether to settle at mediation. They may decide not to do so if it means losing causes of action they would otherwise have. Along with hearing the benefits of mediation confidentiality, parties should learn the possible detriments. Only with knowledge may parties make voluntary and informed decisions, exercising self-determination.[87]

11.4.4. Mediators' Ethical Obligations Regarding Mediated Agreement Formation

Mediated-agreement drafting does not occur in a vacuum. All that happens before the drafting shapes the extent to which parties understand their role and make decisions during the process. Commentators have expressed concern that with the institutionalization of mediation in the court system, there has been an overemphasis on case settlement[88] with underemphasis on party self-determination.[89] Commentators have also expressed concern that some mediators are using questionable tactics to secure settlement.[90] Notably, mediators must be aware that the manner in which they conduct the process greatly impacts the parties' ability to make voluntary settlement-agreement decisions. The comfortable mediation setting with the mediator's thoughtful and helping demeanor may leave parties susceptible to actual or perceived pressure by the mediator.[91] In a federal employment discrimination case, a party sought to overturn the mediated agreement, alleging that the mediator coerced him to settle his case.[92] The court found the mediator "simply served his facilitative function of relaying the Defendant's settlement offer, together with posturing, to the Plaintiff."[93] The plaintiff had mistaken the words of defendant's counsel conveyed by the mediator for the message of the

---

87. GA. ETHICAL STANDARDS FOR MEDIATORS, *supra* note 2, Standard I.C.; "An informed decision must be based on the hazards of mediation as well if it is to be a true exercise of self-determination." SHAPIRA, *supra* note 8, at 155.

88. Kimberlee K. Kovach, *Musings on Idea(l)s in the Ethical Regulation of Mediators: Honesty, Enforcement and Education*, 21 OHIO ST. J. ON DISP. RESOL. 123, 132–33 (2005).

89. Nancy A. Welsh, *The Thinning Vision of Self-Determination in Court-Connected Mediation: The Inevitable Price of Institutionalization?*, 6 HARV. NEGOT. L. REV. 1, 7 (2001).

90. *See generally* James J. Alfini, *Thrashing, Bashing and Hashing It Out: Is This the End of "Good Mediation"?*, 19 FLA. ST. U. L. REV. 47 (1991).

91. Thompson, *supra* note 25, at 530–31.

92. Rodriquez v. Hiday & Ricke, P.A., No. 14-CV-61509, 2015 WL 1470513 (S.D. Fla. Mar. 31, 2015).

93. *Id.* at *4.

mediator.[94] To minimize the likelihood of being named as the wrongdoer in a lawsuit seeking to overturn a mediated agreement, and to avoid an appearance of partiality, mediators should clearly advise when they are conveying the message of another and carefully monitor the content and tone of their communication.

Standards of Practice provide guidance on the role of the mediator in the agreement-memorialization phase. They contemplate mediators serving to memorialize the parties' mediated agreement, providing that the mediator may prepare a memorandum of understanding/agreement that documents the participants' resolution, with the participants' agreement.[95] While attorneys often draft the mediated agreement, mediators may be requested to act as scribe to capture the agreement, especially if parties are not represented by counsel. The Florida Rules provide that even though mediators have an obligation to ensure the agreement is properly memorialized, they do not have the obligation to write the parties' agreement.[96] Mediators may, however, consistent with party self-determination and mediator impartiality, serve as scrivener to memorialize the parties' mediated agreement without adding terms to the agreement.[97] It is not acceptable for a mediator to create new terms[98] or operative language.[99]

The ABA Section of Dispute Resolution addressed the issue of mediation and the unauthorized practice of law with recognition of the principle that "[m]ediation is not the practice of law."[100] Lawyer mediators who discuss legal matters with parties during mediation are not providing legal advice and have not established an attorney-client relationship.[101] When mediators prepare a mediated agreement or memorandum of understanding simply incorporating the parties' settlement terms, they are not practicing law.[102] In contrast, if mediators go beyond the parties' settlement terms when drafting the mediated agreement, they may be engaging in the practice of law.[103] When parties are represented by

94. *Id.*

95. STANDARDS OF PRACTICE FOR PROF'L FAMILY MEDIATORS, Standard VI.C.6 (Acad. of Prof'l Family Mediators 2014).

96. FLA. RULES FOR CERTIFIED & CT.-APPOINTED MEDIATORS R. 10.420(c) with Comm. Notes.

97. Press & Lurie, *supra* note 13.

98. *Id.*

99. ABA Section of Disp. Resol., Resolution on Mediation and the Unauthorized Practice of Law (Feb. 2, 2002).

100. *Id.*

101. *Id.* at 1.

102. *Id.*

103. *Id.*

counsel, mediators are less constrained and may make proposals for settlement terms if they disclose that the proposals are merely informational, for the parties to consider in consultation with their attorneys.[104]

Lawyer mediators will be wise to faithfully stay in the role of mediator and not stray to the practice of law. This requires compliance with the ethical standards for lawyers as well as mediators. Fortunately, the American Bar Association Model Rules of Professional Conduct are in line with ethical guidelines for mediators. Lawyers serving as third-party neutrals are required to inform unrepresented parties that they are not representing them.[105] If the parties do not understand the mediator's role, the lawyer mediator shall explain the difference between the two roles.[106] Consistently, mediators' responsibilities include informing the parties that the role of the mediator is to assist them in reaching a voluntary agreement and does not include legal representation.[107] Ethical rules vary on mediators' obligations to inform parties about mediated agreements. The ABA Resolution on the Unauthorized Practice of Law states mediators should inform the parties that the mediated agreement may affect their legal rights and they should seek the advice of counsel before signing the agreement.[108] The Standards of Practice for Professional Family Mediators provide that the mediator may inform participants that the agreement can be reviewed by an attorney before they sign it[109] and may suggest that the participants obtain legal representation before completing their agreement.[110] The Florida Rule on Independent Legal Advice does not generally apply to all mediation parties.[111] If the mediator believes the party does not understand how the mediated agreement might adversely affect legal rights or obligations, then the mediator has the obligation to advise the party of the right to obtain legal counsel.[112] The mediator does not have a duty to advise a party of legal ramifications of an agreement but does have a duty to advise parties of the importance of knowing such

104. *Id.*
105. Model Rules of Prof'l Conduct R. 2.4(b) (Am. Bar Ass'n 2020).
106. *Id.*
107. *Id.*
108. ABA Resolution on Mediation, *supra* note 99, at 1.
109. Standards for Family Mediators, *supra* note 95, Standard VI.C.4.
110. *Id.* Standard VI.C.3.
111. Fla. Rules for Certified & Ct.-Appointed Mediators R. 10.370(c).
112. *Id.*

information and to give the parties the opportunity to seek the advice of counsel.[113]

Likewise, mediators do not have an ethical duty to sign mediated agreements. Ethical rules do not address mediators signing the mediated agreement, although they are sometimes asked to do so. As mediators are not parties to the agreement, they are not signatories agreeing to and bound by the agreement. Further, mediators should not insert their own language for their purposes, such as including that the parties agree the mediator has complied with the ethical rules.[114] Including issues that are extraneous to the parties' dispute is improper, as the mediated agreement is a memorialization of the terms that resolve the parties' dispute.[115] For reasons other than serving as signatory, mediators may identify themselves as the mediator for the case or confirm the parties' agreement.[116]

11.5. Mediators' Ethical Obligation to Prevent the Formation of Certain Mediated Agreements

Ethical obligations regarding the mediated agreement may require the mediator to decline or discontinue service on a case. Even when parties want to enter into an agreement, mediators may be obligated to intervene or terminate formation of the mediated agreement if the agreement terms would be illegal, unconscionable, or grossly unfair.[117] While party decision making is a fundamental feature of mediation, mediators are obligated to conduct a quality process.[118] Having the parties settle at mediation is secondary in importance to the mediator conducting the mediation in accordance with ethical standards.[119] The public's continued use of and satisfaction with mediation depend on mediators embracing the highest ethical principles.[120]

---

113. Fla. Rules for Certified & Ct.-Appointed Mediators R. 10.370 Comm. Notes.

114. Fla. Mediator Ethics Advisory Comm. [hereinafter MEAC] Advisory Op. 2018-001 (2018).

115. *Id.*

116. *See, e.g.*, Colo. Rev. Stat. § 13-22-308 (2019) (requiring mediators to make a written summary of the parties' agreement for their and their attorneys' signatures).

117. Shapira, *supra* note 8, at 247–49.

118. Model Standards, *supra* note 10, Standard I.A.

119. *See, e.g.*, Fla. Rules for Certified & Ct.-Appointed Mediators R. 10.200.

120. *Id.*

Mediators need to balance party self-determination with their duty to conduct a quality process consistent with their standards of conduct.[121] Party self-determination is not absolute.[122] Even if parties would like to reach a mediated agreement, the mediator has the responsibility to determine if the case is appropriate for mediation and to safeguard the mediation process.[123] The Theory of Shared Decision-Making offered by Omer Shapira provides guidance to mediators who are contemplating terminating a mediation due to the parties' proposed problematic mediated agreement.[124] Premised on the parties' right to make mediation decisions in conjunction with the mediator's duty to conduct the mediation according to the applicable rules, it recognizes that there are some decisions that parties cannot ethically or practically make.[125] At times, mediators will have to balance the parties' right to decide their mediated agreement with the mediator's obligation to follow rules of conduct to protect not only the parties but also the integrity of mediators, the mediation process, and the court, if a court-connected matter.[126] Mediated agreements that are illegal, immoral, unconscionable, grossly unfair, or likely to cause harm to nonparticipants may jeopardize the public's trust in the mediation process.[127] Mediator intervention is justified when the mediation outcome is "incompatible with the goals of mediation and could cause the process to be perceived as defective or abused."[128]

For example, the Virginia Standards of Ethics for Mediators provide that "[t]he mediator shall terminate the mediation when, in the mediator's judgment, the integrity of the process has been compromised."[129] The provided examples include gross inequality of bargaining power or ability, fraud, unfairness resulting from nondisclosure when disclosure was legally required, and a party unable or unwilling to effectively participate in the mediation.[130] Similarly, the Georgia Ethical Standards for Mediators provide that the mediator is the guardian of the fairness of the

121. MODEL STANDARDS, *supra* note 10, Standard I.A.1.

122. SHAPIRA, *supra* note 8, at 135.

123. FLA. RULES FOR CERTIFIED & CT.-APPOINTED MEDIATORS R. 10.400.

124. Omer Shapira, *A Theory of Sharing Decision-Making in Mediation*, 44 MCGEORGE L. REV. 923 (2013).

125. *Id.* at 925.

126. *Id.* at 957.

127. SHAPIRA, *supra* note 8, at 251.

128. *Id.*

129. VA. STANDARDS OF ETHICS & PROF'L RESPONSIBILITY FOR CERTIFIED MEDIATORS, Standard K.4 (Jud. Council of Va. 2011).

130. *Id.*

process and must protect the integrity of the mediation.[131] This includes not playing a part in the formation of an illegal agreement or one impossible to execute.[132] As a further illustration, think, for example, of a party who is trying to quickly settle a case at mediation before the opposing party realizes that the statute of limitations has run, a party hiding assets that are legally required to be disclosed, or an attorney attending mediation for the sole purpose of gathering information from the unrepresented opposing party for use at trial. "These are cases of bad faith, fraud, or unconscionability that had a reasonable party been aware of, he or she would not have agreed to participate in the mediation or accept its outcome. This kind of information might significantly affect the mediation outcome and thus the mediator in such cases has a duty to terminate the mediation."[133]

Similarly, Florida rules advise that a mediator shall terminate a mediation if it entails fraud, duress, unconscionability, or absence of bargaining ability[134] or endangers the physical safety of any person.[135] Additionally, a mediator shall cancel or postpone a mediation if a party is unable to freely exercise self-determination.[136] For example, the Florida Mediator Ethics Advisory Committee (MEAC) decided that if "the mediator believes the party is unable to rationally and intelligently assess the terms of the agreement . . . then the mediator must adjourn, terminate or withdraw from the mediation."[137] In another decision, the Florida MEAC was concerned about a practice described in a mediator's query according to which "the judge indicated to the parties how s/he was likely to rule" before sending them to mediation.[138] The Committee opined that "[f]or some parties, a suggestion from the judge may be treated not as an option, but as a requirement or an order, thus potentially compromising the parties' self-determination." The Committee advised that "[g]iven the judge's intervention, the mediator must carefully monitor the parties' participation in the mediation to ascertain the parties' ability to exercise

---

131. Ga. Ethical Standards for Neutrals, app'x C, ch. 1, A. Ethical Standards for Mediators, Rule IV.

132. *Id.*

133. Shapira, *supra* note 8, at 158.

134. Fla. Rules for Certified & Ct.-Appointed Mediators R. 10.420(b)(4).

135. *Id.* R. 10.420(b)(5).

136. *Id.* R. 10.310(d).

137. Fla. MEAC Advisory Op. 2010-005 (2010), *available at* https://www.flcourts.org/content/download/216890/1967286/MEACOpinion2010-005.pdf.

138. Fla. MEAC Advisory Op. 2006-002 (2006), *available at* https://www.flcourts.org/content/download/216899/1967340/MEAC-Opinion-2006-002.pdf.

self-determination and must be prepared to terminate the mediation if any party is unable or unwilling to participate meaningfully in the process."

When courts refer cases to mediation, the process has the courts' imprimatur. The mediator must conduct the mediation "according to the practices and procedures outlined in the applicable statutes and rules."[139] Mediators' failures to comply with the required practices and procedures may cause the public to lose faith in the process of mediation and courts to limit or discontinue referrals to mediation. As mediators have standards for conducting mediations, the courts have an obligation to protect the integrity of its processes.[140] During a mediation for a dissolution-of-marriage case, the wife handed the husband a note that read: "If you can't agree to this, the kids will take what information they have to whomever to have you arrested, etc. Although I would get no money if you were in jail—you wouldn't be living freely as if you did nothing wrong."[141] After receiving this note, the husband, who had been in trouble for photographing underage nude girls, reached a mediated agreement with the wife. When the husband sought to overturn the mediated agreement, the appellate court advised that it will not condone extortion. Further, the court stated that presenting an extorted agreement to the court was a fraud on the court, making it an instrument of extortion.[142] The case does not suggest that the mediator knew of the wife's threat, but the knowledge would have triggered the need for the mediator to terminate the mediation to prevent the extorted mediated agreement.[143]

11.6. Mediators' Ethical Obligations Postmediation

Whether or not parties reached agreement at mediation, mediators have a postmediation responsibility to preserve the confidentiality of the process, maintain impartiality, and steer clear of conflicts of interest. Mediation communications are protected from subsequent disclosure as provided by law unless a recognized exception applies,[144] and mediators have an

139. Vitakis-Valchine v. Valchine, 793 So. 2d 1094, 1099 (Fla. Dist. Ct. App. 2011).

140. Tetunic, *supra* note 74.

141. Cooper v. Austin, 750 So. 2d 711 (Fla. Dist. Ct. App. 2000).

142. *Id.* at 713.

143. *See, e.g.*, Model Standards of Practice for Family & Divorce Mediators, Standard XI.5 (Ass'n Fam. & Conciliation Cts.) (discussing mediator suspending or terminating mediation when "a participant is using the mediation to further illegal conduct").

144. *See, e.g.*, Fla. Stat. § 44.405(1); Unif. Mediation Act § 4.

ongoing obligation to preserve that confidentiality.[145] If the parties do not reach agreement during mediation, the mediator is limited as to what can be reported to the court regarding the mediation. The Model Standards of Conduct provide that if required, the mediator may report whether the parties appeared for mediation and whether they resolved their dispute.[146] This is consistent with rules of court, which also limit the mediators' communication about the case following the mediation process.[147]

11.6.1. Conflicts of Interest and Impartiality

Standards of conduct for mediators consistently require mediators to avoid conflicts of interest and guard against them or their appearance both during and following mediation.[148] Conflicts of interest arise from the mediator's involvement with the subject matter of the dispute or relationships the mediator has or had with mediation participants.[149]

The Model Standards of Conduct for Mediators address a mediator's conflict obligations following mediation, advising that a mediator "shall not establish another relationship with any of the participants in any matter that would raise questions about the integrity of the mediation."[150] Factors for the mediator to consider when deciding if the relationship might create an actual or perceived conflict of interest include the nature of the relationships and services offered, as well as the time elapsed subsequent to the mediation.[151]

When deciding whether to take a future case, mediators will need to consider their concurrent ethical obligations. Lawyer mediators will be guided by the rules of their licensing jurisdiction, many of which are based on the ABA Model Rules of Professional Conduct, including those for third-party neutrals and conflict of interest. The ABA Model Rules advise that "a lawyer shall not represent anyone in connection with a matter in which the lawyer participated personally and substantially as a . . .

145. *See, e.g.*, Model Standards, *supra* note 10, Standard V.; Fla. Rules of Certified & Ct.-Appointed Mediators R. 10.360(a).

146. Model Standards, *supra* note 10, Standard V.2.

147. *See, e.g.*, *id.* Standard III; Fla. Rules of Certified & Ct.-Appointed Mediators R. 10.340.

148. Model Standards, *supra* note 10, Standard III.A; Minn. Gen. Rules R. 114 app'x, Code of Ethics.

149. Model Standards, *supra* note 10, Standard III.A.

150. *Id.* Standard III.F.

151. *Id.*

mediator . . . unless all parties to the proceeding give informed consent, confirmed in writing."[152]

Mediator rules also prohibit conflicts based on prior relationships and may be more restrictive than the rules for lawyers. For example, the Florida Rules for Mediators do not permit parties to waive conflicts if the conflicts are clear. The Florida MEAC has issued various opinions on conflicts of interest when mediators switch to the role of lawyers following mediation. The committee has advised that a mediator is not permitted to serve as counsel[153] or cocounsel[154] for the case he mediated. It would be inappropriate for the mediator to represent either one or both parties in a dissolution-of-marriage case or any matter arising from the mediation.[155] Consistently, it would be a clear conflict for the mediator, following the mediation, to represent or take a position against a party in a related matter, such as serving as an expert witness on attorneys' fees.[156]

Mediators must also be mindful of their actions that may present issues of partiality as well as conflicts of interest following mediation.[157] They should not act with either partiality or bias based on a participant's characteristics, values, beliefs, or background or for other reasons.[158] The Georgia Ethics Commission on Dispute Resolution has issued opinions arising from complaints parties filed alleging that their mediators violated ethical rules following the mediations they conducted. The husband in a divorce case questioned the mediator's impartiality and integrity when after the 12-hour divorce mediation, the mediator had two dinner dates with the wife—one before the divorce was final.[159] Similarly, in another divorce case, the husband again found the mediator to be partial toward the wife when the psychologist mediator provided counseling to the parties' children, at the wife's request, following the mediation and voluntarily filed an affidavit with the court blaming the husband for the case not settling.[160] Both complaints were determined to have merit and to portray mediators in a bad light. Mediators' actions affect not only the parties but also the larger community whose impression of mediation is formed by what they hear about mediators and the mediation process.

---

152. Model Rules of Prof'l Conduct R. 1.12(a) (Am. Bar Ass'n 2020).
153. Fla. MEAC Advisory Op. 1994-003 (1994).
154. Fla. MEAC Advisory Op. 1994-002 (1994).
155. Fla. MEAC Advisory Op. 2005-004 (2005).
156. Fla. MEAC Advisory Op. 2008-008 (2008).
157. Ga. Comm'n on Disp. Resol. Comm. on Ethics, Advisory Op. 5 (2004).
158. Model Standards, *supra* note 10, Standard II.B.1.
159. Ga. Comm'n on Disp. Resol. Comm. on Ethics, Ethics Op. 5 (2012).
160. *Id.* Ethics Op. 3 (2009).

11.6.2. Mediator Serving in Another Dispute-Resolution Capacity

Parties may want to assign the mediator a future role in a different capacity for the same case or subject matter. Oftentimes, mediators are requested to serve as arbitrators should a future dispute arise regarding the agreement or because the parties did not settle in mediation.[161] For example, Florida rules acknowledge that a mediator may be asked to serve as a decision maker.[162]

The Florida MEAC suggests that a mediator switching to the role of an arbitrator is laden with hazards.[163] The committee recommends that the mediator ensure that the parties understand the role change.[164] In the course of mediation, mediators obtain confidential information that was not meant to be used outside of the mediation, yet the mediator would be carrying that information to the decision-making role.[165] Furthermore, a change in the process would result in a change from the ethical rules that had governed the mediation, including party self-determination, mediator impartiality, and confidentiality.[166] Therefore, mediators contemplating conducting another dispute-resolution process in the same matter as the mediation must obtain the consent of all the parties.[167] For example, Virginia Standards require that before requesting the parties' consent to arbitrate or conduct another dispute-resolution process, the mediator must inform the parties of the procedures used in the new process and the implications of the same person conducting two distinct processes.[168] A court was determined to have abused its discretion when it appointed the mediator in a divorce case as arbitrator for the same case when the parties had not agreed to the arbitrator.[169] Consistently, mediators should decline to serve as special masters for the cases they mediated.[170]

---

161. MEAC Advisory Op. 2009-002 (2009).

162. Fla. Rules for Certified & Ct.-Appointed Mediators R. 10.340 cmt.

163. Fla. MEAC Advisory Op. 2015-003 (2015).

164. *Id.*

165. Fla. MEAC Advisory Op. 96-002 (1996).

166. Fla. Rules for Certified & Ct.-Appointed Mediators R. 10.340 cmt.

167. *See, e.g.*, Model Standards, *supra* note 10, Standard VI.8; Va. Standards, *supra* note 129, at E.5.

168. Va. Standards, *supra* note 129, at E.5. *See also* Model Standards, *supra* note 10, Standard VI.8 (requiring mediators to advise the parties of the implications of the change in processes before obtaining their consent to the change).

169. *In re* Daniel S. Cartwright, 104 S.W.3d 706 (Tex. Ct. App. 2003).

170. Fla. MEAC Advisory Op. 1996-002 (1996).

11.6.3. Mediator's Obligation of Confidentiality

"Confidentiality is forever."[171] Mediators have a continuing obligation not to disclose protected mediation communications unless the protection has been properly waived or a recognized exception applies.[172] Unfortunately, mediation confidentiality law is highly variable.[173] Depending on the state in which they mediated, mediators might be required to testify in an action for overturning or reforming mediated agreements. The states that have adopted the UMA recognize an exception to mediation privilege for "a proceeding to prove a claim to rescind or reform or a defense to avoid liability on a contract arising out of mediation"[174] but do not compel a mediator to provide evidence for this purpose.[175] In contrast, the Florida Mediation Confidentiality and Privilege Act delineates an exception for legally recognized bases for voiding or reforming a mediated agreement but does not exempt mediators from testifying.[176]

Mediators have been subpoenaed for deposition and called to testify in court regarding mediations they have conducted. In Georgia, mediators are advised to file a motion to quash the subpoena.[177] Similarly, in Florida, mediators are advised to decline to voluntarily testify, filing for a protective order or advising the court of their obligation to preserve mediation confidentiality.[178] However, if the judge orders them to testify, they should do so.[179] In camera determinations may be appropriate before mediators are required to testify.[180]

Despite confidentiality and privilege protections, there will be times when mediators do testify because either the testimony is not privileged or confidential, or it fits within a recognized exception.[181]

---

171. Ga. Comm'n on Disp. Resol. Comm. on Ethics, Advisory Op. 8 (2013).

172. *See, e.g.*, Fla. Stat. § 44.405 (2019); Model Standards, *supra* note 10, Standard V.

173. *See generally* Tetunic & Firestone, *supra* note 73.

174. Unif. Mediation Act § 6(b)(2).

175. *Id.* § 6(c).

176. Fla. Stat. § 44.405(4)(a)5.

177. Ga. Comm'n on Disp. Resol. Comm. on Ethics, Advisory Op. 8 (2013).

178. Mediator Qualifications Advisory Panel, Advisory Ops. 99-012 (1999), 96-005 (1996). The Mediator Ethics Advisory Committee was previously titled the Mediator Qualifications Advisory Panel.

179. *Id.*

180. *See, e.g.*, Unif. Mediation Act § 6(b).

181. *See* Chapter 12, "Mediation Confidentiality: Mediators as Witnesses."

11.7. Conclusion

This chapter offers a basis for discussing current law and rules regarding mediated agreements, recognizing that the existing disparity does not minimize mediators' obligations. Rather, it underscores the importance of mediators knowing and following the applicable law and ethical precepts. Codes of conduct and ethical rules will guide the mediators as they honor the integrity of the mediation process, respecting party self-determination and preserving mediation confidentiality, along with following the applicable law and rules for the matters they mediate. However, more is required of mediators. Notably, mediators must exhibit professional integrity. This will at times require terminating a mediation that would have led to an illegal, unconscionable, or grossly unfair mediated agreement. The future of mediation is in the hands of the mediators so it may live up to its promise.

Chapter 12

Mediation Confidentiality: Mediators as Witnesses

Ellen E. Deason

12.1. Introduction

This chapter concerns the ethical principles of confidentiality that guide mediators in the role of witnesses in court and as the sources of reports about a mediation to judges, mediation program sponsors, or others. Unlike a mediator's obligations of confidentiality during caucuses with the parties, which are discussed in Chapter 6, this chapter examines disclosures a mediator might make outside a mediation session, when serving as a witness in an adjudicatory proceeding or reporting mediation events. While much of the analysis of mediation confidentiality has dealt with legal protections,[1] this chapter will apply ethical principles on disclosure to mediators. However, it is important to note that legal provisions interact with and influence the ethical principles. Because mediators have a general professional obligation to follow the law,[2] state law may affect the application of ethical principles.

1. For notable exceptions, see OMER SHAPIRA, A THEORY OF MEDIATION ETHICS: FOUNDATIONS, RATIONALE, AND APPLICATION 271–301 (2016); Kevin Gibson, *Confidentiality in Mediation: A Moral Reassessment*, 1992 J. DISP. RESOL. 25 (1992).
2. SHAPIRA, *supra* note 1, at 289.

The term "confidentiality" is used in this chapter as an umbrella concept to describe all forms of communication protections for mediation.[3] This includes testimony in court and interactions with adjudicators. It also includes disclosures mediators might make outside legal proceedings, such as to public officials or the mediation program that sponsors their work. This comprehensive application reflects the common usage of the term "confidentiality" and corresponds to the definition in many statutes. To avoid confusion, however, it is important to note that this usage is different from the technical statutory definition used in states that have adopted the Uniform Mediation Act (UMA). In that act, the term "confidentiality" is used in contrast to an evidentiary privilege that may prevent disclosure in court. This sense is narrower and covers only obligations to maintain confidentiality outside legal proceedings, which the UMA does not impose by law but leaves to agreement of the parties.

12.2. Mediator Confidentiality as a Professional Obligation

Mediators' obligations to maintain confidentiality are grounded in their professional role in service to the parties. They also flow from the duty they owe to their fellow mediators, the profession of mediation, and the public to preserve the integrity of the mediation process. These obligations to maintain confidentiality are not absolute, and they are not mediators' only professional obligations. Mediators therefore need to apply confidentiality principles, not in isolation, but in the context of the full array of professional ethics that guide mediation. These other professional obligations, which both support and limit the extent of confidentiality duties, include providing a quality mediation process, supporting the parties' self-determination, and maintaining impartiality.

12.2.1. Mediators' Professional Obligation to Maintain Confidentiality

Maintaining confidentiality is an important element of professional codes of conduct for mediators,[4] which tend to set forth a general broad rule

---

3. This sense of the term "confidentiality" has alternatively been labeled "privadentiality." Gregory Firestone & Sharon Press, *Privadentiality: Developing a Coherent Framework for Establishing Communication Protections in Family and Child Protection Dispute Resolution Methods*, 58 FAM. CT. REV. 9, 11 (2020) (developing a framework for disclosures by parties in mediation).

4. *See, e.g.*, FLA. RULES FOR CERTIFIED & CT.-APPOINTED MEDIATORS R. 10.360(a) (2003) [hereinafter FLA. RULES]; ILL. STANDARDS OF PRAC. FOR MEDIATORS § II (1999) [hereinafter ILL. STANDARDS]; N.C. STANDARDS OF PROF'L CONDUCT FOR MEDIATORS § 3 (2020) [hereinafter N.C. STANDARDS]; N.Y. STANDARDS

that mediators shall maintain confidentiality and then provide for limited exceptions permitting some disclosures. The exceptions can be created by parties exercising their self-determination or dictated by strong public policies. For example, the Model Standards of Conduct for Mediators provide that "[a] mediator shall maintain the confidentiality of all information obtained by the mediator in mediation, unless otherwise agreed to by the parties or required by applicable law."[5]

Unless parties tailor confidentiality narrowly to fit their circumstances, they are justified in expecting—based on the ethical codes for mediators, state legal frameworks, and the profession's public portrayal of mediation—that mediation will be a reliably private process.[6] This expectation, subject to the exceptions discussed below, creates a professional duty for mediators to safeguard any information that could adversely affect a party's interests or portray them in a bad light.[7] And in addition to an obligation to the parties, mediators also owe a professional duty to the mediation profession and to the public to maintain the confidentiality standards the profession has espoused.

Consistent with this broad reading of their obligation, mediators should not limit protection to oral statements; confidentiality should also cover written communications and conduct.[8] In addition, mediators should protect information over the complete time frame of the process, including communications before and after mediation sessions that relate to the mediation.[9] And, when the parties reasonably expect anonymity, mediators should not disclose information connecting them with a

---

of Conduct for N.Y. Cmty. Disp. Resol. Ctr. Mediators § V(A) [hereinafter N.Y. Standards]; Tenn. Sup. Ct. Rules R. 31, app. A, § 7 (2007); Tex. Ethical Guidelines for Mediators § 8 (2005).

5. Model Standards of Conduct for Mediators, Standard VI.A (2005) [hereinafter Model Standards]; *see also* Model Standards of Practice for Family & Divorce Mediators, Standard VII (2000) [hereinafter Model Family Standards] ("A family mediator shall maintain the confidentiality of all information acquired in the mediation process, unless the mediator is permitted or required to reveal the information by law or agreement of the participants.").

6. Shapira, *supra* note 1, at 272–73.

7. *Id.* at 281.

8. *E.g.*, Model Standards, *supra* note 5, Standard V.A.2; Or. Mediation Ass'n Core Standards of Mediation Prac., Standard IV, cmt. 4 (2005) [hereinafter Or. Standards]; Va. Standards of Ethics & Prof'l Resp. for Certified Mediators, Standard H(4) (2011) [hereinafter Va. Standards]; Ga. Comm'n on Disp. Resol., Advisory Op. 8, at 3 (2013) [hereinafter Ga. Comm'n Op. 8].

9. *E.g.*, N.C. Standards, *supra* note 4, Standard 3(a); Ga. Comm'n Op. 8, *supra* note 8, at 6.

mediation.[10] These ethical principles find support in legislation and court cases;[11] however, mediators should be aware that their ethical obligations may extend further than the scope of the applicable legal provisions. Statutes and rules vary greatly among jurisdictions, and many are narrower,[12] or silent, on these aspects of the scope of confidentiality coverage.

12.2.2. The Role of Confidentiality in Providing an Effective Process

The need for mediators to maintain the confidentiality of the information they obtain during a mediation process is fundamental to their professional obligation to provide a quality process for the benefit of the parties and in the eyes of the public. As one crucial element of a quality process, a mediator should "promote honesty and candor between and among all participants."[13] Information exchanged directly between parties or provided to a mediator is central to the functioning of mediation; it is the basis on which resolutions acceptable to the parties can be built. Yet revealing information and offering concessions can create vulnerabilities in the complex three-way communication dynamics that characterize mediation. The parties are adversaries with a dispute; the mediator is not aligned with either but is instead an impartial facilitator. Without adequate confidentiality, these relationships create an inherently risky situation for the parties; one of them may try to use information from the mediation to their advantage against the party who provided the information, and the mediator may become embroiled in that effort.[14]

The parties are not likely to enter mediation trusting each other, but trust in the mediator and the mediation process can create an atmosphere that allows parties to take the risks necessary to participate effectively. Building this trust is one of the most important functions of a mediator, and confidentiality is one of the most important tools. As stated by the

10. *E.g.*, Model Standards, *supra* note 5, Standard V.A.3; N.C. Standards, *supra* note 4, Standard 3(d).

11. *See, e.g.*, Unif. Mediation Act § 2(2) (Unif. Law Comm'n 2003) (broad definition of "mediation communication" including nonverbal behavior for purposes related to mediation).

12. *See, e.g.*, Folb v. Motion Picture Indus. Pension & Health Plans, 16 F. Supp. 2d 1164 (C.D. Cal. 1998), *aff'd*, 216 F.3d 1082 (9th Cir. 2000) (limiting protection of common-law privilege to communications before and during mediation sessions); Fla. Stat. Ann. § 44.403(1) (2004) (same).

13. Model Standards, *supra* note 5, Standard V.A.4.

14. *See* Ellen E. Deason, *The Quest for Uniformity in Mediation Confidentiality: Foolish Consistency or Crucial Predictability*, 85 Marq. L. Rev. 79, 80–82 (2001) (discussing the importance of confidentiality in fostering communication between the parties and with the mediator).

New York State Community Dispute Resolution Center Mediator Ethics Advisory Committee (MEAC): "Confidentiality is integral to the mediation process. It fosters trust among the parties and between each party and the mediator, and it promotes trust among parties in the mediation process itself."[15]

It is usually unrealistic to expect adversarial parties to embrace a deep form of interpersonal trust. But when personal trust is low, mediation confidentiality can provide what is termed "institutional trust."[16] This form of trust rests on external controls and safeguards to reduce the risks and uncertainties that created the need for trust in the first place. For mediation, these safeguards are confidentiality's legal and ethical limitations on disclosures.[17] This is what encourages parties to participate fully in mediation, despite the risks and vulnerabilities it can entail. Therefore, it is widely recognized that the parties' expectations of confidentiality play a crucial role in encouraging the candor in communication on which a quality mediation process depends. As stated in the Georgia Standards, "Without the protection of confidentiality, parties would be unwilling to communicate freely, and the discussion necessary to resolve disputes would be seriously curtailed."[18]

12.2.3. The Role of Mediator Confidentiality in Self-Determination

Parties' expectations of confidentiality by the mediator are expressly justified and encouraged by the explanations—and explicit promises of confidentiality—that mediators typically convey at the start of the session. The explanation allows parties to predict what aspects of their mediation will be protected from disclosures. They can then exercise self-determination to determine their level of participation and perhaps set limits on the information they might share. The parties' need to anticipate the extent and limits of confidentiality translates into an obligation

15. N.Y. MEAC, Op. 2006-01, at 2 (2006).

16. *See* Ellen E. Deason, *The Need for Trust as a Justification of Confidentiality in Mediation: A Cross-Disciplinary Approach*, 54 U. Kan. L. Rev. 1387, 1403–06 (2006) (describing institutional trust).

17. *Id.* at 1392–95, 1406–18 (analyzing the importance of confidentiality for developing trust and its crucial role in mediation).

18. Ga. ADR Rules, App. C, Ch. 1(A), Ethical Standards for Mediators, Standard II (1994) [hereinafter Ga. Standards]; *see also* N.C. Disp. Resol. Comm'n, Op. 09 (2006). For a classic judicial statement of this principle, see *Lake Utopia Paper Ltd. v. Connelly Containers, Inc.*, 608 F.2d 928, 930 (2d Cir. 1979) (explaining that, without confidentiality, mediation participants "of necessity will feel constrained to conduct themselves in a cautious, tight-lipped, non-committal manner more suitable to poker players in a high-stakes game").

for the mediator to inform the parties, not only about the legal provisions that govern the parties' obligations and choices, but also what to expect from the mediator.[19]

An excellent statement of the comprehensive goal underlying the mediator's role in informing the parties about confidentiality comes from the Georgia Commission on Dispute Resolution: "It is the mediator's responsibility to ensure that all mediation attendees understand the concept and benefit of, and the obligation embedded in, mediation confidentiality."[20] The Model Standards instruct that a "mediator shall promote understanding among the parties of the extent that the parties will maintain confidentiality of information they obtain in a mediation."[21] This standard does not explicitly require informing the parties of the *mediator's* obligations to maintain confidentiality, but an understanding of confidentiality would be incomplete without it.

At one time, mediation participants were often given the impression that confidentiality was absolute and that they would be completely protected from disclosures or investigation.[22] Hopefully that is no longer ever the case, for it is inconsistent with law and ethical standards. If the mediator states falsely that mediation is completely confidential, parties—especially those who are self-represented—will be denied their opportunity to exercise informed self-determination in deciding about their participation. And there is a risk that a party's trust in the process will be undermined if an unexpected exception to confidentiality later disadvantages the party. The Model Family Standards reflect a modern view of the appropriate content. They endorse an expansive discussion of confidentiality prior to mediation. It should include not only the "participants' expectations of confidentiality" but also information from the mediator on "the limitations of confidentiality, such as statutory, judicially or ethically mandated reporting."[23] And these confidentiality provisions should be included in the written agreement to mediate.[24]

A mediator should consider, however, how much detail about confidentiality exceptions to convey. A full explanation of all the possibilities for disclosures can be overwhelming and might undermine the parties' confidence in the effectiveness of confidentiality to the detriment of their

19. Va. Standards, *supra* note 8, Standard H(6).

20. Ga. Comm'n Op. 8, *supra* note 8, at 1.

21. Model Standards, *supra* note 5, Standard III.C.

22. *See* Gibson, *supra* note 1, at 28 & n.169.

23. Model Family Standards, *supra* note 5, Standard VII.A, B; *see also* Ga. Standards, *supra* note 18, Standard II; Or. Standards, *supra* note 8, Standard IV.

24. Model Family Standards, *supra* note 5, Standard VII.A.

willingness to participate in the process. This effect is exacerbated if a mediator delivers a full list of complex confidentiality exceptions orally at the start of the mediation session, especially when parties have little experience with mediation or are self-represented. To avoid this problem, the Florida MEAC recommends providing a mediation agreement in advance of the session to promote trust and self-determination and avoid an environment in which the parties may feel coerced into signing it.[25]

Guidance varies on the level of detail a mediator should provide. For example, the California Rules require only "a general explanation of the confidentiality of a mediation proceeding."[26] At the other end of the spectrum, the Virginia Standards require mediators to specify all the legal limitations on confidentiality using "an Agreement to Mediate that contains the statutory language relating to confidentiality and any requirements for mandatory reporting that are applicable to the mediation."[27]

When there is no explicit state guidance, a mediator should at least describe her legal and ethical obligations to make mandatory reports when that might be relevant in the mediation. In any mediation that concerns a minor or vulnerable person, the mediator should inform the parties of the mediator's ethical obligation to report abuse (discussed later). Depending on the disputed issues and context of the mediation, it may also be appropriate to alert the participants to the mediator's obligation to report certain threats of violence or an attempt to use the mediation to plan a crime (also discussed later). The content and detail of the explanation of permissive disclosures by the mediator may vary depending on the legal sophistication of the parties and whether they are participating with an attorney who can take responsibility for counseling them. In any event, a mediator should convey enough about the limits on confidentiality and her own disclosure obligations so that the parties can exercise informed self-determination.

12.2.4. The Role of Mediator Confidentiality in Promoting Impartiality

Impartiality—meaning "freedom from favoritism, bias, or prejudice"—is a central value in mediation.[28] Along with confidentiality, it contributes to parties' trust in the mediator and, by extension, trust in the process. The mediator's obligation to avoid favoring one party or that party's

25. Fla. MEAC Op. 2017-007, at 3–4 (2017).

26. Cal. Rules of Conduct for Mediators in Ct.-Connected Cases R. 3.854(b) (2013).

27. Va. Standards, *supra* note 8, Standard H(1).

28. Model Standards, *supra* note 5, Standard II.A.

interests or proposed solutions is at the core of what makes the mediator's role professional.[29]

Mediator testimony about what occurred in a mediation has the potential to undermine the perception of impartiality, no matter how well the mediator maintained it during the mediation process. One can understand why mediators would be sought to testify, for they are valuable witnesses. Their nonaligned status, enhanced by their reputation for impartiality, makes them especially credible.[30] If the mediation does not resolve all the issues, a party may seek to bolster its position using mediator testimony in a later stage of the ongoing dispute. Or, if the parties do reach a settlement, a party may later try to attack it in court using information from the mediation proceeding. In these situations, the mediator's testimony will inevitably function to favor one of the opposing parties (or will be interpreted as doing so), which will destroy the perception of impartiality.[31]

It is not only the mediator's reputation for impartiality that is placed at risk by serving as a witness or reporting on a mediation but also that of the mediation process in general. From the perspective of the public, or of a party deciding whether to engage in mediation, "if a mediator can be converted into the opposing party's weapon in court, then her neutrality is only temporary and illusory."[32] This broader consequence of a confidentiality breach carries special consequences for court-sponsored mediation programs, where the parties and the public may be concerned about informal channels of communication between mediators and the judge responsible for deciding the dispute if there is no settlement. In this setting, confidentiality principles play an important role by keeping the mediation process separate from judicial decision making and safeguarding the integrity of both processes.[33]

---

29. *See, e.g.*, Joseph B. Stulberg, *The Theory and Practice of Mediation: A Reply to Professor Susskind*, 6 VT. L. REV. 85, 86 (1981) (asserting that it is neutrality that "permits mediation to be an effective, principled dispute resolution procedure").

30. Olam v. Congress Mortg. Co., 68 F. Supp. 2d 1110, 1138 (N.D. Cal. 1999) (observing that the "mediator was the only source of presumptively disinterested, neutral evidence").

31. *In re* Anonymous, 283 F.3d 627, 639 (4th Cir. 2002) (quoting NLRB v. Joseph Macaluso, Inc., 618 F.2d 51, 55–56 (9th Cir. 1980)); *see also* Scott H. Hughes, *The Uniform Mediation Act: To the Spoiled Go the Privileges*, 85 MARQ. L. REV. 9, 70–71 (2001).

32. Deason, *supra* note 14, at 82.

33. *See id.* at 83.

12.2.5. Summary

In summary, expectations that mediators will keep mediation information confidential, combined with other fundamental mediation values, provide a foundation for a robust professional ethical norm of confidentiality for mediators. Mediators must observe this norm rigorously by avoiding disclosures unless they are justified.

12.3. Ethical Grounds for Mediators to Depart from Complete Confidentiality

The professional norm of confidentiality for mediators is not, however, absolute. First, consistent with party self-determination, a mediator may be justified in making a disclosure when the parties waive their confidentiality protections or authorize a disclosure. Second, even when the parties do not agree with disclosure, ethical principles justify exceptions to confidentiality when the benefits of confidentiality and the harm to the parties from disclosure are outweighed by public policy or the interests of the profession.[34] Mediator disclosures may consist of testimony in a court or arbitral proceeding when summoned by a subpoena, under a court order, or on a voluntary basis. Disclosures may also take the form of a report to an adjudicator, an appropriate public authority, or the mediator's sponsoring program. Generally, if a mediator decides to report during a mediation, he must withdraw to avoid the appearance of partiality. The mediator should determine on a case-by-case basis whether it is appropriate to adjourn or to terminate the mediation, based on the severity or nature of the communication.[35]

In addition to situations in which a mediator is *permitted* to disclose mediation communications, there are also some situations when a mediator is ethically *required* to disclose. This section will first consider the few situations that can require disclosure. Second, it will discuss permissive disclosure.

12.3.1. Ethical Duty to Disclose Mediation Communications

From a professional ethics perspective, a mediator is required to disclose information when failure to do so would violate norms of morality and law. Parties and the public cannot reasonably expect mediators to maintain confidentiality when it would violate these norms. This duty concerns information that, if the mediator's failure to disclose were revealed,

34. Shapira, *supra* note 1, at 282.
35. Fla. MEAC Op. 2012-001, at 2 (2012).

would damage the reputation of the mediation profession and the public's ability to trust in the process.[36] Stated succinctly, there is an ethical duty to disclose mediation information when disclosure is necessary "to prevent serious harm to individuals or important public interests."[37]

Deciding when such a report is required can be a difficult question for a mediator. Without adequate justification, it would be unethical to file a report based on mediation communications because the report would impinge on multiple mediator obligations: to promote self-determination, act impartially, and maintain confidentiality.[38] This means that mediators must educate themselves about the applicable law and ethics regarding their obligation to report and be very cautious in considering whether to disclose information from a mediation. There are three types of mediation information that may trigger a mediator's obligation to disclose in some circumstances: information indicating abuse of children or vulnerable adults, serious threats of imminent physical harm, and serious violations of attorneys' ethical rules.

12.3.1.1. Child or Elder Abuse

The obligation for mediators to report child or elder abuse is based on both ethical and legal duties. While legal reporting requirements may not explicitly cover all mediators, the "desire to protect abused children through mandatory reporting is perceived to be as much of a moral and ethical duty as it is a legal duty."[39] In many states, mediators do have a legal duty to report abuse to child protection authorities under a child protection reporting statute. Statutes often cover reporting about harm to vulnerable adults as well.[40] In some states, "any person" who has knowledge of abuse (which obviously includes mediators) is a mandatory reporter.[41] In a few states, child protection statutes explicitly list mediators as mandatory reporters.[42] Other states identify professionals subject

---

36. SHAPIRA, *supra* note 1, at 282, 288–90.

37. *Id.* at 289.

38. Art Hinshaw, *Mediators as Mandatory Reporters of Child Abuse: Preserving Mediation's Core Values*, 34 FLA. ST. U. L. REV. 271, 302–03 (2007).

39. *Id.* at 299.

40. *E.g.*, OHIO REV. CODE ANN. §§ 2151.421, 5101.63.

41. Hinshaw, *supra* note 38, at 289 & n.120 (identifying 19 states that impose reporting duties on "any person").

42. *Id.* at 289–90 & n.121 (identifying Kansas, Louisiana, Virginia, and Wisconsin as states that explicitly require mediators to report child abuse).

to mandatory reporting obligations but do not list mediators.[43] However, these statutes typically list professions in which many mediators are trained, such as law and social work, and a prudent mediator in this situation would identify herself as a mandatory reporter by extension of her other professional obligations.[44] This interpretation of reporting statutes is supported by many state mediation statutes. Occasionally a state, such as Florida, identifies reports of child or elder abuse as mandatory.[45] More commonly, mediation statutes enable mediators to fulfill reporting requirements without creating a conflict with their obligation to maintain confidentiality through a confidentiality exception for suspected child or elder abuse.[46]

However, even if a mediator is not covered by any statutory category designating mandatory reporters and thus is not legally obligated to report abuse, there is a strong argument for required reporting based on professional ethical principles. Reports of child or elder abuse may fit within a professional ethical duty to warn of serious bodily harm (discussed in Section 12.3.1.2). In addition, such reports are independently justified based on a strong public interest: protection of children and vulnerable adults. Furthermore, this public interest is intertwined with an important mediation goal—improving outcomes for all parties who are affected by the dispute, which includes potential victims of abuse. It is not in the abused person's interest, nor that of society, for the abuse to continue unabated.[47]

Definitions of abuse and neglect vary from state to state, but most include four categories of harm: physical abuse, neglect, emotional/mental injury, and sexual molestation/abuse. The reporting standards also vary,[48] but a commentator helpfully summarizes them by suggesting that a mediator "should report when she feels there is enough evidence to

---

43. One explanation for this omission may be that most of the statutes were originally enacted in the 1960s, before mediation was a common process. *See id.* at 285–86 (describing impetus for mandatory reporting statutes).

44. *See id.* at 290–93 (noting that most codes and commentators employ a conservative approach and conclude that mandatory reporting duties apply to a professional listed as a reporter when they mediate).

45. Fla. Stat. § 44.405(4)(a)(3) (2004); *see also* Fla. MEAC Op. 2012-007 (2013).

46. *See, e.g.*, Unif. Mediation Act §§ 6(a)(7), 7(b)(3); *see also* Unif. Mediation Act § 6 cmt. 8 (listing statutes).

47. Hinshaw, *supra* note 38, at 273, 300.

48. *Id.* at 286–89.

support a belief of abuse."[49] There is no need for ironclad proof, but innuendo, hints, or indirect allusions to potential abuse are not enough.

In terms of process, when a mediator considers reporting, he should verify as much as possible the basis for his suspicion of abuse. One commentator suggests that, to minimize the harm to confidentiality and self-determination, the mediator should discuss her suspicions with the parties and see if they will agree to disclose the information themselves or consent to disclosure by the mediator.[50] Another commentator suggests that the mediator should promptly remind the parties of his status as a mandatory reporter so that they may make an informed decision about what to share with him. If the evidence supports a reasonable suspicion and triggers a report of abuse, then the mediator should terminate the mediation.[51] When making the report, the mediator should limit the information to that which is necessary to support an investigation.

12.3.1.2. Threat of Serious Physical Harm

In some states, courts have established a legal duty for certain professionals to warn an intended victim or report a threat to inflict serious bodily harm to the authorities. This duty developed in the wake of the California *Tarasoff* case, in which a psychotherapist failed to warn a victim after threats of serious bodily harm by his patient.[52] The legal duty has been extended beyond psychotherapists to other professionals, and some assume it covers mediators.[53] Other commentators question the duty for mediators because it is usually premised on "greater expertise to assess the danger and a closer relationship to the person who poses the danger" than occurs in most mediations, possibly excepting environmental and family matters.[54]

Despite lack of clarity regarding a legal duty to report or warn of serious harm, as an ethical matter, a mediator is arguably required to warn an

49. *Id.* at 304.

50. Shapira, *supra* note 1, at 290.

51. Hinshaw, *supra* note 38, at 303–05.

52. Tarasoff v. Regents of Univ. of Cal., 551 P.2d 334 (Cal. 1976).

53. *See* James Bartens, Note, *If a Threat of Violence Is Presented, When Does the Law Require Family Mediators to Breach Confidentiality? Guiding Family Mediators through the Application of* Tarasoff *Principles*, 42 Fam. Ct. Rev. 641 (2004); John R. Murphy III, Comment, *In the Wake of* Tarasoff: *Mediation and the Duty to Disclose*, 5 Catholic U. L. Rev. 209, 210–11 (1985).

54. Sarah R. Cole et al., Mediation: Law, Policy, and Practice § 11.14 (2020).

intended victim or report to the appropriate authorities.[55] When there is a credible threat of bodily injury or violence, disclosure serves the public interest in safety and the protection of others.[56] Some codes of conduct for mediators recognize this duty. For example, the Family Mediation Model Standards instruct that "[t]he mediator *shall* disclose a participant's threat of suicide or violence against any person to the threatened person and the appropriate authorities if the mediator believes such threat is likely to be acted upon as permitted by law."[57] Other standards permit but do not mandate reporting.[58] The Illinois Standards, for instance, require mediators to "inform the participants in writing that confidentiality will not apply when there is a threat to inflict bodily harm."[59] As with reports of child or elder abuse, many mediation statutes avoid subjecting mediators to contradictory mandates by excluding from confidentiality protection communications that would justify warning of a threat of violence.[60]

12.3.1.3. Attorneys' Ethical Violations

A third type of mandatory reporting obligation applies only to mediators who are attorneys. Attorneys are required by professional ethics rules to report serious violations of those rules by other attorneys.[61] This duty is rooted in important ethical goals: to "maintain the integrity of the legal profession, further the ends of justice, and protect the public from unscrupulous attorneys."[62] Attorneys carry this duty with them when they serve as mediators, reflecting their multiple professional ethical obligations. For example, in Florida, the mediation statute *permits* any mediator to report

---

55. SHAPIRA, *supra* note 1, at 289.

56. UNIF. MEDIATION ACT § 6 cmt. 4.

57. MODEL FAMILY STANDARDS, *supra* note 5, Standard VII.C (emphasis added).

58. *See, e.g.*, N.C. STANDARDS, *supra* note 4, Standard 3(d)(4)(a).

59. ILL. STANDARDS, *supra* note 4, Standard II; *see also* FAMILY MEDIATION CAN. CODE art. 7.1(d) (establishing an exception to mediation confidentiality "when the information discloses an actual or potential threat to human life or safety").

60. *See, e.g.*, UNIF. MEDIATION ACT § 6(a)(3); COLO. REV. STAT. § 13-22-307(2)(b) (1991); OR. REV. STAT. § 36.220(6) (1997); WYO. STAT. § 1-43-103(c)(ii) (1991); *see also* Fla. MEAC Op. 2012-001 (2012) (communications that threaten violence are not confidential).

61. *See* MODEL RULES OF PROF'L CONDUCT R. 8.3 (requiring attorneys to report violations of the Rules that raise a substantial question as to a lawyer's honesty, trustworthiness, or fitness as a lawyer).

62. Skolnick v. Altheimer & Gray, 730 N.E.2d 4, 13 (Ill. 2000). *See generally* Mori Irvine, *Serving Two Masters: The Moral Obligation under the Rules of Professional Conduct to Report Attorney Misconduct in a Confidential Mediation*, 26 RUTGERS L.J. 155 (1994).

professional misconduct during a mediation for the internal use of a body conducting an investigation.[63] But in the opinion of the Florida MEAC, if the mediator is an attorney, reporting is not an option; it is instead an obligation under the rules regulating the Florida Bar.[64] Similarly, an Illinois State Bar Association Advisory Opinion concluded that lawyer mediators have an "absolute duty" to report an attorney's misconduct during a mediation.[65]

The importance of reporting an attorney's serious ethical violations is reenforced by the limited case law interpreting this obligation for lawyer mediators. *In re Waller*[66] upheld the suspension of an attorney in a disciplinary action following a lawyer mediator's report of the attorney's conflict of interest, even though the order of reference to mediation prohibited disclosures to the court. The court reasoned that the disclosure was justified because of the public importance of the matter and because the communication regarding the conflict did not concern the dispute being mediated.[67]

12.3.2. Permissible Grounds to Testify or Report Mediation Communications

It is more common for a mediator to be in a position where she is permitted, but not required, to disclose mediation information than to be ethically required to do so. A disclosure by a mediator is permissible from a professional ethics perspective if it is not harmful to the parties or, even if it may be harmful, if it is justified. Disclosures can be ethically justified in two situations: (1) when the parties have waived their objections or agreed to a narrow scope of confidentiality protections that do not include the information; or (2) when "the harm of nondisclosure to important professional and public interests" is greater than the potential harm of disclosure.[68] This topic will be covered in two parts: first, the mediator's obligations when the parties have waived their confidentiality protections, and second, when the parties have not waived confidentiality protections and a mediator must determine if he is nonetheless justified in disclosing information.

63. Fla. Stat. § 44.405(a)(6) (2004); *see also* Unif. Mediation Act §§ 6(a)(6), 6(c); Va. Code Ann. § 8.01-581.22(vii) (2013).

64. Fla. MEAC Op. 2011-003 (2011).

65. Ill. State Bar Ass'n Advisory Op. on Prof'l Conduct, Op. 11-01 (2011).

66. *In re* Waller, 573 A.2d 780 (D.C. 1990).

67. *Id.* at 785.

68. Shapira, *supra* note 1, at 282.

12.3.2.1. Disclosures When the Parties Waive Confidentiality

When all the participants in a mediation have waived their legal right to confidentiality protection, this usually means that they believe that disclosure of mediation information will help them reach their goals. There are two different perspectives on how a mediator should react if all the parties seek her testimony about mediation information. One view is that the principles of party autonomy and self-determination mean that mediators should abide by the parties' choice and disclose communications from the mediation. According to this view, "parties should be able to . . . mutually agree on the disclosure of any [dispute resolution] communication."[69] A second perspective is that mediators need to make independent ethical determinations about whether or not to testify. This is because mediator testimony, even when agreed to by the parties, threatens another core value of mediation: impartiality. Importantly, a mediator's ethical responsibilities are intended not only to support the parties but also to maintain the reputation of the profession in the public's eye. As described previously, the perception of partiality created by mediator testimony (see Section 12.2.4) poses a danger of harm to the integrity of the process and erosion of public trust.

The Model Standards firmly support the second approach. Standard V provides: "If the parties to a mediation agree that the mediator may disclose information obtained during the mediation, the mediator *may* do so."[70] In other words, "even if the parties agree that the mediator shall disclose [information] . . . Standard V(A)(1) states that the mediator may do so but is not required to do so."[71] This approach reflects the principle that disclosures by mediators must be consistent with all the ethical norms applicable to mediators, including impartiality.[72]

Disclosure by mediators when the parties have waived confidentiality is an aspect of confidentiality that is heavily influenced by the law, which varies among the states and influences the content of ethical guidance. In many states, including those that have enacted the UMA, mediators have an evidentiary privilege to avoid testifying and to prevent other mediation participants from testifying about mediator communications.[73] A privilege permits mediators to testify (which they should do only if ethically permissible) but gives them the option to invoke their

69. *See, e.g.*, Firestone & Press, *supra* note 3, at 19 & nn.102–03.
70. Model Standards, *supra* note 5, Standard V.A.1 (emphasis added).
71. *Id.* Reporter's Notes, *Notes on Construction* 8.
72. *See* Shapira, *supra* note 1, at 282.
73. Unif. Mediation Act § 4(b)(2).

privilege and refuse to testify even when the parties agree it would be desirable. In other states, mediators lack this flexibility; only the parties may block disclosures. Florida, for example, provides a privilege for parties but no independent privilege for mediators. The Florida Rules require a mediator to "maintain confidentiality of all information revealed during mediation *except* where disclosure is required or permitted by law or is *agreed to by all the parties*."[74] The mediation statute puts control even more squarely in the hands of the parties by declaring that "there is no confidentiality or privilege . . . for any mediation communication . . . [f]or which the confidentiality or privilege against disclosure has been waived by all the parties."[75]

Mediators need to educate themselves on the applicable law. Unless they are required by state law to abide by the parties' choice, mediators should follow the Model Standards and apply their own judgment in deciding whether to disclose. Parties are likely to consider only their own interests in making their determination to waive confidentiality, whereas a mediator is in a better position to factor in all the consequences of testifying, including damage to the perception of impartiality and potential harm to the integrity of the mediation process. If a mediator works with a program, he should consult with the program leadership in considering whether to testify or report.

12.3.2.2. Disclosures When the Parties Do Not Waive Confidentiality

A mediator may be subpoenaed to testify by a single party against the wishes of other parties or by someone who was not a participant in the mediation. There may also be situations in which a mediator wishes to report, such as when mediation is being used to commit a crime, or to testify, such as with claims between the mediator and parties. Even when the parties have not waived their confidentiality protections, mediators may testify ethically if the need for disclosure based on public and professional values exceeds the benefits of maintaining confidentiality for the parties and public interests.

Mediators are not entirely on their own in determining the appropriate ethical and public policy balance. In states with mediation confidentiality statutes, a legislature has weighed the relevant factors and determined when the need for disclosure outweighs the value of confidentiality. Or, in some cases, the legislature has determined that it is not possible to make a judgment in the abstract and has instructed courts to

74. FLA. RULES, *supra* note 4, R. 10.306(a) (emphasis added).
75. FLA. STAT. § 44.405(4)(a)(1) (2004).

evaluate the balance in each case. In addition to providing guidance on the balance of public interests, there are legal consequences for mediators: they may be called to testify about communications that are subject to an exception from state confidentiality protections unless there is a provision specifically limiting mediator subpoenas (see Section 12.4).

Legislatures commonly make exceptions from confidentiality protection for communications such as those that trigger a duty to report (see Section 12.3.1), planning or committing a crime, and professional misconduct by a mediation participant. Some states also make confidentiality exceptions for testimony in legal proceedings to enforce a mediated agreement and/or in criminal proceedings. But the legal treatment for this testimony varies greatly from state to state and so there is no generally accepted balance to guide a mediator's judgment.

12.3.2.2.1. Disclosures about Crimes

The ethical duty to warn of a credible threat of a crime of violence was discussed in Section 12.3.1.2. It is important to note that the justification for reporting—to prevent serious physical harm—does not extend to mediation communications concerning past crimes, even if they involved violence. Prevention does not factor into the calculus when a crime is completed, so the social benefits of disclosure are not as strong as maintaining the confidentiality of mediation. There is no duty for mediators to report past crimes, and mediators should not voluntarily disclose that a party might have committed a crime.[76]

In contrast, many states withhold confidentiality protection from communications about an ongoing or future commission of a crime.[77] Under such exceptions, a mediator has no duty to warn but may legally report or testify. One reason for this exception to confidentiality is a concern that participants might use mediation itself to plan or commit a crime. For example, two gangs might meet to arrange a drug deal and claim they are mediating so they can benefit from a cloak of confidentiality in a future prosecution. Or, even if the purpose of the mediation is not criminal, a party may attempt to protect communications that concern a future crime. If a mediation is being used to further criminal conduct, the Model Standards require that "a mediator should take appropriate steps including, if necessary, postponing, withdrawing from or terminating the

76. N.Y. MEAC Op. 2006-03 (2013).

77. *See, e.g.*, UNIF. MEDIATION ACT §§ 5(c), 6(a)(4); FLA. STAT. § 44.405(4)(a)(2) (2004); CAL. EVID. CODE § 703.5 (1994).

mediation."[78] While the Model Standards do not endorse reporting, some disclosures may be appropriate in some situations to maintain public confidence that mediation will not be misused for criminal purposes. In the opinion of the New York MEAC, if a mediation is being used for criminal activity, the mediator should terminate the mediation and report to the sponsoring organization. The mediator may not report directly to the authorities.[79]

In terms of testimony, statutes are split or silent on whether confidentiality protections apply beyond civil cases, or they leave the decision for a court to weigh in each case. These differences reflect competing policy views and fail to give clear guidance to mediators on the balance of the values of confidentiality versus disclosure. On one hand, any mediator testimony threatens to impair the integrity of the process, and resolving a conflict that implicates a crime may require exactly the candor that confidentiality is designed to further. On the other hand, there can be a strong need for evidence in a criminal proceeding to avoid an inaccurate decision—for the prosecution, the defense, and society—because of the high stakes for public safety and human liberty. In addition, defendants' constitutional protections may require disclosure.[80] In applying a professional ethics perspective, a mediator should consider not only the circumstances of the mediation and the proceeding but also whether the testimony she might give is necessary for a fair outcome. If the information is available from any other source, the justification for disclosure is greatly diminished.[81]

12.3.2.2.2. Disclosures Regarding Enforcement of Mediated Agreements

Proceedings seeking, or resisting, the enforcement of an agreement reached in mediation are another topic for which legislatures' policies provide little guidance to mediators about whether the need for disclosure is great enough to justify an exception to confidentiality. Approaches vary among the states: some prohibit disclosure, some provide an exception to confidentiality, and some delegate case-by-case balancing to the courts.[82] In a dispute between the parties about enforcement, they tend to seek the mediator's testimony as a tie-breaker, and harming impartiality

78. Model Standards, *supra* note 5, Standard VI.A.9.

79. N.Y. MEAC Op. 2008-01 (2008).

80. *See generally* Unif. Mediation Act § 6 cmt. 10.

81. *Cf. id.* § 6(b)(1) (evidence must be not otherwise available).

82. *See generally* Ellen E. Deason, *Enforcing Mediated Settlement Agreements: Contract Law Collides with Confidentiality*, 35 U.C. Davis L. Rev. 33 (2001).

is thus unavoidable. But the weight on the other side of the scale—the harm of nondisclosure—will vary with the case.

If the issue is the existence of an oral agreement, the testimony that would be required to prove a settlement has the potential to severely undermine confidentiality. And because parties could have avoided the dispute by making a record and signing it, this situation does not justify the harm to the value of confidentiality that would result from mediator testimony.[83] The balance is not as straightforward, however, when a party claims that an agreement is unenforceable due to fraud or duress. If that allegation is false, it is merely a way to interfere with the result of the mediation process and undermine its integrity. But if it is true, mediation failed as a consensual process for the party who was tricked or forced into an agreement.[84] With duress, sometimes the case includes allegations that the mediator contributed to or was aware of the pressure to agree.[85] In this situation, the mediator may be justified in testifying to maintain the legitimacy of mediation. Otherwise, a mediator should resist testifying unless ordered by a court.

12.3.2.2.3. Disclosures Regarding Professional Misconduct

In addition to mediators' reports of professional misconduct by a mediation participant (see Section 12.3.1.3), occasionally a party may allege mediator professional misconduct.[86] If a party names a mediator as a defendant in a malpractice suit or in a disciplinary complaint filed with a mediation program or state regulatory office, this will necessarily involve examining mediation information to establish or refute the claim. From a professional ethics standpoint, it would be fundamentally unfair to prevent a mediator from defending himself, and parties cannot reasonably expect a mediator to maintain the confidentiality of information needed for that defense.[87] Some mediation codes of conduct explicitly include this exception to confidentiality,[88] and their rules for filing complaints

---

83. *Id.* at 73–87.

84. *Id.* at 89–90.

85. *See, e.g.*, Allen v. Leal, 27 F. Supp. 2d 945 (S.D. Tex. 1998); Olam v. Cong. Mortg. Co., 68 F. Supp. 2d 1110 (N.D. Cal. 1999).

86. *See* James Coben, *Evaluating the Singapore Convention through a U.S.-Centric Litigation Lens: Lessons Learned from Nearly Two Decades of Mediation Disputes in Federal and State Courts*, 20 Cardozo J. Conflict Resol. 1063, 1073–74 (2019); Michael Moffitt, *Suing Mediators*, 83 B.U. L. Rev. 147 (2003).

87. *See* Shapira, *supra* note 1, at 285.

88. *E.g.*, Va. Standards, *supra* note 8, Standard H(1)(ii), (vi); N.C. Standards, *supra* note 4, Standard 3(d)(5), (6).

provide procedures for mediators to respond to the allegations.[89] In addition, there is support in law in some states through an explicit exception to confidentiality provisions that permits testimony regarding a claim or complaint of professional misconduct or malpractice filed against a mediator.[90] Both the ethical and legal exceptions are limited, however, to information that is necessary to process the allegations against the mediator, and the mediator should make the disclosures only to the court or body that is deciding the claim.

12.3.2.2.4. Disclosures in Fee Disputes

A dispute over fees is another situation in which a mediator may find herself in the role of witness in opposition to a party. Parties' reasonable expectations of a confidential process do not include denying the mediator the agreed compensation for his services, so a mediator who has not received payment may ethically file suit against the delinquent party to seek payment.[91] This is a narrow exception to confidentiality that allows disclosures only as required to show the amount of agreed fees and expenses owed.[92] State ethics bodies have issued opinions consistent with this course of action. For example, the Alabama Supreme Court Commission for Dispute Resolution decided that the Alabama Code of Ethics does not prohibit a mediator from reporting to the court that her fee has not been paid.[93]

12.3.2.2.5. Reports to Courts and Mediation Programs

Mediators in disputes referred to them by a court or mediation organization need to abide by the rules of the program that sponsors the mediation. However, these rules may not infringe on a mediator's ethical obligations to the parties, the profession, and the public to maintain the integrity of the process. This means that a mediator must justify disclosures to program staff or judges based on not only the program's rules but also professional ethics principles. Disclosures to the program can be justified for two limited purposes: to facilitate monitoring and developing mediators and when the information is needed to administer the program.[94]

---

89. *E.g.*, FLA. RULES, *supra* note 4, R. 10.810(g).

90. *E.g.*, UNIF. MEDIATION ACT § 6(a)(5); FLA. STAT. § 44.405(4)(a)(4), (6) (2004); VA. CODE ANN. § 8.01-581.22(vi) (2013).

91. SHAPIRA, *supra* note 1, at 285–86.

92. *See, e.g.*, N.C. STANDARDS, *supra* note 4, Standard 3(d)(2).

93. Ala. Sup. Ct. Comm'n for Disp. Resol., Op. 001-10 (2010); *see also* Fla. MEAC Op. 2006-08 (2007).

94. SHAPIRA, *supra* note 1, at 287.

Disclosures to program staff are justified for mediator education, which serves a legitimate purpose by supporting the professional obligation of competence and promoting quality mediation.[95] Allowing disclosures in this context encourages mediators to discuss issues with those more experienced and permits seasoned mediators to use examples to guide others. But disclosures as part of training are permissible only if the participants consent or if their identity remains confidential. Parties' reasonable expectations of confidentiality are not infringed if they cannot be identified in connection with the dispute or mediation events, so a mediator must disclose the information in anonymous form.[96]

The general consensus is that for administrative purposes, mediators may report only "whether parties appeared at a scheduled mediation and whether or not [they] reached a resolution."[97] This limitation is especially important for court-sponsored mediation programs in order to avoid an appearance that mediation information might flow through a back-door channel to a judge. The Florida MEAC has concluded that this narrow exception allows mediators in court-connected programs to report attendance[98] and either "full agreement," "partial agreement," or "no agreement."[99] This information is necessary because the court needs to know if the case will continue. But mediators must make this report without comment or recommendation, and if the mediation was terminated, they may not report the reason but should simply report "no agreement."[100] The scope of disclosure should be strictly limited to avoid any appearance of impropriety and to protect the integrity of both judicial and mediation processes. This ethical guidance is supplemented by law in many states where mediators are prohibited by statute from reporting to any judicial officer who will make a ruling on the dispute unless the subject falls within a delineated exception to confidentiality.[101]

In some states and court programs, mediators may find themselves expected to report when parties have not complied with a requirement

95. *See* Model Standards, *supra* note 5, Standards IV, VI.

96. *See, e.g.*, Shapira, *supra* note 1, at 288; N.Y. MEAC Op. 2006-01, at 4–5 (2006); Va. Standards, *supra* note 8, Standard H(7).

97. Model Standards, *supra* note 5, Standard V.A.2.

98. Fla. MEAC Op. 2019-006 (2020), Op. 2006-008 (2007); *see also* N.Y. Standards, *supra* note 4, Standard V(A) cmt. 4.

99. Fla. MEAC Op. 2014-007 (2014).

100. *Id.*

101. *See* Unif. Mediation Act § 7.

that they participate in mediation in good faith.[102] These statutes and rules were enacted to counter resistance to mandatory mediation, and many threaten the parties with sanctions for noncompliance,[103] although the definition of "good faith" is hazy and variable.[104] The relationship of these requirements to confidentiality provisions is not clear, but if the applicable professional standards include the common exception to confidentiality for disclosures "required by law," mediators would be permitted to report bad-faith participation. Although many commentators support some form of good-faith requirement,[105] mediator disclosures about party participation need to delve into details of mediation communications if they are to establish any allegation of bad faith. Other commentators have objected that such reporting requirements jeopardize the confidentiality and neutrality of the mediation process[106] and "corrupt" it by causing distrust.[107] As stated in the Georgia Standards, "the possible damage to the process by reporting more than offsets the benefit in a given case."[108] Because the need for confidence in confidentiality outweighs the benefits of sanctions for bad-faith participation, reports that disclose bad-faith participation are not justified.

12.3.2.3. A Note on Applicable Law

There are several references in this chapter to the applicable law of mediation and how it intersects with ethical principles, along with examples of how law can vary significantly among the states. If a dispute concerns parties and activities in only one state and a mediation is held in that state,

---

102. *See, e.g.*, John Lande, *Using Dispute System Design Methods to Promote Good-Faith Participation in Court-Connected Mediation Programs*, 50 UCLA L. Rev. 69, 78–79 (2002) (listing 22 states, 21 federal district courts, and 17 state courts with good-faith participation requirements).

103. *Id.* at 81 (describing sanctions).

104. *See, e.g., id.* at 86–98.

105. *See, e.g.*, Peter Thompson, *Good Faith Mediation in the Federal Courts*, 26 Ohio St. J. on Disp. Resol. 363 (2011).

106. *See, e.g.*, James Alfini & Catherine McCabe, *Mediating in the Shadow of the Courts: A Survey of Emerging Caselaw*, 54 Ark. L. Rev. 171, 182–95 (2001); Alexandria Zylstra, *The Road from Voluntary Mediation to Mandatory Good-Faith Requirements*, 17 J. Am. Acad. Matrim. Law. 69, 94–97 (2001); *see also In re* AT Reynolds & Sons, Inc., 452 B.R. 374, 482–84 (S.D.N.Y. 2011) (confidentiality considerations preclude the court from inquiring into the level of a party's participation).

107. Wayne Brazil, *Continuing the Conversation about the Current Status and the Future of ADR: A View from the Court*, 2000 J. Disp. Resol. 11, 31–33 (2000).

108. Ga. Standards, *supra* note 18, Standard IV(B) (concluding confidentiality precludes mediators from reporting bad faith); *see also* Lande, *supra* note 102, at 106.

one can predict with confidence that this "home" state will likely be both the forum and the source of applicable law if there is a later dispute about the mediation. However, if the dispute has a multistate dimension and mediation is private rather than court-connected, it is possible that a party may later file a case in a state other than the site of the mediation or that a court may decide to apply another state's confidentiality law. Consider, for example, a case in which a Delaware court enforced an agreement the parties had reached through mediation in Florida to settle patent litigation originally filed in South Carolina.[109] And if a dispute about a mediation is filed in federal court—typically an enforcement action under diversity jurisdiction—the outcome is even more unpredictable: in addition to state-to-state choice-of-law issues, the applicable confidentiality law may be either state or federal.[110] The complexities of conflicts of law mean that the parties in cases with a multistate dimension should be alert to the possibility that another state's law, or even federal law, might govern limits on disclosures in a subsequent suit. Advising the parties is a matter that may be left to the parties' attorneys, but a mediator in such a case should be aware that he too may be subject to legal obligations of confidentiality in other states.

12.4. Response to a Subpoena to Testify

12.4.1. Legal Tools That Protect Mediators

Many states support the ethical limitations on mediator testimony with mediation statutes or court rules. They typically empower mediators to avoid testifying in many circumstances or disqualify them from testifying as a matter of law. First, in some states, mediators hold their own privilege as described in Section 12.3.2.1. This evidentiary tool gives mediators power to refuse to testify about mediation communications and to block other participants from testifying about the mediator's own communications.[111] Note, however, that there is no privilege if the communication falls within a statutory exception.[112] When that is the case, the mediator typically may be subpoenaed.

Second, other states declare that mediators are incompetent to testify or lacking in capacity to serve as a witness about mediations they

109. Asten, Inc. v. Wangner Sys. Corp., No. C.A. 15617, 1999 WL 803965 (Del. Ch. Sept. 23, 1999).

110. *See generally* Ellen E. Deason, *Predictable Mediation Confidentiality in the U.S. Federal System*, 17 Ohio St. J. on Disp. Resol. 239 (2002).

111. *See, e.g.*, Unif. Mediation Act § 4(b)(2).

112. For a typical list of exceptions, see Unif. Mediation Act § 6.

have facilitated.[113] Unlike a privilege, this legal format does not provide a mediator with the opportunity to waive confidentiality and testify voluntarily in appropriate circumstances. And the result can be controversial: California has interpreted its statute as brooking no exceptions except those specified in the statute, even for testimony about attorney or mediator misconduct.[114]

Finally, some states declare that mediators may not be subpoenaed in court proceedings or in specific court proceedings. This leaves mediators the option to testify voluntarily, unlike when they are declared incompetent to testify. The Georgia ADR Rules, for example, provide that a neutral may not "be subpoenaed or otherwise required to testify concerning a mediation . . . in any subsequent administrative or judicial proceeding." The Rules include exceptions that are consistent with the ethical limits on confidentiality discussed previously: threats of imminent violence to self and others; when the mediator believes a child is abused; or communications relevant to legal claims or disciplinary proceedings against the mediator arising out of a mediation.[115] In UMA states, mediators may not be called to testify about professional misconduct of other participants or enforcement of a mediated agreement, even though those topics are not covered by confidentiality.[116]

12.4.2. Techniques to Help Avoid Subpoenas from the Parties

These legal protections are not universally available, but there are practical measures that mediators can take to minimize the risk of a subpoena. First, many mediators ask the parties to sign an agreement to mediate at the beginning of the process. This agreement can provide that the parties will not ask or seek to compel the mediator to provide information about the mediation in a court proceeding.[117] In jurisdictions where mediators do not hold a privilege, such an agreement can provide a contractual basis to protect mediators from being subpoenaed by a party. Mediators should realize, however, that if a nonparticipant brings a lawsuit,

113. *See, e.g.*, Minn. Stat. Ann. § 595.02 (sub. 1a) (2020); Cal. Evid. Code § 703.5 (1994).

114. *See* Foxgate Homeowners Ass'n v. Bramalea Cal., Inc., 25 P.3d 117 (Cal. 2001) (rejecting a judge-made exception to confidentiality that would permit a mediator to disclose sanctionable attorney conduct).

115. Ga. ADR Rules R. VII(A) (2013).

116. Unif. Mediation Act § 6(c).

117. *See, e.g.*, *Agreement to Mediate Forms—Civil*, Resol. Sys. Inst., *available at* https://www.aboutrsi.org/files/CivAgrmtMed.pdf (last visited Mar. 9, 2021) (examples from Cobb Cnty., Ga., & Cook Cnty. Cir. Ct., Ill.).

the contract will not provide protection because the mediation agreement does not bind nonparticipants.[118] Mediators should, in addition, check the applicable state's policies on such agreements. In Florida, consistent with the mediator's inability to refuse to testify when the parties have waived confidentiality (see Section 12.3.2.1), a mediator's confidentiality agreement cannot ethically require parties to agree they will not subpoena the mediator.[119]

Second, the mediator should try to make sure that every agreement between the parties is recorded in writing (or using acceptable electronic means) and signed by the parties. In the United States, by far the largest category of litigation about mediation issues concerns the enforcement of agreements reached in mediation.[120] Some of these disputes are challenges to the existence and/or the terms of an agreement that one party alleges was reached orally during the mediation. State laws that treat oral agreements as privileged protect the mediator from being required to submit information about a putative settlement.[121] But even in the absence of such legal protection, if there is a signed record, it may provide evidence that precludes the dispute entirely. The writing need not be a full contract; it can be a list of the terms of the agreement or a memorandum of understanding. It does need to be complete enough to be enforceable and should include all material aspects of the resolution.[122] For example, a divorce settlement that neglected to record the conditions the couple had agreed upon for the sale of their house led to litigation over those terms, with mediator testimony that was ruled inadmissible on appeal.[123]

12.4.3. When a Mediator Is Subpoenaed

If a mediator is nonetheless subpoenaed to testify or provide documents, the mediator should inform the parties immediately. The mediator must then decide her course of action against the backdrop of her obligation to maintain confidentiality and the applicable exceptions to that obligation. Many standards provide an exception that permits a mediator to

---

118. *See, e.g.*, Folb v. Motion Picture Indus. Pension & Health Plans, 16 F. Supp. 2d 1164 (C.D. Cal. 1998), *aff'd*, 216 F.3d 1082 (9th Cir. 2000).

119. Fla. MEAC Op. 2017-007 (2017) (reasoning that only parties, not mediators, can waive confidentiality in Florida).

120. Coben, *supra* note 86, at 1073–74.

121. *See, e.g.*, Akron v. Carter, 942 N.E.2d 409 (Ohio Ct. App. 2010) (refusing to enforce an oral settlement agreement, which is privileged and not discoverable under the Uniform Mediation Act).

122. *See* Deason, *supra* note 82, at 84–88.

123. *See, e.g.*, Winegart v. Winegart, 910 N.W.2d 906 (S.D. 2018).

disclose information when "required by applicable law."[124] "Applicable law" includes court orders, so it is technically not an ethical violation to testify under a court order. A subpoena from a party is not, however, an order of the court, and a mediator or mediation program may move to quash it.

What actions to protect confidentiality are ethically required? When asked what a mediator should do when faced with a subpoena seeking disclosure of mediation communications, the ABA Section of Dispute Resolution Committee on Ethical Guidance observed that the Model Standards do not provide an answer: they do not indicate to what extent a mediator should protect mediation communications or what means a mediator should use.[125] Given the expectations of confidentiality in the Model Standards, however, the ABA ethical guidance concludes that mediators who have been subpoenaed should "strive" to maintain the confidentiality of communications.[126]

What does "strive" mean? There is no single prescribed course of action. According to the Model Family Standards, if a mediator "reasonably believes [testifying] would violate an obligation of confidentiality to the participants," he "should not testify . . . in response to a subpoena without an order of the court."[127] In contrast, the Florida MEAC concluded that a mediator may appear in response to a subpoena. A mediator may file a motion to quash a subpoena for the purpose of bringing confidentiality provisions to the attention of the court but is not required to do so.[128] The ABA ethical guidance helpfully recognizes that there may be practical limits on the extent to which a mediator can defend confidentiality and that these limits will vary with the resources of the mediator. At a minimum, the mediator should remind the judge of the confidentiality requirement and provide the judge with the applicable standards and laws. If the subpoena is not withdrawn or denied, a mediator with legal resources could move to quash it or file for a protective order. A mediator working for an organization or program can reasonably expect the organization, with its greater resources, to provide a thorough defense. But the Model Standards themselves do not impose an affirmative duty to resist

124. *See, e.g.*, Model Standards, *supra* note 5, Standard V.A; Model Family Standards, *supra* note 5, Standard VII.

125. ABA Section of Disp. Resol. Comm. on Mediator Ethical Guidance, Op. 2008-3, at 2 (2008) [hereinafter ABA Ethical Guidance].

126. *Id.* at 5 (2008); *see also* Ga. Comm'n Op. 8, *supra* note 8, at 4 (recommending a mediator file a motion to quash a subpoena).

127. Model Family Standards, *supra* note 5, Standard VII.E.

128. Fla. MEAC Op. 2017-119 (2017).

compelled disclosure of confidential mediation information.[129] If a court, after considering confidentiality obligations, rules that a mediator should testify, she should comply with the court order.

12.5. Conclusion

The principle of confidentiality in mediation requires mediators to avoid testifying or reporting mediation information in almost all circumstances. The assurance of confidentiality is crucial to developing sufficient trust to encourage candor by the parties, which is essential to a quality process. This professional value also supports the principle of impartiality by avoiding any perception that the mediator is supporting one party.

Confidentiality is not an absolute value, but it should yield only when there is a need for disclosure to accommodate a compelling societal interest. Because of their professional duty to the parties, mediators should resist testifying and refrain from reporting on mediation activities with only a few exceptions. They may testify when all the parties agree, in recognition of party self-determination, but mediators should also consider the harm of disclosure to the profession's standing and the public interest in settling disputes through effective mediation. Otherwise, mediators should disclose mediation information only if the need for disclosure substantially outweighs the public interest in preserving confidentiality. Exceptions to confidentiality with the strongest justifications are reports of child or elder abuse, warnings of serious physical harm, using mediation to further crime, and complaints about ethical violations by mediators or other professionals. In addition, mediators may ethically report to mediation programs for administrative and training purposes. Testimony in criminal proceedings or concerning enforcement of mediated agreements may be justified in specific cases. Mediators should be especially careful to limit the content of reports to courts, which has consequences for the integrity of both the mediation and adjudicatory systems.

129. ABA Ethical Guidance, *supra* note 125, at 5.

Chapter 13

Disciplining Mediators

Michael Moffitt

13.1. Introduction

A book devoted to questions of mediator ethics appropriately spends most of its time devoted to questions of line-drawing. What behavior is/is not ethical? How do various aspirational ethical standards intersect with each other? To what extent are ethical lines dependent on context? As a process matter, who gets to (should get to?) draw these lines? And so on.

This chapter takes up the important, if perhaps subsidiary, question of what might happen to mediators who do not adhere to ethical directives. Most mediators consider themselves to be ethical practitioners, and probably all mediators *aspire to be* ethical practitioners. That intrinsic motivation to practice within some set of parameters is surely the most immediate—and maybe the most important—factor affecting mediators' routine decision making. Most mediators would, most of the time, probably practice exactly as they do even if they operated under no threat of sanction or discipline. Yet understanding the landscape of ethics—particularly in a practice so tightly bound up in the legal system more broadly—requires some understanding of the potential consequences of noncompliance. This chapter takes up that "or else what" question.

13.2. Forms of Accountability for Mediators

Broadly speaking, there are five different avenues of formal, external accountability for mediators. There are surely informal factors at play (mediators' interests in being well regarded by their peers, for example). There are surely internal factors at play (the desire to look in the mirror with pride each morning, for example). But if discipline or sanction is to be meted out on a transgressing mediator, it will almost certainly come in one of five forms:

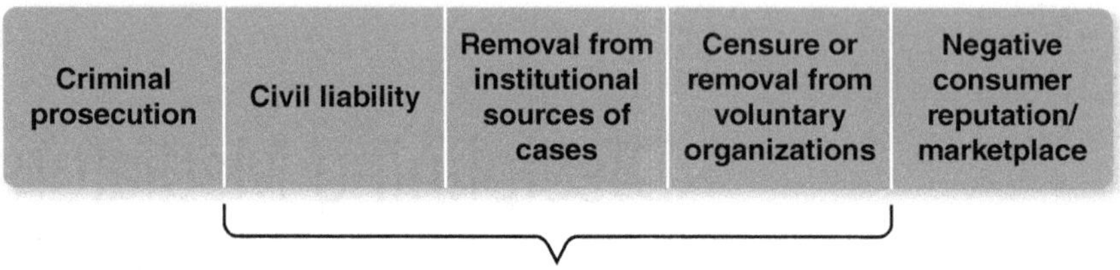

Figure 13.1 Forms of Accountability

This chapter focuses on the middle three of these potential vehicles for mediator discipline. On the far end of the spectrum, the threat of criminal prosecution is real but remote. In most mediation contexts, a mediator would have to be entrepreneurially awful to engage in behavior that runs afoul of criminal laws. It is not inconceivable that some mediator somewhere could engage in fraud, collusion, corruption, or embezzlement. But these are such extreme versions of misconduct that the "ethics" frame on such behavior is evidently inadequate. On the other end of the spectrum, mediators' everyday actions surely affect their current clients' perceptions. Mediators who engage in *perceivable* unethical practices run some risk of damaged reputations in the marketplace. But the marketplace for mediators is problematic because of a number of information asymmetries. Most significantly for purposes of this chapter, mediation clients have only partial visibility into their mediators' practices.[1] Just as it can be difficult for clients to know whether a mediator is skilled, it can be difficult for clients to know if mediators' conduct is aligned with ethical standards. I focus, therefore, on the middle three of these avenues of potential discipline for mediators.

Note that each of these three is ex post. That is, they are mechanisms by which mediators may be *punished* for having failed to adhere to some standard. Most systems of quality assurance, in most professional

1. *See* Michael Moffitt, *Casting Light on the Black Box of Mediation: Should Mediators Make Their Conduct More Transparent?*, 13 Ohio St. J. on Disp. Resol. 1 (1997).

or quasiprofessional practice areas, rely on a combination of four factors, only two of which are after the fact:

Examples of the Four Ways to Assure Quality Services		
	FRONT-END	BACK-END
	(steps aimed at assuring quality by limiting the intial pool to those practioners deemed competent or qualifed)	(steps aimed at assuring quality by punishing or removing from practice those whose conduct is deemed unacceptable)
PUBLIC		
(steps taken by the state)	❶ For example, requiring a license in order to join the practice	❷ For example, upon finding of misconduct, revoking a license or otherwise banning a practioner from future practice
PRIVATE		
(steps taken by private parties or organizations)	❸ For example, consumers using reputations to make hiring decisions	❹ For example, unhappy consumers filing a complaint or suing bad practioners for malpractice

Figure 13.2 Four Ways to Assure Mediator Quality[2]

As this is a chapter focusing on mediator discipline, a "back-end" or after-the-fact enterprise, I will describe the range of private, governmental, or organizational sanctions mediators could face if they engage in unethical practice.[3]

2. Figure taken from Michael Moffitt, *The Four Ways to Assure Mediator Quality (and Why None of Them Work)*, 24 Ohio St. J. on Disp. Resol. 191 (2009).

3. There is a separate question about remedies available to *clients* in cases in which the mediator has acted unethically. Civil lawsuits, sounding contract or tort, for example, provide the prospect of monetary recovery. See Section 13.3. Separately, injured clients can seek to have mediation outcomes set aside, in cases where the mediator engaged in ethical misconduct. For more on this prospect, see Fran L. Tetunic, *The Irony of Mediator as Problem Maker: Mediator Misconduct Setting Aside Mediated Agreements*, 23 Harv. Negot. L. Rev. 177 (2017). *See also* Vitakis-Valchine v. Valchine, 793 So. 2d 1094 (Fla. App. 4th Dist. 2001); Melvin A. Rubin, *Mediator Malpractice: A Proposed Defensive Path through the Minefield*, 17 Disp. Resol. Mag. 23 (2010). In many cases, this remedy will be more significant to former mediation

13.3. Civil Liability of Mediators

With respect to the specific question of mediators engaging in an unethical practice, the most intuitive potential sanction is probably the prospect of a civil lawsuit brought by unhappy clients against the transgressing mediator. If your doctor, lawyer, plumber, or therapist engages in substandard practice in a way that harms you, you will almost always have recourse in the form of a civil lawsuit against them. The same is true, at least in theory, with respect to mediators.

The reality on the ground, however, is that there are a number of aspects of mediation practice that make it considerably more challenging for clients to recover against mediators for misconduct. If we focus specifically on alleged *ethical* lapses by the mediator (for example, breaching confidentiality or failing to address conflicts of interest appropriately), mediators' exposure to liability narrows even further. There may be an amorphous ethical duty of competence (demonstrated, for example, by being up to date on the standards of mediation practice), but even if such a duty is recognized, generalized claims against mediators are unlikely to be successful. Rather, claims are more likely to be successful if they allege that a mediator has breached some specific duty—and even these kinds of claims face real challenges for the reasons I outline below.

Depending on the jurisdiction and the specific factual context, there are roughly three avenues of possible action in a civil complaint against a mediator.

13.3.1. Breach of Contract (Explicit)

In some cases, a mediator may have created a contractual obligation regarding a specific ethical principle. For example, a mediator might have a clause in her standard Agreement to Mediate reading "I will keep everything confidential and will assure the confidentiality of all mediation communications." If a party believes that the mediator has breached this exacting level of confidentiality,[4] that party would have a straightforward contract basis for raising the claim. The party would not need to refer to external codes or standards of practice in arguing that

---

clients. However, because such remedies do not, strictly speaking, serve as a form of discipline against the mediator, I exclude further detailed treatment in this chapter.

4. For an interesting perspective on the incoherence of confidentiality assurances and expectations, see Gregory Firestone & Sharon Press, *Privadentiality: Developing a Coherent Framework for Establishing Communication Protections in Family and Child Protection Dispute Resolution Methods*, 58 FAM. CT. REV. 9 (2020).

confidentiality attaches to the mediator's set of duties. The party would simply point to the explicit promise in the mediator's agreement.

Most mediators' engagement agreements do not commonly provide explicit, unambiguous reference to ethical obligations. In a study of mediator agreements some years ago, I found that most mediation contracts contained vague promises, such as the commitment to "endeavor to facilitate communication between the parties with the goal of discovering possible terms of a mutually agreeable resolution."[5] Although this description might serve as a generalized definition[6] of good mediation, it provides little by way of explicit recourse for a party who believes a mediator's conduct has been substandard. How, after all, would one demonstrate that a mediator had breached such a commitment?

Still, there are contractual terms that at least raise the specter of creating ethical obligations and the corresponding threat of civil liability for breaches. Does it mean anything if a mediator promises the mediation will be "efficient" or that its outcomes will be "fair"? What about mediators who promise that a process will be "impartial," that the mediator will "offer suggestions," or that the parties' "ability to decide for themselves" will be preserved? What about mediators who promise they "will not tell the parties what to do"?[7] Might there be a context in which one of these kinds of clauses is deemed a promise—one that a mediator voluntarily undertook and then breached?[8]

13.3.2. Breach of Contract (Implied)

Even if a mediator's agreement doesn't include specific commitments, there are contexts in which the mediator may be held to have impliedly promised to adhere to one or more ethical tenets. For example, a mediator who advertises himself as a member of a particular ADR organization could be held to have impliedly promised adherence to that organization's published standards of ethical practice. Are all of those who advertise

---

5. Michael Moffitt, *Promises, Promises: Mediators Must Exercise Contract Caution*, 22 ALTS. TO HIGH COST LITIG. 1, 10 (2004).

6. *See* Michael Moffitt, *Schmediation and the Dimensions of Definition*, 10 HARV. NEGOT. L. REV. 69 (2005).

7. Moffitt, *supra* note 5, at 11.

8. *See* Michael Moffitt, *Suing Mediators*, 83 B.U. L. REV. 147 (2003); Michael Moffitt, *Ten Ways to Get Sued: A Guide for Mediators*, 8 HARV. NEGOT. L. REV. 81 (2003); Michael Moffitt, *What Me Liable? A Checkup for Mediators*, DISP. RESOL. MAG. 25 (Summer 2003).

their memberships in the Association for Conflict Resolution impliedly committing to adhere to ACR's published Ethical Principles?[9]

Additionally, mediators' advertisements sometimes contain exuberantly optimistic language about mediation—and in particular about the likelihood of settlement. An unsophisticated consumer could easily understand some of these as constituting a promise to resolve disputes.

> [A] careful examination of some mediators' materials shows the possibility that some could be considered a promise of settlement. The caption under one mediator's photo reads, in bold letters, "I settle cases" and the contract says nothing further about mediation outcomes or about the mediation process. Another mediator's contract says, "At the conclusion of the mediation, the mediator and the parties will jointly draft the settlement document."[10]

Although the prospect of promising settlement is anathema to most professional articulations of mediators' roles, some mediators' public-facing materials lean toward propaganda—raising the risk that they are creating contractual obligations.

Furthermore, even without any communications from mediators about the obligations they *intend* to take on, there are those who have suggested that certain duties may automatically attach to mediators. Might, for example, a mediator be held liable for an undisclosed conflict of interest, even if nothing in her explicit assertions speaks to the question of neutrality or impartiality? A number of scholars have suggested that such a duty should be an unwaivable, inherent duty attaching to mediators,[11] although I am aware of no court cases that have arrived at this conclusion.

13.3.3. Malpractice

Even in the absence of any specific contractual obligations, mediators face the prospect of a civil action alleging that the mediator's conduct constituted actionable malpractice, typically sounding in tort.[12] Like

---

9. *See Final Report of the ACR Ethics Comm.: Ethical Principles*, Ass'n for Conflict Resol. (May 2010), https://acrnet.org/general/custom.asp?page=EthicalPrinciples.

10. Moffitt, *supra* note 5, at 12.

11. Amanda K. Esquibel, *The Case of the Conflicted Mediator: An Argument for Liability and against Immunity*, 31 Rutgers L.J. 131, 168 (1999).

12. For a comparative perspective on malpractice actions against mediators, see A.K.C. Koo, *Exploring Mediator Liability in Negligence*, 45 Common L. World Rev. 165 (2016).

almost any other practitioner, a mediator surely owes certain duties to his client. If a mediator's actions breach one or more of those duties, causing harm to one or more of his clients, it would stand to reason that that mediator would be exposed to the prospect of tort-based malpractice liability.

As an empirical matter, successful malpractice actions against mediators are vanishingly rare.[13] The absence of successful, published negligence cases against mediators does not prove that mediators are perfect or that clients are never harmed by mediators. It does not even prove that no such lawsuits are filed against mediators. After all, many cases settle, and obtaining information about settled cases is difficult. At a minimum, mediators' misconduct at least creates the *potential* for exposure to liability. There are, however, at least six barriers facing prospective plaintiffs who are contemplating bringing malpractice claims against mediators. I explore those six next because to understand the range of potential sanctions against mediators requires an understanding of not only the theoretical sanctions but also the likelihood of those sanctions attaching.

13.3.3.1. Invisible (or at Least Hard-to-Spot) Harms

Mediation clients are only likely to file complaints against mediators if they believe (a) that they have been injured, (b) that the mediator was the cause of that injury, and (c) that there is some prospect of recovery or relief available to the injured party. In some contexts, the first of these may be entirely obvious. A mediator writes a tell-all book, describing salacious aspects of the celebrity divorce on which she worked. A mediator holds a press conference, sharing details of the options each side had explored during a brainstorming session that had been characterized to the parties as off the record. A mediator provides inaccurate assurance about the legal implications of a clause he has suggested to an unsophisticated party, and he then prevents further consultation with counsel. In such cases, a client would immediately feel the harm associated with the mediator's behavior.

Harms from mediators' errors are not, however, always so conspicuous. Just as certain kinds of injuries stemming from doctors' errors are often invisible to the patient,[14] mediation parties do not always have visibility into the impacts of mediators' decisions. Would clients know

13. *See* Moffitt, *Suing Mediators*, *supra* note 8, at 150–51.

14. *See* Michael Moffitt, *Settlement Malpractice*, 86 U. Chi. L. Rev. 1825, 1841 n.38 (2019) (describing information asymmetries and their effects on injured parties' assessments of professionals' conduct).

immediately if a mediator had misrepresented their credentials? When would a client learn of a mediator's undisclosed conflict of interest?

The fact that a client might, on reflection, be disappointed with the substantive outcome of a mediation does not produce any reliable indication that the mediator was somehow to blame, of course. There are plenty of examples of unhappy mediation clients who may (inappropriately) direct anger toward a mediator. ("If only the mediator had been competent, the other side would have agreed to the terms I was seeking.") But regarding the prospect of tort liability, the prerequisite that a prospective plaintiff perceives an injury attributable to the mediator is a real hurdle.

13.3.3.2. Challenges Establishing a Duty

No tort claim can survive without establishing that the prospective defendant (here, a mediator) owes some level of care or duty to the prospective plaintiff (here, an unhappy client). With respect specifically to *ethical* duties, the topic of this book, there are fundamentally only two different mechanisms by which a plaintiff could seek to meet that threshold requirement. First, the plaintiff could assert that the mediator voluntarily assumed specific obligations that would not otherwise attach. For example, the plaintiff may point to the mediator's contractual promises or membership in an organization that holds its members out as adhering to a particular set of obligations. Second, the plaintiff could assert that a particular ethical duty is *universal*, such that it applies to all mediators, not just this one. As an example, some scholars have urged that mediators should broadly be assumed to have fiduciary duties with respect to clients.[15] Others have argued that mediation depends so heavily on impartiality that a duty to disclose potential conflicts should be considered implied in every mediation agreement.[16] Such arguments toward the universal, however, have generally failed—principally because mediation is not a licensed practice. One part of the reason there is no licensure for mediation is the (sometimes beautiful but always breathtakingly broad) diversity of practices taking place under the umbrella label "mediation." Without a consensus on what "mediation" is, the state cannot establish any regulatory monopoly over mediation.[17] Without a regulatory monopoly, the prospect of universal ethical duties attaching in a way that permits tort claims becomes harder.

---

15. *See* Arthur A. Chaykin, *Mediator Liability: A New Role for Fiduciary Duties*, 53 U. Cin. L. Rev. 731 (1984).

16. *See* Esquibel, *supra* note 11.

17. *See* Moffitt, *supra* note 6.

Lange v. Marshall[18] provides an early illustration of the courts' hesitance to impose particular ethical duties on mediators. In that case, a personal friend of a divorcing couple agreed to work with them jointly as they sought to arrive at a settlement. Ms. Lange was hospitalized at the time the settlement talks concluded, and the mediator, Marshall, drafted up the terms of the agreement. Ms. Lange subsequently challenged the provisions and also filed a claim against Marshall. In her complaint, she alleged that Marshall failed to protect her interests, failed to inquire about Mr. Lange's true assets, provided no information about her rights in the divorce, and provided no information comparing the settlement's terms with what she could expect if the case went to court. The defendant mediator admitted that he took none of the steps the plaintiff sought, but "contended that he had no duty to do them."[19] The court wrote, "We need not resolve the exact nature of the defendant's status nor the duties which this status imposed upon him." The court instead resolved the case in favor of the defendant on appeal, holding that the plaintiff had failed to establish proximately caused damages (see later for more on that).

DiGiuseppe v. Talbot[20] illustrates many courts' reluctance to bind mediators to duties not explicitly appearing in a mediation agreement. Elizabeth and Vincent DiGiuseppe engaged the services of a mediator, Jeannine Talbot. Talbot, who was also an attorney but who specifically indicated that she would represent neither of the DiGiuseppes, met with the couple on multiple occasions over several years "to assist them in settling the issues arising from the impending dissolution of their marriage."[21] The parties eventually settled, without consulting separately with counsel. Subsequently, Vincent DiGiuseppe believed that the agreement's provision regarding educational expenses would be capped by a Connecticut statute. The court rejected his argument, however, pointing to the clear language of the mediated agreement. He then brought an action against Talbot, alleging that she had "drafted a flawed agreement" in a manner constituting malpractice. The court granted Talbot summary judgment, noting that no attorney-client relationship was established contractually and that "no duty arises in the present case outside of the contract."[22]

---

18. Lange v. Marshall, 622 S.W.2d 237 (Mo. Ct. App. 1981).
19. *Id.* at 238.
20. DiGiuseppe v. Talbot, 2017 WL 2324303 (Conn. Super. Ct. May 4, 2017).
21. DiGiuseppe v. DiGiuseppe, 2015 Conn. Super. LEXIS 2900 at 2 (Super. Ct. Nov. 23, 2015).
22. *DiGiuseppe*, 2017 WL 2324303 at 2.

13.3.3.3. Challenges Establishing a Breach

A typical negligence-based tort claim against a practitioner involves demonstrating that the practitioner's actions fall outside of the appropriate standards of practice or care. Often, a plaintiff accomplishes this by demonstrating that there is a customary set of practices and then demonstrating that the defendant's actions were inconsistent with that customary practice. The challenge with mediation is that

> mediation practice is gloriously diverse. Mediators as a community include members of many different cultures, socio-economic backgrounds, education, and political leanings. The diversity of their approaches to the basic undertaking of facilitating negotiations or conversations is similarly rich. While some have argued strongly for a more unified, restrictive understanding of what constitutes "mediation," the practice continues to elude restriction. Even efforts at defining sub-categories of mediators, often framed in terms of "style," "model," "approach," or "orientation," have been similarly less than exact. Experienced, educated, well-intending practitioners engage in a wide variety of activities under the rubric of mediating, and no indication exists of an emerging consensus on practice decisions. Who should be in the room? How should the agenda be established? How should possible settlement options be discussed? How should non-settlement alternatives be considered? What role should the law or other external standards play? How transparent should the mediator be about the actions he or she takes? How and by whom should the problems be defined? For better or worse (and I largely think it is for the better), the diversity of mediation renders the articulation of an identifiable customary practice difficult.[23]

With respect specifically to *ethical* practices, the picture is not much clearer. Consider, for example, some of the kinds of in-the-room decisions a mediator makes through the lens of impartiality, neutrality, impartial regard, or whatever thesaurus-related articulation of that bucket of concepts one uses. Or consider those same moves through the lens of self-determination, party autonomy, or whatever label best attaches.

> Almost anything a mediator does during the course of a mediation might be explained by one or more of the current, competing

23. Moffitt, *Suing Mediators*, *supra* note 8, at 149.

> theories of mediation practice. Some mediators keep the parties separated almost exclusively. Others keep them together in almost every circumstance. Some mediators play an active role in structuring conversation during the mediation. Others view such procedural decisions as part of the parties' role. A mediator who decides to offer suggestions or to evaluate the merits of the disputants' claims is either right on track or wildly out of bounds, depending on the school of mediation. One mediator might cajole, strong-arm, threaten, argue with, beg, or even bribe the disputants to reach a compromise. Another would view each of these as anathema to the role of a mediator. In short, a mediator can do few things that will constitute a clear breach of all conceptions of acceptable mediator practice.[24]

To be clear, some of these behaviors would find little defense in modern articulations of mediator ethics, almost all of which elevate party autonomy or voluntariness, for example.[25] From the narrow perspective of a tort-based inquiry, however, a prospective plaintiff would have a challenging time pegging any particular mediator behavior as falling outside of customary practices.

13.3.3.4. Challenges Establishing a Causation

Even if a former client establishes that a mediator did [x] and that [x] constituted a breach of that mediator's duty, the client must still demonstrate that [x] caused some identifiable injury to the client. Among other things, the fact that there are almost always intervening decision makers makes this challenging, in practice. For simplicity's sake, a complaining mediation party has to choose from one of two avenues: (a) "The case did not settle, but if the mediator had behaved correctly, it would have settled on favorable terms," or (b) "The case settled, but if the mediator had behaved correctly, the outcome would have been more favorable to me (either with better settlement terms or no settlement)." Both present causation challenges.

If the case failed to settle, a plaintiff faces two challenges. First, the plaintiff must show that the mediator's actions are the reason it failed to settle. In most circumstances, courts will treat such a clock-rewinding exercise as intolerably speculative.[26] Second, even if a plaintiff were to

---

24. *Id.* at 157.

25. *See, e.g.*, Omer Shapira, A Theory of Mediators' Ethics: Foundations, Rationale, and Application 140–48 (2016).

26. *See* Moffitt, *supra* note 14, at 1853–55.

succeed in demonstrating that the case was undeniably settleable, the complaining party would then have the problem of the duty to mitigate. In other words, "If it was so easily settled, then why didn't you parties just settle it on your own?"[27]

If the case settled, but on terms the former client now regrets, the same kinds of causation challenges arise. A party might claim that *she* would have never agreed to the final terms if the mediator had provided fuller information, for example. But how can that party prove that the *other party* would have agreed to a different set of terms in this alternate universe?[28] In most cases, because of the presence of intervening decision makers,[29] establishing causation will be a real hurdle in complaints against mediators.

For example, in *Lehrer v. Zwernemann*,[30] a former mediation client brought an action against the mediator alleging that the mediator had breached a duty to be impartial by, among other things, failing to disclose a prior relationship with opposing counsel. The plaintiff alleged that he would not have agreed to this particular mediator if he had known about the prior relationship. However, the plaintiff did not provide evidence that he would not have entered the eventual mediation *settlement* if the conflict had been disclosed. Without evidence of legal injury, the court dismissed the claim.

13.3.3.5. Challenges Establishing Damages

Even if a mediator has breached an ethical duty *and* at least one party suffered an injury directly tied to that breach, the question in a malpractice action remains, "How much injury did that client suffer?" And the nature of mediation practice makes this a hard question to answer. With legal malpractice, the case-within-a-case method of assessment provides one possible avenue for answering questions of damage. It compares the actual outcome of the trial (which included the legal malpractice) with what we expect the outcome of a properly conducted trial would have been. There is no shortage of critiques of this approach to assessing misconduct, but its fundamental structure persists in the legal malpractice context.[31]

---

27. *See* Moffitt, *Suing Mediators*, *supra* note 8, at 176–78.

28. *See* Moffitt, *supra* note 14, at 1850.

29. In some contexts, judicial approval of a settlement may introduce yet another intervening decision maker, breaking the chain of causation. *See* Moffitt, *supra* note 14, at 1852–53.

30. Lehrer v. Zwernemann, 14 S.W.3d 775 (Tex. App. 2000).

31. *See* Restatement (Third) of the Law Governing Lawyers § 53 (2000).

With mediation, however, I am aware of no courts that have entertained the suggestion of a settlement-within-a-settlement analysis. How much more would the other side have conceded if the mediator had not engaged in misconduct? How much worse is this settlement than the probabilistic assessment of what would have happened if this case had gone to trial? How can we compare a multifaceted, creative settlement (for example, with an apology, payment over time, a contingent reopener, and a confidentiality clause) with a theoretical, dollars-only court judgment?[32] Instead, as a practical matter, a mediator's fees may be the only thing easily recovered in an action against a mediator. And in most cases, that sum is not significant enough to warrant the time and expense of litigating.

13.3.3.6. Mediator Immunity

Even if a complaining party were to overcome the obstacles just listed, there is some possibility that the mediator might nevertheless enjoy some form of immunity from suit. Such immunity may come in one of three forms: quasi-judicial immunity, statutory immunity, or immunity through contractual waiver.

In some jurisdictions, mediators may enjoy a form of immunity akin to that protecting judges from facing the prospect of individual liability stemming from their judicial decisions—even if those decisions ultimately prove demonstrably wrong. The concept of judicial immunity dates back at least 400 years under English common law, although its application to mediators is far more recent.[33] In the case underlying *Howard v. Drapkin*,[34] a psychologist who rendered a nonbinding opinion in a custody dispute was sued by one of the divorcing parents. The California Court of Appeals extended quasi-judicial immunity to the psychologist and, more sweepingly, to "neutral third persons who are engaged in mediation, conciliation, evaluation, or similar dispute resolution efforts."[35] The court specifically rejected the suggestion that such neutrals are not sufficiently judicial to warrant immunity, writing that "those

32. For some examples of courts coming *close* to considering nonstandard, nonmonetary aspects of settlement agreements, see Moffitt, *supra* note 14, at 1874–78 and cases cited therein.

33. For a useful survey of the history of judicial immunity, quasi-judicial immunity, and the extension of these principles to mediators, see Scott Hughes, *Mediator Immunity and Inequitable Shifting of Risk*, 83 Or. L. Rev. 107 (2004). *See also* Cassondra E. Joseph, *The Scope of Mediator Immunity: When Mediators Can Invoke Absolute Immunity*, 12 Ohio St. J. on Disp. Resol. 629 (1997).

34. Howard v. Drapkin, 271 Cal. Rptr. 893 (Cal. Ct. App. 1990).

35. *Id.*

persons are similar to a judge who is handling a voluntary or mandatory settlement conference, no matter whether they are (1) making binding decision[s] . . . , (2) making recommendations to the court . . . , or (3) privately attempting to settle disputes."[36] The D.C. Circuit Court followed similar logic in *Wagshal v. Foster*,[37] extending quasi-judicial immunity to a court-appointed case evaluator in an action alleging that the evaluator had been biased and had inappropriately forced an unfavorable settlement. As with the *Howard v. Drapkin* opinion, the court in *Wagshal v. Foster* found both functional similarities between mediators and judges and policy considerations weighing in favor of blanket shields against claims. There has been considerable outcry against the idea of extending quasi-judicial immunity to mediators, and some jurisdictions have rejected its application to mediators.[38] Still, one piece of the landscape, in at least some jurisdictions, includes common-law immunity protecting mediators against civil malpractice claims.

In other contexts, mediators enjoy immunity that derives from statutory, rather than common-law, protections. For example, Florida state law provides that mediators operating under a court-ordered mediation program "shall have judicial immunity in the same manner and to the same extent as a judge."[39] Other states provide qualified immunity to mediators, leaving open the prospect of only a narrow range of claims—claims that are exceedingly unlikely to be the result of alleged breaches of the ethical duties described in this book.[40]

Finally, some mediation agreements include contractual waivers that have the effect of shielding mediators from virtually any subsequent complaint. Some of these waivers seek to create contractual equivalents to immunity. ("The parties agree that the mediator shall have immunity in the same manner and to the same extent as a judge in the state in which the mediation is conducted.")[41] Other waiver provisions provide sweeping scope. ("The mediator shall not be liable to any person or entity, including the parties, for any act or omission including negligence or breach of

36. *Id.* at 903.

37. Wagshal v. Foster, 28 F.3d 1249 (D.C. Cir. 1994).

38. *See* Hughes, *supra* note 33, at 111 n.14.

39. Fla. Stat. § 44.107 (2020). *See also* Ind. Code Ann. § 4-21.5-3.5-4; N.C. Gen. Stat. § 7A-38.1(j).

40. For a useful summary of the statutory landscape, see Esquibel, *supra* note 11, at 141–48.

41. John R. Van Winkle, Mediation: A Path Back for the Lost Lawyer 127 (2001).

confidentiality or for any advice or opinion or comment associated with his engagement as mediator and involvement in the dispute.")[42] Not all mediators include this kind of language in their contracts, and few cases have tested the enforceability of such clauses. Furthermore, attorneys are generally prohibited from including malpractice liability waivers in their contracts, raising potentially interesting questions about cross-professional practice.[43] Still, an understanding of the landscape of potential liability must include reference to waivers because "even if the provisions were not enforceable, it is reasonable to assume that some parties may be deterred from suing based on an assumption that they had contractually waived their right to do so."[44]

13.3.3.7. The Prospect of Malpractice Exposure

For the range of reasons just described, mediators face little practical prospect of significant civil liability stemming from their mediation practices. There have been virtually no reported cases in which complaining parties succeeded in raising malpractice claims. The current rates for malpractice insurance suggest that the market shares the view that mediators face relatively small exposure to liability for their mediation activities. Anecdotal evidence suggests that many mediators "operate without a net," in the sense that they carry no liability insurance whatsoever. And many who do have insurance report that they carry it for the defense coverage, more than for the prospect of covering liability payouts.[45] Whatever other mechanisms may exist to assure that mediators act ethically, the threat of civil lawsuits by former clients does not present a significant piece of the puzzle.

13.4. Institutional Discipline

A large number of court systems maintain rosters of mediators—practitioners who hold themselves out as available to provide mediation

42. Moffitt, *Suing Mediators*, *supra* note 8, at 165 n.60.

43. *See* Model Rules of Prof'l Conduct R. 1.8(h). *Cf.* Michael Moffitt, *Loyalty, Confidentiality, and Attorney-Mediators: Professional Responsibility in Cross-Profession Practice*, 1 Harv. Negot. L. Rev. 203 (1996).

44. Moffitt, *Suing Mediators*, *supra* note 8, at 167.

45. For more on the often-misunderstood aspects of mediators and liability insurance, see Paula Young, *The Crisis in Insurance Coverage for Mediators: Even Lawyer-Mediators Are "Going Bare,"* 15 Appalachian J.L. 1 (2016).

services related to the types of cases that court system routinely hears.[46] One ABA study suggested that court-connected rosters are "the single most important form of credentialing for mediators today."[47] Although parties are often free to choose mediators who are not on one of these rosters, as a practical matter, inclusion on such rosters is a key element of many practicing mediators' businesses. Eligibility to appear on most court rosters hinges on a range of criteria, including "minimum standards of education, training, experience, or performance, alone or in various combinations."[48] And each of the programs has some articulated set of ethical standards or codes to which its mediators at least theoretically adhere.

In most court-connected mediation programs, unhappy former mediation clients have a formal mechanism by which they can register complaints about some aspect of a mediator's conduct. Although Florida was not the first state to adopt mediator ethics provisions broadly in its court-connected mediation programs, it was "the first to recognize the importance of including a disciplinary procedure for handling mediator misconduct along with its standards."[49] The Florida Supreme Court "recognized that absent a means of enforcement, [articulating ethical] standards would be insufficient."[50] Many states have since followed with mediator grievance systems in one form or another.[51]

In these complaints filed against court-connected mediators, one can find illustrations of virtually every recognized aspect of mediator

46. For a survey of what is known (and what is yet to be known) about existing court system ADR programs, see Nancy Welsh, *Bringing Transparency and Accountability (with a Dash of Competition) to Court-Connected Dispute Resolution*, 88 Fordham L. Rev. 2449 (2020).

47. *Alternative Dispute Resolution Section of the American Bar Association Task Force on Mediator Credentialing: Final Report* (Aug. 2012), *available at* https://www.americanbar.org/content/dam/aba/images/dispute_resolution/CredentialingTaskForce.pdf.

48. Dorothy J. Della Noce, *Communicating Quality Assurance: A Case Study of Mediator Profiles on a Court Roster*, 84 N.D. L. Rev. 769, 770–71 (2008).

49. Sharon Press, *Mediator Ethical Breaches: Implications for Public Policy*, 6 Y.B. on Arb. & Mediation 107, 120 (2014). Professor Press also provides a helpful history of the evolution of Florida's grievance system more broadly.

50. *Id.*

51. For a comprehensive view of the systems that existed at the time of the article's publication, see Paula Young, *Take It or Leave It. Lump It or Grieve It: Designing Mediator Complaint Systems That Protect Mediators, Unhappy Parties, Attorneys, Courts, the Process, and the Field*, 21 Ohio St. J. on Disp. Resol. 721 (2006).

ethics. A mediator charged clients a higher rate than was advertised,[52] and another charged the parties for more hours than he actually spent.[53] A mediator interfered with the parties' right to self-determination by fighting a party's decision not to select him as a mediator.[54] A mediator breached confidentiality.[55] A mediator made repeated comments about a party's appearance and her jewelry, in a manner suggesting partiality and bias.[56] A mediator refused to permit parties to take adequate breaks.[57] A mediator seeking to renew her membership on a roster failed to disclose that her bar license had been suspended for forging signatures on foreclosure documents.[58] A mediator changed terms of a proposed settlement without informing one of the parties.[59]

To be clear, such conduct is hardly the norm among mediators, and formal complaints about mediators' conduct are rare. In Florida, for example, "conservative estimates place [the number of mediations conducted in Florida at] at least 100,000 cases annually."[60] Between 2000 and 2014, there were, however, fewer than 200 total complaints filed against mediators in Florida.[61] That amounts to roughly one complaint for every 7,500 mediations. Still, the mechanisms by which complaints are processed provide an illustration of the potential for (and the limitations of) institutional discipline.

Given the prominent role roster membership plays in the mediation market, complaint mechanisms associated with mediation rosters provide

52. *In re* Nadine Mitchells, QCC 2012-037 (Fla. 2018), *available at* https://www.flcourts.org/content/download/532260/5909444/admission-and-stipulation-qcc-2012-037.pdf.

53. *In re* Saul Cimbler, MQB2015-007 (Fla. 2016), *available at* https://www.flcourts.org/content/download/215930/1961526/DecisionofPanelMQB2015-007.pdf.

54. *Id.*

55. *Alternative Dispute Resolution (ADR) Ethics Board Public Reprimands* (Apr. 1, 2016), http://www.mncourts.gov/mncourtsgov/media/scao_library/ADR/ADR-Ethics-Board-Public-Sanctions-list.pdf.

56. *In re* William J. Jatczak, MQB 2010-010 (Fla. 2012), *available at* https://www.flcourts.org/content/download/215952/1961658/JatczakSactions.pdf.

57. *In re* Mark London, MQB 2005-002 (Fla. 2006).

58. *Public Sanctions Imposed* (May 1, 2017), https://www.nccourts.gov/assets/inline-files/Mann_Public_Admonishment.pdf?YACeuCYB857nXOVMVzPJVp6BzUceKI9Y.

59. *In re* Darlene J. Brower, MQB 2005-002 (Fla. 2015), *available at* https://www.flcourts.org/content/download/215936/file/OrderAdmissionStipandFCmqb2013-015.pdf.

60. Press, *supra* note 49, at 110.

61. *Id.* at 131.

at least three types of potential discipline, each different from the prospect of private liability—membership sanctions, reputational sanctions, and educational opportunities.

13.4.1. Sanction or Exclusion from Mediation Rosters

Given the prominent role roster membership plays in many mediators' practices, the most severe form of discipline associated with a mediation complaint would be removal from the court system's mediation roster. Such sanctions are comparatively rare. In Florida, for example, fewer than 5 percent of grievances filed even reached the hearing stage, a necessary precursor in Florida's procedures regarding the imposition of formal sanctions.[62] Furthermore, from 2000 through 2014, only one Florida case resulted in a mediator being suspended from a roster, and it was a case involving "issues of alcoholism . . . [and] two first degree misdemeanors."[63] Even *that* mediator was later reinstated to the roster in question.[64] The same pattern exists around the country. Fewer than 1 percent of the mediators against whom complaints were filed were ultimately removed—*even temporarily*—from state rosters.[65] In short, removal from program rosters may be a possible sanction in the most egregious circumstances, but most mediator grievance systems look to other remedies as the more common avenues for imposing discipline.

13.4.2. Reputational and Other Sanctions for Roster Mediators

The fact that mediators are rarely removed from court rosters does not mean that mediators face no real or potential risk of discipline resulting from parties' complaints. For example, remedies or sanctions have sometimes included tangible restrictions on mediators' practices.[66] Mediators have agreed to (or been ordered to) refund client fees.[67] And in some jurisdictions, mediators found to have violated certain standards have been held responsible for the costs of the disciplinary proceedings.[68]

Short of formal sanctions, some court systems also have mechanisms in place through which they can accomplish some measure of publicity associated with mediators' negative behavior.[69] In Georgia, for example,

62. *Id.* at 133.
63. *Id.*
64. *Id.*
65. Young, *supra* note 51, at 775.
66. *See* Press, *supra* note 49, at 130 n.164.
67. *Id.* at 135–36.
68. *Id.* at 160.
69. *See* Art Hinshaw, *Regulating Mediators*, 21 HARV. NEGOT. L. REV. 163 (2016).

the Committee on Ethics may issue written decisions and may also issue advisory opinions. "Ethics opinions relate to conduct giving rise to a specific complaint and can function as a sanction because the committee may, by rule, reveal the name of the mediator in the opinion. The opinions serve an education and cautionary role."[70] This approach is not universal. In Minnesota, for example, the public learns only about the existence of a finding against a mediator and the rule(s) the mediator is deemed to have violated—but none of the facts or details of that violation.[71] At the national level, information about grievances against mediators is even more challenging to access.[72] Still, one important component of the landscape of discipline against mediators stems from the potential for reputational sanction.

Finally, mediators' conduct may be constrained at least to some extent by the *fear* of a complaint. Even if mediators perceive no significant risk of removal from a roster or any lesser formal remedy, they may legitimately want to stay out of any complaint system entirely. A "victory" for a mediator against whom a complaint has been filed still involves time and money spent defending against a charge. It may, depending on the state, also involve some form of public reporting. It may require mediators to appear before panels of judges or peers, put in a posture of defending their mediation decisions. Even if the eventual potential sanctions were insignificant, the complaint procedures themselves might serve some deterrent effect.

---

70. Young, *supra* note 51, at 843. The Committee on Ethics of the Georgia Commission on Dispute Resolution has published only six ethics opinions, and although they are empowered to name names, they have never opted to do so. *See Ethics Information for Registered Neutrals*, GA. OFF. OF DISP. RESOL., https://godr.org/registered-neutral/ethics-information/ (last visited Mar. 10, 2021). Similar processes exist in Florida and North Carolina; *see Sanctions—Imposed*, FLA. CTS., https://www.flcourts.org/Resources-Services/Alternative-Dispute-Resolution/Mediation-in-Florida/Discipline-Proceedings-Sanctions/Sanctions-Imposed (last visited Mar. 10, 2021); *see also Public Sanctions Issued*, N.C. JUD. BRANCH, https://www.nccourts.gov/commissions/dispute-resolution-commission/public-sanctions-issued (last visited Mar. 10, 2021).

71. *See, e.g.*, *Alternative Dispute Resolution (ADR) Ethics Board Public Reprimands*, *supra* note 55. Further illustrating the paucity of information in many contexts, Minnesota has published *zero* ethics board sanctions since at least 2016; *Alternative Dispute Resolution (ADR) / Mediation*, MINN. JUD. BRANCH, http://www.mncourts.gov/Help-Topics/AlternativeDisputeResolution.aspx (last visited Mar. 10, 2021).

72. The American Bar Association Section of Dispute Resolution maintains a National Clearinghouse of Mediator Ethics Opinions, available at https://www.americanbar.org/groups/dispute_resolution/resources/Ethics/, but it includes only a few dozen entries.

13.4.3. Rehabilitative or Educational Opportunities

Recognizing that a system of discipline that relies solely on punishment for deterrence is necessarily limited, many states have designed complaint mechanisms aimed at resolving issues early, informally, and often with an eye toward rehabilitation or education. In some circumstances, complaining parties are seeking nothing more than some assurance that the mediator in question will not repeat the complained-about behavior.[73] Even in complaints that move through the entire grievance procedure, the resolution often reflects the kind of custom-tailored outcomes for which mediation itself is commonly known. For example, mediators have sometimes agreed to remedies such as "making an apology, accepting oral reprimands or admonishments, agreeing to attend additional training programs, gaining experience by working with a supervising mediator, and accepting a written reprimand."[74] Consensual resolutions have also sometimes included "researching and writing an article clarifying the procedural and ethical issues related to the alleged violation."[75]

13.5. Voluntary Organizations and Accountability

Many mediators belong to one or more voluntary professional organizations. For example, the Association for Conflict Resolution (ACR) has operated as an international professional organization since 2001, and its predecessor organizations operated for decades before that. Thousands of mediators have voluntarily joined ACR. Why? Some join to find a community of practitioners. ("I'm the only environmental mediator in my town who focuses on water rights.") Some join to lend their voices and their dues to the cause of promoting public understanding of quality conflict-resolution practices. ("I want a promediation agenda in any court reform movement.") Some join for the signaling function. ("Prospective clients will view my membership in ACR as evidence of my seriousness as a mediator.")

Most voluntary professional organizations of mediators have some ethical statements or principles. ACR is a good example of this. The Model Standards ACR promulgates, along with the AAA and the ABA, have served as the primary model for mediation ethics in the United

73. *See* Press, *supra* note 49, at 134.
74. Young, *supra* note 51, at 749.
75. Press, *supra* note 49, at 135–36.

States.[76] Most of its foundational ethical premises—including impartiality, confidentiality, and self-determination—appear prominently elsewhere in this book.

Might one find, therefore, some prospect of discipline or sanction through ACR? If a client complains that an ACR member has run afoul of one or more of these ethical norms, is there any prospect of censure or sanction? I can find no examples of voluntary mediation organizations voicing public concern about the conduct of one of their members. And I can find no provision in ACR's bylaws for the removal of a member for *any* reason other than failure to pay "all annual dues and any other monies owed ACR when they are due and payable."[77]

The American Bar Association's Section of Dispute Resolution is the other prominent, national dispute-resolution organization that operates like a professional organization. Like ACR, it provides community, education, networking, and educational opportunities. Although a part of the Bar, the Section does not require its members to be licensed to practice law. The disciplinary mechanisms in place for the legal profession do not, therefore, carry over to the Section. As a result, the Section of Dispute Resolution operates much like ACR when it comes to the prospect of mediator discipline.

The CPR International Institute for Conflict Prevention and Resolution is structured differently than the two voluntary organizations just described. Membership on its panel is by invitation and application only. Nevertheless, in its more than 40 years of existence, no member has been removed from the CPR panel for disciplinary reasons.[78] CPR maintains a procedure for challenging the neutrality of a proposed arbitrator,[79] but these provisions neither include mediators nor provide ex post opportunities for discipline.

Outside of the United States, voluntary mediation associations may play a more prominent role in potential discipline for mediators. For example, the ADR Institute of Ontario provides a complaint mechanism that includes the prospect of sanctions up to and including removal from

76. The structure of the Model Standards is not without controversy. *See, e.g.*, Michael Moffitt & Jamie Henikoff, *Remodeling the Model Standards of Conduct for Mediators*, 2 Harv. Negot. L. Rev. 87 (1997).

77. ACR Bylaws, § 5.2 (June 22, 2016), *available at* https://cdn.ymaws.com/acrnet.org/resource/resmgr/docs/acr_bylaws_approved_june_201.pdf.

78. E-mail from Kai Sass-Hauschildt, CPR Manager of Int'l Programs, to Michael Moffitt (July 1, 2020) (on file with author).

79. *Challenge Protocol*, CPR, https://www.cpradr.org/resource-center/protocols-guidelines/ethics-codes/challenge-protocol (last visited Mar. 10, 2021).

their roster.[80] The same is true of the Family Mediation Council in the UK.[81] I can intuit no reason why voluntary organizations in the United States could not play similar roles, but they do not presently do so.

A cynical view of the landscape would suggest, "This conflates dues-paying with quality control," noting that people are removed from membership only for financial reasons. A more sympathetic perspective would say, "These organizations exist, in part, to educate—to promulgate information about ethical mediation practices. They don't exist to police individual mediators' behaviors. The field is better for the work they do. Discipline is not their job." Whether the better perspective is that these organizations are (1) appropriately staying in their lanes or (2) inappropriately engaging in NIMBYism with respect to ethically problematic mediator behaviors is a debatable normative question. The undebatable descriptive reality, however, is that as a practical matter, voluntary mediation organizations in the United States play limited formal disciplinary functions. As with court-connected programs' discipline, if voluntary mediation associations dissuade mediators from unethical behavior, it is for procedural ("I don't want the costs associated with defending my mediation actions") and reputational ("I don't want the shame associated with defending my mediation actions") reasons rather than for formal remedial reasons.

13.6. Conclusion

Mediators have many good reasons to engage in ethical practices. It's the right thing to do. It's what the parties expect. It's what we expect of ourselves. And my strong impression is that the vast majority of mediators practice ethically the vast majority of the time. However, the principal question motivating this chapter was "Or else what?" What happens to mediators if they stray from established ethical norms in their practices?

Mediators face the prospect of discipline in a number of different forms. At a minimum, they may face reputational costs and transaction costs associated with having to defend themselves against complaints. Many of these costs are incurred even if a mediator is ultimately deemed

80. *See Complaints Policy*, ADR Inst. of Ont. (Oct. 13, 2011), https://adr-ontario.ca/rules-codes/complaints-policy/. *See also Discipline Procedure*, ADR Inst. of Can. (rev. Sept. 7, 1995), https://adric.ca/rules-codes/complaints-discipline-policy/ (similar procedures for the ADR Institute of Canada).

81. *See Complaints about Mediators*, Family Mediation Council, https://www.familymediationcouncil.org.uk/complaints-about-mediators/ (last visited Mar. 10, 2021).

to have practiced ethically. Those mediators found to have violated one or more established ethical mandates face the real prospect of low-level sanctions such as returning clients' fees. They may also face real, if difficult to quantify, injury to their public reputations if they are the subject of civil litigation or if they are in a jurisdiction in which mediators' names are associated with negative findings stemming from ethics complaints.

As a practical matter, each of the most serious of the potential disciplinary sanctions is vanishingly rare. Mediators face very low exposure to civil liability for their mediation conduct, little likelihood of permanent removal from court-connected rosters, and virtually no chance of being removed from voluntary mediation organizations. Instead, the landscape of mediator discipline depends more significantly on informal pressures and on less punitive or exclusionary means of assuring compliance with ethical norms.

Given the shortcomings or unavailability of retributive sanction, some have called for the adoption of more restorative practices as a means of responding to mediators' ethical lapses.[82] Others have argued for more front-end efforts (like education or credentialing) rather than ex post punishment for ethically problematic behavior.[83] Still others suggest structuring institutional systems to prevent mediator "burnout" and the associated challenges of maintaining the kinds of creativity, compassion, flexibility, and impartiality demanded by most ethical conceptions of mediators' roles.[84] The landscape of mediator ethics includes *some* risk of formal or informal discipline associated with unethical behavior. Given the limited role formal discipline plays, however, the fact that most mediators behave ethically is likely a function of other important considerations.

---

82. Sharon Press, *Mediator Ethical Breaches: Implications for Public Policy*, 6 Y.B. Arb. & Mediation 107 (2014).

83. *See, e.g.*, Hinshaw, *supra* note 69, at 197–201.

84. *See* Lydia Nussbaum, *Mediator Burnout*, 34 Ohio St. J. on Disp. Resol. 171, 213–20 (2019).

Part V

Developing Ethical Skills

Chapter 14

Continuing Mediation Ethics Education

Gregory Firestone, Ph.D.

14.1. Introduction

Continuing mediator ethics education (CMEE) is an essential necessity for practicing mediators. Given the limited time that mediators are generally required to attend formal mediation training—40-hour basic training is commonly used as a standard[1]—mediators must continually strive to improve their overall mediation competence as well as sharpen their understanding of the critical ethical elements of mediation practice.

This chapter is divided into five sections. The first section addresses the extent to which CMEE is required in some U.S. jurisdictions, the second considers why CMEE is necessary, the third explores how mediators can increase their professional ethics capacities and knowledge, the fourth

---

Acknowledgment: I would like to thank Doug Frenkel, Susan Raines, Omer Shapira, and Paula Young for their careful review and invaluable feedback on earlier drafts of this chapter.

1. Ana Maria Gonçalves & Daniel Rainey, *Standards, Qualifications, and Certification for e-Mediators*, 5 INT'L J. ON ONLINE DISP. RESOL. 82–93 (2018) ("Requirements vary from jurisdiction to jurisdiction and from country to country, but a de facto standard seems to exist on the basis of the 40-hour basic training outlined by courts as a way to certify mediators accepting court-referred cases. Some distinctions are usually made among civil cases, family mediation cases, and the like, but the 40-hour basic training is commonly used as a starting point." *Id.* at 83.).

contains a conclusion along with some recommendations for CMEE, and the last section offers a limited sample of resources for pursuing CMEE.

14.2. Is Continuing Mediation Ethics Education Required?

Mediation is generally an unregulated field where no state regulates the entire field of mediation. Those mediators most likely to be regulated are those practicing within the scope of the court-connected or court-referred cases in certain states.[2]

While voluntary professional codes do exist, for most mediators, adherence to these codes is optional. For those who choose to comply with these codes, there is some guidance regarding a mediator's ethical obligation to pursue continuing mediator education (CME). For example, Standard IV (Competence) of the Model Standards of Conduct for Mediators (Model Standards)[3] states the following: "A.2. A mediator should attend educational programs and related activities to maintain and enhance the mediator's knowledge and skills related to mediation."[4]

Similarly, Standard XIII of the AFCC Model Standards of Practice for Family and Divorce Mediation (AFCC Model Standards)[5] provides:

> A family mediator shall acquire and maintain professional competence in mediation.
>
> A. Mediators should continuously improve their professional skills and abilities by, among other activities, participating in relevant continuing education programs and should regularly engage in self-assessment.
>
> B. Mediators should participate in programs of peer consultation and should help train and mentor the work of less experienced mediators.
>
> C. Mediators should continuously strive to understand the impact of culture and diversity on the mediator's practice.[6]

---

2. ABA Section of Disp. Resol. Ethics Subcomm., *Behind the Curtain: Ethics for Mediators*, 26(1) PROF'L LAW. (Summer 2019).

3. MODEL STANDARDS OF CONDUCT FOR MEDIATORS (Am. Arb. Ass'n, Am. Bar Ass'n & Ass'n for Conflict Resol. 2005). These standards can be found at https://www.americanbar.org/groups/dispute_resolution/policy_standards/.

4. *Id.* Standard IV.A.2.

5. MODEL STANDARDS OF PRACTICE FOR FAMILY AND DIVORCE MEDIATION (Ass'n of Family & Conciliation Cts. (2000) & Am. Bar Ass'n (2001)). The standards can be found at https://www.afccnet.org/Portals/0/PublicDocuments/CEFCP/ModelStandardsOfPracticeForFamilyAndDivorceMediation.pdf.

6. *Id.* § XIII.

Interestingly, both standards only provide that continuing mediator education "should" be obtained and do not require such. However, one less widely adopted set of standards developed by the Academy of Professional Family Mediators does require that CME be mandatory even though no minimum amount of CME is specified.[7]

A number of jurisdictions in the United States, including but not limited to Alabama,[8] Florida,[9] Georgia,[10] Idaho,[11] Indiana,[12] Minnesota,[13] Mississippi,[14] Nevada,[15] New Jersey,[16] Oregon,[17] and Virginia,[18] have gone a step further by making CME mandatory for certain mediators. While some states do not specify whether CMEE is required, others do. For example, Florida requires four hours of mediator ethics every two years for mediator recertification by the Florida Supreme Court,[19] Ore-

7. APFM Standards of Practice for Prof'l Family Mediators (Feb. 2, 2014), Standard IIC: "Family mediators shall continuously improve their professional skills and abilities by participating in relevant continuing education courses and programs." (*available at* https://apfmnet.org/standards-practice-professional-family-mediators/).

8. Ala. Code of Ethics for Mediators (effective Mar. 1, 1996), Standard III(1)(2), https://alabamaadr.org/web/roster-documents/documents/med_Mediator_Code_of_Ethics_150501_updated.pdf.

9. Sup. Ct. of Fla., No. AOSC19-26, *In re Procedures Governing Certification of Mediators* (May 28, 2019), https://www.flcourts.org/content/download/533913/5930214/AOSC19-26.pdf.

10. Ga. Alt. Disp. Resol. Rules § II (Jan. 3, 2019), https://georgiacourts.gov/wp-content/uploads/2019/07/ADR-Rules.pdf.

11. Idaho Ct. Admin. R. 73(a)2. Qualifications of Civil Mediators (effective July 1, 2016), https://isc.idaho.gov/icar73.

12. Ind. Rules of Ct. Rules for Alt. Disp. Resol. R. 2.5(D) Qualifications of Mediators, https://www.in.gov/courts/rules/adr/index.html#_Toc60037263 (last updated Jan. 1, 2021).

13. Minn. General Rules of Practice R. 114.13(g), https://www.revisor.mn.gov/court_rules/gp/id/114/ (last visited Mar. 10, 2021).

14. *Qualifications*, Miss. Bar, https://www.msbar.org/for-members/mediators-directory/qualifications/ (last visited Mar. 10, 2021).

15. Nev. Rules Governing Alt. Disp. Resol. § C. Mediation R. 4(D) (Nev. Sup. Ct. Rules, effective Mar. 3, 2005, including amendments through Jan. 1, 2020).

16. Rules Governing the Cts. of the St. of N.J. Part I. Rules of General Application ch. IV. Administration Rule 1:40-12(b)(2), https://www.njcourts.gov/attorneys/assets/rules/r1-40.pdf (last visited Mar. 10, 2021).

17. Or. Jud. Dep't Ct.-Connected Mediator Qualifications Rules § 3.6 Continuing Mediator Education Requirements (Aug. 1, 2005), https://www.courts.oregon.gov/rules/Other%20Rules/05cER001sh.pdf.

18. Sup. Ct. of Va. Guidelines for the Training & Certification of Ct.-Referred Mediators D.4. (adopted by the Jud. Council of Va. Oct. 22, 2020, effective Nov. 1, 2020).

19. Fla. Sup. Ct. Admin. Order No. AOSC19-26 (ordered May 28, 2019).

gon requires one hour every year for approved general civil mediators and two hours every two years for approved domestic relations custody and parenting or domestic relations financial mediators,[20] and Virginia requires two hours of CMEE every two-year period for court-referred mediators.[21] However, in these cases, no specific guidance is given as to what constitutes CMEE. For example, does CME focusing upon the laws and rules governing mediation privadentiality[22] constitute the study of mediation ethics, or is it only the interpretation of mediation privadentiality laws and rules as they apply to a specific ethical scenario that constitutes the study of mediation ethics? While understanding the laws and rules that govern a key aspect of most mediations provides a foundation upon which ethical decision making begins, it is not quite CMEE. When such CME includes ethical decision making building upon this legal foundation, it constitutes CMEE because it teaches ethical decision making within a legal context.

Certainly, CME focused upon the study of ethical standards would seem to be a good start for furthering a mediator's ethical competence. However, which ethical standards should a mediator study? In addition to the two national standards already mentioned, there are a host of other, somewhat differing mediation standards in the United States. As Ellen Waldman points out, "[T]he codes governing professional conduct in mediation are inconsistent."[23] This can be confusing and problematic for some mediators who may be bound to comply with more than one set of standards given the organizations to which they belong, the mediation panels on which they serve, and/or the jurisdictions in which they mediate. As Waldman points out, "[R]ules binding on mediators at the

---

20. Or. Jud. Dep't Ct.-Connected Mediator Qualifications Rules, *supra* note 17.

21. Va. Guidelines for Training, *supra* note 18, at D.4.b.

22. *See* Gregory Firestone & Sharon Press, *Privadentiality: Developing a Coherent Framework for Establishing Communication Protections in Family and Child Protection Dispute Resolution Methods*, 58 Fam. Ct. Rev. 9, 11 (2020) ("[W]e propose a new umbrella term, privadentiality, to replace the term confidentiality when referring to the umbrella of all communication protections including: confidentiality, privilege, incompetency to testify, evidentiary exclusions, and the privacy of proceedings. Privadentiality would encompass all of these concepts, as well as other variations of communication protections established by contract, common law, or court or administrative rule . . . . Privadentiality would apply when all participants and the professional(s) are prohibited from disclosing DR process communications and where the presence of other parties (even those with adverse interests) would not result in a loss of DR communication protections.").

23. Mediation Ethics 12 (Ellen Waldman ed., 2011).

state level may not jibe with either the Model Standards or the specialized codes developed for particular types of cases."[24] Furthermore, as Suzanne McCorkle notes, differences between state mediation standards are problematic for mediators who may mediate in more than one jurisdiction because "permissible behavior in one state may be deemed unethical in a neighboring state."[25]

For some mediators who may not be governed by any state, court rule, mediation panel, or professional organization, there may be no applicable standards to which they are required to adhere. One can only wonder what yardstick a mediator would draw upon when an ethical problem arises and whether parties are sufficiently protected in the event the mediator fails to appreciate the ethical issues raised in a particular circumstance.

14.3. Why Is Continuing Mediation Ethics Education Necessary?

If one assumes that mediation ethics is a universal given based upon fundamental ethical principles, then CMEE would appear to be less of a concern. However, mediation is context specific, and one needs to understand what guiding mediation principles apply in order to find an appropriate ethical path in a given circumstance in mediation. As Shapira states, "[M]ediation ethics cannot rely on abstract principles alone, and must be contextualized, grounded in the particularities of mediation cases."[26]

As most mediators have no formal training in the study of ethics in general, mediation guidelines are a crucial starting point for most beginning mediators. From my perspective as mediation trainer for more than 25 years, it's safe to say that new mediators tend to rely on the standards of professional conduct more than applying general ethical principles to their mediation work. In other words, they are looking for specific guidance on what to do and what not to do because they often don't fully appreciate the ethical principles inherent in the practice of mediation.

Typically, new mediation trainees are learning a new role and can struggle with letting go of the ethical standards associated with their previous or concurrent profession or occupation. For example, lawyers and

---

24. *Id.* at 12–13.

25. Suzanne McCorkle, *The Murky World of Mediation Ethics: Neutrality, Impartiality, and Conflict of Interest in State Codes of Conduct*, 23 Conflict Resol. Q. 165, 182 (2005).

26. Omer Shapira, A Theory of Mediator's Ethics: Foundations, Rationale, and Application 345 (2016).

judges who become mediators sometimes have a difficult time directing their focus from the outcome of a mediation (which is more the focus of an attorney or judge) toward the mediation process itself (which is more the focus of a mediator). Lawyers are used to being advocates for a particular outcome, and judges are more oriented toward determining the outcome, rather than helping the parties to freely reach their own agreements.

There are a number of reasons for mediators to pursue ongoing mediation ethics training, including the following.

14.3.1. Evolution of Mediation Standards and Ethics Advisory Opinions

The ethical standards for mediators and the regulatory world in which mediation is embedded continue to evolve over time. Similarly, mediator ethical advisory opinions issued by the ABA Section of Dispute Resolution and different state mediation ethics advisory groups upon which a mediator has relied may be revised or rescinded over time due to revisions to standards of professional conduct for mediators, laws and rules governing mediation, etc.

For example, under the Florida Rules of Civil Procedure, a party must appear to mediation with full authority to settle.[27] In 2001, the Florida Mediator Ethics Committee (MEAC) decided: "If a party's representative reveals a lack of 'full authority' in joint session and the other party decides to end the mediation, the mediator may report to the court such 'nonappearance' without violating the confidentiality of mediation if the lack of authority was not revealed in caucus."[28]

Five years later, the MEAC changed its opinion and advised:

> Yes, it would be an ethical violation to report to the court that a party did not have full settlement authority. Under the circumstances presented, the mediator is limited to reporting that no agreement was reached . . . . In light of the foregoing, the MEAC is obligated to recede from the opinions offered in 95-009, 99-002, and 2001-010 relating specifically to the mediator's report to the court based on nonappearance.[29]

27. *See, e.g.*, Fla. Rules of Civil Procedure R. 12.720(b) Appearance at Mediation.

28. Fla. Mediator Ethics Advisory Op. 2001-010, at 2.

29. Fla. Mediator Ethics Advisory Op. 2006-003, at 2.

The change in opinions was triggered, in part, by the enactment of the Florida Mediation Confidentiality and Privilege Act,[30] which significantly enhanced mediation confidentiality and privilege protections in Florida and provided no exception to allow the mediator to report "non-appearance" to the court.

14.3.2. Increasing Use of Court-Ordered Mediation

Given the increasing use of mandatory mediation where parties, not always represented by counsel, are ordered by the court to mediation prior to trial, the ethical conduct of mediation becomes even more important. Nancy Welsh raised awareness of the "thinning vision of self-determination in court-connected mediation"[31] and identified the framework in which self-determination has often been compromised in court-connected mediation.

> In searching for an effective means of protecting self-determination, it is important to remember that high-pressure settlement tactics, or muscle mediation, are not effective in a vacuum. Rather, these tactics derive their effectiveness from the framework within which they operate. They are effective because: 1) self-determination is now understood quite narrowly as a party's power to choose to agree or not to agree to a settlement; 2) this narrowed vision is consistent with courts' and attorneys' understanding of parties' free will; 3) courts are eager to enforce settlements and have established a strong presumption that a settlement reflects the exercise of parties' free will (or self-determination); and 4) courts require a strong showing to overcome this presumption and generally perceive coercion only in its most blatant forms.[32]

Welsh also identifies a number of troubling trends in court-connected mediation, including the following:

> [A] few of the adaptations in court-connected mediation that make bargaining more efficient and settlement more likely (e.g., the de facto exclusion of disputants and the marginalization or abandonment of the joint session) . . . the reduced role of the

30. Fla. Stat. § 44.401044.406.

31. Nancy A. Welsh, *The Thinning Vision of Self-Determination in Court-Connected Mediation: The Inevitable Price of Institutionalization?*, 6 Harv. Negot. L. Rev. 1 (2001).

32. *Id.* at 78.

> disputants who attend mediation sessions, attorneys' strong preference for evaluative interventions, and even the focus on monetary settlements have the potential to cause problems if mediation continues to evolve in order to fit exclusively within a bargaining paradigm.[33]

Welsh warns that these trends, if not suitably addressed, may reduce the party's perception of justice and "could tarnish the legitimacy and authority of the courts."[34] Given these dire warnings, one important way to address these concerns would involve ongoing CMEE.

14.3.3. Increasing Prevalence of Pro Se Parties

In some areas of mediation, such as family mediation, an increasing number of parties appear pro se.[35] When parties attend mediation represented by counsel, the parties have the benefit of mediation preparation, legal advice, and advocacy as needed. Pro se parties, however, have to fend for themselves. As Ellen Waldman and Lola Akin Ojelabi point out:

> Mediation's relationship to social justice is both muddled and fraught. A rich body of literature critiques mediation as a regressive process impeding disadvantaged groups' access to justice, while mediation defenders reject rights-based notions of fairness and focus on the value of voice and autonomy in the disputing process. Ethics codes reflect this muddle, emphasizing both the importance of party self determination and mediator impartiality, while, in some instances, suggesting that grossly one-sided agreements might require mediator intervention or withdrawal.[36]

Clearly, mediating with pro se parties presents additional ethical challenges. The AFCC Model Standard XI is an example of an ethical code that imparts an obligation upon the mediator to be mindful of the substantive issues in a mediation along with managing the procedural aspects by providing that

> [a] family mediator shall suspend or terminate the mediation process when the mediator reasonably believes that a participant

---

33. Nancy A. Welsh, *Making Deals in Court-Connected Mediation: What's Justice Got to Do with It?*, 79 Wash. U. L.Q. 787, 860 (2001).

34. *Id.* at 861.

35. Debra Berman & James Alfini, *Lawyer Colonization of Family Mediation: Consequences and Implications*, 95 Marq. L. Rev. 887 (2012).

36. Ellen Waldman & Lola Akin Ojelabi, *Mediators and Substantive Justice: A View from Rawls' Original Position*, 30 Ohio St. J. on Disp. Resol. 429 (2016).

> is unable to effectively participate or for other compelling reasons. A. Circumstances under which a mediator should consider suspending or terminating the mediation, may include, among others . . . 4. the participants are about to enter into an agreement that the mediator reasonably believes to be unconscionable . . . .[37]

Ongoing CMEE is critical for the mediator to find ways to empower pro se parties to exercise self-determination while at the same time being mindful of a mediator's responsibility to suspend or terminate a mediation when the parties approach reaching an unconscionable agreement.

14.3.4. Wide Variety of Disputes Mediated

Utilization of mediation to resolve an ever-widening array of disputes tends to complicate the practice of mediation, as mediating different types of disputes may raise different ethical concerns.

One example was the implementation of child protection mediation beginning more than 20 years ago. For a family mediator, the concept of self-determination largely relates to the ability of both spouses to negotiate in a manner where neither side can dictate the terms to the other party. However, in a child protection mediation, self-determination takes on new meaning as now one or both parents, who might have had their child or children removed from their home due to allegations of child abuse or neglect, must, with the assistance of their attorney(s), negotiate with a child protection agency and an attorney representing the state (or prosecutor) likely along with other parties including a guardian ad litem (and possibly attorney for the guardian ad litem), foster parents, the child(ren), other relatives, etc. From a parent's perspective, it can easily feel as if the child protection agency is holding the child hostage until the parent agrees to the demands of the agency. For a mediator to mediate such a case requires a great deal of skill to empower the parent(s) to be able to exercise self-determination when facing a significant power imbalance.[38] Thus, addressing the mediator's obligation to enable the parents to exercise self-determination requires deeper understanding of the meaning of self-determination and different, and perhaps greater, skill to facilitate such a process.

---

37. Model Standards of Practice for Family and Divorce Mediation, *supra* note 5, Standard XI.A.4.

38. For more on empowering parents in a child protection mediation, see Gregory Firestone, *Empowering Parents in Child Protection Mediation: Challenges and Opportunities*, 47 Fam. Ct. Rev. 98 (2009).

Given the wide range of disputes being mediated, including but not limited to bankruptcy, child protection, civil rights, construction, community, contractual, disability, employment, family, intellectual property, medical malpractice, personal injury, etc.; the differing sophistication of mediation participants; and the presence of pro se parties as well as parties represented by counsel, mediators face the potential for a wide range of challenging ethical issues, which must each be considered within the case-specific circumstances of the mediation.

14.3.5. Recent Research on Human Decision Making

Behavioral economics, which is the study of human decision making and the biases affecting human preferences and decision making,[39] demonstrates that human behavior can be modified in subtle ways that people often may not recognize. One way in which people can be "nudged"[40] is described by Richard Thaler and Cass Sunstein as follows:

> [M]any people will take whatever option requires the least effort, or the path of least resistance. Recall the discussion of inertia, status quo bias, and the 'yeah whatever' heuristic. All these forces imply that if, for a given choice, there is a default option—an option that will obtain if the chooser does nothing—then we can expect a large number of people to end up with that option, whether or not it is good for them. And as we have also stressed, these behavioral tendencies toward doing nothing will be reinforced if the default option comes with some implicit or explicit suggestion that it represents the normal or even the recommended course of action.[41]

Thaler and Sunstein define arranging the context in which choices are made in order to manipulate the final selection as "choice architecture."[42] As an example of the influence of choice architecture, Daniel Kahneman reports research that indicates that countries with opt-in questions (where there is no default option) show dramatically lower organ donation rates when compared to countries using opt-out questions (where organ donation is the default option and people must intentionally opt out). According to Kahneman, "The best single predictor of whether or not people

39. For an excellent introduction to behavioral economics, see Daniel Kahneman, Thinking Fast and Slow (2011).

40. Richard Thaler & Cass Sunstein, Nudge (2009).

41. *Id.* at 93.

42. *Id.* at 3.

will donate their organs is the designation of the default option that will be adopted without having to check a box."[43]

As such, the field of behavioral economics challenges our understanding of self-determination. While only one example is provided here, there are numerous other strategies available for nudging behavior or altering decision making. While Thaler and Sunstein's notion of "libertarian paternalism" (where principles of behavioral economics are applied to nudge people to make better choices) may make sense for certain governmental actions such as to encourage organ donation or promote saving for retirement, it would not seem to fit the role of a mediator, whose responsibility is to emphasize the parties' right to determine their own agreement without substantive interference from the mediator.

For example, might divorce mediators get a different response with some couples if they ask about the issue of parental decision making by saying either "Most divorcing couples agree to shared decision making for their children. What would you both like to do?" or "How would you both like to make decisions for your children?" While generally one would expect most parents to agree to shared parenting, might the first question lead to more agreement on shared parenting than the second question and perhaps inhibit some parties from expressing their preferences and concerns regarding parental decision making?

Omer Shapira makes a distinction between "soft forms of deception,"[44] such as reframing a hostile comment into something more acceptable to the other party, and a more manipulative withholding of relevant information from one party, which he says should be avoided. In the same manner, mediators must grapple with which soft forms of choice architecture[45] or other application of behavioral economics research help to facilitate the mediation communication and negotiation and which might covertly compromise self-determination to such an extent as to be unethical.

The Model Standards state, in part, that "[a] mediator shall not undermine party self-determination by any party . . . ."[46] As such, the challenge for mediators is sorting out what forms of soft manipulation may be permissible and what forms of manipulation may unduly compromise self-determination and therefore be unethical. Increasingly, mediators will need to reflect on the growing "technology" for nudging decision

43. Kahneman, *supra* note 39, at 373.
44. Shapira, *supra* note 26, at 267.
45. Thaler & Sunstein, *supra* note 40, at 3.
46. Model Standards, *supra* note 3, Standard I.B.

making and determine where the line is between ethically promoting dialogue and negotiation in the service of promoting self-determination and otherwise undermining self-determination by employing hidden methods of manipulation to nudge the parties to an agreement selected by the mediator.

Of course, a related issue is understanding the extent to which a mediator's own preferences and decision making may be biased by the manner in which mediation parties frame their negotiation and communication. This is also worthy of CMEE, as it pertains to ways in which a mediator may be impacted by the parties that could possibly compromise a mediator's impartiality or neutrality.

14.3.6. Implicit Bias

Implicit bias research challenges our understanding of a mediator's unconscious bias and raises concerns about the extent to which a mediator may unconsciously fail to act impartially with mediation parties. As Carol Izumi points out:

> Research shows that unconscious mental processes involving stereotypes and attitudes affect our judgments, perceptions, and behavior toward others. Implicit bias, the automatic association of stereotypes and attitudes with social groups, may produce discriminatory responses toward parties despite a mediator's best efforts at creating an outwardly evenhanded process. Even the most well-intentioned and egalitarian mediators must actively engage in bias reduction strategies to mitigate prejudice in mediation.[47]

As such, implicit bias research challenges our understanding of the concept of mediator impartiality and requires mediators to not only understand the concept of implicit bias but also continually strive to improve their understanding of their own potential unconscious biases and seek to become less influenced by these unconscious processes.

14.3.7. Increased Use of Online Dispute Resolution Involving Mediation

Mediation is increasingly utilizing online technology to support and/or conduct the mediation process. Beginning in the mid-1990s, online dispute resolution (ODR) including mediation has grown significantly since

47. Carol Izumi, *Implicit Bias and Prejudice in Mediation*, 70 SMU L. Rev. 681 (2017).

then.[48] Some of the challenges associated with the use of ODR identified by Noam Ebner and John Zeleznikow include establishing "criteria for what constitutes professionally acceptable platforms for conducting an online mediation—in terms of allowing both parties to speak or to be seen, protecting security, and so on."[49] Certainly a variety of other issues come to mind in terms of whether a mediator can adequately address issues of power imbalances, safety, etc., if the mediator is limited to online interaction. Also, the mediator's choice of an online platform might affect the degree to which mediation communications are private. While these problems can be overcome, they do have the potential to raise new ethical issues for mediators as they address the unique features of online mediation. For this reason, the Ethical Principles for ODR Initiative[50] were developed to delineate many additional ethical issues that a mediator must consider when practicing mediation online.

ODR using artificial intelligence raises yet more concerns for the ethical practice of mediation. According to Ayelet Sela,

> In both private and public justice systems, online dispute resolution (ODR) technologies are profoundly affecting people's access to justice and redress and the nature of their procedural experiences. Automation and artificial intelligence play a key role in delivering the promise of ODR. At the same time, there are challenging normative and practical concerns regarding the ability of "machine made justice" to meet appropriate procedural and substantive standards.[51]

Thus, in addition to the role of using electronic means of communication, ODR can now embrace automation and artificial intelligence in ways that may impact the integrity of the mediation practice. For example, algorithms designed for one purpose may inadvertently affect some parties differently than other parties due to gender, culture, education, or other factors.[52]

---

48. Noam Ebner & John Zeleznikow, *No Sheriff in Town: Governance for Online Dispute Resolution*, 32 NEGOT. J. 297 (2016).

49. *Id.* at 315.

50. Leah Wing et al., *Ethical Principles for ODR Initiative*, NAT'L CTR. FOR TECH. & DISP. RESOL. (2016).

51. Ayelet Sela, *Can Computers Be Fair? How Automated and Human-Powered Online Dispute Resolution Affect Procedural Justice in Mediation and Arbitration*, 33 OHIO ST. J. OF DISP. RESOL. 92 (2018).

52. A good example of the unintended effects of algorithms occurred when Apple rolled out the Apple Pay Card and it was reported to be gender biased. *See* Neil Vigdor,

Mediators who include online mediation as part or all of their practice will need to further study implications of online mediation and how an ethical mediation practice can be best achieved.

14.3.8. Improving Ethical Analysis and Decision-Making Skills

The previous reasons are only provided as examples of the evolving nature of the world in which mediation is practiced. Even if the field of mediation were not changing and our understanding of biases in human decision making were not growing, mediators still need to move from merely following ethical standards to ethically applying mediation principles in more difficult cases. As Ellen Waldman points out, "Because the codes only take us so far, we must acknowledge the need to exercise discretion and balance competing ethical objectives. Adopting a practical approach to mediation ethics requires recognizing that value compromises and trade-offs are an integral part of doing ethics in this field."[53]

Most mediators don't develop effective ethical decision-making skills in basic mediation training, and competent mediators must continually strive to improve their ethical competence over the course of their mediation career.

14.4. How Can Mediators Increase Their Professional Ethics Capacities and Knowledge?

Figure 14.1 lays out the multidimensional approach to building ethical decision-making competence.

At the most basic level, mediators' CMEE should focus upon the applicable laws and court rules pertaining to mediation in their jurisdiction or court mediation program and how they apply to mediation practice. From there, applicable mediation standards and codes and applicable ethics opinions should be considered along with published mediator grievances that apply to a particular mediator.[54] In addition, mediators need to be mindful of other comparable mediator standards and codes along with any related ethics opinions or grievances that may be available.

Apple Card Investigated after Gender Discrimination Complaints, N.Y. Times, Nov. 10, 2019, *available at* https://www.nytimes.com/2019/11/10/business/Apple-credit-card-investigation.html.

53. Mediation Ethics, *supra* note 23, at 15.

54. Paula M. Young, *Teaching the Ethical Values Governing Mediator Impartiality Using Short Lectures, Buzz Group Discussions, Video Clips, a Defining Features Matrix, Games, and an Exercise Based on Grievances Filed against Florida Mediators*, 11 Pepp. Disp. Resol. L.J. 309 (2011).

Figure 14.1: Building Ethical Decision-Making Competence

Mediators also need to develop the capacity to reflect internally on their own personal feelings and/or biases in order to optimize their ethical decision making and ethical mediation practice.

Omer Shapira suggests professional mediators need to be mindful of their ethical obligations to their clients, the mediation profession, the public, and employers and principals (including the referring court when applicable).[55] These obligations are delineated in 15 ethical standards: "Competence, Conflicts of Interest, Party Self-determination, Professional Integrity, Impartiality, Diligence, Respect and Dignity, Honesty, Confidentiality, Fairness, Maintaining the Profession's Standing and Public Trust in the Profession, Advancement of the Profession, Advertising and Solicitation, Fees, and Obligations to Employers and Principals."[56] The professional ethics perspective supplements the previous levels of mediator ethics education with meaning, content, and structure. As such, mediators' ethical decision making must consider all of these ethical obligations in relation to their clients as well as to the mediation profession, the public, and employers or principals.[57]

55. Shapira, *supra* note 26.
56. *Id.* at 114.
57. *Id.*

Mediators can also increase their professional ethics capacity by developing a method for ethical decision making such as the following steps: (1) Identify the Ethical Conflict(s), (2) Research Applicable Standards of Conduct for Mediators, Rules, Statutes, etc., (3) Research Applicable Mediator Ethical Advisory Opinions and Grievances, (4) Generate Possible Options for the Mediator, (5) Evaluate the Options, and (6) Select the Best Option. Experienced mediators may develop more elaborate models for ethical decision making[58] and will weave in a self-reflection process as well.

The most common mediation ethical issues typically involve one or more of the following ethical values: confidentiality, self-determination of the parties, and impartiality of the mediator.[59] While these three areas perhaps deserve a greater amount of study than other areas, all of the aspects delineated by Shapira previously are worthy of further study. While some might be viewed as more important than others, the goal of a mediator should be to find solutions to ethical dilemmas that best satisfy a particular situation while keeping all of a mediator's ethical obligations in mind.

In order to pursue mediator ethics education at a minimum, mediators must stay apprised of the ever-changing set of laws, rules, standards of professional conduct, mediator ethics opinions, local administrative orders, etc., within which mediation is embedded. For many mediators who practice within different jurisdictions governed by different laws such as the differences between state and federal disputes, legal vs. administrative proceedings, or presuit and court-ordered mediations, the need to stay current on the varied legal and ethical guidelines becomes even more essential and challenging.

While studying specific codes of conduct and mediator ethics advisory opinions would seem to be a useful form of furthering one's ethical development, it is really only just the beginning. The problem with such codes is that these standards give the impression that the codes are absolute and can easily be applied to all situations rather than viewing ethical decision making as being context specific. As Julie Macfarlane points out:

58. See *id.* at 346 for a more detailed discussion of "milestones for ethical decision making."

59. *Mediation Self-Reflection Treasury*, Sup. Ct. of Va. Div. of Disp. Resol. Servs. (2018), http://www.vacourts.gov/courtadmin/aoc/djs/programs/drs/mediation/resources/treasury.pdf.

> Codes that attempt to provide classifications and definitions of bad behaviour and follow these with prescriptions about appropriate responses by mediators reinforce the widely held misconception that it is possible to describe and prescribe behaviour and response in mediation independent of context. In this way, codes of conduct for mediators appear to be guilty of raising expectations about ethical certainties that cannot be met.[60]

As standards may conflict in mediation, mediators must often weigh how best to address a given problem in a specific situation. For this reason, mediators cannot rely upon mediator ethics advisory opinion summaries without reading the full question and understanding the context upon which the opinion is issued.

Following are some ways in which mediators can further their mediation ethical understanding and capacities.

14.4.1. Stay Abreast of Current Events in the Field of Mediation

Mediators should monitor applicable mediation standards and codes, mediation ethics advisory opinions, published mediator grievances,[61] mediation law (such as portions governing mediation privadentiality), relevant mediation court rules and codes, etc., to ensure that they are up to date with their understanding of their ethical obligations and the legal world in which they mediate. Joining professional mediation groups and, where applicable, joining mediator panels or becoming certified or otherwise qualified by courts can help to keep the mediator informed of changes in the field.

14.4.2. Attend Mediation Ethics Workshops and Webinars

Interactive workshops and synchronous webinars provide constructive opportunities to practice ethical analysis and decision making. Passive attendance at or listening to presentations and webinars can be very educational but generally are not as useful for learning critical ethical decision-making skills, as there is no opportunity for more interactive participation and discussions.

---

60. Julie Macfarlane, *Mediating Ethically: The Limits of Codes of Conduct and the Potential of a Reflective Practice Model*, 40 Osgoode Hall L.J. 49, 71 (2002).

61. One good resource of published mediator grievances can be found on the Florida Courts website: https://www.flcourts.org/Resources-Services/Alternative-Dispute-Resolution/Rules-Discipline-Sanctions.

14.4.3. Read Mediation Ethics Books and Articles

There are a growing number of excellent books and articles on mediation ethics, and a sample of suggested reading is provided in Section 14.6.

14.4.4. Participate in Peer Consultation and Education

The AFCC Model Standards recommend peer consultation as a type of CME.[62] Mediators can form a mediator ethics workgroup with other mediators who meet regularly (in person or virtually) to discuss mediation cases that raise interesting ethical issues. Note that mediators are able to discuss cases as long as identifying details (such as the names of the parties, date of mediation, personally identifying details of the parties, etc.) are omitted. As an added layer of protection, mediators can also change minor details so as to disguise the specific case mediated.

One model of peer consultation described by Beryl Minkle, Anthony S. Bashir, and Claudia Sutulov involves creating a safe and private interdisciplinary group of about 12 diverse professionals who meet monthly to "share cases and talk openly about misgivings or mistakes in their mediation practices."[63] According to these authors,

> Through questioning and reframing, for example, the mediator can assess the influences of feelings, thoughts, and beliefs on attitudes and actions. The resulting insights enable the mediator to reconsider his or her mental frameworks and the influence of his or her internal landscape on the mediation, and to choose possible alternative ways of understanding the process and of determining if different actions are necessary. He or she is now better able to support the goals of the parties, protecting the mediation process by hewing to practice guidelines, acceptable limits, and professional boundaries in providing responsible, ethical service . . . .[64]

---

62. MODEL STANDARDS OF PRACTICE FOR FAMILY AND DIVORCE MEDIATION, *supra* note 5, Standard XIII.B: Mediators should participate in programs of peer consultation and should help train and mentor the work of less experienced mediators.

63. Beryl Minkle, Anthony S. Bashir & Claudia Sutulov, *Peer Consultation for Mediators: The Use of a Holding Environment to Support Mediator Reflection, Inquiry, and Self-Knowing*, 24 NEGOT. J. 303, 305 (2008).

64. *Id.* at 316.

14.4.5. Self-Assessment

The AFCC Model Standards specifically mention self-assessment as another recommended form of CME.[65] As Julie Macfarlane points out: "Reflective practice seems to offer the potential for self-conscious and context-responsive approaches to ethical choices in mediation without advocating for a single 'right' way."[66]

A good example of a self-assessment tool is the Mediator Self-Reflection Form[67] promulgated by the Virginia Division of Dispute Resolution Services.[68] Mediators are encouraged to select one of their mediation cases and self-reflect on the case. If Virginia mediators complete and submit the form, they can earn continuing mediator education credit for completing the survey.[69] The form is broken down into five sections: Visualize the Mediation, What Stands Out?, What Was My Self-Awareness?, Learning, and Professional Development.[70] Woven into these categories are a variety of questions from which mediators can select to answer. Included among the questions are the following ethics-focused questions:

- How did my actions fit with my beliefs about the role of a mediator and the goals of mediation—were they consistent with those beliefs?
- How did my actions fit with mediator ethics? Was I mindful of ethical considerations as I mediated?
- Did I step outside the mediator role into another professional role? If so, what were my thoughts/intentions?
- Did ethical issues arise? If so, how did I handle it? Would I do anything differently next time? Why or why not?
- Did all my actions stem from the principles of mediation? Would I do anything differently next time? What might have changed if I had acted differently?
- Can I improve my understanding of mediator ethics? How?

---

65. MODEL STANDARDS OF PRACTICE FOR FAMILY AND DIVORCE MEDIATION, *supra* note 5, Standard XIII.A: "A family mediator shall acquire and maintain professional competence in mediation. A. Mediators should continuously improve their professional skills and abilities by, among other activities, participating in relevant continuing education programs and should regularly engage in self-assessment."

66. Macfarlane, *supra* note 60, at 73.

67. *See Mediator Self-Reflection*, OFF. OF THE EXEC. SEC'Y OF THE SUP. CT. OF VA. (Sept. 2018), http://www.vacourts.gov/courtadmin/aoc/djs/programs/drs/mediation/forms/adr1011.pdf.

68. *Mediation Self-Reflection Treasury*, *supra* note 59.

69. VA. GUIDELINES FOR TRAINING, *supra* note 18, at D.4.9.

70. *See Mediator Self-Reflection*, *supra* note 67.

Learning to become a reflective practitioner takes time and need not be done independently. Certainly, learning to be self-reflective can also be achieved through individual mentorship and peer group consultation. As Michael Lang suggests:

> If the field of conflict resolution is to be credible and accepted as a distinct profession, then we must, without sacrificing the inclusivity that has been its hallmark, address concerns about competence. We must be concerned with nurturing excellence in practice. I believe we can achieve this goal by utilizing elicitive teaching methods and by training mediators to be reflective practitioners.[71]

14.4.6. Mindfulness

Leonard Riskin defines mindfulness as "a certain way of paying attention—intentionally, moment-to-moment, with equanimity and without attachment—to whatever passes through the conventional senses and the mind."[72] A mindful mediator is attentive not only to others but also to the internal processes within the mediator. By becoming more mindful, the mediator can be more present and attuned to emotional factors that may interfere with a mediator's ability to practice ethically. As Riskin states:

> Each of us, no matter how much we meditate and try to maintain present moment awareness in life, will encounter situations in which we lose it. On the other hand, of course, mindfulness training and practice, especially those techniques meant to help us bring mindful awareness into daily life, can increase the proportion of time when we are likely to behave ethically or skillfully, either because we are in tune with others or in control of our responses to circumstances. Perhaps that's all we can expect from mindfulness training. And perhaps that's enough.[73]

As such, learning and practicing mindfulness can be another way for mediators to improve their ethical mediation skills. While studying and

71. Michael Lang, *Becoming Reflective Practitioners*, MEDIATE (July 2000), https://www.mediate.com/articles/reflect.cfm (originally published in the January 1998 issue of *Consensus*, a publication of the MIT-Harvard Public Disputes Program).

72. Leonard L. Riskin, *Annual Saltman Lecture: Further beyond Reason: Emotions, the Core Concerns, and Mindfulness in Negotiation*, 10 NEV. L.J. 290, 308 (2010).

73. Leonard L. Riskin, *Awareness and Ethics in Dispute Resolution and Law: Why Mindfulness Tends to Foster Ethical Behavior*, 50 S. TEX. L. REV. 493, 503 (2009).

practicing mindfulness might not be considered CMEE in the narrow definition of CMEE, it certainly can lead to a mediator practicing more ethically, nonetheless.

14.4.7. Implicit Bias

Developing a better understanding of a mediator's own implicit bias is another opportunity for mediators to enhance their ethical mediation practice. The path for such insight can include taking implicit bias tests such as one of the many Implicit Association Tests that are currently offered for free by Harvard University[74] and learning to become more self-aware of and less controlled by the mediator's unconscious biases.

14.5. Conclusion and Recommendations

For most mediators, the amount of mediation training required to become a practicing mediator is minimal at best. While there may be many ways to get parties to reach an agreement, ethical and otherwise, the skilled mediator finds ways to promote meaningful dialogue and successful negotiation between the parties in ways that adhere to the highest standards of mediation ethics respecting party self-determination, mediator impartiality, and the many other important ethical obligations of a mediator. Understanding mediation ethics, developing ethical awareness and skills, and acquiring a professional ethics perspective are a continuous and long-term effort. By continually pursuing CMEE, mediators can learn to improve their collaborative skillset and raise the overall level of their ethical mediation practice. In order to enhance the skillful and ethical practice of mediation, three recommendations are offered.

14.5.1. CME Should Be Required for Mediators

Simply taking a mediation course, often for only five days, does not provide mediators with sufficient training to sustain a mediation career. If one looks at requirements for other professions, continuing education generally is a standard practice. For example, the American Bar Association Model Rule for Minimum Continuing Legal Education requires 15 CLE credit hours per year.[75]

---

74. *Project Implicit*, HARV. UNIV., https://implicit.harvard.edu/implicit/takeatest.html (last visited Mar. 10, 2021).

75. MODEL RULE FOR MINIMUM CONTINUING LEGAL EDUC. § 3(A) (2017).

14.5.2. CMEE Should Be a Required Portion of CME and, If Not Specifically Required, CMEE Should Be Considered an Ethical Obligation of All Mediators

Initial mediation training cannot provide mediators with sufficient training to grapple with important ethical issues facing a mediator. Initial training at best teaches mediators the fundamental elements of mediation ethics and provides a limited number of examples to demonstrate the principles. Advanced CMEE is essential for the mediator to adequately address their obligations to their clients, the mediation profession, the public and employers or principals.

Other professions have ethics education requirements. For example, the American Bar Association Model Rule for Minimum Continuing Legal Education requires 15 CLE credit hours per year, which must include one hour of Ethics and Professionalism Programming.[76] While one hour seems insufficient, it is a recognition by the ABA of the importance of ongoing ethics training.

All Florida Supreme Court–certified mediators are required to complete four hours of CMEE each two-year renewal cycle of their certification. Given that the integrity of the mediation process is ultimately the responsibility of the mediator, completing two hours of CMEE on average each year seems to be a reasonable CMEE requirement.

CMEE should be multidimensional focusing upon all the levels of mediation ethics. As described earlier in Figure 14.1, mediator ethics builds a multilayered foundation, and there is merit to furthering one's understanding of all levels. As mediators develop real-world experience, they have a better context for more deeply appreciating the complex ethical issues inherent in their mediation practice.

14.5.3. Self-Reflection Tools, Implicit Bias Tests, and Similar Activities That Encourage Greater Awareness of a Mediator's Internal Processes Should Be Considered as a Valuable Component of CMEE

Virginia provides a good example for recognizing the value of self-reflection and provides a useful tool for promoting such. Ideally, such self-reflection tools could expand the number of ethics-related questions to better assist mediators to integrate their self-reflection with ethical decision making.

76. *Id.* § 3(A)(2).

In *When Breath Becomes Air*, neurosurgeon Paul Kalanithi describes his struggle to save lives:

> Even if you are perfect, the world isn't. The secret is to know that the deck is stacked, that you will lose, that your hands or judgment will slip, and yet still struggle to win for your patients. You can't ever reach perfection, but you can believe in an asymptote toward which you are ceaselessly striving.[77]

Mediators similarly practice in an imperfect world with clients who despite our best efforts can't always be helped as much as we would like. Recognizing this, we owe it to ourselves, our clients, the mediation profession, the public, and our employers and principals to pursue the asymptote of a truly ethical mediation practice, knowing we are on a never-ending journey where there will always be room for improvement.

14.6. Resources for Continuing Mediation Ethics Education

Following is a sample of resources available for mediators to further their CME and CMEE offered to help mediators find useful CME and CMEE opportunities. As the list does not include all resources and likely will become outdated over time, mediators are encouraged to explore other mediation ethics learning opportunities that may be more timely, focused to their particular interests, and conveniently available.

14.6.1. Mediator Ethics Advisory Opinions around the United States

Advisory Opinion of the North Carolina Dispute Resolution Commission: https://www.nccourts.gov/assets/inline-files/Complied-AO-website.pdf?XqasfznyPt8NP4ivASbNCJfLZwSr_6L5

Board of Professional Responsibility of the Supreme Court of Tennessee Formal Ethics Opinion: https://www.tncourts.gov/programs/mediation/resources-mediators/opinions

Florida Mediator Ethics Advisory Opinions: http://videosurvey.flcourts.org/gen_public/adr/MEACOpinions/index-opinions.shtml

Georgia Commission on Dispute Resolution, Committee on Ethics: https://godr.org/about-us/rules/

National Clearinghouse for Mediator Ethics Opinions: https://www.americanbar.org/groups/dispute_resolution/resources/dispute-resolution-resource-database/ (Note: This is a search page and resources can be found by typing in the desired search criteria.) and

77. Paul Kalanithi, When Breath Becomes Air 114 (2016).

https://www.americanbar.org/groups/dispute_resolution/resources/mediator_ethics_opinions/

New York Mediator Ethics Advisory Opinions: http://ww2.nycourts.gov/ip/adr/meac.shtml

14.6.2. Mediation Ethics Books

MEDIATION ETHICS (Ellen Waldman ed., 2011)

OMER SHAPIRA, A THEORY OF MEDIATOR'S ETHICS: FOUNDATIONS, RATIONALE, AND APPLICATION (2016)

14.6.3. Mediation Ethics Articles

The references cited in this chapter provide a wide range of mediation ethics articles worth reading.

14.6.4. Mediation Self-Reflection Resources

Beryl Minkle, Anthony S. Bashir & Claudia Sutulov, Peer Consultation for Mediators: The Use of a Holding Environment to Support Mediator Reflection, Inquiry, and Self-Knowing, 24 NEGOT. J. 303 (2008)

DONALD SCHON, THE REFLECTIVE PRACTITIONER: HOW PROFESSIONALS THINK IN ACTION (1983)

Julie Macfarlane, Mediating Ethically: The Limits of Codes of Conduct and the Potential of a Reflective Practice Model, 40 OSGOODE HALL L.J. 49 (2002)

Mediation Self-Reflection Resources recommended by the Supreme Court of Virginia Division of Dispute Resolution Services: http://www.courts.state.va.us/courtadmin/aoc/djs/programs/drs/mediation/resources/treasury.pdf

MICHAEL LANG, THE GUIDE TO REFLECTIVE PRACTICE IN CONFLICT RESOLUTION (The ACR Practitioner's Guide Series, 2019)

14.6.5. Implicit Bias

AN INTRODUCTION TO IMPLICIT BIAS: KNOWLEDGE, JUSTICE, AND THE SOCIAL MIND (Erin Beeghly & Alex Madva eds., 2020)

MICHAEL BROWNSTEIN, THE IMPLICIT MIND COGNITIVE ARCHITECTURE, THE SELF, AND ETHICS (2018)

Project Implicit, https://implicit.harvard.edu/implicit/takeatest.html

14.6.6. Mediation and Mindfulness

Leonard L. Riskin, Annual Saltman Lecture: Further beyond Reason: Emotions, the Core Concerns, and Mindfulness in Negotiation, 10 Nev. L.J. 290 (2010)

Leonard L. Riskin & Rachel Wohl, *Mindfulness in the Heat of Conflict: Taking STOCK*, 20 Harv. Negot. L. Rev. 121 (2015)

Leslie Larkin Cooney, *Surfing to Success as a Mindful Negotiator*, 17 Pepp. Disp. Resol. L.J. 131 (2017)

14.6.7. Behavioral Economics

Daniel Kahneman, Thinking Fast and Slow (2011)

Michael Lewis, The Undoing Project (2017)

Richard Thaler & Cass Sunstein, Nudge (2009)

14.6.8. Professional Mediation Organization Conferences and Training

Academy of Professional Family Mediators: www.apfmnet.org

American Arbitration Association: https://aaamediation.org/

American Bar Association Section of Dispute Resolution Annual Conference: https://www.americanbar.org/groups/dispute_resolution/events_cle/annual/

Association for Conflict Resolution Annual Conference: www.acrnet.org

Association of Family and Conciliation Courts Annual and State Conferences: www.afccnet.org

International Mediation Institute Global Pound Conference: https://www.imimediation.org/

Ohio Mediation Association Annual Conference: https://www.mediateohio.org/

National Association for Community Mediation: www.nafcm.org

Wisconsin Association of Mediators Annual Conference: https://www.wamediators.org/

14.6.9. State and Court Conferences

Florida Dispute Resolution Center Annual Conference: https://www.flcourts.org/Resources-Services/Alternative-Dispute-Resolution/Annual-Conference

North Carolina Dispute Resolution Commission: https://www.nccourts.gov/assets/documents/publications/Current-CME-Programs-04292020.pdf?GTjAtN8f9TvYNkYv91FpgOkSqOvqUXpb

Tennessee State Courts Continuing Mediator Education: http://www.tncourts.gov/programs/mediation/resources-mediators/continuing-mediation-education

Virginia Mediation Network: https://www.vamediation.org/conferences-learning-opportunities

14.6.10. Law Schools

Many law schools offer mediation conferences available to mediators in the field. At the time of writing this chapter, the 12 best law school dispute resolution programs included, in order of ranking, the following law schools: Harvard University, Ohio State University (Moritz), Pepperdine University (Caruso), University of Missouri, Yeshiva University (Cardozo), Mitchell Hamline School of Law, Northwestern University (Pritzker), Texas A&M University, University of Nevada–Las Vegas, Arizona State University (O'Connor), Marquette University, and University of Oregon.[78] Certainly, other law schools also offer excellent mediation conferences as well.

14.6.11. Graduate Dispute Resolution Programs

Many universities and colleges also offer graduate study in alternative dispute resolution (ADR). The following, listed in alphabetical order, include a list of programs that offer online graduate study in mediation, conflict resolution, and/or ADR: Abilene Christian University, Arizona State University, California State University–Dominguez Hills, Creighton University, Dallas Baptist University, Dominican University, George Mason University, Norwich University, Nova Southeastern University, and the University of Denver.

14.6.12. Teaching Mediation Ethics

Mary Thompson, *Teaching Ethical Competence*, 10 Disp. Resol. Mag. 23 (2004)

Paula M. Young, Teaching Professional Ethics to Lawyers and Mediators Using Active Learning Techniques, 40 Sw. L. Rev. 127 (2010)

78. *Best Dispute Resolution Programs*, U.S. News & World Report, https://www.usnews.com/best-graduate-schools/top-law-schools/dispute-resolution-rankings (last visited Mar. 11, 2021).

Paula M. Young, Teaching the Ethical Values Governing Mediator Impartiality Using Short Lectures, Buzz Group Discussions, Video Clips, a Defining Features Matrix, Games, and an Exercise Based on Grievances Filed against Florida Mediators, 11 PEPP. DISP. RESOL. L.J. 309 (2011)

APPENDIX A

State Mediation Codes of Conduct and Mediation Ethical Advisory Opinions

Susan Nauss Exon

An online version of this appendix, with live hyperlinks, is available at http://ambar.org/mediation-ethics.

Alabama — ALA. CODE OF ETHICS FOR MEDIATORS (Sup. Ct. of Ala., amended 2015), https://alabamaadr.org/web/resources/resources_ethics.php.
Alabama Supreme Court Commission on Dispute Resolution issues ethical guidance opinions.

Alaska* — No Mediator Ethical Standards.

Arizona* — No Mediator Ethical Standards.
Ethics opinions relating to lawyer mediators can be requested by contacting the Arizona Supreme Court's Attorney Ethics Advisory Committee.

Arkansas* — REQUIREMENTS FOR THE CONDUCT OF MEDIATION & MEDIATORS (Ark. Alt. Disp. Resol. Comm'n 2001), https://www.arcourts.gov/sites/default/files/2019-06/CONDUCT%202012.pdf.

California* — RULES OF CONDUCT FOR MEDIATORS IN CT.-CONNECTED MEDIATION PROGRAMS FOR CIVIL CASES, CAL. RULES OF CT. 3.850–3.872 (amended 2011), https://www.courts.ca.gov/cms/rules/index.cfm?title=three.
STANDARDS OF PRACTICE FOR CAL. MEDIATORS (Cal. Disp. Resol. Council 2000), https://www.cdrc.net/standards-of-practice-for-californi.

Colorado*	The Colorado Mediation Association, formerly the Colorado Council of Mediators (CCMO), adopted the August 2005 Model Standards of Conduct for Mediators (ABA Model Standards), http://coloradomediation.org/pg.cfm. COLO. MODEL STANDARDS OF CONDUCT FOR MEDIATORS (CBA, CJI, DOL, CCMO & Off. of Disp. Resol. of the Colo. Jud. Dep't 2000) is a voluntary code and appears to be the ABA Model Standards. http://www.Coloradomediation.org/docs/code%20of%20conduct.pdf.
Connecticut*	No Mediator Ethical Standards.
Delaware*	No Mediator Ethical Standards.
Florida	FLA. RULES FOR CERTIFIED & CT.-APPOINTED MEDIATORS, PART II (Fla. Disp. Resol. Ctr. 2018), https://www.flcourts.org/Resources-Services/Alternative-Dispute-Resolution/Rules-Discipline-Sanctions. The Florida Mediator Ethical Advisory Committee (MEAC) issues Ethics Opinions. https://www.flcourts.org/Resources-Services/Alternative-Dispute-Resolution/Mediator-Ethics-Advisory-Committee-Opinions-MEAC (last visited Feb. 24, 2021).
Georgia	ETHICAL STANDARDS FOR MEDIATORS, GA. ALT. DISP. RESOL. RULES, app. C, ch. 1 (Ga. Comm'n on Disp. Resol., amended 2013), https://godr.org/registered-neutral/ethics-information/. The Committee on Ethics issues both Advisory Opinions (advice on how a mediator should operate within a certain situation) and Ethics Opinions (instances of mediator misbehavior). *Ethics Information for Registered Neutrals*, GA. OFF. OF DISPUTE RESOL., https://godr.org/registered-neutral/ethics-information/ (last visited Feb. 24, 2021).
Hawaii*	GUIDELINES FOR HAW. MEDIATORS (Haw. Comm. on Mediation Standards 2002), http://www.courts.state.hi.us/services/alternative_dispute/selecting/guidelines/introduction.html.

Idaho*	STANDARDS OF PRACTICE FOR IDAHO MEDIATORS (Idaho Mediation Ass'n), https://www.idahomediationassociation.org/Standards-of-Practice (last visited Feb. 24, 2021).
Illinois	MCI PROF'L STANDARDS OF PRACTICE FOR MEDIATORS (Mediation Council of Ill. 2009), http://www.mediationcouncilofillinois.org/sites/default/files/MCI Professional Standards of Practice.pdf. The Illinois State Bar Association issues Ethics Opinions on Arbitration and Mediation. https://www.isba.org/ethics/bysubject/Arbitration%20and%20Mediation (last visited Apr. 29, 2020).
Indiana*	RULES FOR ADR, IND. RULES OF CT. (1992; includes amendments through Jan. 1, 2019), http://www.in.gov/judiciary/rules/adr.
Iowa*	IOWA SUP. CT. RULES 11.1–11.10 (2012), https://www.legis.iowa.gov/docs/ACO/CourtRulesChapter/08-28-2019.11.pdf.
Kansas*	KAN. R. REL. MED. 918, Ethics (Kan. Sup. Ct. 2020), https://casetext.com/rule/kansas-court-rules/kansas-rules-relating-to-mediation-dispute-resolution/rule-918-ethics.
Kentucky*	Supreme Court of Kentucky Order 2005-02: *In re* Amendment to the Rules of Administrative Procedure AP Part XII. Mediation Guidelines for Court of Justice Mediators, Section 3, Ethical Guidelines (2005), https://kycourts.gov/courtprograms/mediation/Documents/AdminOrder200502.pdf. MODEL MEDIATION RULES, KY. RULES ANNOTATED establish procedures for mediation. https://kycourts.gov/courtprograms/mediation/Pages/modelmediation.aspx. The Kentucky Bar Association issues ethics opinions regarding its Rules of Professional Conduct and Ethics.

Louisiana*	LA. REV. STAT. ANN. § 9:4107 (Westlaw through 2019 Reg. Sess.) (Louisiana Mediation Act adopted the ABA Model Standards).
Maine*	STANDARDS OF CONDUCT (Me. Ass'n of Mediators), https://mainemediators.org/Standards-of-Conduct (last visited Feb. 24, 2021).
Maryland*	MD. STANDARDS OF CONDUCT FOR CT.-DESIGNATED MEDIATORS (Jud. Council ADR Comm. 2020) (these standards are identical to MD. STANDARDS OF CONDUCT FOR CT.-DESIGNATED MEDIATORS (2020)), https://www.courts.state.md.us/macro/adrresources.
Massachusetts*	UNIFORM RULES ON DISP. RESOL., MASS. SUP. JUD. CT. RULE 1:18, R. 9. Ethical Standards (1999), https://www.mass.gov/supreme-judicial-court-rules/supreme-judicial-court-rule-118-uniform-rules-on-dispute-resolution. The Massachusetts Bar Association issues ethical opinions for lawyer mediators.
Michigan*	MICH. SUP. CT. MEDIATOR STANDARDS OF CONDUCT (Off. of Disp. Resol. 2013), https://courts.michigan.gov/administration/scao/officesprograms/odr/pages/mediator-standards-of-conduct.aspx. The Michigan Bar Association issues ethical opinions for lawyer mediators.
Minnesota*	MINN. GEN. R. OF PRAC. FOR THE DIST. CTS. 114 app., CODE OF ETHICS (amended 2019), https://www.revisor.mn.gov/court_rules/rule/gp-114~a0/.
Mississippi*	CT. ANNEXED MEDIATION RULES FOR CIVIL LITIG. (amended 2002), https://courts.ms.gov/research/rules/msrulesofcourt/court_annexed_mediation.pdf.

Missouri*	No Court-Connected Mediator Ethical Standards. SUP. CT. RULES GOVERNING THE MO. BAR & THE JUDICIARY R. 17 (1997) relates to ADR, https://www.courts.mo.gov/courts/ClerkHandbooksP2RulesOnly.nsf/c0c6ffa99df4993f86256ba50057dcb8/a5a360d73fae04fa86256ca600521250?OpenDocument. The Association of Missouri Mediators adopted the 2005 ABA Model Standards. http://www.momediators.org/conduct.html (last visited Apr. 29, 2020).
Montana*	CODE OF ETHICS & STANDARDS OF PRACTICE (Mont. Mediation Ass'n 2014), https://mtmediation.org/wp-content/uploads/2015/04/mtma-code-of-ethics-standards-of-practice-rev-2-13-14-reviewed-by-committee.pdf.
Nebraska	MANUAL OF STANDARDS & ETHICS FOR CTR. MEDIATORS, DIRECTORS & STAFF (Neb. Off. of Disp. Resol., amended 2009), https://supremecourt.nebraska.gov/administration/professional-ethics/professional-ethics-mediators. The Nebraska Supreme Court Counsel for Discipline issues ethical opinions for lawyer mediators. https://supremecourt.nebraska.gov/administration/professional-ethics/professional-ethics-mediators.
Nevada*	No Court-Connected Mediator Ethical Standards. NEV. MEDIATION RULES 1–11 (2005) address mediation for court-annexed mediation, including mediator qualifications, immunity, and confidentiality. https://www.washoecourts.com/OtherDocs/Arbitration/NMR.pdf.

New Hampshire*	Each New Hampshire court has individual rules regarding mediation ethical standards. Some are included in local rules, and some relate to specific subjects such as family law and probate. The following rules relate to general civil matters: N.H. Sup. Ct. Rules R. 12-A (cases pending in the Supreme Court may be referred to mediation), https://www.courts.state.nh.us/rules/scr/scr-12-a.htm (last visited Apr. 26, 2021). Alt. Disp. Resol., N.H. R. Super. Ct., Civil Rule 32 (includes impartiality, conflicts of interest, confidentiality, and immunity rules for Superior Court neutrals), https://www.courts.state.nh.us/rules/supercr-new/supercr-new-32.htm (last visited Apr. 26, 2021). Mediation, N.H. R. Super. Ct., Civil Rule 30 relates to mediation but does not include ethical standards. https://www.courts.state.nh.us/rules/supercr-new/supercr-new-30.htm (last visited Apr. 26, 2021). Civil Writ Mediation Rules, N.H. Rules of the Cir. Ct.—District Div. R. 3.28, https://www.courts.state.nh.us/rules/dmcr/dmcr-3_28.htm (last visited Apr. 26, 2021). Mediation, N.H. Rules of the Cir. Ct.—District Div. R. 3.30, https://www.courts.state.nh.us/rules/dmcr-civil-efile/dmcrcivil-VI-3-30-3-34.html#r3-30 (last visited Apr. 26, 2021).

New Jersey*	STANDARDS OF CONDUCT FOR MEDIATORS IN CT.-CONNECTED PROGRAMS (N.J. Sup. Ct. 2000), https://njcourts.gov/courts/assets/civil/mediatorstandards.pdf. Questions to the Advisory Committee on Mediator Standards may be directed to Manager, CDR Programs, Administrative Office of the Courts, P.O. Box 988, Trenton, NJ 08625; phone 609-984-2337. CODE OF PROF'L ETHICS (N.J. Ass'n of Prof'l Mediators 2007), https://njapm.org/njapm-mediator-standards-of-conduct/.
New Mexico*	GUIDELINES FOR CT.-CONNECTED MEDIATION SERVS. (N.M. Statewide ADR Comm'n 2016), https://adr.nmcourts.gov/adr-commission-information.aspx. The New Mexico Mediation Procedures Act, N.M. STAT. ANN. §§ 44-7B-1 *et seq.* (Westlaw, current with 2020 Reg. Sess. laws in effect through May 20, 2020), defines mediation and sets forth confidentiality provisions. ETHICS & STANDARDS OF PRACTICE (N.M. Mediation Ass'n), https://newmexicomediationassociation.org/standards/ (last visited Apr. 26, 2021). CODE OF ETHICAL CONDUCT (N.M. Mediation Ass'n 2014), https://newmexicomediationassociation.org/standards/.

New York	STANDARDS OF CONDUCT FOR N.Y. ST. CMTY. DISP. RESOL. CTR. MEDIATORS (N.Y. State Unified Ct. Sys., Div. of Prof'l and Ct. Servs., amended 2009), http://ww2.nycourts.gov/ip/adr/Publications.shtml. The New York State Mediation Association has adopted the ABA Model Standards with changes. The New York State Unified Court System Mediator Ethics Advisory Committee (MEAC) issues Ethics Opinions. http://ww2.nycourts.gov/ip/adr/meac.shtml.
North Carolina	STANDARDS OF PROF'L CONDUCT FOR MEDIATORS, N.C. SUP. CT. RULES (Disp. Resol. Comm'n 2020), https://www.nccourts.gov/courts/supreme-court/court-rules/standards-of-professional-conduct-for-mediators. The North Carolina Dispute Resolution Commission issues Advisory Opinions. https://www.nccourts.gov/commissions/dispute-resolution-commission/drc-advisory-opinions-and-policy.
North Dakota*	CODE OF MEDIATION ETHICS, N.D. RULES OF CT. R. 8.9, app. A (2007), https://www.ndcourts.gov/legal-resources/rules/ndrct/appendix-a-to-rule-8-9.
Ohio*	RULES OF SUPERINTENDENCE FOR THE CTS. OF OHIO R. 16 MEDIATION FINAL RULE AMENDMENTS (2020) creates a Commission on Dispute Resolution. Rule 16.21 allows for local courts to adopt their own rules. Rule 16.22 requires mediators to adhere to the ABA Model Standards. SUP. CT. OF OHIO CORE VALUES FOR MEDIATION (Disp. Resol. Section & Comm'n on Disp. Resol. 2017).

Oklahoma* Rules and Procedures for the Dispute Resolution Procedure Act, OKLA. STAT. ANN. tit. 12, ch. 37, app. A (Westlaw, current through Mar. 1, 2020).
ETHICAL GUIDELINES FOR MEDIATORS (Okla. Chapter of Ass'n of Attorney-Mediators), https://www.attorney-mediators.org/ethicalguidelines (last visited Apr. 29, 2020).

Oregon* No Court-Connected Mediator Ethical Standards. OR. REV. STAT. ch. 36 (Mediation and Arbitration); OR. REV. STAT. § 36.262 (confidentiality); OR. REV. STAT. § 36.264 (immunity).
CORE STANDARDS OF MEDIATION PRACTICE (Or. Mediation Ass'n 2005), http://ormediation.org/what-is-mediation/guidelines-for-mediators/.

Pennsylvania* The Pennsylvania Council of Mediators has endorsed the 2005 ABA Model Standards. https://www.pamediation.org/recommended-guidelines.html (last visited Apr. 29, 2020).
The Council cites to the Advisory Opinions of the ABA Committee on Mediator Ethical Guidance.

Rhode Island* No Court-Connected Mediator Ethical Standards. The Rhode Island Judiciary has an appellate mediation program and does not include any ethical guidance for mediators. https://www.courts.ri.gov/AppellateMediationProgram/Pages/default.aspx (last visited Apr. 26, 2021).
The Rhode Island Mediators Association has approved the ABA Model Standards. http://www.rimediators.org/Mediator-Code-of-Conduct (adopted 2009).

South Carolina*	STANDARDS OF CONDUCT FOR MEDIATORS, CT.-ANNEXED ALT. DISP. RESOL. (ADR) RULES, app. B, https://www.sccourts.org/courtReg/indexadr.cfm (last visited Apr. 26, 2021).
South Dakota*	No Mediator Ethical Standards.
Tennessee	STANDARDS OF PROF'L CONDUCT FOR RULE 31 NEUTRALS, TENN. SUP. CT. RULE 31, app. A (amended 2019), http://tncourts.gov/rules/supreme-court/31. The Alternative Dispute Resolution Commission issues Ethics Advisory Opinions and Formal Grievance Decisions. The Board of Professional Responsibility issues Formal Ethical Opinions. http://tncourts.gov/programs/mediation/resources-mediators/opinions (last visited Apr. 26, 2021). The Tennessee Judicial Ethics Committee issues Advisory Opinions on mediation issues with respect to judges.

Texas*

TEX. CIV. PRAC. REM. CODE §§ 154.023 (2001), 154.053 (amended effective 1999).

ETHICAL GUIDELINES FOR MEDIATORS (2011) (Tex. Sup. Ct. adopted 2005, amended 2011), https://www.txmediator.org/members/resources/ethics/Amendment_to_Ethical_Guidelines_for_Mediators%202011.pdf.

ETHICAL GUIDELINES FOR MEDIATORS (St. Bar of Tex. 1994), https://www.txmediator.org/aboutmediation/guidelines.php.

Texas Judicial Ethics Opinions discuss mediation issues with respect to judges and former judges. https://www.txcourts.gov/media/678096/JudicialEthicsOpinions.pdf (last visited Apr. 26, 2021).

The Professional Ethics Committee of the State Bar of Texas issues ethical opinions for lawyer mediators. https://www.legalethicstexas.com/Ethics-Resources/Opinions/Search-Results.aspx?searchtext=mediation+ethics&searchmode=AllWords (last visited Apr. 26, 2021).

Utah*

CODE OF ETHICS FOR ADR PROVIDERS, UTAH RULES OF CT.-ANNEXED ALT. DISP. RESOL. R. 104 (2008).

The Utah Mediation Best Practice Guide (rev. Nov. 2018) was prepared by a subcommittee of the Utah Judicial Council's Ad Hoc Committee on Alternative Dispute Resolution (ADR Committee), https://www.utahbar.org/wp-content/uploads/2019/11/Mediation-Best-Practices-Guide-Final-Draft.pdf.

Vermont*

VT. CT. R. 16.3 (2019) addresses mediation, including impartiality, conflicts of interest, and confidentiality.

Virginia*	STANDARDS OF ETHICS & PROF'L RESPONSIBILITY FOR CERTIFIED MEDIATORS (Jud. Council of Va. 2011), http://www.courts.state.va.us/courtadmin/aoc/djs/programs/drs/mediation/soe.pdf.
Washington*	STANDARDS OF PRACTICE FOR MEDIATORS (Wash. Mediation Ass'n 1997) (the original 1994 version of the ABA Model Standards), https://washingtonmediation.org/standards-of-practice/.
West Virginia*	W. VA. TRIAL CT. R. 25.01–25.16 (2004) (procedural rules regarding mediation, confidentiality, and immunity), https://casetext.com/rule/west-virginia-court-rules/west-virginia-trial-court-rules/chapter-2-civil-matters/rule-25-mediation.
Wisconsin	ETHICAL GUIDELINES FOR THE PRACTICE OF MEDIATION (Wis. Ass'n of Mediators 1997), https://www.wamediators.org/ethical-practices. WIS. STAT. § 802.12 (Westlaw, current through 2019 Act 184, published Mar. 6, 2020) provides for ADR processes, including mediation. The State Bar of Wisconsin Ethics Counsel issues ethical opinions regarding lawyer mediators.
Wyoming*	No Mediation Ethical Standards. WYO. STAT. ANN. §§ 1-43-101 to 1-43-104 (Westlaw, current through chapters effective Mar. 26 of the 2020 Budget Sess. of the Wyoming Legislature) provides for mediation, including confidentiality and immunity.

*Has no Mediator Ethical Advisory Committee (MEAC) Opinions.

APPENDIX B

The Model Standards of Conduct for Mediators

American Arbitration Association
(Adopted September 8, 2005)
American Bar Association
(Approved by the ABA House of Delegates August 9, 2005)
Association for Conflict Resolution
(Adopted August 22, 2005)
September 2005

2005

The Model Standards of Conduct for Mediators was prepared in 1994 by the American Arbitration Association, the American Bar Association's Section of Dispute Resolution, and the Association for Conflict Resolution.[1] A joint committee consisting of representatives from the same successor organizations revised the Model Standards in 2005.[2] Both the original 1994 version and the 2005 revision have been approved by each participating organization.[3]

1. The Association for Conflict Resolution is a merged organization of the Academy of Family Mediators, the Conflict Resolution Education Network and the Society of Professionals in Dispute Resolution (SPIDR). SPIDR was the third participating organization in the development of the 1994 Standards.

2. Reporter's Notes, which are not part of these Standards and therefore have not been specifically approved by any of the organizations, provide commentary regarding these revisions.

3. The 2005 version to [sic] the Model Standards were approved by the American Bar Association's House of Delegates on August 9, 2005, the Board of the Association of Conflict Resolution on August 22, 2005 and the Executive Committee of the American Arbitration Association on September 8, 2005.

Preamble

Mediation is used to resolve a broad range of conflicts within a variety of settings. These Standards are designed to serve as fundamental ethical guidelines for persons mediating in all practice contexts. They serve three primary goals: to guide the conduct of mediators; to inform the mediating parties; and to promote public confidence in mediation as a process for resolving disputes.

Mediation is a process in which an impartial third party facilitates communication and negotiation and promotes voluntary decision making by the parties to the dispute.

Mediation serves various purposes, including providing the opportunity for parties to define and clarify issues, understand different perspectives, identify interests, explore and assess possible solutions, and reach mutually satisfactory agreements, when desired.

Note on Construction

These Standards are to be read and construed in their entirety. There is no priority significance attached to the sequence in which the Standards appear.

The use of the term "shall" in a Standard indicates that the mediator must follow the practice described. The use of the term "should" indicates that the practice described in the standard is highly desirable, but not required, and is to be departed from only for very strong reasons and requires careful use of judgment and discretion.

The use of the term "mediator" is understood to be inclusive so that it applies to co-mediator models.

These Standards do not include specific temporal parameters when referencing a mediation, and therefore, do not define the exact beginning or ending of a mediation.

Various aspects of a mediation, including some matters covered by these Standards, may also be affected by applicable law, court rules, regulations, other applicable professional rules, mediation rules to which the parties have agreed and other agreements of the parties. These sources may create conflicts with, and may take precedence over, these Standards. However, a mediator should make every effort to comply with the spirit and intent of these Standards in resolving such conflicts. This effort should include honoring all remaining Standards not in conflict with these other sources.

These Standards, unless and until adopted by a court or other regulatory authority do not have the force of law. Nonetheless, the fact that these Standards have been adopted by the respective sponsoring entities, should alert mediators to the fact that the Standards might be viewed as establishing a standard of care for mediators.

Standard I. Self-Determination

A. A mediator shall conduct a mediation based on the principle of party self-determination. Self-determination is the act of coming to a voluntary, uncoerced decision in which each party makes free and informed choices as to process and outcome. Parties may exercise self-determination at any stage of a mediation, including mediator selection, process design, participation in or withdrawal from the process, and outcomes.
   1. Although party self-determination for process design is a fundamental principle of mediation practice, a mediator may need to balance such party self-determination with a mediator's duty to conduct a quality process in accordance with these Standards.
   2. A mediator cannot personally ensure that each party has made free and informed choices to reach particular decisions, but, where appropriate, a mediator should make the parties aware of the importance of consulting other professionals to help them make informed choices.

B. A mediator shall not undermine party self-determination by any party for reasons such as higher settlement rates, egos, increased fees, or outside pressures from court personnel, program administrators, provider organizations, the media or others.

Standard II. Impartiality

A. A mediator shall decline a mediation if the mediator cannot conduct it in an impartial manner. Impartiality means freedom from favoritism, bias or prejudice.

B. A mediator shall conduct a mediation in an impartial manner and avoid conduct that gives the appearance of partiality.
   1. A mediator should not act with partiality or prejudice based on any participant's personal characteristics, background, values and beliefs, or performance at a mediation, or any other reason.
   2. A mediator should neither give nor accept a gift, favor, loan or other item of value that raises a question as to the mediator's actual or perceived impartiality.

3. A mediator may accept or give de minimis gifts or incidental items or services that are provided to facilitate a mediation or respect cultural norms so long as such practices do not raise questions as to a mediator's actual or perceived impartiality.

C. If at any time a mediator is unable to conduct a mediation in an impartial manner, the mediator shall withdraw.

Standard III. Conflicts of Interest

A. A mediator shall avoid a conflict of interest or the appearance of a conflict of interest during and after a mediation. A conflict of interest can arise from involvement by a mediator with the subject matter of the dispute or from any relationship between a mediator and any mediation participant, whether past or present, personal or professional, that reasonably raises a question of a mediator's impartiality.

B. A mediator shall make a reasonable inquiry to determine whether there are any facts that a reasonable individual would consider likely to create a potential or actual conflict of interest for a mediator. A mediator's actions necessary to accomplish a reasonable inquiry into potential conflicts of interest may vary based on practice context.

C. A mediator shall disclose, as soon as practicable, all actual and potential conflicts of interest that are reasonably known to the mediator and could reasonably be seen as raising a question about the mediator's impartiality. After disclosure, if all parties agree, the mediator may proceed with the mediation.

D. If a mediator learns any fact after accepting a mediation that raises a question with respect to that mediator's service creating a potential or actual conflict of interest, the mediator shall disclose it as quickly as practicable. After disclosure, if all parties agree, the mediator may proceed with the mediation.

E. If a mediator's conflict of interest might reasonably be viewed as undermining the integrity of the mediation, a mediator shall withdraw from or decline to proceed with the mediation regardless of the expressed desire or agreement of the parties to the contrary.

F. Subsequent to a mediation, a mediator shall not establish another relationship with any of the participants in any matter that would raise questions about the integrity of the mediation. When a mediator develops personal or professional relationships with parties, other individuals or organizations following a mediation in which they were involved, the mediator should consider factors such as time elapsed following the mediation, the nature of the relationships established, and services offered when determining whether the relationships might create a perceived or actual conflict of interest.

Standard IV. Competence

A. A mediator shall mediate only when the mediator has the necessary competence to satisfy the reasonable expectations of the parties.
   1. Any person may be selected as a mediator, provided that the parties are satisfied with the mediator's competence and qualifications. Training, experience in mediation, skills, cultural understandings and other qualities are often necessary for mediator competence. A person who offers to serve as a mediator creates the expectation that the person is competent to mediate effectively.
   2. A mediator should attend educational programs and related activities to maintain and enhance the mediator's knowledge and skills related to mediation.
   3. A mediator should have available for the parties' [sic] information relevant to the mediator's training, education, experience and approach to conducting a mediation.

B. If a mediator, during the course of a mediation determines that the mediator cannot conduct the mediation competently, the mediator shall discuss that determination with the parties as soon as is practicable and take appropriate steps to address the situation, including, but not limited to, withdrawing or requesting appropriate assistance.

C. If a mediator's ability to conduct a mediation is impaired by drugs, alcohol, medication or otherwise, the mediator shall not conduct the mediation.

Standard V. Confidentiality

A. A mediator shall maintain the confidentiality of all information obtained by the mediator in mediation, unless otherwise agreed to by the parties or required by applicable law.
   1. If the parties to a mediation agree that the mediator may disclose information obtained during the mediation, the mediator may do so.

2. A mediator should not communicate to any non-participant information about how the parties acted in the mediation. A mediator may report, if required, whether parties appeared at a scheduled mediation and whether or not the parties reached a resolution.
3. If a mediator participates in teaching, research or evaluation of mediation, the mediator should protect the anonymity of the parties and abide by their reasonable expectations regarding confidentiality.

B. A mediator who meets with any persons in private session during a mediation shall not convey directly or indirectly to any other person, any information that was obtained during that private session without the consent of the disclosing person.

C. A mediator shall promote understanding among the parties of the extent to which the parties will maintain confidentiality of information they obtain in a mediation.

D. Depending on the circumstance of a mediation, the parties may have varying expectations regarding confidentiality that a mediator should address. The parties may make their own rules with respect to confidentiality, or the accepted practice of an individual mediator or institution may dictate a particular set of expectations.

Standard VI. Quality of the Process

A. A mediator shall conduct a mediation in accordance with these Standards and in a manner that promotes diligence, timeliness, safety, presence of the appropriate participants, party participation, procedural fairness, party competency and mutual respect among all participants.
   1. A mediator should agree to mediate only when the mediator is prepared to commit the attention essential to an effective mediation.
   2. A mediator should only accept cases when the mediator can satisfy the reasonable expectation of the parties concerning the timing of a mediation.
   3. The presence or absence of persons at a mediation depends on the agreement of the parties and the mediator. The parties and mediator may agree that others may be excluded from particular sessions or from all sessions.

4. A mediator should promote honesty and candor between and among all participants, and a mediator shall not knowingly misrepresent any material fact or circumstance in the course of a mediation.
5. The role of a mediator differs substantially from other professional roles. Mixing the role of a mediator and the role of another profession is problematic and thus, a mediator should distinguish between the roles. A mediator may provide information that the mediator is qualified by training or experience to provide, only if the mediator can do so consistent with these Standards.
6. A mediator shall not conduct a dispute resolution procedure other than mediation but label it mediation in an effort to gain the protection of rules, statutes, or other governing authorities pertaining to mediation.
7. A mediator may recommend, when appropriate, that parties consider resolving their dispute through arbitration, counseling, neutral evaluation or other processes.
8. A mediator shall not undertake an additional dispute resolution role in the same matter without the consent of the parties. Before providing such service, a mediator shall inform the parties of the implications of the change in process and obtain their consent to the change. A mediator who undertakes such role assumes different duties and responsibilities that may be governed by other standards.
9. If a mediation is being used to further criminal conduct, a mediator should take appropriate steps including, if necessary, postponing, withdrawing from or terminating the mediation.
10. If a party appears to have difficulty comprehending the process, issues, or settlement options, or difficulty participating in a mediation, the mediator should explore the circumstances and potential accommodations, modifications or adjustments that would make possible the party's capacity to comprehend, participate and exercise self-determination.

B. If a mediator is made aware of domestic abuse or violence among the parties, the mediator shall take appropriate steps including, if necessary, postponing, withdrawing from or terminating the mediation.

C. If a mediator believes that participant conduct, including that of the mediator, jeopardizes conducting a mediation consistent with these Standards, a mediator shall take appropriate steps including, if necessary, postponing, withdrawing from or terminating the mediation.

Standard VII. Advertising and Solicitation

A. A mediator shall be truthful and not misleading when advertising, soliciting or otherwise communicating the mediator's qualifications, experience, services and fees.
   1. A mediator should not include any promises as to outcome in communications, including business cards, stationery, or computer-based communications.
   2. A mediator should only claim to meet the mediator qualifications of a governmental entity or private organization if that entity or organization has a recognized procedure for qualifying mediators and it grants such status to the mediator.

B. A mediator shall not solicit in a manner that gives an appearance of partiality for or against a party or otherwise undermines the integrity of the process.

C. A mediator shall not communicate to others, in promotional materials or through other forms of communication, the names of persons served without their permission.

Standard VIII. Fees and Other Charges

A. A mediator shall provide each party or each party's representative true and complete information about mediation fees, expenses and any other actual or potential charges that may be incurred in connection with a mediation.
   1. If a mediator charges fees, the mediator should develop them in light of all relevant factors, including the type and complexity of the matter, the qualifications of the mediator, the time required and the rates customary for such mediation services.
   2. A mediator's fee arrangement should be in writing unless the parties request otherwise.

B. A mediator shall not charge fees in a manner that impairs a mediator's impartiality.
   1. A mediator should not enter into a fee agreement which is contingent upon the result of the mediation or amount of the settlement.
   2. While a mediator may accept unequal fee payments from the parties, a mediator should not allow such a fee arrangement to adversely impact the mediator's ability to conduct a mediation in an impartial manner.

Standard IX. Advancement of Mediation Practice

A. A mediator should act in a manner that advances the practice of mediation. A mediator promotes this Standard by engaging in some or all of the following:
   1. Fostering diversity within the field of mediation.
   2. Striving to make mediation accessible to those who elect to use it, including providing services at a reduced rate or on a pro bono basis as appropriate.
   3. Participating in research when given the opportunity, including obtaining participant feedback when appropriate.
   4. Participating in outreach and education efforts to assist the public in developing an improved understanding of, and appreciation for, mediation.
   5. Assisting newer mediators through training, mentoring and networking.

B. A mediator should demonstrate respect for differing points of view within the field, seek to learn from other mediators and work together with other mediators to improve the profession and better serve people in conflict.

About the Editor

Dr. Omer Shapira is a Senior Lecturer at the Faculty of Law, Ono Academic College, Israel, and a mediator. He teaches courses and seminars on law, ADR, mediation, and mediation ethics at both undergraduate and postgraduate levels and lectures on mediation ethics in mediator training courses, professional conferences, and continuing education programs for mediators. He is the author of *A Theory of Mediators' Ethics: Foundations, Rationale, and Application* (Cambridge University Press, 2016); *Use of Power and Influence in Mediation: Practice and Applied Ethics* (Ono Academic College Press, 2007) (Heb.); and *Mediation Ethics: Codes of Ethics and Dealing with Dilemmas* (The Hebrew University Magnes Press, 2018) (Heb.) (coedited with Carmela Zilberstein). Dr. Shapira sits on a Mediator Ethics Committee (Israel) that receives ethical inquiries from practitioners and drafts reasoned ethical opinions that are informed by the theoretical work in which he engages. He also chairs IMI—International Mediation Institute Ethics Committee.

About the Contributors

James J. Alfini is Dean and Professor Emeritus at South Texas College of Law Houston. He previously was a member of the law faculty at Florida State University, where he also served as Director of Education and Research for the Florida Dispute Resolution Center. He has served as Chair of the ABA Dispute Resolution Section and Chair of the Association of American Law Schools ADR Section. His publications in the ADR field include the coauthored *Mediation Theory and Practice*, a law school textbook published by Lexis Law Publishing. He received his undergraduate degree from Columbia University and his J.D. from Northwestern University.

Kristen M. Blankley is Professor of Law and Director of the Robert J. Kutak Center for the Teaching and Study of Applied Ethics at the University of Nebraska. Her teaching and research focus on arbitration, mediation, and the intersection of ethics and dispute resolution.

Ellen E. Deason is the Joanne Wharton Murphy/Classes of 1965 and 1973 Professor of Law Emerita at the Ohio State University Moritz College of Law. She is a coauthor of casebooks on Civil Procedure and Alternative Dispute Resolution and, most recently, Global Issues in Mediation (with Jacqueline Nolan-Haley and Mariana H.C. Gonstead). Her scholarship focuses on mediation and other settlement processes. The Association of American Law Schools Section of ADR recognized her article on appropriate roles for judges in settlement by selecting it as the Article of the Year for 2017. Ms. Deason was honored with the Ohio State University Alumni Award for Distinguished Teaching in 2016 and chosen by the students as College of Law Professor of the Year in 2015. She has also taught at universities in China, Spain, and England. She would like to thank Raegan Hudson for her excellent research assistance.

Bill Eddy is a mediator, lawyer, and therapist. He was the Senior Family Mediator at the National Conflict Resolution Center in San Diego, California, for 15 years. He is also the cofounder and Chief Innovation Officer of the High Conflict Institute, for which he has trained lawyers, mediators, judges, mental health professionals, and others on managing high-conflict personalities in over 30 states and ten countries. He has written 20 books and manuals, most recently *Mediating High Conflict Disputes* (Unhooked Books, 2021). He is the developer of the New Ways for Families skills-training method for high-conflict divorce and the New Ways for Mediation method for high-conflict cases.

Donna Erez-Navot is the Assistant Director of the Kukin Program for Conflict Resolution at Cardozo Law School, where she also directs the Cardozo Mediation Clinic. Before joining the faculty at Cardozo, Ms. Erez-Navot was the founding Director of the Mediation Clinic at University of Wisconsin. As part of the Clinic, she was instrumental in setting up several mediation programs including Waukesha County Child Protection Mediation Program, Dane County Small Claims Mediation Program, and Dane County Child Protection Mediation Pilot Program. Before moving to Madison in 2009, she was employed as a mediator in the Child Permanency Mediation Program in the NYC Family Court, where she mediated issues surrounding placement of children in foster care. She is a graduate of Cardozo Law School. After attaining her undergraduate degree at Emory University, Ms. Erez-Navot studied Social Work at Tel Aviv University.

Susan Nauss Exon is Professor Emerita, University of La Verne College of Law, having retired in June 2020 after 21 years of teaching. She currently mediates and arbitrates on several panels, including the American Arbitration Association and California Arbitration & Mediation Services. Ms. Nauss Exon speaks frequently regarding mediation ethics, ODR, and trust building in online mediation. She has numerous published papers and articles in these areas. Her book, *Advanced Guide for Mediators*, is available from Carolina Academic Press. Ms. Nauss Exon has been active in the ABA Section of Dispute Resolution, as a past cochair of its Ethics Committee and past member of its Ethical Guidance Committee.

Gregory Firestone, Ph.D., is a mediator, mediation trainer, and licensed psychologist who founded and directed the University of South Florida (USF) Conflict Resolution Collaborative from 1994 until retiring in 2016. Dr. Firestone is currently a USF Affiliate Associate Professor. He served as Vice Chair of the Florida Supreme Court ADR Rules and Policy Committee for seven years and for three years represented national mediation organizations in the National Conference of Commissioners on Uniform State Laws (aka Uniform Law Commission) drafting of the Uniform Mediation Act. Dr. Firestone has published and lectured widely and received numerous awards including the Florida Supreme Court Excellence in Alternative Dispute Resolution Award.

Elayne E. Greenberg is Assistant Dean of Dispute Resolution, Professor of Legal Practice and Faculty Director of the Hugh L. Carey Center for Dispute Resolution at St. John's Law School. She has educated, trained, and written internationally on the subject of dispute resolution ethics. Professor Greenberg's deep involvement in the field is evidenced by the innovative dispute resolution programs that she has developed and implemented. In her many leadership roles, she has helped shape the development of dispute resolution policy. In her long-standing column, the Ethical Compass, in *The New York Dispute Resolution Lawyer*, she discusses emerging ethical issues.

Michael Moffitt is the Philip H. Knight Chair in Law at the University of Oregon, where he has been a professor since 2001 and served as Dean from 2011 through 2017. He was formerly the Roger D. Fisher Visiting Professor in Negotiation and Conflict Resolution at Harvard Law School, where he also served as the Clinical Supervisor of the Harvard Mediation Program. A graduate of Harvard Law School and Marietta College, he has worked in more than 20 countries on public-sector and private-sector negotiations.

Jacqueline Nolan-Haley directs the ADR & Conflict Resolution Program and the Mediation Clinical Program at Fordham University Law School. She teaches courses in ADR, Mediation, and Conflict Resolution at Fordham and at its Queens University Belfast and University College Dublin Summer Programs and has been a Visiting Scholar at the Harvard Program on Negotiation. She has trained lawyers, judges, and public officials in mediation in the United States, Ghana, and Northern Ireland. She is a member of the Ethics Committee of the ABA Section of Dispute Resolution, chair of the CLE & Education Committee of the New York Bar Association's Dispute Resolution Section, member of the American Arbitration Association ICDR Council and the Mediation Advisory Committee, and former chair of the Association of American Law Schools' ADR Section. Her research focuses on justice and ethics issues in ADR, and in 2020 she was awarded the ABA Section of Dispute Resolution Award for outstanding scholarly work.

Sharon Press is Director of the Dispute Resolution Institute and Professor of Law at Mitchell Hamline School of Law. Ms. Press is Co-President of Community Mediation Minnesota and serves on the boards of the Institute for the Study of Conflict Transformation and Community Mediation and Restorative Services. She is a Florida Supreme Court–certified county and family mediator and on Minnesota's Roster of Civil Facilitative and Hybrid Neutrals and mediates regularly. Prior to joining Mitchell Hamline, Ms. Press was director of the Florida Dispute Resolution Center, where she was responsible for the ADR programs for the Florida state court system, including the grievance process and advisory ethical opinions for mediators. She was the Association for Conflict Resolution's representative to the Drafting Committee for the Model Standards of Conduct for Mediators adopted by the AAA, ABA, and ACR. She received both her B.A. and J.D. from The George Washington University.

Fran Tetunic is a Professor of Law at Nova Southeastern University Shepard Broad College of Law and directs its Dispute Resolution Clinic. An attorney licensed to practice law in Florida, Ms. Tetunic served on the Florida Supreme Court's Alternative Dispute Resolution Rules and Policy Committee and as chair of the Mediator Ethics Advisory Committee, signing 65 opinions on behalf of the committee. Certified as a Florida Supreme Court Circuit Civil, Family, and County Mediator, Ms. Tetunic has mediated approximately 2,000 cases and provides continuing education training regarding mediation. Her publications include articles on mediation case law and ethics and an article on mediator misconduct setting aside mediated agreements.

Ellen Waldman is Professor of Law and founding Director of the Mediation Clinic at Thomas Jefferson School of Law. In the area of dispute resolution, she writes, trains, consults, and mediates in a broad range of cases, including end of life in the health care context. A member of the American Bar Association Dispute Resolution Section subcommittee on ethics, former cochair of the Section's committee on health care, and participant in the California judicial council's task force on training requirements for court-connected mediators, Ms. Waldman has been deeply involved in policy questions relating to the training and education of mediators. She has published more than 25 articles on numerous dispute resolution topics, including, in 2011, the first full-length book treatment of mediation ethics entitled *Mediation Ethics: Cases and Commentaries.*

Nancy A. Welsh is University Professor, Professor of Law, and Director of the Dispute Resolution Program of Texas A&M University School of Law and was previously William Trickett Faculty Scholar and Professor of Law at Penn State University, Dickinson School of Law, and Executive Director of Mediation Center in Minnesota. She presents nationally and internationally and has written more than 70 articles and chapters on dispute resolution and procedural law. She is coauthor of *Dispute Resolution and Lawyers* (6th ed.) and coeditor of *Evolution of a Field: Personal Histories in Conflict Resolution*. She also conducted research and taught as a Fulbright Scholar in the Netherlands, is an elected member of the American Law Institute, and has served as Chair of both the ABA Dispute Resolution Section and the AALS Alternative Dispute Resolution Section.

Index

J

K

L

M

Q

R

S